Worlds of Music

AN INTRODUCTION TO THE MUSIC OF THE WORLD'S PEOPLES

Shorter Version

Jeff Todd Titon
General Editor

Linda K. Fujie
David Locke
David P. McAllester
David B. Reck
John M. Schechter
Mark Slobin
R. Anderson Sutton

SCHIRMER
THOMSON LEARNING™

Australia • Canada • Mexico • Singapore • Spain
United Kingdom • United States

SCHIRMER
THOMSON LEARNING

Music Editor: Clark G. Baxter
Assistant Editor: Jennifer Ellis
Editorial Assistant: Dulce Moreno
Executive Marketing Manager: Diane McOscar
Project Editor: Dianne Jensis Toop
Print Buyer: Tandra Jorgensen
Associate Permissions Editor: Stephanie Keough-Hedges
Production Service: Greg Hubit Bookworks
Text Designer: Harry Voigt
Copy Editor: Molly Roth
Cover Designer: Steven Rapley
Cover Printer: Phoenix Color Corp.
Compositor: TBH Typecast, Inc.
Printer: Quebecor/Taunton

Printed in the United States of America
1 2 3 4 5 6 7 04 03 02 01 00

Library of Congress Cataloging-in-Publication Data

Worlds of music : an introduction to the music of the world's peoples / Jeff Todd Titon, general editor.—Shorter ed.
p. cm.
Includes bibliographical references and index.
Contents: The music-culture as a world of music / Jeff Todd Titon and Mark Slobin—North America/Native America / David P. McAllester—Africa/Ewe / David Locke—North America/Black America/Blues / Jeff Todd Titon—Europe/Bosnia / Mark Slobin—India/South India / David B. Reck—Asia/Indonesia / R. Anderson Sutton—East Asia/Japan / Linda K. Fujie—Latin America/Ecuador / John M. Schechter—Discovering and documenting a world of music / David B. Reck, Mark Slobin, and Jeff Todd Titon.
ISBN 0-534-58545-0
1. Folk music—History and criticism. 2. Music—History and criticism. 3. Ethnomusicology. I. Titon, Jeff Todd. II. Title.
ML3545.W67 2001
780'.9—dc21 00-050493

Wadsworth/Thomson Learning
10 Davis Drive
Belmont, CA 94002-3098
USA

For more information about our products, contact us:
Thomson Learning Academic Resource Center
1-800-423-0563
http://www.wadsworth.com

International Headquarters
Thomson Learning
International Division
290 Harbor Drive, 2nd Floor
Stamford, CT 06902-7477
USA

UK/Europe/Middle East/South Africa
Thomson Learning
Berkshire House
168–173 High Holborn
London WC1V 7AA
United Kingdom

Asia
Thomson Learning
60 Albert Street, #15-01
Albert Complex
Singapore 189969

Canada
Nelson Thomson Learning
1120 Birchmount Road
Toronto, Ontario M1K 5G4
Canada

THIS BOOK PRINTED ON ACID-FREE RECYCLED PAPER

Contents

8 East Asia/Japan 211

9 Latin America/Ecuador 243

Recorded Selections

CD 1

1. *Postal workers canceling stamps at the University of Ghana post office* (2:57). Field recording by James Koetting, Legon, Ghana, 1975.

2. *Songs of Hermit Trushes* (0:32). Field recording by Jeff Todd Titon, Little Deer Isle, Maine, 1999.

3. *Yeibichai* song (2:07). Sandoval Begay, leader. Field recording by Willard Rhodes (no date) in Library of Congress Archive of Folk Culture AFS L41. 12″ LP. Used by permission of Willard Rhodes.

4. *Folsom Prison Blues* (2:48). Words and music by Johnny Cash. Published by Hi-Lo Music. Performed by The Fenders on *The Fenders, Second Time Roun'*, 12″ LP. Thoreau, New Mexico, 1966. Used by permission from The Harry Fox Agency, Inc.

5. *Shizhané'é* ("I'm in Luck"), Navajo Circle Dance song (1:16). Performed by Albert G. Sandoval, Jr., and Ray Winnie. Field recording by David P. McAllester, Sedona, Arizona, 1957. Used by permission of Albert G. Sandoval and Ray Winnie.

6. Hymn of the Native American Church, *Navajo Peyote song* (1:11). Performed by George Mitchell and Kaya David. Field recording by Willard Rhodes (no date) in Library of Congress Archive of Folk Culture AFS 14. 12″ LP. Used by permission of Willard Rhodes.

7. *Mother Earth* (2:59) from *Yazzie Girl* (CR-534) by Sharon Burch. © 1989 Sharon Burch. Used by permissions of Canyon Records Productions, 3131 West Clarendon Avenue, Phoenix, Arizona 85017.

8. *Origins* (3:43), R. Carlos Nakai, from *Cycles: Native American Flute Music*, Canyon Records Productions 614, 1985. Used by permission of Canyon Records Productions, 3131 West Clarendon Avenue, Phoenix, Arizona 85017.

9. *Agbekor*: Five songs performed by an Ewe *Agbekor* ensemble. Three slow-paced songs (2:45); one song in free rhythm (1:16); one fast-paced song (1:05). Field recording by David Locke, Anlo-Afiadenyigba, Ghana, 1976.

10. *Nag Biegu* ("Ferocious Wild Bull") Praise Name Dance song (2:06). Performed by *lunsi* drummers of the Dagbamba people. Field recording by David Locke, Ghana, 1984.

11. *Poor Boy Blues* (3:14). Lazy Bill Lucas Trio. Field recording by Jeff Todd Titon, Minneapolis, Minnesota, 1970. (Background noise from the apartment is audible.)

12. *Sweet Home Chicago* (3:09). Words and Music by Robert Johnson. © (1978), 1990, 1991 King of Spades Music, BMI/Administered by Delta Haze Corporation. Performed by The Fieldstones on *Memphis Blues Today*, High Water 12″ LP 1001 ℗1983, Memphis State University (now HighTone Records, Oakland, CA). Used by permission.

13. *You Don't Love Me* (3:34). Words and Music by Magic Sam. Performed by Magic Sam. Field recording by Jeff Todd Titon, Ann Arbor, Michigan, August 1969.

14. *Ain't Enough Comin' In* (5:58). Words and Music by Otis Rush. © 1994 Otis Rush Publishing, BMI/Administered by BUG. Performed by Otis Rush on *Otis Rush: Ain't Enough Comin' In*, Mercury 314518769-2, 1994. Used by permission.

15. *Pararuda* ("Come, little rain") performed by Gypsy children in Giestetsi village, Romania. From *Folk Music of Romania*, Columbia Records, 12″ LP, KL 5799.

16. Muslim highlander women's *ganga* song (0:39). Performed by Šecira Kadrić, Aiša Kadrić, Enisa Trešnjo. Field recording by Mirjana Laušević, Gornji Lukomir village, Bosnia, 1990. Used by permission.

17. Muslim highlander men's *ganga* song (1:22). Performed by Safet Elezović, Muhamed Elezović, Zejnil Masleša. Field recording by Mirjana Laušević, Gornji Lukomir village, Bosnia, 1990. Used by permission.

18. Muslim lowlands song with *sargija* lute (1:05). Performed by Skiba and friends. Field recording by Mirjana Laušević, Bosnia, 1989. Used by permission.

19. *Trepetljika trepetala* ("That which trembles") lowlands *sevdalinka* song (1:17). Written and performed by Himzo Polovina with *tamburitza* orchestra. Live radio performance, 1986. Used by permission of Edmir Polovina.

20. *Mani zemlju koja Bosnu nema* (1:53). Written and performed by Lepa Brena. From *Lepa Brena I Slatki Greh,* 1984. RTS Records 12" LP 2113473, Belgrade, Yugoslavia.

21. *Da zna zora* (2:40). Words and music by Željko Bebek. Performed by Željko Bebek and Halid Beslić. From *Bebek: Niko Viša Ne Sanja,* 1989. Croatia Records, Zagreb, Croatia.

22. *Train Piece* (3:33). Written and performed by Mensur Hatić. Field recording by Mark Slobin, Detroit, Michigan, 1994.

23. *Klaro del dija* (1:24). Performed by Flory Jagoda on *Kantikas Diminona,* Global Village Music CD C139, 1989. Used by permission of Global Village Music, 245 West 29th Street, New York, New York 10001.

24. *Engal Kalyanam* ("Our Wedding"), cinema song (3:23). Music by M. S. Viswanathan, lyrics by Vali. Performed by P. Susheela, T. M. Soundararajan, P. B. Sreenivos, and L. R. Eswari. From *Hits from Tamil Films,* Vol. 6, EMI Odeon (India) 12" LP 3AECS 5519, Calcutta, India, 1969. Published and copyrighted to The Gramophone Company of India, Ltd. Used by permission.

CD 2

25. *Ivaraku jucinadi* by Tyagaraja, *raga sankarabharanam, adi tala,* karnataka sangeeta performance segment: improvisation with *kriti*. Performed by T. Viswanathan, flute; Ramnad V. Raghavan, *mridangam*. Recording by David B. Reck, Amherst, MA, 1995.

26. *Bubaran Kembang Pacar* ("Red Flower") *pélog pathet nem* (2:58). Central Javanese *gamelan* music in loud-playing style, performed by musicians affiliated with the royal palace in Yogyakarta. Field recording by R. Anderson Sutton, Yogyakarta, Java, Indonesia, 1980.

27. *Playon Lasem, sléndro pathet nem,* Rendition 1 (1:18). Central Javanese *gamelan* music for shadow puppetry performed by gamelan group of Ki Suparman. Field recording by R. Anderson Sutton, Yogyakarta, Java, Indonesia, 1974.

28. *Playon Lasem, sléndro pathet nem,* Rendition 2 (0:30). Central Javanese *gamelan* music for shadow puppetry performed by gamelan group of Ki Suparman. Field recording by R. Anderson Sutton, Yogyakarta, Java, Indonesia, 1974.

28. *Tabuh Gari* (6:18) Various Artists. From *Gamelan Semar Pegulingan: Music from Bali,* recorded by Robert E. Brown, Nonesuch Explorer H-72046. ℗1972 Nonesuch Records. Produced under License from Nonesuch Records.

30. *Indonesia Maharddhika* ("Indonesia Is Free") (3:19). Words and music by Guhru Sukarno Putra. Performed by heavy pop group Guruh Gipsy, under the direction of Guhru Sukarno Putra for *Guruh Gipsy,* 1976, PT Dela Rahita, Jakarta, Java, Indonesia. Used by permission of Guhru Sukarno Putra.

31. *Tsuru no sugomori* ("Nesting Cranes") (3:40). Performed by Kawase Junsuke, *shakuhachi* (flute), and Kawase Hakuse, *shamisen* (lute). Field recording by Linda Fujie, Tokyo, Japan, 1989.

32. *Hakusen no* ("A White Fan") (3:22). Performed by Shitaya Kotsuru for Nippon Columbia WK-170.

33. *Nikata-bushi* (4:07). Performed by Asano Sanae. Field recording by Karl Signell, Washington, D.C., 1986. Used by permission of performer and collector.

34. *Naite Nagasaki* ("Crying Nagasaki") (3:34). Performed by Kanda Fukumaru for Nippon Columbia AH-210.

35. *Cascarón, sanjuán* of Ecuador (3:26). Performed by Quichua harpist Efraín. Field recording by John Schechter, outside Cotacachi, Ecuador, April 1980.

36. *Rusa María wasi rupajmi* ("Rosa Maria's house is burning"), *sanjuán* of Ecuador (2:30). Performed by three Quichua musicians. Field recording by John Schechter, outside Cotacachi, Ecuador, January 1980. (Microphone noise in original recording.)

37. *Ilumán tiyu* ("Man of Ilumán"), *sanjuán* of Ecuador (3:20). Performed by the Quichua ensemble Conjunto Iluman. Field recording by John Schechter, Iluman, Ecuador, October 1990.

38. *Vacación* (1:30). Performed by Quichua harpist Sergio at a child's wake. Field recording by John Schechter, outside Cotacachi, Ecuador, February 1980.

39. Lament by Ecuadorian Quichua mother for her deceased two-year-old girl the morning after the child's wake (3:11), preceded by fifteen seconds of Sergio's *Vacación*. Field recording by John Schechter, outside Cotacachi, Ecuador, January 1980.

Preface

Why study music? There are many reasons, but perhaps the most important are pleasure and understanding. We have designed this book and its accompanying CDs to introduce undergraduates to the study of music the world over. Although *Worlds of Music* contains musical notation, the notation is only illustrative, not essential. The book may be used by students who do not read music. The only prerequisites are a curious ear and a curious mind.

This shorter version is a condensation of *Worlds of Music,* third edition (1996), in response to requests from students and teachers who wanted a more compact package. The first chapter has been extensively rewritten to introduce the elements of world music in greater detail. It now has many more illustrations and cross-references to musical examples in the various parts of the book/CD set. Using as illustrations the popular Ghanaian postal workers' stamp-canceling music and the song of the hermit thrush, Chapter 1 asks students how one draws the line between music and nonmusic. Using students' everyday ideas of rhythm, meter, melody, and harmony, it sharpens these rudimentary concepts and shows how they apply to many of the musics of the world's peoples that will be studied in this book. Our consideration of rudiments in a world music context includes not only musical sounds and structures but also basic concepts of the music-culture, people's ideas about music, social activities involving music, and the material culture of music. The last chapter guides students through a fieldwork project; it has been updated and retained almost in its entirety. The other chapters, also updated, have been shortened without sacrificing the depth and integrity of the case-study approach that has been the hallmark of this book since the first edition appeared in 1984.

University courses in music of the world's peoples have increased dramatically since World War II, and the reasons are easy to comprehend. Students who love music are alive to all music. So are composers, and many use the world's musical resources in their newest works. This is an important feature of today's music, and the people who listen to it—now and in the future—will want to keep their musical horizons broad. Another reason for the interest in all kinds of music is the upsurge in ethnic awareness. As modern people try to locate themselves in a world that is changing with bewildering speed, they find music especially rewarding, for music is among the most tenacious of cultural elements. Music symbolizes a people's way of life; it represents a distillation of cultural style. For many, music *is* a way of life.

Interest in and appreciation of world music has grown enormously just in the past ten years. World music has become a significant part of the surrounding concert world. More recordings and videos are available than ever before, world music is now a part of the cable television mix, and many students actively seek world music on the World Wide Web. Musicians from all over the globe now appear on college and university campuses. Not only is world music now important in the mass media, but multiculturalism—the celebration of the multiethnic heritage of the United States—has brought a flood of ethnic festivals, always featuring music. Many younger people searching for musical roots have looked into their ethnic pasts and chosen to learn the music of their foreparents, while others view the variety of musics in the world as a vast resource to be drawn on in creating their own sounds.

The authors of this book are ethnomusicologists; our field, *ethnomusicology,* is usually defined as the study of music in culture. Some ethnomusicologists define the field as the study of music *as* culture, underlining the fact that music is a way of organizing human activity. By *culture* we do not mean "the elite arts," as it is sometimes used. Rather, we use the term as anthropologists do: Culture is a people's way of life, learned and transmitted through the centuries of adapting to the natural and human world. *Ethnomusicology is the study of music in the context of human life.*

I like to think of ethnomusicology as the study of people making music. People "make" music in two ways: They make or construct the *idea* of music—what it is (and is not) and what it does—and they make or produce the *sounds* that they call music. Although we experience music as something "out there" in the world, our response to music depends on the ideas we associate with that music, and those ideas come from the people (ourselves included) who carry our culture. In other words, people "make" music into a cultural domain, with associated sets of ideas and activities. We could not even pick out musical form and structure, how the parts of a piece of music work together to form a whole, if we did not depend on the idea that music must be organized rather than random, and if we had not learned to make music that way. Analyzing form and structure is characteristic of some cultures, including Western ones, but in other areas of the world people do not habitually break a thing down into parts to analyze it.

As students of music in culture, ethnomusicologists have every reason to investigate Western art music, that is, the tradition of Palestrina, Bach, Beethoven, Verdi, Stravinsky, and the like. But with some recent exceptions, ethnomusicologists in North America have specialized in music outside this tradition. They know the Western classics well, but their interest embraces all music. Indeed, many have devoted years to performing music outside the Western mainstream. Further, because ethnomusicologists study more than the music itself (and some even deny that there is such a thing), they are not satisfied merely to analyze and compare musical forms, structures, melodies, rhythms, compositions, and genres. Instead, they borrow insights and methods from anthropology, sociology, literary criticism, linguistics, and history to understand music as human expression. In fact, until the 1950s ethnomusicology courses in United States' universities were more likely to be found in anthropology departments than music departments, and some nineteenth-century founders of ethnomusicology were psychologists. Ethnomusicology is therefore interdisciplinary, combining elements of the arts, humanities, and social sciences. Because of its eclectic methods and worldwide scope, ethnomusicology is well suited to students seeking a liberal arts education.

The number of world-music textbooks in print is very small, and most are theory and method books aimed at graduate students. The rest are world-music surveys, but we think there are good reasons to avoid a survey course at the beginning level. In its broad sweep a survey offers only a passing acquaintance with the music of many peoples. Too often a survey turns into a superficial musical tour: If today is Tuesday, this must be India. The inevitable result is musical overkill; by the term's end students are so overloaded they can barely recognize different musics of the world, let alone understand any one.

Instead of surveying the whole world of music, then, the best introduction, we think, explores in depth the music of a small number of representative human groups. This approach is not new; it adapts to ethnomusicology the case method in anthropology, the touchstone approach in literature, and the problems approach in history. Its object is not primarily to pile up factual knowledge about various musical worlds, though certainly many facts will be learned. Rather, the point is to experience something of what it is like to be an ethnomusicologist puzzling out his or her way toward understanding an unfamiliar music. This process, we believe, is the best foundation for either future coursework (including surveys and seminars) or self-directed study and enjoyment of world music after college.

We decided on a small number of case studies because that is how we teach the introductory-level world-music course at our universities. We thought also that by writing about music in societies we know firsthand, we could write an authoritative book. Ethnomusicologists are a notoriously independent bunch, and the idea of adopting a textbook may strike some as a trifle confining. That is why we have tried to leave plenty of room for instructors to add examples and case studies of their own. Each chapter, then, reflects our own choice of subject. It also reflects our different ways of approaching music, for we agree that music cannot be "caught" by one method only. Most important, we have tried to present an introduction to world music that provides pleasure as well as knowledge.

We suggest that students begin with Chapter 1. The case studies, Chapters 2 through 9, make be taken in any order. Many colleges and universities have a one-term introductory world-music course, often called something like "Music of the World's Peoples." In a one-term course the teacher might choose the five or six case studies from the shorter edition that best suit the course's pace and purpose, perhaps adding a unit based on the teacher's own research.

Because any fieldwork project should begin well before the end of the term, we suggest that Chapter 10 be read just after the first case study and that students begin fieldwork immediately afterward. Many students say the field projects are the most valuable experiences they take away from this course, particularly when they must make sense of what they document in the field. The field project encourages original research. Students find it attractive and meaningful to make an original contribution to knowledge.

We have appreciated the assistance over the years of several editors at Schirmer Books—Maribeth Anderson Payne, Ken Stuart, Richard Carlin, and Jonathan Wiener—and Clark Baxter and Abbie Meyer at Wadsworth in seeing this project through production. We would be pleased to hear from our readers, and we may be reached by writing the publisher or any of us at our respective universities.

Jeff Todd Titon
General Editor

The Authors

Linda K. Fujie received the Ph.D. in ethnomusicology from Columbia University, where she was a student of Dieter Christensen and Adelaida Schramm. She has conducted field research in Japan, mainly concerning urban festival and popular music, under grants from the National Endowment for the Humanities, Columbia University, and Colby College. Her interest in overseas Japanese culture has also resulted in research on Japanese-American and Japanese-Brazilian communities, the latter funded by the German Music Council. Her research has been published in articles in the *Yearbook for Traditional Music,* publications on popular music, and Japanese journals. Other research interests, on which she has also written articles and delivered papers at European conferences, include the music of the Shaker community in Maine and folk music in Germany. She has taught at Colby College as an assistant professor and at the East Asian Institute of the Free University of Berlin. For German radio she regularly writes and delivers radio programs on topics related to traditional music. She also lectures on ethnomusicology at the University of Bamberg.

David Locke received the Ph.D. in ethnomusicology from Wesleyan University, where he studied with David P. McAllester, Mark Slobin, and Gen'ichi Tsuge. At Wesleyan his teachers of traditional African music included Abraham Adzinyah and Freeman Donkor. He conducted doctoral dissertation fieldwork in Ghana from 1975 to 1977 under the supervision of Professor. J. H. K. Nketia. In Ghana his teachers and research associates included Godwin Agbeli, Midawo Gideon Foli Alorwoyie, and Abubakari Lunna. He has published numerous books and articles on African music and regularly performs the repertories of music and dance about which he writes. He teaches at Tufts University, where he currently serves as the chair of the music department, director of the master's degree program in ethnomusicology, and faculty advisor in the Tufts-in-Ghana Foreign Study Program. His current projects include an ethnomusicological study of the music-culture of Dagbon, the documentation and analysis of repertories of African music, and the preparation of multimedia materials on music and culture. He is active in the Society for Ethnomusicology and has served as president of its northeast chapter.

David P. McAllester received the Ph.D. in anthropology from Columbia University, where he studied with George Herzog. He has been a student of American Indian music since 1938. He has undertaken fieldwork among the Comanches, Hopis, Apaches, Navajos, Penobscots, and Passamaquoddies. He is the author of such classic works in ethnomusicology as *Peyote Music, Enemy Way Music, Myth of the Great Star Chant,* and *Navajo Blessingway Singer* (coauthored with Charlotte Frisbie). He is one of the founders of the Society for Ethnomusicology, and he has served as its president and the editor of its journal, *Ethnomusicology.* He is professor emeritus of anthropology and music at Wesleyan University.

David B. Reck received the Ph.D. in ethnomusicology from Wesleyan University, where he was a student of Mark Slobin and David P. McAllester. He has studied and traveled in India, Southeast Asia, and the Far East under grants from the American Institute of Indian Studies, the Rockefeller Foundation, the John Simon Guggenheim Memorial Foundation, and the JDR IIIrd Fund. An accomplished musician on the South-Indian *veena,* he has performed extensively in the United States, Europe, and India both as a soloist and accompanist and as a member of the group Kirtana. As a composer, he has received commissions from the Library of Congress, the Koussevitsky Foundation, and the Fromm Music Foundation and has had his music performed at Tanglewood and Carnegie Hall. The author of *Music of the Whole Earth,* his research and publications include work on India's music; American popular styles; the music of J. S. Bach, Bartók, and Stravinsky; and cross-influences between the West and the Orient. Currently he is professor of music and of Asian languages and civilizations at Amherst College.

John M. Schechter received the Ph.D. in ethnomusicology from the University of Texas at Austin, where he studied ethnomusicology with Gérard Béhague, Andean anthropology with Richard Schaedel, and Quichua with Louisa Stark and Guillermo Delgado. Following his Peace Corps service in Colombia in the 1960s, he pursued ethnomusicological fieldwork in the Andes of Ecuador in 1979, 1980, and 1990. He is the author of *The Indispensable Harp: Historical Development, Modern Roles, Configurations, and Performance Practices in Ecuador and Latin America* (1992). He is the general editor of, and a contributing author to, *Music in Latin American Culture: Regional Traditions* (1999), a volume examining music-culture traditions in distinct regions of Latin America, with chapters by ethnomusicologists specializing in those regions. Schechter's other recent publications have explored formulaic expression in Ecuadorian Quichua *sanjuán;* recent evolution in the *bomba,* a focal African-Ecuadorian musical genre; the syncretic nature of the Andean Corpus Christi celebration; and the ethnography and cultural history of the Latin-American/Iberian children's wake music-ritual. He is associate professor of music at the University of California, Santa Cruz, where he teaches ethnomusicology and music theory, directs two Latin-American ensembles, and serves as provost of Merrill College.

Mark Slobin received the Ph.D. in musicology at the University of Michigan. He is the author, editor, or translator of many books, some on the music of Afghanistan and Central Asia and others on Jewish music in Europe and the United States, East-European music, and the theory and method of studying subcultural musics in Euro-America. *Tenement Songs: The Popular Music of the Jewish Immigrants* won the ASCAP-Deems Taylor Award. He is a past president of the Society for Ethnomusicology and of the Society for Asian Music, having edited the latter's journal, *Asian Music,* from 1971 to 1987. He has taught at Wesleyan University, where he is professor and chair of the music department, and has visited at Harvard, Berkeley, and NYU.

R. Anderson Sutton received the Ph.D. in musicology from the University of Michigan, where he studied with Judith Becker and William Malm. He was introduced to Javanese music while an undergraduate at Wesleyan University, and made it the focus of his master's study at the University of Hawaii, where he studied gamelan with Hardja Susilo. On numerous occasions since 1973 he has conducted field research in Indonesia, with grants from the East-West Center, Fulbright-Hays, Social Science Research Council, National Endowment for the Humanities, Wenner-Gren Foundation, and American Philosophical Society. He is the author of *Traditions of Gamelan Music in Java, Variation in Central Javanese Gamelan Music,* and numerous articles on Javanese music. He has recently completed a book on music and cultural politics in South Sulawesi, Indonesia, and his current research concerns music and the Indonesian media. Active as a gamelan musician since 1971, he has performed with several professional groups in Indonesia and directed numerous performances in the United States. He has served as first vice president and book review editor for the Society for Ethnomusicology, and as a member of the Working Committee on Performing Arts for the Festival of Indonesia (1990–92). He has taught at the University of Hawaii and the University of Wisconsin–Madison, where he is professor of music and past director of the Center for Southeast Asian Studies.

Jeff Todd Titon received the Ph.D. in American Studies from the University of Minnesota, where he studied ethnomusicology with Alan Kagan and musicology with Johannes Riedel. He has done fieldwork in North America on religious folk music, blues music, and old-time fiddling. with support from the National Endowment for the Arts and the National Endowment for the Humanities. For two years he was rhythm guitarist in the Lazy Bill Lucas Blues Band, a group that appeared in the 1970 Ann Arbor Blues Festival. The author or editor of five books, including *Early Downhome*

Blues, which won the ASCAP-Deems Taylor Award, and *Powerhouse for God,* he is also a documentary photographer and filmmaker. In 1991 he wrote a hypermedia computer program about old-time fiddler Clyde Davenport that is now regarded as a model for weblike interactive computer representations of people making music. Smithsonian Folkways recently published a CD from his fieldwork with Old Regular Baptists in eastern Kentucky; an anthology of old-time fiddle tune transcriptions is forthcoming from the University Press of Kentucky, and he is the coeditor of the forthcoming five-volume *American Musical Traditions,* a production of Schirmer Books with the Smithsonian Institution. He developed the ethnomusicology program at Tufts University, where he taught from 1971 to 1986. From 1990 to 1995 he served as the editor of *Ethnomusicology,* the journal of the Society for Ethnomusicology. Since 1986 he has been professor of music and director of the Ph.D. program in ethnomusicology at Brown University.

CHAPTER

1

The Music-Culture as a World of Music

Jeff Todd Titon and Mark Slobin

The world around us is full of sounds. All of them are meaningful in some way. Some are sounds you make. You might sing in the shower, talk to yourself, shout to a friend, whistle a tune, beep the horn in your car, sing along with a song on your Walkman or CD player, practice a piece on your instrument, play in a band or orchestra, or sing in a chorus or an informal group on a street corner. Some are sounds from sources outside yourself. If you live in the city, you hear a lot of human-made sounds. You might be startled by the sound of a police siren or a car alarm. You may notice the noise of the garbage trucks for an early morning pickup, and the drone of a motor in a parked truck can irritate you, but usually you block out the traffic noise that is there most of the time. In the country you can more easily hear the sounds of nature. In the spring and summer you may hear birds singing and calling to each other, the snorting of deer in the woods, or the warning bark of a distant dog. By a river or the ocean you can hear the sounds of surf or boats loading and unloading or the deep bass of foghorns. Stop for a moment and listen to the sounds around you. Become alive to the soundscape.

The Soundscape

Just as landscape refers to land, *soundscape* (a term developed by the Canadian composer R. Murray Schafer) refers to sound: the characteristic sounds of a particular place, both human-made and nonhuman sounds (Schafer 1980). The examples so far present soundscapes in the present, but it is also interesting to think about what they were like in the past. What kinds of sounds did the dinosaurs make? With our wristwatches we can always find out what time it is, but in medieval Europe people told time by listening to the bells on the clock tower. Today we take the sounds of a passing railroad train for granted, but its sounds were arresting when first heard.

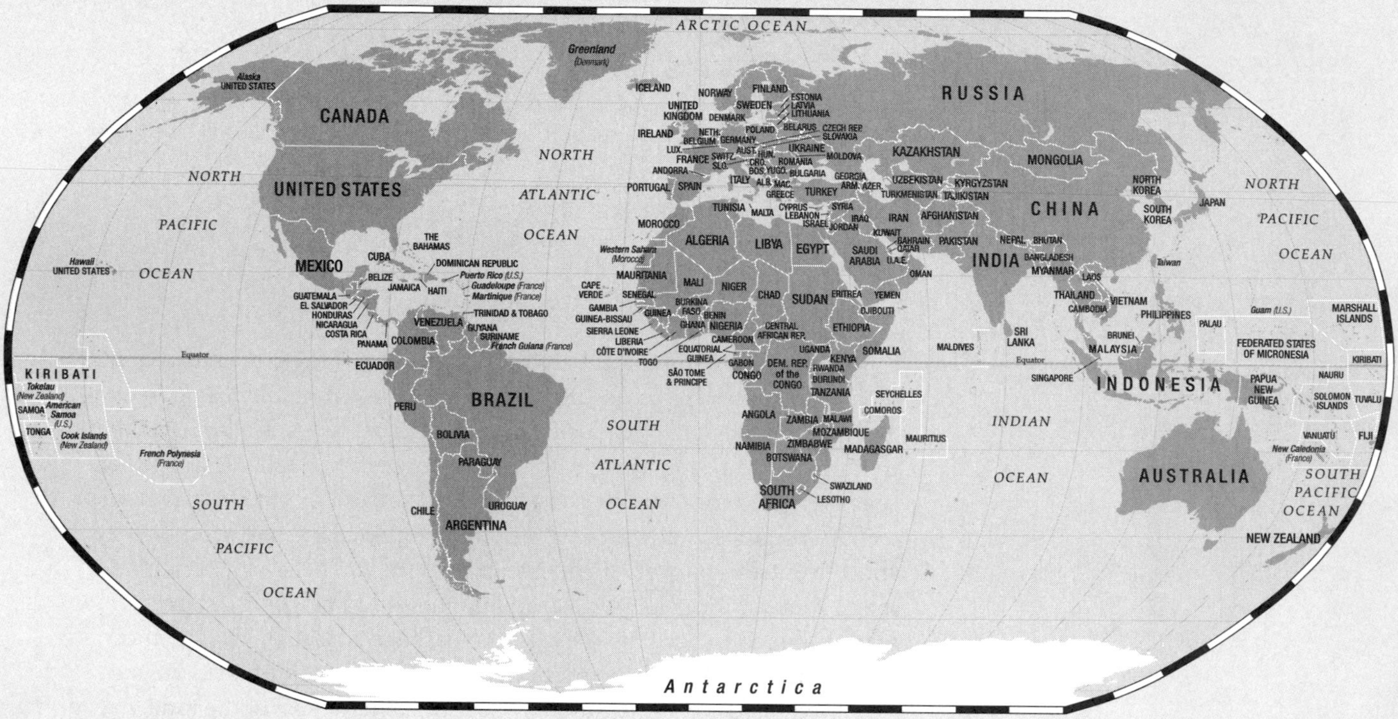
ARCTIC OCEAN
Greenland
(Denmark)
Alaska
UNITED STATES
CANADA
ICELAND
NORWAY
FINLAND
ESTONIA
LATVIA
LITHUANIA
SWEDEN
UNITED KINGDOM
DENMARK
RUSSIA
IRELAND
NETH.
BELGIUM
GERMANY
POLAND
BELARUS
CZECH REP.
SLOVAKIA
LUX.
FRANCE
SWITZ.
SLO.
AUST.
HUN.
UKRAINE
MOLDOVA
ROMANIA
CRO.
BOS.
YUGO.
BULGARIA
ANDORRA
PORTUGAL
SPAIN
ITALY
ALB.
MAC.
GREECE
KAZAKHSTAN
MONGOLIA
GEORGIA
ARM.
AZER.
UZBEKISTAN
KYRGYZSTAN
TURKMENISTAN
TAJIKISTAN
TURKEY
NORTH KOREA
SOUTH KOREA
JAPAN
CHINA
NORTH
ATLANTIC
OCEAN
NORTH
PACIFIC
OCEAN
UNITED STATES
TUNISIA
MALTA
CYPRUS
LEBANON
SYRIA
ISRAEL
JORDAN
IRAQ
IRAN
KUWAIT
AFGHANISTAN
PAKISTAN
NEPAL
BHUTAN
BAHRAIN
QATAR
U.A.E.
OMAN
MOROCCO
ALGERIA
LIBYA
EGYPT
SAUDI ARABIA
INDIA
BANGLADESH
MYANMAR
Taiwan
NORTH
PACIFIC
OCEAN
Hawaii
UNITED STATES
MEXICO
CUBA
THE BAHAMAS
DOMINICAN REPUBLIC
Puerto Rico (U.S.)
Guadeloupe (France)
Martinique (France)
BELIZE
JAMAICA
HAITI
GUATEMALA
EL SALVADOR
HONDURAS
NICARAGUA
COSTA RICA
PANAMA
TRINIDAD & TOBAGO
VENEZUELA
GUYANA
SURINAME
French Guiana (France)
COLOMBIA
Western Sahara
(Morocco)
MAURITANIA
CAPE VERDE
SENEGAL
GAMBIA
GUINEA
GUINEA-BISSAU
SIERRA LEONE
LIBERIA
CÔTE D'IVOIRE
BURKINA FASO
GHANA
TOGO
BENIN
NIGERIA
MALI
NIGER
CHAD
SUDAN
ERITREA
YEMEN
DJIBOUTI
ETHIOPIA
CENTRAL AFRICAN REP.
CAMEROON
EQUATORIAL GUINEA
GABON
SÃO TOME & PRINCIPE
CONGO
DEM. REP. of the CONGO
UGANDA
KENYA
RWANDA
BURUNDI
SOMALIA
TANZANIA
LAOS
THAILAND
CAMBODIA
VIETNAM
PHILIPPINES
PALAU
Guam (U.S.)
MARSHALL ISLANDS
FEDERATED STATES OF MICRONESIA
SRI LANKA
MALDIVES
BRUNEI
MALAYSIA
SINGAPORE
INDONESIA
Equator
KIRIBATI
NAURU
PAPUA NEW GUINEA
SOLOMON ISLANDS
TUVALU
ECUADOR
KIRIBATI
Tokelau
(New Zealand)
SAMOA
American Samoa
(U.S.)
TONGA
Cook Islands
(New Zealand)
French Polynesia
(France)
PERU
BRAZIL
BOLIVIA
PARAGUAY
CHILE
URUGUAY
ARGENTINA
SOUTH
ATLANTIC
OCEAN
ANGOLA
ZAMBIA
MALAWI
MOZAMBIQUE
NAMIBIA
ZIMBABWE
BOTSWANA
MADAGASCAR
SEYCHELLES
COMOROS
MAURITIUS
SWAZILAND
SOUTH AFRICA
LESOTHO
INDIAN
OCEAN
AUSTRALIA
VANUATU
FIJI
New Caledonia
(France)
SOUTH
PACIFIC
OCEAN
NEW ZEALAND
SOUTH
PACIFIC
OCEAN
Antarctica

The American naturalist Henry David Thoreau was alive to the soundscape when he lived by himself in a cabin in the woods at Walden Pond 150 years ago. As he writes in *Walden,* "The whistle of the steam engine penetrated my woods summer and winter—sounding like the scream of a hawk sailing over some farmer's yard." The hawk is a bird of prey. It is an ominous comparison. Thoreau then describes the train as an iron horse (a common comparison at the time) and then a dragon, a threatening symbol of chaos rather than industrial progress: "When I hear the iron horse make the hills echo with his snort like thunder—shaking the earth with his feet, and breathing fire and smoke from his nostrils, what kind of winged horse or fiery dragon they will put into the new mythology I don't know." Writing about his wilderness soundscape, Thoreau first made sure his readers knew what he did not hear: the crowing of the rooster, the sounds of animals—dogs, cats, cows, pigs—the butter churn, the spinning wheel, children crying, the "singing of the kettle, the hissing of the urn"—this was the soundscape of a farm in 1850, quite familiar to Thoreau's readers—and we might stop to notice which of these sounds has disappeared from the soundscape altogether—who today hears a butter churn or spinning wheel? In his wilderness soundscape Thoreau heard "squirrels on the roof and under the floor; a whippoorwill on the ridge-pole, a bluejay screaming in the yard, a hare or woodchuck under the house, a screech-owl or a cat-owl behind it, a flock of wild geese or a laughing loon in the pond, a fox to bark in the night"; but no rooster "to crow nor hens to cackle in the yard—no yard!" In Thoreau's America you could tell, blindfolded, whether you were in the wilderness, on a farm, or in a town or city. How have those soundscapes changed since 1850? What might Thoreau have written about automobiles in the countryside, tractors on the farms, trucks on the interstate highways, and jet planes everywhere?

CD 1
Track 1

Listen now to CD Selection 1. The soundscape is a post office, but it is unlike any post office you will likely encounter in North America. You are hearing men canceling stamps at the University of Accra, in Ghana, Africa. Two of the men whistle a tune while three make percussive sounds. A stamp gets canceled several times for the sake of the rhythm. You will learn more about this example shortly. For now, think of it as yet another example of a soundscape: the acoustic environment where sounds, including music, occur.

The Music-Culture

Every human society has music. Music seems so universal that scientists send it out in space capsules, figuring that music is the way to communicate with intelligent beings in distant solar systems who could not be expected to understand human language. Though music is universal, its meaning is not. A famous musician from Asia attended a European symphony concert approximately 150 years ago. He had never heard a performance of Western music before. The story goes that after the concert, his hosts asked him how he had liked it. "Very well," he replied. Not satisfied with this answer, his hosts asked (through an interpreter) what part he liked best. "The first part," he said. "Oh, you enjoyed the first movement?" "No, before that." To the stranger, the best part of the performance was the tuning-up period. His hosts had a different opinion. Who was right?

Different cultures give music different meanings. Recall from the preface that by *culture* we mean the way of life of a people, learned and transmitted from one generation to the next. We stress the word *learned* because we differentiate a people's cultural inheritance from what is passed along genetically. From birth, a person absorbs the cultural inheritance of family, community, schoolmates, and increasingly the mass-media—magazines, movies, television, and computers. This cultural inheritance tells us how to understand the situations we are in (what the situations mean) and how we might behave in those situations. It works so automatically that we are aware of it only when it breaks down, as it does on occasion when we misunderstand a situation we are in. Cultures, like the people who carry them, do not function perfectly all the time. Musical situations and the very concept of music mean different things and involve different activities around the globe. Because music and all the beliefs and activities associated with it are a part of culture, we use the term *music-culture* to mean a group's total involvement with music: ideas, actions, institutions, material objects—everything that has to do with music. In our example, the European music-culture dictates that the sound made by symphony musicians tuning up is not music. But to the stranger from Asia, it was music. Considered from within their own cultural contexts, both the stranger and his hosts were correct.

People may be perplexed by music that comes from outside their own music-culture. They may grant that it is music but find it difficult to hear and enjoy. In Victorian England, people said they had a hard time listening to the strange music of the native peoples within the British Colonial Empire. For example, the expansive and exciting improvisations of India's classical music were ridiculed because the music was not written down "as proper music should be." The subtle tuning of Indian *raga* scales was considered "indicative of a bad ear" because it did not match the tuning of a piano (see Chapter 6). What the British really were saying was that they did not know how to understand Indian music on its own cultural terms. Any music sounds out of tune when its tuning system is judged by the standards of another.

Recently a person from Armenia, who had grown up listening only to Armenian music in the family and community, wrote about hearing European classical music for the first time:

> I found that most European music sounds either like "mush" or "foamy," without a solid base. The classical music seemed to make the least sense, with a kind of schizophrenic melody—one moment it's calm, then the next moment it's crazy. Of course there always seemed to be "mush" (harmony) which made all the songs seem kind of similar. (posted to SEM public listserver 9 July 1998)

From the Armenian music-culture, this listener had gotten an idea of what makes a good melody and found European classical music melodies lacking because they changed mood too quickly. Nor did this Armenian respond to the harmonic practice of Western art music. Many different kinds of harmony are found throughout the world of music. The Armenian who did not like Western classical music also felt that popular music in the United States lacked interesting rhythms and melodies:

> The rock and other pop styles then and now sound like music produced by machinery, and rarely have I heard a melody worth repeating. The same with "country" and "folk" and other more traditional styles. These musics, while making more sense with their melody (of the most undeveloped type), have killed off any sense of gracefulness with their monotonous droning and machine-like sense of rhythm. (posted to SEM public list-server 9 July 1998)

You might find these remarks offensive or amusing—or you might agree with them. Like the other examples, they are here to illustrate that listeners all over the world have prejudices based on the music they know and like. On the contrary, listening to music all over the planet fosters an open ear and an open mind. Learning to hear a strange music from the viewpoint of the people who make that music enlarges our understanding and increases our pleasure.

Music or Nonmusic?

Sound is anything that can be heard, but what is music? As we have seen, not all music-cultures have the same idea of music; some music-cultures have no word for it, while others have a word that roughly translates into English as music-dance because to them music is inconceivable without movement. Writing about Rosa, the Macedonian village she lived in, Nahoma Sachs points out that "traditional Rosans have no general equivalent to the English 'music.' They divide the range of sound which might be termed music into two categories: pesni, songs, and muzika, instrumental music" (Sachs 1975:27). Of course, this distinction between songs and music is found in many parts of the world, even in North America. Old-time Baptists in the southern Appalachian Mountains sometimes say, "We don't have music in our service," meaning they do not have instrumental music accompanying their singing. Other music-cultures have words for song types (lullaby, epic, historical song, and so on) but no overall word for music. Nor do they have words or concepts that directly correspond to what Euro-Americans consider the elements of music: melody, rhythm, harmony, and so forth.

Most of the readers of this book (and its authors) have grown up within the cultures of Europe and North America. Consciously and unconsciously our approaches and viewpoints reflect this background. However, it is important to "get out of our cultural skins" as much as possible, to view music through cultural windows other than our own. We may even learn to view our own music-culture from a new perspective. Today, because of the widespread distribution of music on radio, television, film, video, sound recordings, and computers, people in just about every music-culture are likely to have heard some of the same music. It is helpful to think about the interaction between the local and the global. This thread runs throughout our book. Though we emphasize the local, music-cultures should not be understood as isolated and untouched, but rather as ways of life that resist homogenization.

If we want to understand the different musics of the world, we need to understand them on their own terms—that is, as the music-cultures whose music we are studying do. We also need a way to talk about music as a whole without imposing our ideas of music inappropriately. To start, we can ask whether there is something about music common to all music-cultures, no matter whether the people in those cultures are aware of it. If we do find what that something is, then we can use it to guide our study of all music.

To approach this question, we might think about certain sounds that may or may not be music. We do not mean simple disagreements over whether a particular sound is music: Some people do not think rap is music, but what they are really saying is that to them it is not good or meaningful music. We mean more difficult cases that test the boundaries, such as the songs of birds or dolphins or whales—are these music?

CD 1
Track 2

Think for a moment about bird songs. Everyone has heard birds sing, but not everyone has paid attention. Try it for a moment: Listen to the songs of a hermit thrush at dusk in a spruce forest (CD Selection 2). At Walden Pond, Thoreau heard hermit thrushes that sounded like these. Many think that the thrush has the most beautiful song of all the birds native to North America. Most bird songs consist of a single phrase, repeated, but the hermit thrush's melody is more complicated. You hear a vocalization (phrase) and then a pause, then another vocalization and pause, and so on. Each vocalization has a similar rhythm and is composed of five to eight tones. The phrase is a little higher or lower each time. If you listen closely, you also hear that the thrush can produce more than one tone at once, a kind of two-tone harmony. This is the result of the way his syrinx (voice box) is constructed.

Is bird song music? The thrush's song has some of the characteristics of music. It has rhythm, melody, repetition, and variation. It also has a function: Scientists believe that birds sing to announce their presence in a particular territory to other birds of the same kind, and that they sing to attract a mate. In some species a bird can tell which other bird it is and how that bird is feeling. Bird song has inspired Western classical music composers. Some composers have taken down bird songs in musical notation, and some have incorporated, imitated or transformed bird song phrases in their compositions. Bird song is also found in Chinese classical music. In Chinese compositions such as "The Court of the Phoenix," for *sona* (oboe) and ensemble, extended passages are a virtual catalog of bird calls and songs imitated by instruments.

Yet, people in the Euro-American music-culture hesitate to call bird songs music. Because each bird in a species sings the same song over and over, bird songs appear to lack the creativity of human expression. Bird songs do not seem to belong to the human world, whereas music is defined in our culture as a human expression. By contrast, people in some other music-cultures think bird songs do have human meaning. For the Kaluli people of Papua New Guinea, bird songs are the voices of their human ancestors who have died and changed into birds. These songs cause humans grief, which expresses itself in weeping (Feld 1990). The Kaluli give a different meaning to bird songs than Euro-Americans do. Does this mean it is impossible to find a single idea of what music is? Not really. Euro-Americans may disagree with the Kaluli over whether bird songs have human meaning, but they both agree that *music* has human meaning.

Our thought-experiment with bird song and its meanings in different music-cultures suggests that music has something to do with the human world. We can go further and say that music is sound that is humanly patterned or organized (Blacking 1973). Let's take another example of a sound that tests the boundary between music and nonmusic. Listen to CD Selection 1 again. These postal workers hand-canceling stamps at the post office of the University of Ghana are making drumming sounds, and two are whistling; but there are no drums, and the workers are just passing the time. How, exactly? James Koetting (in Titon 1992: 98–99) describes the process as follows:

CD 1
Track 1

> Twice a day the letters that must be canceled are laid out in two files, one on either side of a divided table. Two men sit across from one another at the table, and each has a hand-canceling machine (like the price markers you may have seen in supermarkets), an ink pad, and a stack of letters. The work part of the process is simple: a letter is slipped from the stack with the left hand, and the right hand inks the marker and stamps the letter. . . .
>
> This is what you are hearing: the two men seated at the table slap a letter rhythmically several times to bring it from the file to the position on the table where it is to be canceled. (This act makes a light-sounding thud.) The marker is inked one or more times (the lowest, most resonant sound you hear) and then stamped on the letter (the high-pitched mechanized sound you hear) . . . The rhythm produced is not a simple one-two-three (bring forward the letter—ink the marker—stamp the letter). Rather, musical sensitivities take over. Several slaps on the letter to bring it down, repeated thuds of the marker in the ink pad and multiple cancellations of single letters are done for rhythmic interest. Such repetition slows down the work, but also makes it much more interesting.
>
> The other sounds you hear have nothing to do with the work itself. A third man has a pair of scissors that he clicks—not cutting anything, but adding to the rhythm. The scissors go "click, click, click, rest," a basic rhythm used in [Ghanaian] popular dance music. The fourth worker simply whistles along. He and any of the other three workers who care to join him whistle popular tunes or church music that fits the rhythm.

Worksong, found in music-cultures all over the world, is a kind of music whose function ranges from coordinating complex tasks to making boring and repetitive work more interesting. In this instance the workers have turned life imperceptibly into art. Writing further about the postal workers' recording, Koetting says, "It sounds like music and, of course it is; but the men performing it do not quite think of it that way. These men are working, not putting on a musical show; people pass by the workplace paying little attention to the 'music'" (Titon 1992:98). Even though the postal workers do not think of this as music, we have presented it as music here, partly because it is humanly patterned sound. Even so, not all humanly patterned sound is music. Speech, for example, is humanly patterned sound, and at times it shows musical attributes, but we do not claim that speech is music. Whether canceling stamps at the University of Ghana post office "really" is music is a philosophical question. What do you think?

People in various music-cultures pattern sounds differently. What are some of the patterns that musical sounds fall into? Several aspects of musical sound that our music-culture recognizes and talks about in ordinary language should be familiar to most readers of this book: rhythm, meter, melody, and harmony. These are ways of describing patterns or structure (form) in sound. It will be interesting to see what happens to these Western (but not exclusively Western) ideas when for better or worse they are applied to every music-culture throughout this book. Here we briefly review these ideas. Then we consider the four components of a music culture, which in music textbooks are not usually considered rudiments but are no less a part of humanly organized sound: ideas, activities, repertories, and the material culture of music.

Rhythm and Meter

In ordinary language we say *rhythm* when we refer to the patterned recurrence of events, as in "the rhythm of the seasons," or "the rhythm of the raindrops." As Hewitt Pantaleoni writes, "Rhythm concerns time felt as a succession of events rather than as a single span" (1985:211). In music, we hear rhythm when we hear a time-relation between sounds. In a classroom you might hear a pen drop from a desk and a little later a student coughing. You do not hear any rhythm, because you hear no relation between the sounds. But when you hear a person walking in the hall outside, or when you hear a heartbeat, you hear rhythm.

If we measure the time-relations between the sounds and find a pattern of regular recurrence, we have *metrical rhythm.* Think of the way soldiers march: HUP-two-three-four, HUP-two, three, four. This is a metered, regularly recurring sound pattern. You can feel recurring accents on HUP. Most popular, classical, and folk music heard in North America today has metered rhythm. Of course, most of those rhythms are more complex than the march rhythm. But if you are familiar with the plainsong Gregorian chant of the Roman Catholic Church, you know musical rhythm without meter. Although not music, ordinary speech is a common example of nonmetrical rhythm, whereas poetic verse is metrical (unless it is free verse). Think of the iambic penta*meter* in Shakespeare's plays, for example.

Most of the musical examples in this book, including the postal workers' canceling stamps (CD Selection 1), are examples of metrical rhythm. With metrical rhythm you feel the beat and move to it. The song of the hermit thrush, though (CD Selection 2), is both metrically rhythmic and not. You can find a beat while the thrush sings a phrase, but after he stops you cannot predict exactly when the bird will start again.

CD 2
Track 7

"Tsuru no sugmori," the Japanese *shakuhachi* piece (CD Selection 31), lacks a steady, dancelike beat. Its rhythm is flexible and related to the performer's breath. That it is unmetered does not mean that it is undisciplined. On the contrary, with an uneven pulsation it is harder for the student learning *shakuhachi* to convey the required precision in the sounds and silences that enhance one another (see pp. 216–221). On the other hand, the rhythm of *karnataka sangeeta* (CD Selection 25) is intricate in another way. The opening *alapana* section also has a flexible, nonmetered rhythm, but the following sections are metrically organized. This classical music of South India divides a metrical rhythm into long, complex, improvised accent patterns based on various combinations of rhythmic figures. The *mridangam* drummer's art is based on fifteen or more distinct types of finger and hand strokes on different parts of the drumheads. Each stroke has its own *solkattu,* or spoken syllable that imitates the sound of the drum stroke. Spoken one after another, they duplicate the rhythmic patterns and are used in learning and practice.

CD 2
Track 1

Although most North Americans are not usually aware of it, the music they listen to usually has more than one rhythm. The singer's melody falls into one pattern, the guitarist's into another; the drummer usually plays more than one pattern at once. Even though these rhythms are usually tied to the same overall accent pattern, the way they interact with each other sets our bodies in motion as we move to the beat. Still, to a native Armenian who grew up on a diet of more intricate rhythms, this *monometer* is dull.

CD 1
Track 1

Rhythm in the postal workers' canceling stamps (CD Selection 1) emphasizes the tugs of different patterns. For the analysis of the rhythm in this example, we turn to David Locke (Titon 1996:77–78). Locke hears the rhythms in a meter of four beats per measure, as outlined by the whistled melody, where most of the tones mark the downbeats (see Music Example 1-1 on page 10). The most regularly recurring rhythm is the high-pitched, loud, dry sound of the scissors. This is a three-tone phrase that occurs on the upbeat of counts 2, 3, and 4 (line A in Music Example 1-1). The lowest sounds are made by inking the stamp. Although we can hear a variety of "inking" rhythms, one of the favorites is given in line C of Music Example 1-1. It fills the silence after the three scissors-clicks in a question-and-answer pattern. The middle sounds are the slaps of the letters being moved into position. There are more of these sounds than the others. The slap rhythms (line B) emphasize, more than the other rhythms do, the pulse that the whistled melody lays down. All together, the three different rhythms interact with the whistled tune in such a way that we sometimes feel that the pulse has shifted from the downbeat to the upbeat.

Music Example 1-1
Postal workers' percussion "voices."
Transcription by David Locke.

We call this *polyrhythm,* the simultaneous occurrence of several distinct rhythmic phrases. Polyrhythm is characteristic of the music of Africa and wherever on the globe Africans have carried their music. In Chapter 3 you will learn to feel yet another quality of rhythmic design, *polymeter,* or the simultaneous presence of two different metrical systems, as (in Locke's terms) you "construct musical reality in two ways at once" while playing an *Ewe* (pronounced eh-way) bell pattern in *Agbekor* (see pp. 57–76).

Melody

In ordinary language we say "melody" when we want to refer to the tune, the part of a piece of music that goes up and down, the part that most people hear and sing along with. It is hard to argue that melody and rhythm are truly different qualities of music, but it helps our understanding if we consider them separately. When we say that someone has a high-pitched voice, or that someone else has a deep or low-pitched voice, we are calling attention to a musical quality called *pitch.* A sound's pitch refers to how high or low it is. When a sound is made, it sets the air in motion, vibrating at so many cycles per second. This vibrating air strikes the ear drum and we hear how high or low pitched it is depending on the speed of the vibrations. You can experience this yourself if you sing a tone that is comfortable for your voice and then slide the tone down gradually as low as you can go. When your voice goes down to a growl, you can feel the vibrations slow down in your throat. Pitch, then, depends on the frequency of these sound vibrations. The faster the vibrations, the higher the pitch.

Another important aspect of melody is *timbre,* or tone quality. Timbre is caused by the characteristic ways different voices and musical instruments vibrate. Timbre tells us why a violin sounds different from a trumpet when they are playing a tone of the same pitch. We take the timbre of our musical instrument palette for granted, but when we encounter an instrument with a timbre that we may never have heard before, such as the Australian *didgeridoo,* we sit up and take notice. Some music-cultures, like the Euro-

CD 1 Track 3

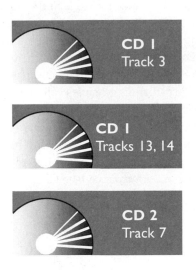

CD 1 Tracks 13, 14

CD 2 Track 7

pean, favor timbres that we may describe as smooth, or liquid; others, like the African, favor timbres that are buzzy; others, like the Asian, favor timbres that we may describe as focused in sound. Other important aspects of melody, besides pitch and timbre, include *volume*—that is, how melodies increase and decrease in loudness. The Navajo yeibichai song (CD Selection 3) begins at the loudest possible volume. Another critical aspect of melody to pay attention to in world music is *emphasis:* the way the major tones of the melody are approached (by sliding up or down to them in pitch, as some singers do; by playing them dead on, as a piano does; by "bending" the pitch, as a blues guitarist does when pushing the string to the side and back (hear CD Selections 13 and 14). Figure 6-9 (p. 160) contrasts notes and melodies on the piano with their counterparts in Indian music. Yet another way to emphasize a point in a melody is by adding decorative tones or what are called *ornaments* in classical music (hear CD Selection 31). These, too, occur in many of the musics of the world. See if you can find them as you listen to the CD set. Concentrate on the way the singers and musicians play with their tones.

Finding how different music-cultures organize sounds into melodies is one of the most fascinating pursuits for the student of music. If we sing the melody of the Christmas carol "Joy to the World," we hear how Westerners like to organize a melody. Try it:

Joy to the world, the Lord has come!
(do ti la so, fa mi re do!)

This is the familiar do-re-mi (solfège) scale, in descending order. Try singing "Joy to the World" backwards, going up the do-re-mi scale and using the syllables in this order: "come has Lord the world the to joy." You might not find that easy! But if you first sing the do-re-mi scale using the solfège syllables, and then replace do-re-me with "come has Lord," and so forth, you will be able to do it.

The white keys of the piano show how most melodies in European and Euro-American music have been organized since the eighteenth century. Do-re-mi (and so forth) comprise a major scale. Notice that these pitches are not equidistant from each other, though. Try singing "Joy to the World" starting on "re" instead of "do." You will see that it throws off the melody. If you are near a keyboard, try playing it by going down the white keys, one at a time. Only one starting key (C) gives the correct melody. This indicates that the interval between each pitch is not the same.

The Euro-American culture prefers the major scale, and Euro-Americans set up many instruments, such as the piano or the flute, so that they can easily play the pitch intervals of this scale. But other music-cultures set up their instruments and their scales differently. For example, Javanese musical gongs organize the octave (the solfège interval between one "do" and another) into nearly five equidistant intervals in their *sléndro* scale. The Javanese have a second scale, *pélog,* which divides the octave into seven tones, but the intervals are not the same as any Western scales (Music Example 7-1, p. 183). The sounds of their *gamelan,* or orchestra, reflect these different tunings (for example, CD Selection 26 is in the *pélog* scale). Japanese music also employs two scales, the *in* and *yo,* which as you may have guessed, are different from the Javanese scales, although the *yo* is a pentatonic scale that is also heard in European folk music (Music Example 8-1, p. 219). In the classical music of South India, known as *karnatic* music, each melody conforms to a set of organizing principles called a *raga.* Although each *raga* has its own scale (based on one of 72 basic scale patterns) it has more than that: characteristic melodic phrases, intonation patterns, and ornaments as well as a mood or feeling associated with it. A *raga* is an organized melodic matrix inside of which the south Indian singer or musician improvises melodically in performance (see Chapter 6, pp. 158–159).

CD 2
Track 2

Harmony

Most readers of this book use the word *harmony* to describe something that can happen to a melody: it can be harmonized. You sing a melody and someone else sings a harmony part, different from the melody, at the same time. You hear the intervals between the tones not only in a sequence, as in a melody, but also simultaneously. These simultaneously sounding tones are called chords. Western music theory is not always useful in describing music outside the Euro-American traditions, but in this case *texture,* a word borrowed from fabrics to describe the interweaving of fibers, helps describe the ways of melody and harmony in the world. Just as threads weave together to make cloth, so melodies can intertwine to make a multimelodic musical whole. *Texture* refers to the nature of these melodic interrelationships.

When the musical texture consists of a single melody only—for example, when you sing by yourself, or when several people sing the same melody in unison—we call the texture *monophonic* (mono = single; phono = voice). If you add one or more voices doing different things, the melodic texture changes and we describe the way the voices relate. In the classical music of India, it is common to have a drone, an unchanging tone or group of tones sounding continuously, against which the melody moves (see Chapter 6). Drones can also be heard on European bagpipes. When two or more voices elaborate the same melody in different ways at the same time, the texture is *heterophonic.* Although infrequent in Western music, it is typical of melodic organization in Japanese traditional music. CD Selection 32 shows heterophony among the voice and *shamisen* parts. When two or more different and distinct melodies are combined, the texture is *polyphonic.* Polyphony can also be heard in New Orleans-style jazz from the first few decades of the twentieth century: Louis Armstrong's earliest recordings offer good examples in which several melodic lines interweave. Javanese *gamelan* and other ensemble music of Southeast Asia (Chapter 7) consists of many layers of melodic activity that some scholars have described as polyphony. Polyphony is characteristic of European

CD 2
Track 8

classical music in the Renaissance period (roughly 1450 to 1600) and the late Baroque (Bach was a master of polyphony).

When two or more voices are combined in a such way that one dominates and the other(s) seem to be accompanying the dominant voice—or what most people mean when they say they hear a harmony (accompanying) part—the texture is *homophonic.* Homophony is typical of folk and popular music throughout the world. A homophonic texture characterizes country music in the United States, such as the Fenders' Navajo rendition of "Folsom Prison Blues" (CD Selection 4) and Efraín's performance of the Ecuadorian Quichua *sanjuán* "Cascarón" on the harp, which is an example of an instrument that can play a melody and an accompaniment simultaneously (CD Selection 35). Piano playing in jazz, rock, and other popular music is homophonic. The pianist usually gives the melody to the right hand and an accompaniment to the left. Sometimes the pianist's role is entirely accompanying, as when "comping" behind a jazz soloist. Blues guitarists such as Blind Blake and Mississippi John Hurt developed a homophonic style in the 1920s in which the fingers of the right hand played melody on the treble strings while the right-hand thumb simultaneously played an accompaniment on the bass strings.

CD 1
Track 4

CD 2
Track 11

Form

The word *form* has many meanings. From your writing assignments you know what an outline is. You might say that you are putting your ideas in "outline form." By form, here, you call attention to the way the structure of your thoughts is arranged. Similarly, in music, painting, architecture, and the other arts, *form* means structural arrangement. To help us understand form in music, we look for patterns of organization in rhythm, melody, and harmony. Patterns of musical organization involve, among other things, the arrangement of small to medium-sized musical units of rhythm, melody, and/or harmony that show repetition or variation. Just as a sentence (a complete thought) is made up of smaller units such as phrases, which in turn are made of individual words, so a musical thought is made up of phrases that result from combinations of sounds. Form can also refer to the arrangement of the instruments, as in the order of solos in a jazz or bluegrass performance, or the way a symphonic piece is orchestrated. Form refers to the structure of a musical performance: the principles by which it is put together and how it works.

Consider the pattern of blues lyrics. The form often consists of three-line stanzas: A line is sung ("Woke up this morning, blues all around my bed"), the line is repeated, and then the stanza closes with a different, third line ("Went to eat my breakfast and the blues were in my bread"). Blues melodies also have a particular form, as do the chord changes (harmony). These are explained in Chapter 4. The form of traditional Native-American melodies (Chapter 2) involves the creative use of small units and variation. This form is not apparent to someone listening to the music for the first time or even the second, which is one of the reasons we pay attention to it (see Music Example 2-1, p. 29). Structural arrangement is an important aspect of the way music is organized, it operates on many levels, and it is a key to understanding not only how music-cultures organize music but how various cultures and subcultures think about time and space in general. For that reason musical form is an important consideration in all the chapters that follow.

Our understanding of rhythm, meter, melody, and harmony is greatly enriched when we consider how these organizing principles of human sound are practiced in music-cultures throughout the globe. Much of the interest in the following chapters lies in seeing how these principles work in different circumstances. But there is more to music than the structure of the sounds. When people make music, they not only produce the sounds, they involve themselves in various social activities and express their ideas about music. To ethnomusicologists considering music as a human phenomenon, these activities and ideas are just as important as the music's structure. In fact, the activities and ideas are also part of the human organization of the sound. We strive for a way to talk about all the aspects of music, not just its sound. Where, for example, is there room to talk about whether musicians are true to an ideal or whether they have sold out to commercial opportunity? We try to present music in relation to individual experience, to history, to the economy and the music industry, and to a music-culture's view of the world and how human beings ought to behave in it. If people all over the world sing the music of the Beatles, we want to know how and why they do it. For that reason, we now introduce a way of talking about all these aspects of music—a model of a music-culture. This model is divided into four components: ideas about music, activities involving music, repertories of music, and the material culture of music (Table 1-1).

Four Components of a Music-Culture

Ideas about Music

Music and the Belief System

What is music, and what is not? Is music human, divine, or both? Is music good and useful for humankind or is it potentially harmful? These questions reach into the music-culture's basic ideas of the nature of human society, art, and the universe. Cultures vary enormously in their answers to these questions, and the answers often are subtle, even paradoxical; they are embodied in rituals that try to reconcile love and hate, life and death, the natural and the cultural. Even within one music-culture, the answers may change with time. For example, a medieval Christian would have trouble understanding one of today's folk masses.

In Chapter 2, for example, we shall see that music is a major part of Navajo ceremonies to cure disease (see Figure 1-1). Navajos understand the medical theories of the Euro-American world, and they use Western medicine. But they also believe that certain kinds of illness, such as depression, indicate that the person's relationship to the natural world is out of balance. Further, Navajos view nature as a powerful force capable of speaking directly to humans and teaching them the songs and prayers for the

Jeff Todd Titon

Figure 1-1
Mr. and Mrs. Walker Calhoun, holding eagle feathers. Big Cove, near Cherokee, North Carolina, 1989. The Calhouns are leaders in preserving traditional songs and dances among the east coast Cherokee.

Table 1-1 The four components of a music culture.

I. Ideas about music
  A. Music and the belief system
  B. Aesthetics of music
  C. Contexts of music
  D. History of music
II. Activities involving music
III. Repertories of music
  A. Style
  B. Genres
  C. Texts
  D. Composition
  E. Transmission
  F. Movement
IV. Material culture of music

curing rituals that restore harmony. Music is so important in the Navajo worldview that their stories of the creation of the universe are expressed traditionally in ceremonial chants. In Chapter 3, you will see that among the Ewe of Ghana, funerals feature singing, dancing, and drumming because the ancestral spirits, as well as their living descendants, love music and dance. Similarly, in Chapter 9 you will find that among the Quichua of Ecuador, and among other Roman Catholic cultures of Latin America, music and dance are integral to the child's wake, a funeral ceremony on the death of a baptized infant. Joyous singing and dancing in the presence of death is understood as an affirmation of life. The *ragas* of India, considered in Chapter 6, are thought to have musical personalities, to express particular moods. As you read through the chapters in this book, see how each music-culture relates music to its worldview.

Aesthetics of Music

When is a song beautiful? When is it beautifully sung? What voice quality is pleasing, and what grates on the ear? How should a musician dress? How long should a performance last? Not all cultures agree on these aesthetic questions involving judgments of what is proper and what is beautiful. Some people in the United States find Chinese opera-singing strained and artificial, but some Chinese find the European bel canto opera style imprecise and unpleasant. Music-cultures can be characterized by preferences in sound quality and performance practice, all of which are aesthetic discriminations.

Javanese *gamelan* music (Chapter 7) is not featured in concert the way we hear classical music in the West; rather, it is usually performed to accompany dance or theater. *Gamelan* music also accompanies a family's celebration of a birth, wedding, or other event, but people are expected to mingle and talk while the music takes place in the background. The aesthetics of Japanese *shakuhachi* flute music (Chapter 8) revolve around the breath, which produces a variety of timbres on the same instrument. Among Zen Buddhists, *shakuhachi* is regarded more as a spiritual tool, a means toward enlightenment, than as a musical instrument.

Contexts for Music

When should music be performed? How often? On what occasions? Again, every music-culture answers these questions about musical surroundings differently (see Figure 1-2). In the modern world, where context can depend on the mere flip of an on-off switch and a portable CD player, it is hard to imagine the days when all music came from face-to-face performances. Our great-grandparents had to sing or play music or hear it from someone nearby; they could not produce it on demand from the disembodied voice of a radio, television, CD player, cassette recorder, or computer. How attentively you would have listened to a singer or a band a hundred years ago if you had thought that the performance might be the only time in your life you would hear that music!

Even though much of the music around the globe today comes through mass media, people in music-cultures still associate particular musics with particular contexts. Navajo ceremonial music is appropriate in certain ceremonial contexts but not others. As we shall see in Chapter 2, these ceremonies have names like Enemyway and Blessingway, and each has a specific music which must be performed properly for the ceremony to be effective. *Vacación* is a special, symbolic composition for the harp that is performed at the start of the Quichuan child's wake, at the late-evening adorning of the corpse, and at the closing of the casket at dawn (Chapter 9).

Figure 1-2
Gospel singers at a pentecostal revival in the southeastern United States. Guitars, banjos, and camp-meeting songs that would be out of place in some U.S. churches are appropriate in this context.

Jeff Todd Titon

The usual context for blues is a bar, juke joint, dance hall, or blues club (Chapter 4). This is a far cry from the concert halls that provide the context for symphony orchestra concerts. For many centuries in India the courts and upper classes supported the classical music that we consider in Chapter 6. But concerts of classical music in India are more relaxed and informal than in Europe, where patronage from the courts and the aristocracy, as well as from the Church, traditionally supported classical music.

Today in Europe and North America the government, the wealthy classes, and the universities supply this patronage. Classical music in various parts of the world, then, usually is associated with patronage from the elite classes, and it is performed in refined contexts that bespeak the wealth and leisure of its supporters. Sometimes, though, governments intervene to support other kinds of music. For example, during the twentieth century the Soviet Union and other Communist states encouraged a certain kind of folk music, or workers' music, thought to inspire solidarity. Typically, under government management what had been a loose and informal village musical aesthetic was transformed into a disciplined, almost mechanized, urban expression of the modern industrial nation-state (see Chapter 5). Folk festivals, supported by Communist governments, showcased this music. In the United States, the last few decades have witnessed the rise of government-supported folk festivals. Here, though, the diversity of ethnic musics is celebrated, and the government encourages the most traditional expressions within the music-cultures that are represented. Folk festivals provide an artificial context for traditional music, but the hope is that in a world where young people are powerfully attracted to new, mass-mediated, transnational popular music, folk festivals will encourage this local music in its home context.

History of Music

Why is music so different among the world's peoples? What happens to music over time and space? Does it stay the same or change, and why? What did the music of the past sound like? Should music be preserved? What will the music of the future be? Some cultures institutionalize the past in museums and the future in world's fairs; they support specialists who earn their living by talking and writing about music. Other cultures pass down knowledge of music history mainly by word of mouth through the generations. Recordings, films, videotapes, CD-ROMs, and now the Internet allow us to preserve musical performances much more exactly than our ancestors could—but only when we choose to do so. One ethnomusicologist was making tapes as he learned to sing Native-American music. His teacher advised him to erase the tapes and reuse them, but he decided to preserve his lessons.

Questions about music history may arise both inside and outside a particular music-culture. Most music-cultures have their own historians or music authorities, formally trained or not, whose curiosity about music leads them to think and talk about music in their own culture, ask questions, and remember answers. In some music-cultures, authority goes along with being a good musician; in others, one need not be a good musician to be a respected historian. Historians usually are curious about music outside their own cultures as well, and they often develop theories to account for musical differences.

The four categories of ideas about music that we have just discussed—music and the belief system, aesthetics, contexts, and history—overlap. Though we separate them here for convenience, we do not want to suggest that music-cultures present a united front in their ideas about music, or that a music-culture prescribes a single aesthetic. People within a music-culture often differ in their ideas about music. Ragtime, jazz, rock and roll, and rap were revolutionary when they were introduced in the United States. They met (and still meet) opposition from some within the U.S. music-culture. This opposition is based on aesthetics (the music is thought to be loud, awful noise) and context (the music's associated lifestyles are thought to involve narcotics, violence, free love, radical politics, and so forth).

When organized divisions exist within a music-culture, we recognize music-subcultures, worlds within worlds of music. In fact, most music-cultures in the modern world may be divided into several subcultures, some opposed to each other: classical versus rock, for example, or (from an earlier era) sacred hymns versus dance music and drinking songs. Many Native-American music-cultures in the northeastern United States, for example, have a subculture of traditionalists interested in older musics that are marked as Native American, while other subcultures are involved more with the music of the Catholic Church, and yet others with forms of contemporary popular music (rock, jazz, country) that they have adapted to their needs and desires. Sometimes the subcultures overlap: The performance of a hymn in a Minnesota church may involve region (the upper

Midwest), ethnicity (German), and religion (Lutheranism)—all bases for musical subcultures. Which musical subcultures do you identify with most strongly? Which do you dislike? Are your preferences based on contexts, aesthetics, or the belief system?

Activities Involving Music

People in a music culture do not just have ideas about music, of course; they put those ideas into practice in a variety of activities—everything from making the sounds to putting music up on the Internet, from rehearsing in their rooms alone to playing in a band to managing a concert to making recordings and marketing them. Increasingly, people are becoming active consumers of music, carefully selecting the music they want to experience from the great variety that is available.

Human activities involving music also include the way people divide, arrange, or rank themselves in relation to music. The sum of musical ideas and performances is unevenly divided among the people in any music-culture. Some perform often, others hardly at all. Some musicians perform for a living, while others are paid little or nothing. People sing different songs and experience music differently because of age and gender. Racial, ethnic, and work groups also sing their own special songs, and each group may develop or be assigned its own musical role. All of these matters have to do with the social organization of the music-culture, and they are based on the music-culture's ideas about music. We may ask, "What is it like in a given music-culture to experience music as a teenage girl, a young male urban professional, a rural grandmother of Swedish ethnic heritage who lives on a farm?"

Sometimes the division of musical behavior resembles the social divisions with the group and reinforces the usual activities of the culture. The Vienna Philharmonic was in the news recently because until 1997 it had no women in its orchestra. In many traditional ceremonies throughout the world, men and women congregate in separate areas; some ceremonies are specifically for men and others for women. On the other hand, music sometimes goes against the broad cultural grain, often at carnival time or at important moments in the life cycle (initiations, weddings, funerals, and so forth). Then people on the cultural fringe become important when they play music for these occasions. In fact, many music-cultures assign a low social status to musicians but also acknowledge their power and sometimes even see magic in their work. The most important features of music's social organization are status and role: the prestige of the music-makers and the different roles assigned people in the music-culture.

Many of the musical situations in this book depend on these basic aspects of social organization. The most spiritual and meditative Japanese *shakuhachi* music was the result of *samurai* (warriors) who became Buddhist priests during the Tokugawa period (1600–1867). Japanese *kouta* is closely linked to the participation of women (Chapter 8). When blues arose early in the twentieth century, middle-class African Americans associated it with the black underclass and tried to keep their youngsters away from it. Blues musicians were assigned a low social status (Chapter 4). Neither the Argentine tango nor the Trinidadian steelband were considered respectable when they arose. Only after they gained popularity abroad and returned to their home countries did they become respectable, even becoming national symbols of music in their respective countries.

Increasingly, ethnomusicologists have turned to the ways in which race, ethnicity, class, gender, region, and identity are embedded in musical activities. When people in a music-culture migrate out of their region, they often use music as a marker of ethnic identity. Flory Jagoda and Mensur Hatic (Chapter 5) are Bosnians who have found an audience for their traditional music among Bosnians who have come to the United States. Throughout North America, ethnic groups perform and sometimes revive music that they consider to be their own, whether Jewish *klezmer* music, Andean panpipe music, central-European polka, or Peking Opera.

In the twentieth century, the music industry has played an especially important role in various music-cultures. Music is packaged, bought and sold. How does a song-commodity become popular? When is popularity the result of industry hype and when does it come from a groundswell of consumer interest? How do new kinds of music break into the media? Why do certain kinds of music gain (or fall) in popularity? What makes a hit song? Fortunes are gained and lost based on music producers' abilities to predict what will sell—yet most of the music released commercially does not sell. How should a group of musicians deal with the industry? How can they support themselves while remaining true to their musical vision? What constitutes selling out? The roles of musicians, consumers, and producers in the popular music industry throughout the world have drawn closer in the last few decades as markets have expanded and musicians from all over the globe now take part. Music has become an enormously important aspect of the global economy. The current struggles over the future of music delivery on the Internet involve profits and losses in the billions of dollars.

Repertories of Music

A *repertory* is a stock of ready performances, and a music-culture's repertory is what most of us think of as the "music itself." It consists of six basic parts: style, genres, texts, composition, transmission, and movement. Think of a music that you are familiar with and see if you can understand it in terms of the following areas.

Style

Style includes everything related to the organization of musical sound itself: pitch elements (scale, melody, harmony, tuning systems), time elements (rhythm and meter), timbre elements (voice quality, instrumental tone color), and sound intensity (loudness and softness). All depend on the music-culture's aesthetics.

Together, style and aesthetics create a recognizable sound that a group understands as its own. The fiddle was the most popular dance instrument in Europe and North America from about the eighteenth century until the turn of the twentieth century. In many areas it is still popular; in others, such as Ireland, it is undergoing a revival. Old-time fiddlers in Missouri prefer their regional dance and contest tunes to the bluegrass tunes of the upper South. Old-time fiddlers in the upper South, on the other hand, prefer their own repertory of breakdown tunes. Yet people new to these repertories do not hear significant differences between them. Are they alike? Not if each group can distinguish its own music. People learning fiddle tunes know they are getting somewhere when they can recognize the differences in national and regional styles and put those differences into words—or music.

Genres

Genres are the named, standard units of the repertory, such as "song" and its various subdivisions (for example, lullaby, Christmas carol, wedding song) or the many types of instrumental music and dances (jig, reel, waltz, schottische, polka, hambo, and so forth). Most music-cultures have a great many genres, but their terms do not always correspond to terms in other music-cultures. Among the Yoruba in the African nation of Nigeria, for example, powerful kings, chiefs, and nobles retained praise singers to sing praises to them (Olajubu 1978:685). The praise songs are called *oriki.* Although we can approximate an English name to describe them (praise songs), no equivalent genre exists today in Europe or America. In Japan, the labels identifying popular music include *gunka* (military songs), *fōku songu* (contemporary folk songs, distinguished from *minyō,* or the traditional folk songs of the countryside), *nyū myushikū* (new music), and *pops* (see Chapter 8). In North America, blues is one genre, country music another. Subdivisions of country music include rockabilly and bluegrass. If you listen to country music stations on the radio, you'll see that some identify themselves as "real country" (along with the latest hits, more of a mix of oldies and southern-oriented country music) and others as "hard country" (more of a mix of rock-oriented country music). Consider electronic dance music and some of its subdivisions; the website mp3.com lists the following: ambient, breakbeat, dance, down tempo, drum 'n' bass, electronica, experimental, game soundtracks, house, industrial electronic, techno, and trance. Subgenres have proliferated as marketing has grown more sophisticated. How many subgenres can you name in your favorite kind of music?

Texts

The words to a song are known as its *text.* Any song with words is an intersection of two very different and profound human communication systems: language and music. A song with words is a temporary weld of these two systems, and for convenience we can look at each by itself. Every text has its own history; sometimes a single text is associated with several different melodies. On the other hand, a single melody can go with several different texts. In blues music, for example, texts and melodies lead independent lives, coupling as the singer desires (Chapter 4). Guruh Sukarnoputra's *pop berat* ("heavy pop") compositions fuse Indonesian patriotic texts, traditional Indonesian musical instruments, and electric guitars and synthesizers (see Chapter 7). Navajo ritual song and prayer texts often conclude by saying that beauty and harmony prevail (see Chapter 2).

Composition

How does music enter the repertory of a music-culture? Is music composed individually or by a group? Is it fixed, varied within certain limits, or improvised spontaneously in performance? Improvisation fascinates most ethnomusicologists: Chapters 3, 4, and 6 consider improvisation in African, African-American, and South-Indian music. Perhaps at some deep level we prize improvisation not just because of the skills involved but because we think it exemplifies human freedom. Composition is another human activity bound up with social organization. Does the music-culture have a special class of composers, or can anyone compose music? Composition is related as well to ideas about music: Some music-cultures divide songs into those composed by people and those "given" to people from deities, animals, and other nonhuman composers.

Transmission

How is music learned and transmitted from one person to the next, from one generation to the next? Does the music-culture rely on formal instruction, as in South India (Chapter 6)? Or is music learned chiefly through imitation (Chapter 4)? Does music theory underlie the process of formal instruction? Does music change over time? How and why? Is there a system of musical notation? Cipher (number) notation in Indonesia arose only in the twentieth century (Chapter 7). In the ancient musical notation for the *ch'in,* the Chinese writing indicates more than what note is to be played because the Chinese pictograms (picture writing) suggest something in nature. For example, the notation may suggest a duck landing on water, telling the player to imitate the duck's landing with his finger when playing the string. Such notation can also evoke the feeling intended in the music.

Some music-cultures transmit music through apprenticeships lasting a lifetime (as in the disciple's relation to a *guru,* Chapter 6). The instructor becomes a parent, teaching values and ethics as well as music. In these situations music truly becomes a way of life, and the apprentice is devoted to the music and the teacher. Other music-cultures have no formal instruction, and the aspiring musician learns by watching and listening, often over a period of years. In these circumstances growing up in a musical family is helpful. When a repertory is transmitted chiefly by example and imitation rather than notation, we say the music exists in oral tradition rather than written. Blues (Chapter 4) is an example of music in oral tradition; so is the *sanjuán* dance genre of highland Ecuadorian Quichua (Chapter 9). Music in oral tradition varies more over time and space than does music tied to a printed musical score. Sometimes the same music exists both in oral and written traditions. People belonging to Primitive Baptist denominations in the upper South sing hymn tunes from notation in tune books such as *The Sacred Harp.* Variants of these hymn tunes also exist in oral tradition among the Old Regular Baptists, who do not use musical notation but who rely instead on learning the tunes from their elders and remembering them.

Movement

A whole range of physical activity accompanies music. Playing a musical instrument, alone or in a group, not only creates sound, but it also moves people literally—that is, they sway, dance, walk, work in response. Even if you cannot see them move very much, their brains and bodies are responding as they hear and process the music. How odd it would be for a rock band to perform without moving in response to their music, in ways that let the audience know they were feeling it. This was demonstrated several years ago by the new-wave rock band Devo when its members acted like robots. In one way or another movement and music connect in the repertory of every culture. Sometimes the movement is very loose, suggesting freedom and abandon, and at other times, as in Balinese dance, it is highly controlled, suggesting that in this culture controlling oneself is beautiful and admirable.

Material Culture of Music

Material culture refers to the material objects—objects that can be seen, held, felt, used—that a culture produces. This book is an example of material culture. So are dinner plates, gravestones, airplanes, hamburgers, pocket calculators, and school buildings. Examining a culture's tools and technology can tell us about the group's history and way of life. Similarly, research into the material culture of music can help us to understand music-cultures. The most vivid body of things in a music-culture, of course, are musical instruments. We cannot hear the actual sound of any musical performances before the 1870s, when the phonograph was invented, so we rely on instruments for important information about music-cultures in the remote past. Here we have two kinds of evidence: instruments preserved more or less intact, such as Sumerian harps over 4,500 years old, and instruments pictured in art. Through the study of instruments, as well as paintings, written documents, and other sources, we can explore the movement of music from the Near East to China over a thousand years ago, we can trace the Guatemalan marimba to its African roots, or we can outline the spread of Near Eastern musical influences to Europe, which resulted in the development of most of the instruments in the symphony orchestra.

We ask questions of today's music-cultures: Who makes instruments and how are they distributed? What is the relation between instrument makers and musicians? How are this generation's musical tastes and styles, compared with those of the previous generation, reflected in the instruments it plays? In the 1950s electric instruments transformed the sound of popular music in the United States, and in the 1960s this electronic musical revolution spread elsewhere in the world. Electric guitars, electric basses, electric pianos, pedal-steel electric guitars—even though we take these for granted today, they represented a musical revolution in the 1950s. Electronic composition was revolutionary in classical music as well. The computer is the most revolutionary musical instrument today. Computer-assisted composition, incorporating sound sampling and other innovations, empowers a new generation of composers to do things they had otherwise been unable to accomplish, while computer-assisted distribution of music through the Internet is thought to be the wave of the future—at least, the near future.

Musical scores, instruction books, sheet music—these too are part of the material culture. Scholars once defined folk music-cultures as those in which people learn to sing music by ear rather than from print, but research shows mutual influence among oral and written sources during the past few centuries in Europe, Britain, and America. Printed versions limit variety because they tend to standardize songs, yet paradoxically they stimulate people to create new and different songs. Also, the ability to read music notation has a far-reaching effect on musicians and, when it becomes widespread, on the music-culture as a whole.

One more important part of a music's material culture should be singled out: the impact of the electronic mass media—phonograph, radios, tape recorders, CDs, movies, televisions, videocassettes, and of course computers. This is all part of the information revolution, a twentieth-century phenomenon as important as the industrial revolution was in the nineteenth. These electronic media have affected music-cultures all over the world. They are one of the main reasons our planet has been called a global village.

Worlds of Music

In the eighteenth century, when Europeans began collecting music from the countryside and from faraway places outside their homelands, they thought that "real," traditional music was dying out. From then on, each time a new music-culture was discovered, the European and American collectors took the music of its oldest generation to be the most authentic, conferring on it a timeless quality and usually deploring anything new. This neither reflected the way music-cultures actually work nor gave people enough credit for creative choice. At any given moment, three kinds of music circulate within most communities: (1) music so old and accepted as "ours" that no one questions (or sometimes even knows) where it comes from; (2) music of an earlier generation understood to be old-fashioned or perhaps classic, and (3) the most recent or current musics, marketed and recognized as the latest development. These recent musics may be local, imported, or a combination of both. The last is most likely, because today the world is linked electronically; musics travel much more quickly than they did a hundred years ago.

Music-cultures, in other words, are dynamic rather than static. They constantly change in response to inside and outside pressures. It is wrong to think of a music-culture as something isolated, stable, smoothly-operating, impenetrable, and uninfluenced by the outside world. Indeed, as we shall see in Chapter 4, the people in a music-culture need not share the same language, nationality, or ethnic origin. At the turn of the twenty-first century, blues is a popular music with performers worldwide. People in a music-culture need not even share all of the same ideas about music—in fact, as we have seen, they do not. As music-cultures change (and they always are changing) they undergo friction, and the "rules" of musical performance, aesthetics, interpretation, and meaning are negotiated, not fixed. Music history is reconceived by each generation.

Music is a fluid, dynamic element of culture, and it changes to suit the expressive and emotional desires of humankind, perhaps the most changeable of the animals. Like all of culture, music is a peculiarly human adaptation to life on this earth. Seen globally, music operates as an ecological system. Each music-culture is a particular adaptation to particular circumstances. Ideas about music, social organization, repertories, and music's material culture vary from one music-culture to the next. It would be unwise to call one music-culture's music "primitive," because doing so imposes one's own standards on a group that does not recognize them. Such ethnocentrism has no place in the study of world musics.

In this book we usually describe the older musical layers first in a given region. Then we discuss increasingly more contemporary musical styles, forms, and attitudes. We wish to leave you with the impression that the world is not a set of untouched, authentic musical villages, but rather a very fluid, interactive, interlocking, overlapping soundscape in which people listen to their ancestors, parents, neighbors, and personal CD and cassette machines all in the same day. We think of people as musical activists, choosing what they like best, remembering what resonates best, forgetting what seems irrelevant, and keeping their ears open for exciting new musical opportunities. This happens everywhere, and it unites the farthest settlement and the largest city.

In the chapters that follow, we explore the acoustic ecologies of several worlds, and worlds within worlds, of music. Although each world may seem strange at first, all are organized and purposeful. Considered as an ecological system, the forces that make up a music-culture exist in a dynamic equilibrium. A change in any part of the acoustic ecology, such as the invention of the electric guitar or the latest computer music technology, may have a far-reaching impact. Viewing music this way leads to the conclusion that music represents a great human force that transcends narrow political, social, and temporal boundaries. Music offers an arena where people can talk and sing and play and reach each other in ways not allowed by the barriers of wealth, status, location, and difference. This book and CD set can present only a tiny sample of the richness of the world's music. The authors hope you will continue your exploration after you have finished this book.

References

Field, Steven. 1990. *Sound and Sentiment: Birds, Weeping, Poetics, and Song in Kaluili Expression,* 2nd ed. Philadelphia: Univ. of Pennsylvania Press.

Olajubu, Chief Oludare. 1978. "Yoruba Verbal Artists and Their Work." *Journal of American Folklore* 91:675–90.

Pantaleoni, Hewitt. 1985. *On the Nature of Music.* Oneonta, N.Y.: Welkin Books.

Sachs, Nahoma. 1975. "Music and Meaning: Musical Symbolism in a Macedonian Village." Ph.D. diss., Princeton Univ.

Schafer, R. Murray. 1980. *The Tuning of the World: Toward a Theory of Soundscape Design.* Philadelphia: Univ. of Pennsylvania Press.

Titon, Jeff Todd, ed. 1992. *Worlds of Music.* 2nd ed. New York: Shirmer Books.

———. 1996. *Worlds of Music.* 3rd ed. New York: Shirmer Books.

Additional Reading

Barz, Gregory and Timothy J. Cooley. 1997. *Shadows in the Field.* New York: Oxford Univ. Press.

Berliner, Paul. 1994. *Thinking in Jazz.* Chicago: Univ. of Chicago Press.

Crafts, Susan D., Daniel Cavicchi, Charles Keil, and the Music in Daily Life Project, 1993. *My Music.* Hanover, N.H.: Univ. Press of New England.

Hamm, Charles, Bruno Nettl, and Ronald Byrnside. 1975. *Contemporary Music and Music Cultures.* Englewood Cliffs, N.J.: Prentice-Hall.

Hood, Mantle. 1982. *The Ethnomusicologist,* 2nd ed. Kent, Ohio: Kent State Univ. Press.

May, Elizabeth, ed. 1981. *Musics of Many Cultures.* Berkeley: Univ. of California Press.

McAllester, David P. 1949. *Peyote Music.* New York:Viking Fund Publications in Anthropology no. 13.

———, ed. 1971. *Readings in Ethnomusicology.* New York: Johnson Reprint Corp.

Merriam, Alan. 1967. *Ethnomusicology of the Flathead Indians.* Chicago: Aldine.

Myers, Helen. 1992. *Ethnomusicology: An Introduction.* New York: Norton.

———. 1993. *Ethnomusicology: Historical and Regional Studies.* New York: Norton.

Nettl, Bruno. 1964. *Theory and Method in Ethnomusicology.* New York: Free Press.

———. 1983. *The Study of Ethnomusicology: Twenty-Nine Issues and Concepts.* Urbana: Univ. of Illinois Press.

———. 1985. *The Western Impact on World Music: Change, Adaptation, and Survival.* New York: Schirmer Books.

———. 1995. *Heartland Excursions: Ethnomusicological Reflections on Schools of Music.* Urbana: Univ. of Illinois Press.

Reck, David. 1977. *Music of the Whole Earth.* New York: Scribner's.

Rice, Timothy, 1994. *May it Fill Your Soul: Experiencing Bulgarian Music.* Chicago: Univ. of Chicago Press.

Shelemay, Kay Kaufman. 1998. *Let Jasmine Rain Down.* Chicago: Univ. of Chicago Press.

Titon, Jeff Todd. 1988. *Powerhouse for God: Speech, Chant, and Song in an Appalachian Baptist Church.* Austin: Univ. of Texas Press.

Turnbull, Colin. 1962. *The Forest People.* New York: Clarion Books.

CHAPTER

2

North America/Native America/Navajo

David P. McAllester

American Indian music is unfamiliar to most non-Indian Americans. We shall look in detail at some of the many types of music being performed today in one group, the Navajos. By studying the music of the Navajos of the Southwestern desert in some detail, we can see how many different kinds of music there are in even one Indian community. When we consider the cultural context of the music, we shall see how closely music is integrated with Indian life.

A Yeibichai Song from the Nightway Ceremony

CD I
Track 3

To begin with sound, we go first to one of the most exciting kinds of Navajo music, the Yeibichai songs. *Yé'ii-bi-chái* (gods-their-grandfathers) refers to ancestor deities who come to dance at one of the major ceremonials, known as Nightway. The masked dancers who impersonate the gods bring supernatural power and blessing to help cure a sick person.

Listen for a moment to the first recording (CD Selection 3; see also Music Example 2-2). When European scholars first heard this kind of sound on wax cylinder field recordings brought back to Berlin in the early 1900s, they exclaimed, "Now, at last, we can hear the music of the true savages!" For four hundred years European social philosophers had thought of American Indians as noble wild men unspoiled by civilization, and here was music that fitted the image.

Nothing known to Europeans sounded like this piercing falsetto, swooping down for more than an octave in a "tumbling strain" that seems to come straight from the emotions. Another feature that intrigued Europeans was the use of vocables (nonlexical or "meaningless" syllables) for the entire texts of the song, as in this Yeibichai song. From north of Mexico

I am grateful to vigilant student-colleagues for several corrections and improvements in this chapter; I would especially like to thank John Kelsey and Patrick Hutchinson. Mr. Hutchinson made a careful study of "Folsom Prison Blues," noting interesting textual and rhythmic elisions and complications not found in the original Johnny Cash recording. These are similar to alterations noted by Robert Witmer in popular music performed by Blood Indians in Canada (1973:79–83).

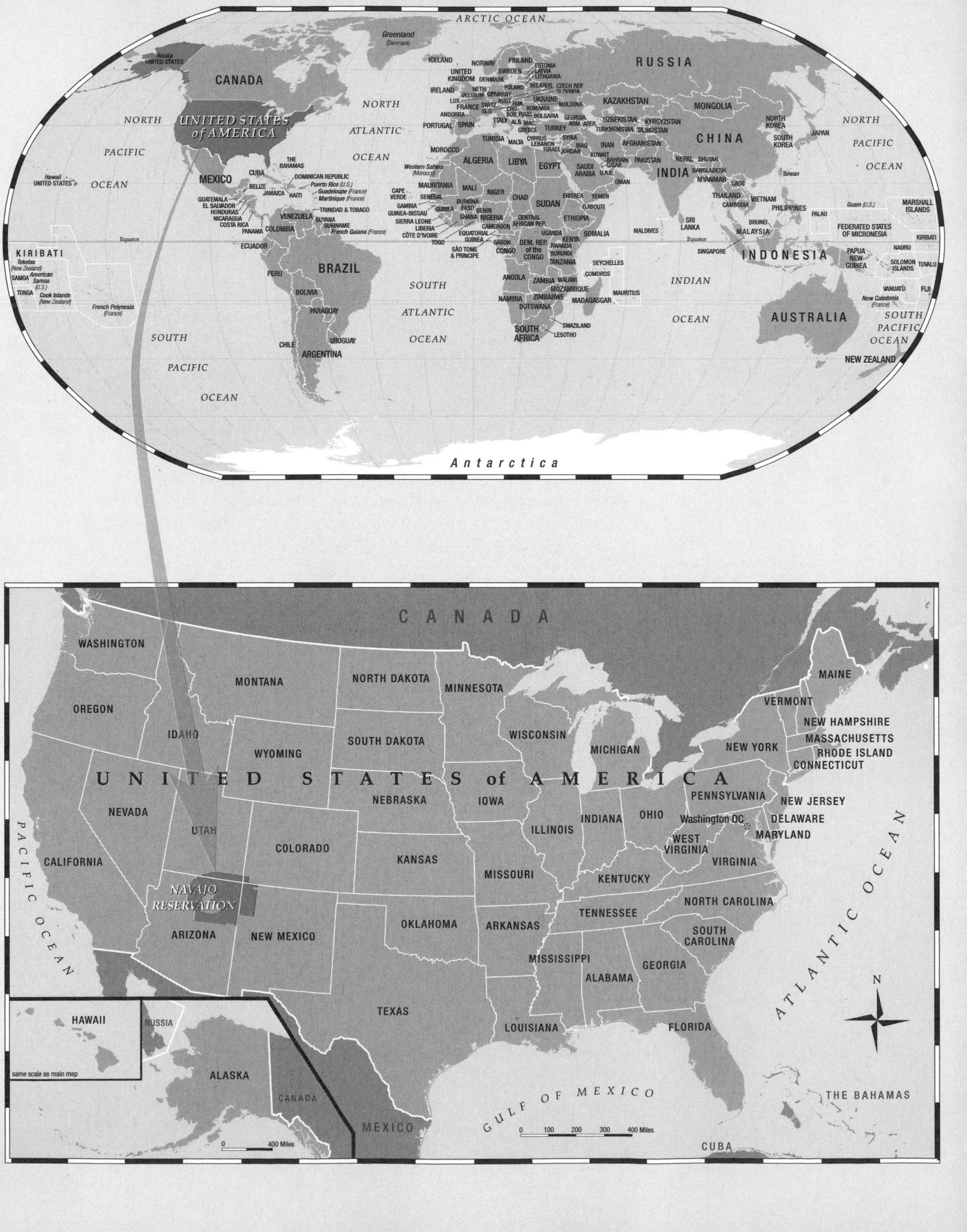

ARCTIC OCEAN
Greenland
(Denmark)
Alaska
UNITED STATES
CANADA
UNITED STATES of AMERICA
ICELAND
NORWAY
FINLAND
SWEDEN
ESTONIA
LATVIA
LITHUANIA
UNITED KINGDOM
DENMARK
IRELAND
NETH.
BELGIUM
GERMANY
POLAND
BELARUS
CZECH REP.
SLOVAKIA
LUX.
FRANCE
SWITZ.
AUST.
HUN.
SLO.
CRO.
BOS./YUGO.
UKRAINE
MOLDOVA
ROMANIA
BULGARIA
ANDORRA
PORTUGAL
SPAIN
ITALY
ALB.
MAC.
GREECE
TURKEY
GEORGIA
ARM.
AZER.
RUSSIA
KAZAKHSTAN
MONGOLIA
UZBEKISTAN
KYRGYZSTAN
TURKMENISTAN
TAJIKISTAN
NORTH KOREA
SOUTH KOREA
JAPAN
CHINA
NORTH PACIFIC OCEAN
NORTH ATLANTIC OCEAN
MOROCCO
TUNISIA
MALTA
CYPRUS
LEBANON
SYRIA
ISRAEL
JORDAN
IRAQ
IRAN
AFGHANISTAN
PAKISTAN
KUWAIT
BAHRAIN
QATAR
SAUDI ARABIA
U.A.E.
OMAN
YEMEN
NEPAL
BHUTAN
BANGLADESH
INDIA
MYANMAR
LAOS
THAILAND
VIETNAM
CAMBODIA
PHILIPPINES
Taiwan
Western Sahara
(Morocco)
ALGERIA
LIBYA
EGYPT
MAURITANIA
MALI
NIGER
CHAD
SUDAN
ERITREA
DJIBOUTI
ETHIOPIA
SOMALIA
CAPE VERDE
SENEGAL
GAMBIA
GUINEA-BISSAU
GUINEA
SIERRA LEONE
LIBERIA
CÔTE D'IVOIRE
BURKINA FASO
GHANA
TOGO
BENIN
NIGERIA
CAMEROON
CENTRAL AFRICAN REP.
EQUATORIAL GUINEA
SÃO TOME & PRINCIPE
GABON
CONGO
DEM. REP. of the CONGO
UGANDA
KENYA
RWANDA
BURUNDI
TANZANIA
SEYCHELLES
COMOROS
ANGOLA
ZAMBIA
MALAWI
MOZAMBIQUE
ZIMBABWE
NAMIBIA
BOTSWANA
MADAGASCAR
MAURITIUS
SOUTH AFRICA
SWAZILAND
LESOTHO
MALDIVES
SRI LANKA
MALAYSIA
BRUNEI
SINGAPORE
INDONESIA
PALAU
Guam (U.S.)
MARSHALL ISLANDS
FEDERATED STATES OF MICRONESIA
KIRIBATI
NAURU
PAPUA NEW GUINEA
SOLOMON ISLANDS
TUVALU
VANUATU
FIJI
New Caledonia
(France)
AUSTRALIA
NEW ZEALAND
SOUTH PACIFIC OCEAN
INDIAN OCEAN
SOUTH ATLANTIC OCEAN
Equator
THE BAHAMAS
CUBA
DOMINICAN REPUBLIC
Puerto Rico (U.S.)
Guadeloupe (France)
Martinique (France)
HAITI
JAMAICA
BELIZE
MEXICO
GUATEMALA
EL SALVADOR
HONDURAS
NICARAGUA
COSTA RICA
PANAMA
TRINIDAD & TOBAGO
VENEZUELA
GUYANA
SURINAME
French Guiana (France)
COLOMBIA
ECUADOR
PERU
BRAZIL
BOLIVIA
PARAGUAY
CHILE
ARGENTINA
URUGUAY
Hawaii
UNITED STATES
NORTH PACIFIC OCEAN
KIRIBATI
Tokelau
(New Zealand)
SAMOA
American Samoa
(U.S.)
TONGA
Cook Islands
(New Zealand)
French Polynesia
(France)
SOUTH PACIFIC OCEAN
Antarctica
CANADA
WASHINGTON
MONTANA
NORTH DAKOTA
MINNESOTA
OREGON
IDAHO
SOUTH DAKOTA
WISCONSIN
MICHIGAN
WYOMING
NEW YORK
MAINE
VERMONT
NEW HAMPSHIRE
MASSACHUSETTS
RHODE ISLAND
CONNECTICUT
UNITED STATES of AMERICA
NEVADA
NEBRASKA
IOWA
PENNSYLVANIA
NEW JERSEY
DELAWARE
MARYLAND
Washington DC
INDIANA
OHIO
ILLINOIS
WEST VIRGINIA
VIRGINIA
UTAH
COLORADO
KANSAS
MISSOURI
KENTUCKY
CALIFORNIA
NAVAJO RESERVATION
ARIZONA
NEW MEXICO
OKLAHOMA
ARKANSAS
TENNESSEE
NORTH CAROLINA
SOUTH CAROLINA
MISSISSIPPI
ALABAMA
GEORGIA
TEXAS
LOUISIANA
FLORIDA
PACIFIC OCEAN
ATLANTIC OCEAN
N
HAWAII
same scale as main map
RUSSIA
ALASKA
CANADA
0
400 Miles
MEXICO
GULF OF MEXICO
0 100 200 300 400 Miles
THE BAHAMAS
CUBA

to the Arctic, the music the Europeans heard was almost entirely vocal and the instruments were chiefly rattles and drums used to accompany the voice. The varieties of rattles and drums invented by North American Indians are legion. There are rattles made from gourds, tree bark, carved wood, deer hooves, turtle shells, spider nests, and, recently, tin cans, to name just a few. There are frame drums and barrel drums of many sizes and shapes, and the water drum, with its wet membrane, is unique in the world. There are a few flutes and flageolets, and one-stringed fiddles played without the voice, but these are rare. Instrumental ensembles like our orchestras are unknown in traditional North American Indian music. The vast majority of traditional songs are still accompanied only by the drum or rattle or sometimes both together.

Native-American traditional musics do not make use of many kinds of accompanying instruments. However, we should not conclude, as the early Europeans did, that we are dealing with a simple, unsophisticated music—or culture.

Survival, whatever the climate, requires encyclopedic knowledge. A language, though it may never have been written down, may contain the most complex grammatical structures known to linguists. Music with no harmonies may contain melodic and rhythmic sophistication unknown to European harmonic music.

CD 1
Track 3

Now for participation: listen again to the *Yeibichai* song and see if you can sing along with it. You may think it is impossible, especially if you are a man and have never tried to sing in the falsetto register before. Until you get your courage up you might find it easier to try singing the song an octave lower than the Navajo singers are. The best way to approach singing this song—and all the songs in this book—is to get the song inside you by hearing it many times. As it gradually becomes part of you, you will be able to sing parts, then all, of it.

Whether you read music or not, relax and do not try to count out the rhythms mechanically. Concentrate on feeling the energy and excitement of this challenging song, with its shouts, melodic ornaments, falsetto voices, and tense singing. Hear how after the first two shouts ("Whooo! whooo!") Sandoval Begay and his group of Yeibichai singers begin by pulsing more or less on one note over and over and how they then leap up to the falsetto range and then move the melody back and forth between falsetto and normal voice.

The text is entirely in vocables, but this song gives a good illustration of how far from "meaningless" vocables can be. From the first calls it is clear to almost any Navajo that this is a Yeibichai song: these and the other vocables all serve to identify the kind of song. Moreover, in this song there is the call of the gods themselves (see Music Example 2-1).

Music Example 2-1
Call of the Yei.

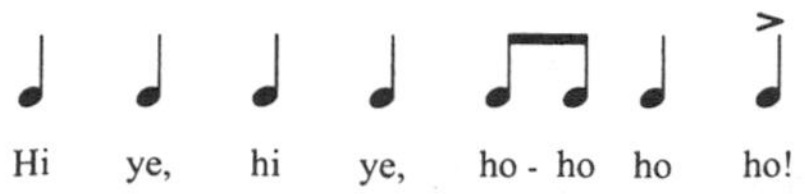

Though there are hundreds of different Yeibichai songs, they usually contain some variation of this call of the Yei. The transcription (Music Example 2-2) will help you with the text and melody. Even if you cannot read notes, think of the transcription as a kind of graph tracing the line of the melody. With no musical training one still can see patterns of movement from high to low and back up again. I have labeled the sections of the song that sound alike with the same letter of the alphabet to help you see where similar musical ideas are repeated. As you listen, pick out the sections that sound the same, or nearly so. Eventually you will hear a structure like this.

Music Example 2-2
Navajo Yeibichai song. Transcription by David P. McAllester from field recording by Willard Rhodes

* Repeat from A twice. High yell replaces 1st 2 notes of A on the first repeat; second repeat ends at "Fine".

After the long introduction (phrases X, Y, and Z), sung almost entirely on the base note (the "tonic") of the song, the melody leaps up an octave. In the first phrase, A, after the introduction, the song comes swooping briskly down to the tonic again to an ending I have labeled "e^1." This ending appears again later on in the song in two variations, "e^2" and "e^3." (I am using capital letters to denote main phrases and small letters for motifs within the phrases.) The same descent is repeated (the second A and e^1) and then another acrobatic plunge takes place in B after two "false starts" that are each very close to the first half of A. I call these ½a and ½a. The song then hovers on the tonic e^2 and e^3 and the phrase *hi ye, hi ye,* which also appears in Y and Z. I call it "z" because it has the weighty function of ending the introduction, and, eventually, the song itself, in the Z phrase. After B, another interesting variation in the use of previous motifs occurs: the *second* half of A is sung twice, a½ and a½, followed by the first half of A, also repeated, ½a and ½a.

The Navajos are noted for their bold experiments in artistic form. This is true in their silversmithing, their weaving, their sandpainting, and their contemporary commercial painting. Here is an example from their music of the play of melodic and rhythmic motifs. Listen again to the CD selection, following the pattern of this complex and intriguing song, and try to sing along.

Yeibichai singers are organized in teams, often made up of men from one particular region or another. They create new songs or sing old favorites, each team singing several songs before the nightlong singing and dancing are over. The teams prepare costumes and masks and practice a dance of the gods that proceeds in two parallel lines with reel-like figures. They also have a clown, who follows the dancers and makes everyone laugh with his antics: getting lost, bumbling into the audience, imitating the other dancers. The teams compete, and the best combination of costumes, clowns, singing, and dancing receives a gift from the family giving the ceremony. The representation of the presence of the gods at the Nightway brings god power to the ceremony and helps the sick person get well.

This dance takes place on the last night of a nine-night ritual that includes such ceremonial practices as purification by sweating and vomiting, making prayer offerings for deities whose presence is thus invoked, and sand-painting rituals in which the one-sung-over sits on elaborate designs in colored sands and other dry pigments. The designs depict the deities; contact with these figures identifies the one-sung-over with the forces of nature they represent and provides their protective power (see Figure 2-1). In the course of the ceremony, hundreds of people may attend as spectators, whose presence lends support to the reenactment of the myth on which the ceremony is based. The one-sung-over takes the role of the mythic hero, and the songs, sand paintings, prayers, and other ritual acts recount the story of how this protagonist's trials and adventures brought the Nightway ceremony from the supernatural world for the use

Figure 2-1
Ceremonial practitioner making a sandpainting of a Lightning Diety in flint armor.

Neg. no. 2A 3634. Courtesy American Museum of Natural History (Photo: Boltin).

of humankind (Faris 1990). Besides the Yeibichai songs, there are hundreds of long chanted songs with elaborate texts of translatable ritual poetry.

Such a ritual drama as Nightway is as complex as "the whole of a Wagnerian opera" (Kluckhohn and Leighton 1938:163). The organization and performance of the whole event is directed by the singer or ceremonial practitioner, who must memorize every detail. Such men and women are among the intellectual leaders of the Navajo communities. Frisbie and McAllester (1978) offer the life story and a rare glimpse into the mind of such a person, Frank Mitchell.

Some readers find the Yeibichai song difficult to learn. The shifts in emphasis, the many variations, and the difficult vocal style demand hours of training before one can do it well. But there are many other kinds of Navajo music.

"Folsom Prison Blues"

Of course you can join in this song (CD Selection 4) right away, especially if you are familiar with country and western music. This version of Johnny Cash's "Folsom Prison Blues" is played and sung by the Fenders,

Figure 2-2
Album cover of the Fenders, an early Navajo country and western group.

an all-Navajo country band from Thoreau, New Mexico, who were popular in the 1960s and 1970s (Figure 2-2). Country music has long been a great favorite with Indian people, especially in the West, just as it is with a large part of the general U.S. public. There are several country and western bands on the Navajo reservation, and some, like the Sundowners and Borderline, have issued records that sell well in Indian country. Even more popular are non-Indian country singers such as Garth Brooks and Tim McGraw. The cowboy and trucker image is appealing to most Westerners, including Indians, who identify with the open life and the excitement of the roundup and the rodeo. The Fenders' liner notes (1966) begin as follows:

> The five Fenders are genuine cowboys . . . as much at home on the back of a bucking rodeo bronc as behind the wild guitar at a good old rodeo dance. These boys believe that to be a No. 1, all-around cowboy, you must be able to play the guitar and sing just as well as you ride, rope and bull-dog.

The Navajo Way of Life

Who are these Navajos we are listening to, and where and how do they live? At more than 200,000, they are our largest Indian tribe. Descended from Athabascan-speaking nomadic hunters who came into the Southwest as recently as six or seven hundred years ago, they now live in scattered communities ranging from extended family groups to small towns on a reservation of some 25,000 square miles (larger than West Virginia) spread over parts of New Mexico, Arizona, and Utah. The exact census of the Navajos is uncertain, since there are thousands living off the reservation in border towns such as Farmington, Gallup, and Flagstaff and such cities as Chicago, Los Angeles, and San Diego. The reason for their move is largely economic: Their population has outgrown the support afforded by the reservation.

On the reservation the Navajos' livelihood is based to a small but culturally significant degree on farming, stock raising, weaving, and silversmithing. But the major part of their $110 million annual income comes from coal, uranium, oil, natural gas, and lumber. Much of their educational and health care funds derive from the Department of the Interior, some of it in fulfillment of the 1868 treaty that marked the end of hostilities between the Navajos and the United States Army. Personal incomes range from the comfortable salaries of tribal administrative and service jobs to the precarious subsistence of marginal farmers. Many Navajos are supported on various kinds of tribal or government relief.

Though much of traditional Navajo culture remains intact, the People (*Diné*), as the Navajos call themselves, also welcome new ideas and change. Their scholarship funds enable hundreds of young people to attend colleges and universities around the country, including their own Navajo Community College on the reservation. A battery of attorneys and a Natural Resources Committee keep watch on the mining leases and lumber operations. The Navajos also operate motels, restaurants, banks, and shopping centers, and they encourage small industries to establish themselves on the

Figure 2-3
Navajos still travel on horseback in many parts of the reservation.

Neg. no. 335258. Courtesy American Museum of Natural History (Photo: Boltin)

reservation. Some Navajos jet to administrative and development conferences in Washington, D.C.; others speak no English and herd sheep on horseback or on foot miles from the nearest paved road (see Figure 2-3).

The men dress in western style, and some of the women still wear skirts and blouses copied from the dresses worn by United States Army officers' wives in the 1860s, during the imprisonment of the Navajos at Fort Sumner, New Mexico. The skirts have shortened in recent years, and Navajo taste demands the addition of buttons, rings, bracelets, necklaces, and heavy belts of silver set with turquoise. The men wear this jewelry, too, sometimes with the added panache of silver hatbands on big cowboy hats. Young people, male and female, are now usually seen in blue jeans like

Figure 2-4
Hand weaving is a source of income for many Navajo women. This scene, from the 1920s, is still common today.

Neg. no. 14471. Courtesy American Museum of Natural History (Photo: P. E. Goddard).

other young people anywhere in the country. The Navajos' famous rugs are woven for cash income; most of them go to the local store, sometimes still called a trading post, to pay for food and other supplies. Some of these rugs are so finely designed and woven that they have brought $20,000 apiece and more in the world market for fine arts (see Figure 2-4).

Navajo houses range from the modern stucco ranch houses and large trailer homes of tribal officials, administrative staff, and school personnel to smaller one-room houses of every description. Some of the old-style circular log hogans (Navajo *hooghan,* place home) can still be seen. Navajo ceremony requires a circular floor plan, and many adaptations of this well-loved and ceremonially important shape are designed into new kinds of structures. The Tribal Council Building in Window Rock, Arizona, is a round sandstone structure with Indian murals inside. The Cultural Center at the Navajo Community College at Traile, Arizona, is six stories of concrete, steel, and glass, but it is octagonal, with a domed roof. Inside, at the heart of the building, is a replica of a traditional log hogan with a dirt floor and a smoke hole that goes up four stories through a shaft to the open sky. It is there as a religious symbol and a meditation room. School buildings, chapter houses, information centers, and arts and crafts outlets exhibit other variations in size and design on the circular shape, which is symbolic of the earth, and on the domed roof, which is symbolic of both mountaintops and the vault of the sky.

Traditional Popular Music

Until the 1940s the most popular musics on the reservation were the different kinds of dance songs from the ceremonials. We have already studied a Yeibichai dance song from Nightway. Corral dance songs from several ceremonies were also popular, but the several different kinds of Ndáá' (war dance)* songs from Enemyway made up the largest body of traditional popular music. These include Circle Dance, Sway songs, Two-step, Skip Dance, and Gift songs. After being eclipsed by country and western music in the 1960s and 1970s, the traditional songs are once again popular on the reservation.

A new recreational pastime called "song and dance" emerged in the 1990s that makes use of Skip Dance and Two-step songs. These can take place in any large hall; couples of all ages, in traditional costumes, participate. Singers or tapes provide the music, and the dancers, identified by large numbered tags, circle the hall while judges note their costumes and dancing skill. Winners receive trophies, and entry fees and donations solicited during the dancing go toward the expenses of the Song and Dance Association hosting the event, or for specified benefits such as school programs.

Some traditionalists have objected to Ndáá' Dance songs being used in this new, secular context, but this is only the latest in a number of new

*Also known as Squaw Dance songs. Many Native Americans now regard the word *squaw* as derogatory, and so we use the Navajo term, *Ndáá'*.

uses. Radio broadcasts have featured Ndáá' Dance songs since the 1930s, and they are having a new wave of radio popularity in the 2000s.

The Circle Dance Song "Shizhané'é"

Ndáá' Dance songs are the hit tunes of traditional Navajo life. Compared with the Yeibichai songs, Ndáá' Dance songs are easy to sing, though to an outsider they can contain some surprises. Many of them are sung entirely on vocables, but the Circle Dance song "Shizhané'é" (CD Selection 1-5; see also Music Example 2-3) contains words that can be translated as well. If you listen to this song a few times, you should be able to get into the swing of this lively melody. Since you do not have to worry about producing the high falsetto sounds of the Yeibichai songs, you can concentrate on other fine points. Pay attention to the sharp little emphases marked with >. See if you can reproduce the nasal tone the Navajos like in their singing. Every phrase ends with

This and the triple meter are characteristic of Circle Dance songs (McAllester 1954:52). Notice how the A phrases in Music Example 2-3 introduce the melodic elements that are more fully developed in B and even more so in C. The whole structure is too long to include on the sound recording.

Music Example 2-3
"Shizhané'é." Navajo Circle Dance song. Transcription by David P. McAllester.

With permission of Albert Sandoval, Jr., and Ray Winnie.

The translatable portion of the text, in the C phrases, is like a nugget in the middle of the song, framed by a vocable chorus before and after it. This is a favorite principle of design in other Navajo arts as well as music. It is the dynamic symmetry discussed by Witherspoon (1977:170–74) and illustrated in weaving and silver jewelry designs. The brief, humorous text is, like many another in Navajo song, intended to make the girls laugh and pay attention to the (male) singers. Though the dance is part of a ceremony, it is also a courtship situation and a social dance.

Shizhané'é

The text as it is sung:

Shizhané'é, shizhané'é, kiya sizini shika nootaał
'aweya he nai ya.

Free translation: I'm in luck, I'm in luck!
She's leaning up against the store front,
Looking everywhere for me!

As the Navajo is spoken, with literal translation:

shizhané'é	me-good luck
kíyah	house-under/against
sizíní	standing-the one who
shíká	me-for/after (as in running after one)
nóotááł	searching for (3rd person)

With permission of Albert Sandoval, Jr., and Ray Winnie.

Linger for a moment on the choices of expression that make the words so witty. The song begins with fatuous self-congratulation. But then we learn both from the form "yah" after "house" and from the neuter static form of sizį́, "the one who is standing," that the girl is really propped against the house. The suggestion is that she has had too much to drink and therefore is unable to be actively searching for ("running after") the singer at all, even though he claims she is. The irony of the situation is combined with a jesting implication that women drink too much and chase after young men. Since the men actually do most of the drinking and chasing after the opposite sex, the song is all the funnier. *Kiyah sizíní* also carries the meaning "prostitute." As in all clever poetry, the zest is in the subtle shades of meaning.

Note on Pronunciation in Navajo

The ´ indicates a glottal stop, as in "oh-oh!" (ó-ó)

ł	is like the Welsh ll in Floyd, unvoiced with the breath coming out on either side of the tongue.	
aa	indicates a long "a"	likewise: oo and other vowels
ą	indicates a nasal "a"	likewise o and other vowels
é	indicates a high "e:"	Navajo has speech tones like Chinese.
ée	indicates a long "e" falling from high to low in tone	

Vowels have "Continental values."

The Enemyway Ceremony

Religion is one of the keys to understanding culture. We will know the Navajos better if we take a closer look at the Enemyway ceremony in which "Shizhané'é" is used. Enemyway is one of the most frequently performed rites in traditional Navajo religion. Like Nightway, discussed earlier, it is a curing ritual. In this case the sickness is brought on by the ghosts of outsiders who have died. Enemyway is often performed for a returned Navajo member of the United States Armed Forces or for others who have been away from home among strangers for a long time. A Navajo who has been in a hospital and returns home cured, in our sense, may have an Enemyway performed because of the inevitable exposure to the spirits of the many non-Navajos who have died in such a place (see Figure 2-5).

The disease theory of the Euro-American world is recognized by the Navajos, and they gladly take advantage of hospitals, surgery, and antibiotics. But, in addition, they see bad dreams, poor appetite, depression, and injuries from accidents as resulting from disharmony with the world of nature. The Navajos see the power of animals, birds, and insects, and also of earth, water, wind, and sky as active potencies that have a direct influence on human life. All of these forces may speak directly to human beings and may teach them the songs, prayers, and ritual acts that make up the ceremonials. At the center of this relationship with the natural world is the concept of ***hózhǫ́ǫ́*** (beauty, blessedness, harmony), which must be maintained, and which, if lost, can be restored by means of ritual. The prayers invoke this state over and over at their conclusions.

Concluding Phrase of Navajo Prayer

Hózhǫ́ǫ́ nahasdlį́į́',
Hózhǫ́ǫ́ nahasdlį́į́',
Hózhǫ́ǫ́ nahasdlį́į́',
Hózhǫ́ǫ́ nahasdlį́į́'!

Conditions of harmony have been restored,
Conditions of harmony have been restored,
Conditions of harmony have been restored,
Conditions of harmony have been restored!

The Enemyway ceremony involves two groups of participants, the "home camp" and the "stick receiver's camp." Members of the latter represent the enemy and are custodians of a stick decorated with symbols of the warrior deity, Enemy Slayer, and of his mother, Changing Woman, who is the principal Navajo deity. The decorated stick is brought from the home camp along with gifts of many yards of brightly colored yarn. The first night of the ceremony consists of singing and dancing at the stick receiver's camp. This kind of dancing is the only time in traditional Navajo life that men and women dance together. It was, and is, a time for fun and courtship. Before the dancing starts there is a concert of "Sway songs," in which the courtship theme may be expressed. A majority of the Sway songs, however, have texts entirely of vocables.

Figure 2-5
Scene by Navajo Painter Andy Tsihuahjinnie shows drumming, singing, and dancing at the public part of an Enemyway ceremony.

Courtesy Andy Tsihuahjinnie

Navajo Sway Song

Heye yeye ya,
Lonesome as I am,
Lonesome as I am, ha-i na,
Lonesome as I am,
Lonesome as I am, ha,
Lonesome as I am, na'a-ne hana. . . .

After an hour or so, the singing shifts to dance songs and the women appear, looking for partners. It is always "ladies' choice," a reflection, perhaps, of the powerful position women have in Navajo society. They own the household; the children belong to the mother's clan, not the father's; and when a couple marry it is traditional for the husband to move in with his wife's family.

Navajo Enemyway Dance Song

He-ne, yane, yana-,
Yala'e-le- yado'eya 'ana he,
Yala'e-le- yado'eya ne. . . .

Your daughter, at night,
Walking around, yado'eya yana hana,
Tomorrow, money,
Lots of it, there will be, yana hana,

Yala'e-le- yado'eya na'ana,
Yala'e-le- yado'eya na'ana he. . . .

In the dance the women are likely to act bashful, but they find partners, and the couples dance along together following other couples in a large circle. The step is simply a light stepping along with a bounce on each step. When a woman is ready to change partners she lets the man know by demanding a token payment. Even some Navajos do not know that this is a symbol of the war booty brought back by Enemy Slayer from a mythical war and given away to Navajo women in the story in celebration of the victory. The song texts of the dance songs often poke fun at the women and sometimes refer to these payments.

After a few hours of dancing, a Signal song (McAllester 1954:27) indicates that the singing is to go back to Sway songs. The dancing stops, and the Sway songs may go on for the rest of the night. Again, the symbolism is of war; the group of singers is divided into two halves, representing the home camp and the enemy, and the singers compete in vigor, repertory, and in seeing who can sing the highest.

They stop at dawn, but after a rest and breakfast a new kind of singing, a serenade of Gift songs, takes place. The home camp people sing outside the main hogan in the stick receiver's camp, and in exchange small gifts like oranges and boxes of Cracker Jack are thrown to the singers through the smoke hole. Larger gifts such as expensive blankets are brought out and handed to responsible members of the singing group; these presents will be reciprocated later in the ceremony. Most of the Gift songs are old and have text entirely in vocables, but a few of the newer ones have words concerning the hoped-for gifts.

Navajo Enemyway Gift Song

Heye yeye yana,
Your skirts, how many? yi-na,
To the store I'm going, 'e hyana heye yeye ya,
To Los Nores I'm going, 'e hya 'ena hya na. . . .

'e-ye yeye yana,
Goats, I came for them, yo'o'o 'ene hanena,
Goats, I came for them yo'o'o 'ene hane,
Yo'o'o 'ena heye yeye yana. . . .

The gifts, like the payments during the dancing, represent war booty. The trip of the home party can be seen as a raid into enemy country and the gifts as the booty they take home with them. But reconciliation is symbolized at the same time, since the stick receiver's camp provides supper and camping facilities, and since the meal and gifts will be returned in a similar exchange on the third morning.

After the breakfast and gift singing on the second day, the stick receiver's party prepares to move toward the home camp. Most of the home camp people leave early, but one of their number remains as an official guide to lead the stick receiver to a good camping place a few miles from the home camp. They time their arrival to take place at about sundown, and another night of singing and dancing follows at this new camp.

Early the next morning the war symbolism of the ceremony is sharply emphasized with a sham battle. The stick receiver's people ride into the home camp with yells and rifle shots, raising a lot of dust and committing small depredations such as pulling down clotheslines. After four such charges they retire to a new campsite a few hundred yards away and a procession from the home camp brings them a sumptuous breakfast. After the meal, the return gift singing takes place at the hogan of the one-sung-over.

Now comes further, heavy war drama. In a secret indoor ritual the afflicted person is given power and protection by sacred chanting and is dressed for battle. At the climax of the ceremony he goes forth and shoots at a trophy of the enemy, thus ritually killing the ghost. The songs used in the preparation of the warrior include long derisive descriptions of the enemy and praise of Navajo warriors (Haile 1938:276–84). If the person being sung over is a woman, a man takes her place when it comes to shooting the enemy ghost.

In the late afternoon a Circle Dance is performed at the stick receiver's new camp. Men join hands in a circle, the two halves of which represent the two camps. Now songs like "Shizhané'é" (Music Example 2-3) are sung. The two sides of the circle take turns singing in a competition to see who can sing the best songs most beautifully. As the songs alternate, so does the direction in which the Circle Dance moves. Most of the songs have no translatable words, and those that do are not overtly about war; however, the presence of the two competing sides is a reminder of conflict, and it is thought that every drumbeat (see Figure 2-6) accompanying the songs drives the enemy ghosts farther into the ground. After a while several other women and a girl carrying the stick may enter the circle and walk around following the direction of the dancing men. The symbols of Changing Woman and her warrior son incised on the sacred stick are further reminders of the meaning of the dance.

After the Circle Dance, another dramatic event takes place: the secret war name of the afflicted person is revealed. Members of the stick receiver's camp walk over to the home camp, singing as they go. Four times on the way, they stop and shout out the identity of the enemy. Then the stick receiver sits down in front of the ceremonial hogan and sings four songs that mention the name of the enemy and that of the one-sung-over. In tra-

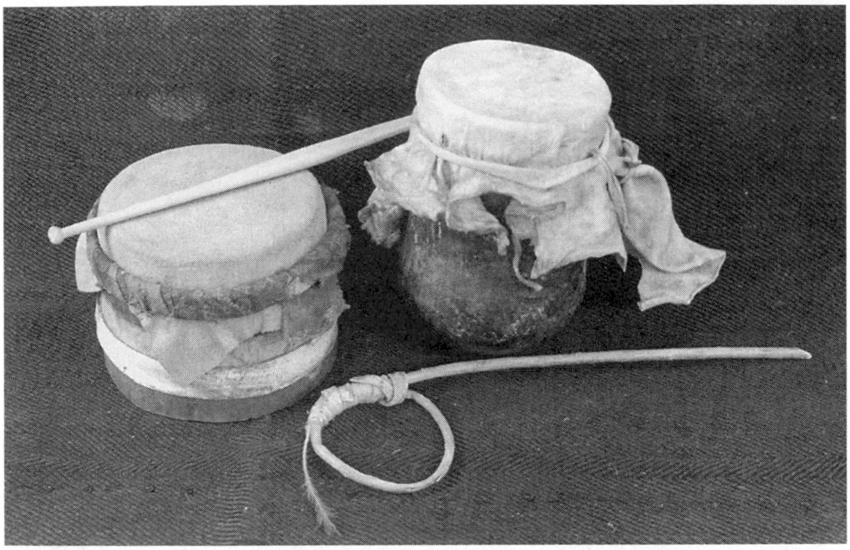

Figure 2-6
Two kinds of water drum. On the left is an Iroquois drum made from a short section of hollowed-out log. On the right is a Navajo pottery water drum, used only in the Enemyway ceremony.

Susan W. McAllester

ditional Navajo life it is impolite to address anyone by name and, in particular, by his or her war name. Polite address is by a kinship term, real or fictitious. Examples of war names are She Went Among War Parties, or He Ran Through Warriors (Reichard 1928:98–99).

The songs describe battle with the enemy and refer to the anguish of the enemy survivors. The death of the enemy ghost is mentioned. Then, after a serenade of Sway songs, the stick receiver's party move back to the dance ground at their camp, and the last night of the ceremony begins with a further selection of Sway songs. After an hour or so the singing changes to dance songs and dancing, which, as on the previous two nights, may go on for several hours. Again the Signal song indicates the end of dancing, and the rest of the night is spent in Sway song competition between the two camps.

At dawn the ceremony ends with a brief blessing ritual conducted while facing the rising sun. The stick receiver's party departs, and the afflicted person, now protected by the many symbolic ways in which the ghost has been eliminated, spends four days in rest and quiet while the effect of the ceremony becomes established over the entire household.

The Native American Church

In their comparatively recent history the Navajos have felt the call of two highly organized religious movements from outside their traditional culture. One is evangelical Christianity. The other is the Native American Church, an Indian movement with roots in ancient Mexico and recent development in Oklahoma. This religion established itself firmly in the United States in the nineteenth century and thereafter developed different perspectives and music from that which can still be seen among the Tarahumare and Huichol Indians of Mexico. It found its way into the

Navajo country in the 1930s. By the 1950s it had grown in this one tribe to a membership estimated at 20,000.

CD I
Track 6

This music is strikingly different from traditional Navajo music. Let us listen to a hymn from the Native American Church and then consider the role of this music in contemporary Navajo life (CD Selection 6; see also Music Example 2-4).

What first arrests the attention is the quiet, introspective quality of the singing in this simple melody. Members of the Native American Church speak of their music as prayer. Although the text has no translatable words, the repetitive simplicity of vocables and music expresses a rapt, inward feeling. According to one theory, Native American Church hymns are derived from Christian hymnody. The quiet, slow movement and the unadorned voice, so unlike the usual boisterous, emphatic, out-of-doors delivery in Indian singing, seem to suggest this interpretation. On the other hand, there are many more features that are all Indian: the rhythmic limitation to only two note values, ♪ ♩ (a specialty of Navajo and Apache music); the descending melodic direction; the rattle and drum accompaniment, the pure melody without harmony; the use of vocables. These features are present in Native American Church music in many different tribes all across the continent to such a marked extent that a distinct, pantribal "Peyote style" can be identified (McAllester 1949:12, 80–82). In the present song, every phrase ends on "he ne yo," anticipating the "he ne yo we" of the last phrase. This ending, always sung entirely on the tonic, is as characteristic of Native American Church music as "amen" is to Christian hymns and prayers.

True to its Oklahoma origin, the Native American Church ideally holds its meetings in a large Plains Indian tipi. This is often erected on Saturday

Music Example 2-4
Navajo Peyote song. Transcription by David P. McAllester from field recording by Willard Rhodes.

evening for the all-night meeting and then taken away to be stored until the next weekend. Such mobility enables the meeting to move to wherever members want a service. Meetings are sometimes held in hogans because they, too, are circular and have an earth floor where the sacred fire and altar can be built.

The Indians of the Native American Church use a water drum and a rattle to accompany their singing. The drum is made of a small, old-fashioned, three-legged iron pot with a wet, almost rubbery, buckskin drumhead stretched over the opening. The pot is half full of water, which is splashed over the inside of the drumhead from time to time by giving the drum a tossing motion. This act serves to keep the drumhead moist and flexible while in use. The player kneels, holding the drum on the ground tipped toward his drumming hand. He controls the tone with pressure on the drumhead from the thumb of his holding hand. He strikes the membrane rapidly and rather heavily with a smooth, hard, slightly decorated drumstick. It is supposed that the water inside the pot has something to do with the strong resonance of this and other kinds of water drums, but no physical studies have yet been made to test the theory.

The peyote rattle is made with a small gourd mounted on a handle stick. The stick fits snugly into a hole in the center of a plug in the mouth of the gourd so that it is wedged tight. The distal (far) end of the stick protrudes two or three inches beyond the gourd, and a tuft of dyed horsehair is attached. This is often red to symbolize the red flower of the peyote cactus. Many Native American Church members hold a beautifully decorated feather fan during the service and use it to waft toward themselves the fragrant incense of cedar needles when these are put into the fire. The feathers of the fan are mounted in separate moveable leather sleeves, like the feathers of the Plains warbonnet. This allows the user to manipulate the fan in such a way that each feather seems to have a quivering life of its own.

The ritual consists of long prayers, many groups of four songs each (sung in turn by members of the meetings), a special water break at midnight, and a fellowship breakfast in the morning. At intervals, under the direction of the leader of the meetings, a Cedar Chief builds up the fire, puts cedar incense on the coals, and passes the cigarettes to make the sacred smoke that accompanies the prayers. He also passes small pieces of a cactus called peyote (from the Aztec *peyotl* "wooly," describing the fine white hairs that grow in tufts on the cactus). When eaten, peyote produces a sense of well-being and, sometimes, visions in vivid color. The peyote is eaten as a sacrament, since Father Peyote is one of the deities of the religion. The Native American Church is sometimes called the Peyote Church.

A crescent-shaped earthen altar six or seven feet long lies west of the fire, and a large peyote cactus, symbolic of Father Peyote, is placed at the midpoint of the crescent. Prayers may be directed to Father Peyote, and some members can hear him responding to their pleas for help in meeting the difficulties of life. The intense feeling of dedication and piety at Peyote Meetings is expressed through prayers and testimonies, often with tears running down the cheeks of the speaker. Prayers include appeals to Jesus and God, as well as to Father Peyote. Peyotists consider that the Native American Church is hospitable to all other religions and includes their ideas in its philosophy and beliefs. Prayers are made for friends and family members who are ill or otherwise in need of help. Leaders of the church, of the Navajo tribe, and of the country at large are also included in the prayers.

The Native American Church was bitterly opposed by tradition-minded Navajos; in the late 1940s meetings were raided by the police and church leaders were jailed. But the church constituency grew so large that the new religion had to be accepted, and today the tipis for peyote meetings can be seen in many Navajo communities. One of these tipis stands near the Cultural Center of Navajo Community College, where participation in the Native American Church's meetings is a recognized student activity.

New Navajo Music

New Composers in Traditional Modes

Among the new kinds of Navajo music is a genre of recently composed songs based, musically, on Enemyway style (usually Sway songs or Dance songs) but not intended for use in that ceremony. The texts are in Navajo, because the songs are intended for Navajo listeners, but they contain social commentary in a different vein from that of the popular songs of Enemyway. The new message is one of protest. A good illustration is the treatment of the use of alcohol in the old songs and the new. The first example in this contrast is a Skip Dance song from Enemyway, probably dating from the 1920s.

Navajo Enemyway Skip Dance Song

'E- ne- ya,

My younger brother,
My whiskey, have some! Nana, he, ne-ye,

My younger brother,
My whiskey, have some! Nana, he, ne-ye,

Your whiskey is all gone, ne,
My whiskey, there's still some, wo,

He yo-o-wo-wo, he yo-o-wo-wo,
Heya, we, heyana, he, nai-ya.

"Navajo Inn" is a recent song by Lena Tsoisdia, a social service worker at Window Rock, the headquarters of the Navajo tribal government. The title takes its name from a drive-in liquor store that used to do a thriving business a few miles from Window Rock. The store was just across the reservation boundary and was thus outside the jurisdiction of the tribal prohibition laws. The lyrics refer to the inn and speak despairingly of women finding their husbands, unconscious, behind "the tall fence."

Ruth Roessel, a prominent Navajo educator, has composed a song about the "Long Walk," when the Navajos were rounded up by Kit Carson and his troops in 1864 and forcibly removed to a large concentration camp at Ft. Sumner, New Mexico. The hardships of the march, which preceded four years of captivity, and the Navajo love for their land are recounted here.

The Long Walk

Long, long ago, our people,
Our grandfathers, our grandmothers,
Walking that long distance,
There was no food, there was no water,
But they were walking a long distance,
But they were walking a long distance!

At Fort Sumner, it was when they got there
They were treated badly,
They were treated badly.

"I wish I were still back in my own home,
I wish I were still back in my own home!
We shall never forget this,
The walk that we are taking now.
We shall never forget this,
The walk that we are taking now.
Even then, we still like our own land,
Even then, we still like our own land!"

With permission of Ruth Roessel.

The two examples here have not been recorded commercially, but several Navajo composers of new songs in styles based on Enemyway popular songs have published their work on popular discs. Kay Bennett (Kaibah) has produced three records on her own label, for example, *Songs from the Navajo Nation* (n.d.). Danny Whitefeather Begay, Cindy Yazzie, and Roger McCabe have released *My Beautiful Land* (n.d.) on the Canyon Records label with fifteen popular songs in this new genre. "Los Angeles Sweetheart" by Danny Whitefeather Begay gives an idea of how those songs go. It is in the Skip Dance style as indicated by the formula

Los Angeles Sweetheart

Heye, yaŋa, heye, yaŋa,

Awe 'a-no 'aweya'a heye, yaŋa,
Awe 'a-no 'aweya'a heye, yaŋa,

Hene ya'o wowo 'awe ya'a heye, yaŋa,
Hene ya'o wowo 'awe ya'a heye, yaŋa,

Oh, that girl, oh, that girl,
To a place called "L.A.," that's where she went,
She went aweya'a heye, yaŋa,
To a place called "L.A.," that's where she went,
She went aweya'a heye, yaŋa,
"All kinds of jobs for you," she wrote,
But she had another man, 'ano 'aweya'a heye, yaŋa,

Hene ya'o wowo 'awe ya'a heye, yaŋa,
Hene ya'o wowo 'awe ya'a heye, yaŋa,

"Los Angeles Sweetheart," by Danny Whitefeather Begay from *My Beautiful Land* (ARP-6078). © Canyon Records Productions.

In this record many of the songs are nostalgic, about Navajos who have left the reservation to find work and wish they could go home again. Others are "flirting songs" referring to the courtship situation at a Ndáá' Dance. The mingling of the new experience in big cities and the traditional dance scene at an Enemyway ceremonial is reflected in the record's cover design, which combines automobiles, hogans, skyscrapers, and the four sacred mountains.

Music with Newly Created Navajo Texts and Melodies

CD I
Track 7

This recent genre is well-represented by Sharon Burch's "Mother Earth" (CD Selection 7; Figure 2-7) from her tape *Yazzie Girl* (1989). She accompanies herself on a guitar in a chantlike melody of her own composition. "She credits her inspiration as a songwriter to the songs, prayers and chants she recalls from her childhood" (Burch 1989).

Mother Earth (in Navajo with English Translation)

Chorus:

Heiyee' t' áá ał tso baa hózhǫ́ǫ́go.	Heiyee' everything brings happiness.
Heiyee' t' áá ał tso baa hózhǫ́ǫ́go.	Heiyee' everything brings happiness.
Heineiyaa.	Heineiyaa.
Nahasdzáán bii' sézį	I am part of Mother Earth
Nahasdzáán bikee' shikee'.	Mother Earth's feet are my feet.
Nahasdzáán bijáád shijáád.	Mother Earth's legs are my legs.
Nahasdzáán bidziil shidziil.	Mother Earth's strength is my strength.
Nahasdzáán bigaan shigaan.	Mother Earth's arms are my arms.
Nahasdzáán bináá' hóló, shináá' hólǫ́	Mother Earth has a vision, I have a vision.

Figure 2-7
Sharon Burch.

Photo © John Running. Courtesy of Canyon Records Productions.

(Chorus)
(first five line of second verse, as in first verse)

Nahasdzáán binitsékees shinitsékees.	Mother Earth's consciousness is my consciousness.

(Chorus)

"Mother Earth" from *Yazzie Girl* (CR-534) by Sharon Burch. ℗ © 1989 Sharon Burch. Use courtesy of Canyon Records Productions.

New Navajo Music with English Texts and Orchestral Accompaniment

Arliene Nofchissey Williams has been called "the Navajo nightingale." Her compositions stem from the Mormon sect of Christianity and express, musically and in words, both her religious perceptions and her Indian identity. She wrote one of her songs, "Proud Earth," when she was a student at Brigham Young University. The words reflect the Mormon respect for Native-American culture and the Indian closeness to nature. At the same time, the song conveys the aspiration of the Latter Day Saints to unite the Indian people under one God. Musically, there are such Indian elements as the use of a steady, repetitive drumbeat and vocables, as well as Euro-American elements such as a string orchestra, harmonies, interpretive dynamics, and a text in English. The use of the voice of the late Chief Dan George, an Indian film star, as narrator adds to the richness of the production. The song has been a "hit" on the Navajo reservation and elsewhere among Indian people. It was produced in Nashville with all the musical technology that the name implies, and at the same time it is an Indian message song, telling the world what the Native Americans feel they have to contribute to world culture from their mythopoeic philosophy of nature.

Lyrics, "Proud Earth (The Song of the People)"

The beat of my heart is kept alive in my drum,
And my plight echoes in the canyons, the meadows, the plains,
And my laughter runs free with the deer,
And my tears fall with the rain,
But my soul knows no pain.

I am one with nature,
Mother Earth is at my feet,
And my God is up above me,
And I'll sing the song of my People.

Come with me, take my hand, come alive with my chant (heya, heya)
For my life already knows wisdom, balance, and beauty.
Let your heart be free from fear (heya, heya)
And your joy meet with mine,
For the peace we can find.

We are one with nature,
Mother Earth is at our feet,
And our God is up above us,
And we'll sing the song, the song of the people (heya, heya),
And we'll sing the song, the song of the people.

The Native-American Flute Revival

The Native-American flute revival probably began in the 1970s in Oklahoma when "Doc Tate" Nevaquaya made the first commercial recording consisting entirely of music of the Plains courting flute (Smythe

Origins

1989:68). But it was a Navajo, R. Carlos Nakai, whose moving, improvisatory compositions, often with synthesizer or orchestral accompaniments, carried the instrument to worldwide popularity and created a large following of imitators, both Indian and non-Indian (McAllester 1994). Nakai's first album appeared in 1982; since then he has made more than twenty others, one of them in Germany and another in Japan. *Cycles* (1985) was chosen by the Martha Graham Dance Company to provide the music for their ballet *Nightchant.* Nakai has performed with several symphony orchestras and was awarded the Arizona Governor's Arts Award in 1992 and an honorary doctorate by Northern Arizona University in 1994. In that same year, *Ancestral Voices,* his third collaboration with guitarist William Eaton, was a Grammy Awards finalist in Best Traditional Folk Music. An example of his improvisation with synthesizer (CD Selection 8) is taken from *Cycles: Native American Flute Music.* It is entitled "Origins"; Nakai comments in the liner notes: "My clan, Naashteezhi dine-e Taachiinii, allows me to be one of the People" (Nakai 1985). Throughout his work the commentary accompanying the music stresses respect for the environment and the Navajo celebration of tribal connections and harmony with nature.

CD I
Track 8

We have ranged over the music of several generations and religions in an effort to find clues to the thought of just one Indian tribe. Even so we have barely touched on the complexities of this rich and rapidly changing culture. One of the most powerful messages that reaches the outsider is that Indian traditional culture is still vital and growing in its own ways even while Native-American people are adopting new ideas and technology from the Euro-American culture around them. This fact is clearly reflected in the many different kinds of music that coexist on the Navajo reservation and in thousands of Navajo homes in Chicago, Los Angeles, San Francisco, and innumerable other locations away from the reservation.

To varying degrees this picture of Navajo music exemplifies what is happening to other Indian communities around the country. The different Indian cultures are on an adventure in which the larger populace around them must inevitably share. Many Indian elements have already become part of the culture that is called "American." Some of these have been superficial: an Indian word such as *squash* or *moose,* or a bit of local legend. Other contributions have had enormous economic import, such as the corn and potatoes that feed much of the world. There is now evidence that some of the music and the other Indian arts, and the religious and philosophical ideas that lie beneath them, are becoming accessible to an increasingly sympathetic American public. No culture remains static, and the Indians will continue to contribute to other world cultures, which are themselves in the process of change.

References

Burch, Sharon. 1989. *Yazzie Girl.* Canyon Records CR534 (Phoenix, Ariz.). Cassette.

Faris, James C. 1990. *The Nightway: A History and a History of Documentation of a Navajo Ceremonial.* Albuquerque: Univ. of New Mexico Press.

The Fenders. 1966. *Second Time 'Round.* Thoreau, N. Mex. 12" LP recording.

Fenton, William. n.d. *Songs from the Iroquois Longhouse.* Library of Congress AFS L6.

Frisbie, Charlotte J. and David P. McAllester. 1978. *Navajo Blessingway Singer: Frank Mitchell, 1881–1967.* Tucson: Univ. of Arizona Press.

Haile, Fr. Berard. 1938. *Origin Legend of the Navajo Enemy Way.* New Haven, Conn.: Yale Univ. Press.

Kluckhohn, Clyde, and Dorothea Leighton. 1938. *The Navajo.* Cambridge, Mass.: Harvard Univ. Press.

McAllester, David P. 1949. *Peyote Music.* New York: Viking Fund Publications in Anthropology, no. 13.

———. 1954. *Enemy Way Music.* Papers of the Peabody Museum of Archaeology and Ethnology, vol. 41, no. 5. Cambridge, Mass.: Harvard Univ. Press.

———. 1994. "The Music of R. Carlos Nakai." In *To the Four Corners: A Festschrift in Honor of Rose Brandel,* ed. Ellen C. Leichtman. Warren, Mich.: Harmonie Park Press.

My Beautiful Land and Other Navajo Songs. n.d. Canyon Records Productions ARP 6078 (Phoenix, Ariz.). Danny Whitefeather Begay, Cindy Yazzi, and Roger McCabe. LP.

Nakai, Carlos. 1985. *Cycles: Native American Flute Music.* Canyon Records Productions CR614-C (Phoenix, Ariz.). Cassette.

Proud Earth. n.d. Salt City Records SC-60 (Provo, Utah). Chief Dan George, Arliene Nofchissey Williams, Rick Brosseau. LP.

Reichard, Gladys A. 1928. *Social Life of the Navajo Indians.* New York: Columbia Univ. Press.

———. 1950. *Navajo Religion.* New York: Bollingen Foundation.

Rhodes, Willard, ed., n.d. *Navajo: Folk Music of the United States.* Washington, D.C.: Library of Congress, Division of Music, Archive of American Folk Song AFS L41.

Smythe, Willie. 1989. "Songs of Indian Territory." In *Songs of Indian Territory: Native American Music Traditions of Oklahoma.* Oklahoma City: Center for the American Indian.

Songs from the Navajo Nation. n.d. Recorded by Kay Bennet (Kaibah). Produced by K. C. Bennet (Gallup, N.Mex.). LP.

Witherspoon, Gary. 1977. *Language and Art in the Navajo Universe.* Ann Arbor: Univ. of Michigan Press.

Witmer, Robert. 1973. "Recent Change in the Musical Culture of the Blood Indians of Alberta, Canada." *Yearbook for Inter-American Musical Research* 9:64–94.

Additional Reading

Bailey, Garrick, and Roberta Glenn Bailey. 1986. *A History of the Navajos: The Reservation Years.* Santa Fe, N.Mex.: School of American Research Press.

Deloria, Vine, Jr. 1969. *Custer Died for Your Sins: An Indian Manifesto.* London: Collier-Macmillan.

Dyk, Walter. 1966. *Son of Old Man Hat.* Lincoln: Univ. of Nebraska Press.

Farella, John R., 1984. *The Main Stalk: A Synthesis of Navajo Philosophy.* Tucson: Univ. of Arizona Press.

Goodman, James B. 1986. *The Navajo Atlas: Environments, Resources, People, and the History of the Diné Bikeyah.* Norman: Univ. of Oklahoma Press.

Griffin-Pierce, Trudy. 1992. *Earth Is My Mother, Sky Is My Father: Space, Time, and Astronomy in Navajo Sandpainting.* Albuquerque: Univ. of New Mexico Press.

Kluckhohn, Clyde, and Leland C. Wyman. 1940. *An Introduction to Navajo Chant Practice.* Menasha, Wis.: Memoirs of the American Anthropological Association, no. 53.

Matthews, Washington. 1894. "Songs of Sequence of the Navajos," *Journal of American Folk-Lore* 7:185–94.

McNeley, James K. 1981. *Holy Wind in Navajo Philosophy.* Tucson: Univ. of Arizona Press.

Neihardt, John G. 1961. *Black Elk Speaks.* Lincoln: Univ. of Nebraska Press.

Wyman, Leland C. 1983. *Southwest Indian Drypainting.* Albuquerque: Univ. of New Mexico Press.

Additional Listening

Anilth, Wilson, and Hanson Ashley. *Navajo Peyote Ceremonial Songs,* vol. 1. Indian House 1541 (Taos, N.Mex.). LP.

Boniface Bonnie Singers. *Navajo Sway Songs.* Indian House 1581 (Taos, N.Mex.). LP.

Boulton, Laura. *Navajo Songs.* Recorded by Laura Boulton in 1933 and 1940. Annotated by Charlotte Frisbie and David McAllester. Washington, D.C.: Smithsonian/Folkways, SF 40403. CD, cassette.

DeMars, James. *Spirit Horses, Concerto for Native American Flute and Chamber Orchestra.* Composed for and performed by R. Carlos Nakai. Phoenix, Ariz.: Canyon Records Productions, CR-7014. CD, cassette.

Four Corner Yeibichai. Canyon Records Productions 7152 (Phoenix, Ariz.). LP, cassette.

Isaacs, Tony. *Night and Daylight Yeibichai.* Indian House IH 1502 (Taos, N.Mex.). LP.

Rhodes, Willard. *Music of the Sioux and the Navajo.* Smithsonian/Folkways 4401 (Washington, D.C.). LP. With 6-page pamphlet.

Williams, Arliene Nofchissey. *Encircle . . . in the Arms of His love.* Composed and performed by Arliene Nofchissey Williams, featuring flutist John Rainer, Jr. Blanding, Utah: Proud Earth Productions, PE-90. Cassette.

XIT. *Plight of the Red Man.* Motown Record Corp. R536L (Detroit). LP. Protest songs in rock style; XIT is an acronym for "Crossing of Indian Tribes," in reference to the pantribal makeup of the group.

Major Sources for Recordings

Canyon Records Productions. 4143 North Sixteenth Street, Phoenix, Ariz. 85016, phone: (602) 266-7835. This is the main distributor of Native-American recordings. It carries recordings of traditional music and also newer genres such as Indian rock, gospel, and country and western.

Indian House. Box 472, Taos, N. Mex. 87571, phone: (505) 776-2953. This company specializes in traditional Indian music and typically devotes an entire recording to one genre such as Taos Round Dance songs, or Navajo Yeibichai songs.

Library of Congress. Archive of Folk Culture, Motion Picture, Broadcast, and Recorded Sound Division, Library of Congress, Washington, D.C. 20540, phone: (202) 707-7833. This collection includes the Willard Rhodes recordings of Native-American music: excellent recordings and notes from all across the country.

Smithsonian/Folkways. The Folkways Collection, Smithsonian Institution, Washington, D.C. 20560, phone: (202) 287-3262. Their holdings include many early and some more recent recordings of Native-American music.

CHAPTER

3

Africa/Ewe

David Locke

Consider a misleadingly simple question: Where does Africa begin and end? At first you might say, "At the borders that mark the continent." But musically, Africa spills over its geographic boundaries. Calling to mind the narrow Strait of Gibraltar, the Suez Canal, the oft-crossed Red and Mediterranean Seas, and the vast Atlantic Ocean, we realize that people from Africa have always shaped world history. If we invoke images—Egypt, Ethiopia, the Moors, Swahili civilization, commerce in humans and precious metals—we know that Africa is not separate from Europe, Asia, and America. As you saw in Chapter 1, music is humanly made sound; it moves with humankind on explorations, conquests, migrations, and enslavements. This chapter, therefore, refers you not only to the African continent but wherever African music-culture is found.

Another question: What music is African music? We could be poetic and say, "Where its people are, there is Africa's music—on the continent and in its diaspora," but the truth is messier. Music is never pure. A music-culture is always a process shaped by many outside influences. From Benin and Luanda to Bahia, Havana, London, and Harlem, music-cultures blend on a subtle continuum. African-influenced music now circulates the planet by means of electronic media. When you learn new things about music, your own personal music-culture changes.

The African continent has two broad zones: (1) the Maghrib, north of the Sahara Desert, and (2) sub-Saharan Africa. North Africa and the Horn of Africa have much in common with the Mediterranean and West Asia; Africa south of the Sahara in many ways is a unique cultural area. But history records significant contacts up and down the Nile, across the Sahara, and along the African coasts. Just as civilizations from the north (Greece, Rome) and east (Arabia, Turkey) have had indelible impacts on northern Africa, the Maghrib has been influenced from the south as well. Similarly, Africa south of the Sahara has never been isolated from the Old World civilizations of Europe and Asia. As this chapter will show, the history and cultural geography of sub-Saharan Africa peoples vary tremendously.

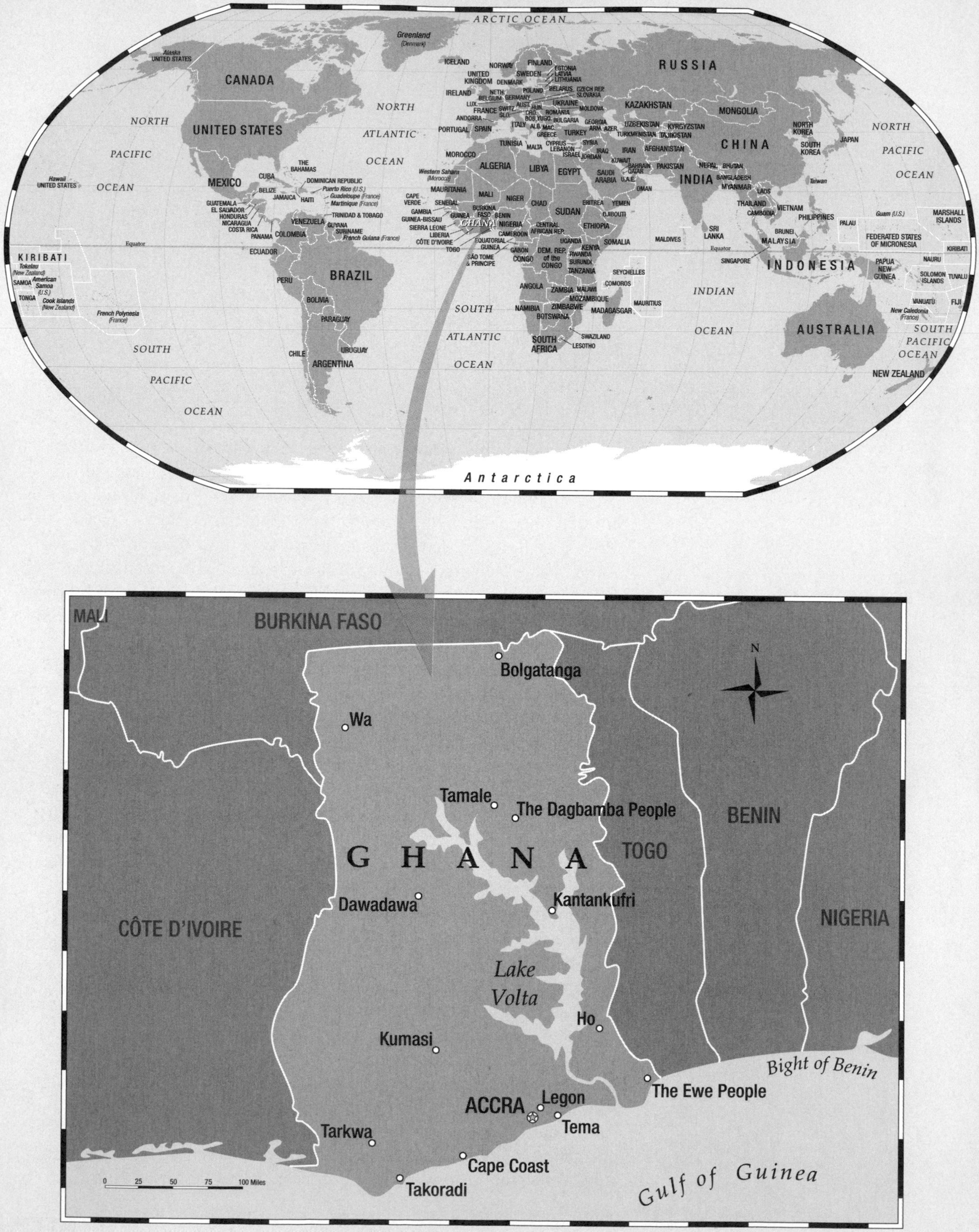

ARCTIC OCEAN
Greenland (Denmark)
Alaska UNITED STATES
CANADA
ICELAND
NORWAY
FINLAND
SWEDEN
ESTONIA
LATVIA
LITHUANIA
UNITED KINGDOM
DENMARK
IRELAND
NETH.
BELGIUM
GERMANY
POLAND
BELARUS
CZECH REP.
SLOVAKIA
UKRAINE
MOLDOVA
ROMANIA
BULGARIA
LUX.
FRANCE
SWITZ.
AUST.
HUN.
SLO.
CRO.
BOS.
YUGO.
ANDORRA
ITALY
ALB.
MAC.
GREECE
PORTUGAL
SPAIN
RUSSIA
KAZAKHSTAN
MONGOLIA
GEORGIA
ARM.
AZER.
UZBEKISTAN
KYRGYZSTAN
TURKMENISTAN
TAJIKISTAN
TURKEY
CYPRUS
SYRIA
LEBANON
ISRAEL
JORDAN
IRAQ
IRAN
AFGHANISTAN
KUWAIT
BAHRAIN
QATAR
U.A.E.
SAUDI ARABIA
OMAN
YEMEN
PAKISTAN
NEPAL
BHUTAN
BANGLADESH
INDIA
CHINA
NORTH KOREA
SOUTH KOREA
JAPAN
MYANMAR
LAOS
THAILAND
VIETNAM
CAMBODIA
PHILIPPINES
Taiwan
SRI LANKA
MALDIVES
BRUNEI
MALAYSIA
SINGAPORE
INDONESIA
PALAU
Guam (U.S.)
MARSHALL ISLANDS
FEDERATED STATES OF MICRONESIA
KIRIBATI
NAURU
PAPUA NEW GUINEA
SOLOMON ISLANDS
TUVALU
VANUATU
FIJI
New Caledonia (France)
AUSTRALIA
NEW ZEALAND
NORTH PACIFIC OCEAN
NORTH ATLANTIC OCEAN
UNITED STATES
MEXICO
Hawaii UNITED STATES
THE BAHAMAS
CUBA
DOMINICAN REPUBLIC
Puerto Rico (U.S.)
Guadeloupe (France)
Martinique (France)
BELIZE
JAMAICA
HAITI
GUATEMALA
EL SALVADOR
HONDURAS
NICARAGUA
COSTA RICA
PANAMA
TRINIDAD & TOBAGO
VENEZUELA
GUYANA
SURINAME
French Guiana (France)
COLOMBIA
Equator
ECUADOR
PERU
BRAZIL
BOLIVIA
PARAGUAY
CHILE
URUGUAY
ARGENTINA
KIRIBATI
Tokelau (New Zealand)
SAMOA
American Samoa (U.S.)
TONGA
Cook Islands (New Zealand)
French Polynesia (France)
SOUTH PACIFIC OCEAN
MOROCCO
Western Sahara (Morocco)
ALGERIA
TUNISIA
MALTA
LIBYA
EGYPT
MAURITANIA
MALI
NIGER
CHAD
SUDAN
ERITREA
DJIBOUTI
ETHIOPIA
SOMALIA
CAPE VERDE
SENEGAL
GAMBIA
GUINEA-BISSAU
GUINEA
SIERRA LEONE
LIBERIA
CÔTE D'IVOIRE
BURKINA FASO
GHANA
TOGO
BENIN
NIGERIA
CAMEROON
CENTRAL AFRICAN REP.
EQUATORIAL GUINEA
SÃO TOME & PRINCIPE
GABON
CONGO
DEM. REP. of the CONGO
UGANDA
KENYA
RWANDA
BURUNDI
TANZANIA
SEYCHELLES
COMOROS
ANGOLA
ZAMBIA
MALAWI
MOZAMBIQUE
ZIMBABWE
NAMIBIA
BOTSWANA
MADAGASCAR
MAURITIUS
SWAZILAND
LESOTHO
SOUTH AFRICA
SOUTH ATLANTIC OCEAN
INDIAN OCEAN
Antarctica
MALI
BURKINA FASO
N
Bolgatanga
Wa
Tamale
The Dagbamba People
BENIN
GHANA
TOGO
Dawadawa
Kantankufri
CÔTE D'IVOIRE
NIGERIA
Lake Volta
Ho
Kumasi
Bight of Benin
The Ewe People
ACCRA
Legon
Tema
Tarkwa
Cape Coast
Takoradi
0 25 50 75 100 Miles
Gulf of Guinea

Permit an ungrammatical question: When is an African? In everyday circumstances, people do not usually think of themselves as "African" (Mphahlele 1962). Identity arises from local connections of gender, age, kinship, place, language, religion, and work. Ethnicity comes into play only in the presence of people from a different group. One "becomes" a Serer, so to speak, in the presence of a Wolof, an African when among the French, a white in the company of a black, a yellow, a red (Senghor 1967). These terms suggest relationships among people more than they mark essential characteristics of individuals. Physical appearance and genetic inheritance do not determine culture, but the bogus concept of "race" is crucial to the ignorance that spawns prejudice and the bigotry that fosters injustice (Appiah 1992). Although they pervade our global village, such labels should be marked: USE WITH CARE.

In an intercultural context, "Africa" is a resonant symbol. People of African descent, wherever they are in the world, may regard Africa as the ancestral homeland, the place of empowerment and belonging (Asante 1987). Industrialized citizens of "information societies" may envision Africa as either a pastoral Eden or the impoverished Third World. Land of "heathens" to the Muslim and Christian, Africa is a fount of ancient wisdom for those who practice religions such as *santería* or *vodun.* Famine relief and foreign aid, wilderness safari and Tarzan, savage or sage—Africa is a psychic space, not just a physical place.

The sections that follow introduce two African music-cultures. They show some of Africa's widely shared characteristics. Information for the sections comes from my own field research.

Agbekor: Music and Dance of the Ewe People

Drawing on my field research in West Africa since the 1970s, we now consider a type of singing and drumming called *Agbekor* (pronounced "ah-*gbeh*-kaw"). As you hear on CD Selection 9, *Agbekor's* music features a percussion ensemble and a chorus of singers. A complex lead drumming part rides on a rich polyrhythmic texture established by an ensemble of bells, rattles, and drums of different sizes. Songs are clear examples of call-and-response. *Agbekor* is a creation of Ewe-speaking people (pronounced "*eh*-way") who live on the Atlantic coast of western Africa in the nation-states of Ghana and Togo.

The Ewe People

History

Triumph over adversity is an important theme in Ewe oral history. Until they came to their present territory, the Ewe people had lived precariously as a minority within kingdoms of more populous and powerful peoples such as the Yoruba and the Fon. Prominent in their oral traditions is the story of their exodus in the late 1600s from Agokoli, the tyrannical king of Notsie, a walled city-state located in what is now southern Togo.

Intimidating Agokoli's warriors with fierce drumming, the Ewes escaped under cover of darkness. Moving southwestward, they founded many settlements along a large lagoon near the mouth of the Volta River. At last Wenya, their elderly leader, declared that he was too tired to continue. Thus, this Ewe group became known as the *Anlo* (pronounced "*ahng-law*"), a word that means "cramped." Other families of Ewe-speakers settled nearby along the coast and in the upland hills.

In these new lands, the Ewe communities grew and multiplied. Eventually, the small Ewe settlements expanded into territorial divisions whose inhabitants all could trace male ancestors to the original villages. Family heads or distinguished war leaders became chiefs. Despite bonds of common culture and history, each division zealously cherished its independence. The Ewe people have never supported a hierarchical concentration of power within a large state (compare them with the Dagbamba kingdom, discussed later in this Chapter).

Ever since those early days, the important units of Ewe social life have been extended families. Members of a lineage—that is, people who can trace their genealogy to a common ancestor—share rights and obligations. Lineage elders hold positions of secular and sacred authority. The ever-present spirits of lineage ancestors help their offspring, especially if the living perform the necessary customary rituals.

The eighteenth and nineteenth centuries saw the Ewes in frequent military conflict with neighboring ethnic groups, European traders, and even among themselves. The Anlo-Ewe gained a fearsome reputation as warriors.

Religious Philosophy

An Ewe scholar has commented on the sacred worldview of his people: "A traveler in Anlo is struck by the predominating, all-pervasive influence of religion in the intimate life of the family and community. . . . The sea, the lagoon, the river, streams, animals, birds and reptiles as well as the earth with its natural and artificial protuberances are worshipped as divine or as the abode of divinities" (Fiawo 1959:35, in Locke 1978:32). The Ewe supreme being, Mawu, is remote from the affairs of humanity. Other divinities, such as Se (pronounced "seh"), interact with things in this world. Se embodies God's attributes of law, order, and harmony; Se is the maker and keeper of human souls; Se is destiny. Many Ewes believe that before a spirit enters the fetus, it tells Se how its life on earth will be and how its body will die. If you ask Ewe musicians the source of their talent, most likely they will identify the ancestor whose spirit they have inherited. Ask why they are so involved in music making, they will say it is their destiny.

According to the worldview of many Ewes, God has endowed certain natural substances with extraordinary force. By combining these special substances in appropriate ways, knowledgeable people can influence what happens in the world. Medicine can heal, protect, or enhance human capability. Performers often use charms to enhance their ability or to defend themselves against jealous rivals. Hunters are among the most learned herbalists.

Ancestral spirits are another crucial spiritual force in the lives of Ewe people.

> The Ewe believe that part of a [person's] soul lives on in the spirit world after his [or her] death and must be cared for by the living. This care is essential, for the ancestors can either provide for and guard the living or punish them. . . . The doctrine of reincarnation, whereby some ancestors are reborn into their earthly kin-groups, is also given credence. The dead are believed to live somewhere in the world of spirits, *Tsiefe,* from where they watch their living decendants in the earthly world, *Kodzogbe.* They are believed to possess supernatural powers of one sort or another, coupled with a kindly interest in their descendants as well as the ability to do harm if the latter neglect them. (Nukunya 1969:27, in Locke 1978:35)

Funerals are significant social institutions because, without ritual action by the living, a soul cannot become an ancestral spirit. A funeral is an affirmation of life, a cause for celebration because another ancestor now is there to watch over the living. Because spirits of ancestors love music and dance, funeral memorial services feature drumming, singing, and dancing. Full of the passions aroused by death, funerals have replaced war as an appropriate occasion for war drumming such as *Agbekor.* Knowledge of Ewe history and culture helps explain the great energy found in performance pieces like *Agbekor.* Vital energy, life force, strength—these are at the heart of the Ewe outlook.

Agbekor History and Contemporary Performance

Legends of Origin

During my field research, I interviewed elders about how *Agbekor* began.* Many people said it was inspired by hunters' observations of monkeys in the forest. According to some elders, the monkeys changed into human form, played drums, and danced; others say that the monkeys kept their animal form as they beat with sticks and danced. Significantly, hunters, like warriors, had access to esoteric power.

> In the olden days hunters were the repository of knowledge given to men by God. Hunters had special herbs. . . . Having used such herbs, the hunter could meet and talk with leopards and other animals which eat human beings. . . . As for Agbekor, it was in such a way that they saw it and brought it home. But having seen such a thing, they could not reveal it to others just like that. Hunters have certain customs during which they drum, beat the double bell, and perform such activities that are connected

*I conducted these interviews with the assistance of a language specialist, Bernard Akpeleasi, who subsequently translated the spoken Ewe into written English.

> with the worship of things we believe. It was during such a traditional hunting custom that they exhibited the monkey's dance. Spectators who went to the performance decided to found it as a proper dance. There were hunters among them because once they had revealed the dance in the hunting customary performance they could later repeat it again publicly. But if a hunter saw something and came home to reveal it, he would surely become insane. That was how *Agbekor* became known as a dance of the monkeys. (Kwaku Denu, quoted in Locke 1978:38–39)

Although many Ewes consider them legend rather than history, stories like this signify the high respect accorded to *Agbekor.* Hunters were spiritually forceful leaders, and the forest was the zone of dangerously potent supernatural forces. We feel this power in a performance of *Agbekor.*

Agbekor As War Drumming

The original occasion for a performance of *Agbekor* was war. Elders explained that their ancestors performed it before combat as a means to attain the required frame of mind, or after battle as a means of communicating what had happened.

> They would play the introductory part before they were about to go to war. When the warriors heard the rhythms, they would be completely filled with bravery. They would not think that they might be going, never to return, for their minds were filled only with thoughts of fighting. (Elders of the Agbogbome Agbekor Society, quoted in Locke 1978:44)
>
> Yes, it is a war dance. It is a dance that was played when they returned from an expedition. They would exhibit the things that happened during the war, especially the death of an elder or a chief. (Alfred Awunyo, quoted in Locke 1978:43)
>
> If they were fighting, brave acts were done. When they were relaxing after the battle, they would play the drums and during the dance a warrior could display what he had done during the battle for the others to see. (Kpogo Ladzekpo, quoted in Locke 1978:43)

The Meaning of the Name *Agbekor*

I asked whether the name *Agbekor* has meaning. "I can say it signifies enjoying life: we make ourselves happy in life. The suffering that our elders underwent was brought out in the dance, and it could be that when they became settled, they gave the dance this name, which shows that the dance expresses the enjoyment of life" (Kwaku Denu, quoted in Locke 1978:47). Another elder told me that when people played *Agbekor* during times of war, they called it *Atamuga* (pronounced "ah-*tam*-gah"), which means "the great oath." Before going to battle, warriors would gather with their war leaders at shrines that housed spiritually powerful objects. They would swear on a sacred sword an oath to their ancestors to obey their leaders' commands and fight bravely for their community. When the Anlo no longer went to war, the name changed to *Agbekor* (Kpogo Ladzekpo, quoted in Locke 1978:45–46).

The word *Agbekor* is a compound of two short words: *agbe* means "life" and *kor* means "clear." The professional performer Midawo Gideon Foli Alorwoyie translates *Agbekor* as "clear life": The battle is over, the danger is past, and our lives are now in the clear (Locke 1978:47). Many people add the prefix *atsia* (plural *atsiawo*), calling the piece *atsiagbekor* (pronounced "ah-chah-*gbeh*-kaw"). The word *atsia* has two meanings: (1) stylish self-display, looking good, or bluffing, and (2) a preset figure of music and dance. As presented below, the form of the lead drumming and the dance consists of a sequence of *atsiawo.*

Learning

In Ewe music-culture, most music and dance is learned through enculturation. *Agbekor,* on the other hand, requires special training. The eminent African ethnomusicologist J.H.K. Nketia describes learning through slow absorption without formal teaching:

> The very organization of traditional music in social life enables the individual to acquire his musical knowledge in slow stages, to widen his experience of the music of his culture through the social groups into which he is progressively incorporated and the activities in which he takes part. . . . The young have to rely largely on their imitative ability and on correction by others when this is volunteered. They must rely on their own eyes, ears and memory. They must acquire their own technique of learning. (Nketia 1964:4)

Midawo Alorwoyie explains how one learns from the performance of an expert:

> All you have to do is know when he is going to play. . . . You have to go and pay attention to what you hear . . . to how the drums are coordinated and to the drum language, to what the responses are to the calls, and so on. You have to use your common sense right there to make sure that you get the patterns clear. Up to today, if you want to be a drummer, you go to the place where people are playing and then pay attention and listen. That's it. (Davis 1994:27)

Because of its complexity *Agbekor* is hard to learn in this informal way. Members of an *Agbekor* group practice in a secluded area for up to a year before they appear in public. Of course, all the novices are familiar with the general style of Ewe music and dance. Instruction entails demonstration and emulation. With adept dancers in front, the whole group performs together. No one breaks it down and analyzes it. Rather than learning elements arranged as exercises, people learn long sequences of movement and music in a simulated performance context (compare this with the teaching of *karnataka sangeeta,* described in Chapter 6).

This style of learning depends on gifted students who can learn long rhythmic compositions merely by listening to them several times. For certain people, drumming comes as easily and naturally as spoken language. Ewes know that drumming talent often comes from one's ancestors. A precocious youngster may be the reincarnation of an ancestor who was a renowned musician. One village drummer told me of a special drummer's ritual: "My father was a drummer and he taught me. It was when he was old and could no longer play that he gave me the curved sticks. A ceremony has to be performed before the curved sticks are handed over to you. . . . If the custom is not done the drum language will escape your mind" (Dogbevi Abaglo, quoted in Locke 1978:53). Midawo Alorwoyie explains the effects of this ritual: "Once the custom has been made, you can't sleep soundly. The rhythms you want to learn will come into your head while you sleep. . . . The ceremony protects the person in many ways. It protects your hands when you play and protects you from the evil intentions of other people who may envy you. . . . Whenever you see a master drummer in Africa, I'm telling you, he has got to have some sort of backbone" (Locke 1978:54–55).

Performing Organizations

Times have changed since Ewe hunters created *Agbekor.* Britain, Germany, and France administered Ewe territory during a brief colonial period (1880s to 1950s); now the Ewe people live in the nation-states of Ghana and Togo. Today, relatively few villages have preserved their heritage of *Agbekor.* But the tradition vigorously continues within drum and dance societies of several types: mutual aid organizations, school and civic youth groups, and theatrical performing companies. Throughout Africa, voluntary mutual aid societies are an important type of performing group (Ladzekpo 1971). *Agbekor* groups of this kind are formal organizations with a group identity, institutionalized procedures, recognized leaders, and so forth. Many group members are poor and cannot afford funeral expenses by themselves. People solve this financial problem by pooling resources. When a member dies, individuals contribute a small amount so the group can give a lump sum of cash to the family. The society's performance of music and dance makes the funeral grand.

In the mid-1970s I studied *Agbekor* with members of this type of cooperative society, the Anya Agbekor Society of Accra (Figure 3-1). One of their leaders recounted how the group came into existence: "The first Anya Agbekor group in Accra was formed by our elder brothers and uncles. They all scattered in the mid-sixties and that group died away. We, the younger ones, decided to revive it in 1970. Three or four people sat down and said, 'How can we let this thing just go away? *Agbekor* originated in our place, among our family, so it is not good to let it go.' We felt that it was something we had to do to remember the old family members. We formed the group to help ourselves" (Evans Amenumey, quoted in Locke 1978:63). I also studied with school groups trained by my teacher Godwin Agbeli. In colonial times, missionaries whipped students for attending traditional performance events. These days, most Ewes value their traditional repertory or music and dance as a cultural resource. Since Ghana achieved statehood in 1957, the national government has held competitions for amateur cultural groups from the country's many ethnic regions. Young people often join

Figure 3.1
The Anya Agbekor Society (with the author) in performance.

Courtesy of Godwin Agbeli

groups because rehearsals and performances provide social opportunities. Like many African nations, Ghana sponsors professional performing arts troupes. With its spectacular, crowd-pleasing music and dance, *Agbekor* is a staple of their repertory.

A Performance

On Sunday, March 6, 1977, in a crowded, working-class section of Accra, the Anya Society performed in honor of the late chief patron of the group. His son may have been thinking of his father when he described a patron's role in a drum society: "A patron is somebody who you can trust, somebody who is sympathetic and has love and interest in the thing the group is doing. He should be someone who can organize and knows how to talk to people. The patron solves many of our problems, quarrels and money matters" (Evans Amenumey, quoted in Locke 1978:61).

The evening before, the group held a wake during which they drummed *Kpegisu,* another prestigious war drumming of the Ewe (Locke 1992). Early Sunday morning, they played *Agbekor* briefly to announce the afternoon's performance. Had the event occurred in Anyako, the group would have made a procession through the ward. People went home to rest and returned to the open lot near the patron's family house by 3:30 in the afternoon for the main event.

The performance area was arranged like a rectangle within a circle. Ten drummers were at one end; fifteen dancers formed three columns facing the drummers; ten singers were in a semicircle behind the dancers; about three hundred onlookers encircled the entire performance area. All drummers and most dancers were male. Most singers were female; several younger women danced with the men. Group elders, bereaved family members, and invited dignitaries sat behind the drummers. With the account book laid out on a table, the group's secretary accepted the members' contributions.

The action began with an introductory section called *adzo* (pronounced "ah-*dzo*"), that is, short sections. Dancers sang songs in free rhythm. After the *adzo,* the main section, *vutsotsoe* (pronounced "voo-*tsaw*-tso-eh"), that is, fast drumming, started. The first sequence of figures had ritual significance: after dancing vigorously forward toward the drums, dancers bent toward the ground and three times intoned, "Aa-oo." The dance leader called out "Kutowo" (pronounced "koo-*taw*-woh"), that is, the dead ones, and the group responded, "Yaa," a vocable indicating strong emphasis. After that, in time to a specific lead drum rhythm, the dancers did an especially strenuous yet graceful movement. The prolonged "Aa-oo" summons the spirits of departed ancestors, especially those slain in battle; the call-and-response "Kutowo-Yaa" honors the dead, reminding everyone of the sacrifices made by the ancestors; the dance figure shows their readiness to act in the manner of the ancestors.

Following this ritually charged passage, the dancers performed approximately ten more *atsiawo,* or "styles."* The lead drummer spontaneously selected these from the many drum and dance sequences known to the group. The singers also were busy. Their song leader raised up each song; the chorus received it and answered. One song was repeated five to ten times before another was begun.

After about twenty minutes the *adzokpi* (pronounced "ah-*dzoh*-kpee") section of the performance began. Group members came forward in pairs or small groups to dance in front of the lead drummer. The dance movement differed for men and women. As in genres of Ewe social dancing, friends invited each other to move into the center of the dance space. When everyone had their fill of this more individualistic display, the lead drummer returned to the group styles. Soon, he signalled for a break in the action by playing the special ending figure.

During the break, the group's leaders went to the center of the dance area to pour a libation. Calling on the ancestors to drink, elders ceremonially poured water and liquor onto the earth. An elder explains: "We pour libation to call upon the deceased members of the dance [group] to send us their blessings [so we can] play the dance the same way we did when they were alive. How the Christians call Jesus, call God, though Jesus is dead—they do not see him and yet they call him—it is in the same manner that

*Perhaps because the word *atsia* means "stylishness," many English speaking Ewe musicians refer to the preformed drum and dance compositions as "styles."

we call upon the members of the dance [group] who are no more so that their blessings come down upon us during the dancing" (Kpogo Ladzekpo, quoted in Locke 1978:82–83).

The performance resumed with *vulolo* (pronounced "voo-*law*-law"), that is, slow drumming, the processional section of *Agbekor.* After about fifteen minutes, they went straight to *vutsotsoe,* the up-tempo section, and then *adzokpi,* the "solos" section. After a brief rest, they did another sequence of group figures at slow and fast pace, followed by individual display.

At the peak of the final *adzokpi* section, elders, patrons, and invited guests came out onto the dance area. These dignitaries danced the stately women's movement rather than the more acrobatic male dance. While they danced, singers and dancers knelt on one knee as a mark of respect. After dancing back and forth in front of the drummers, they returned to their position on the benches in back of the drummers.

By six o'clock, with the equatorial sun falling quickly, the performance was over. As the group members contentedly carried the equipment back to the Anya house, the audience dispersed, talking excitedly about the performance.

Although a performance follows a definite pattern, *Agbekor* is not rigidly formalized. A. M. Jones, a pioneering scholar of African music, has commented on the elasticity of African musical performance: "Within the prescribed limits of custom, no one quite knows what is going to happen: it depends quite a lot on the inspiration of the leading performers. These men [and women] are not making music which is crystallized on a music score. They are moved by the spirit of the occasion" (Jones 1959:108).

Figure 3-2
Agkebor ensemble.
(Drawing by Emmanuel Agbeli)

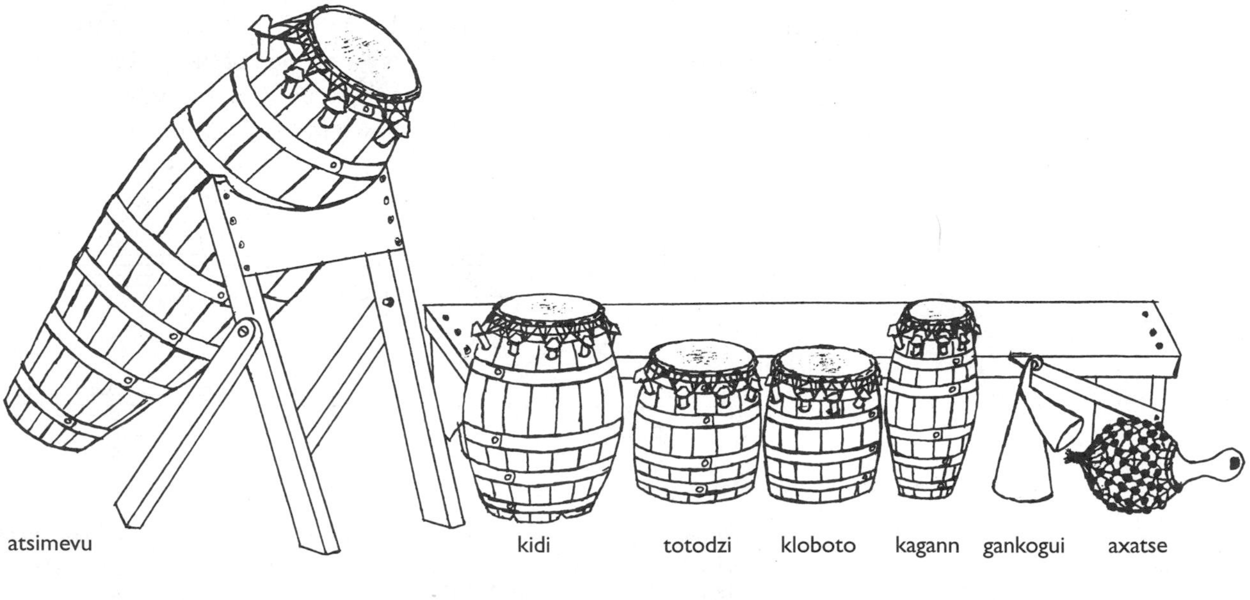

CD 1
Track 9

Music of the Percussion Ensemble

We now turn to music of the percussion ensemble for the slow-paced section of *Agbekor.** Instruments in the ensemble include a double bell, a gourd rattle, and four single-headed drums (see Figure 3-2). One by one the phrases are not too difficult, but playing them in an ensemble is surprisingly hard. The challenge is to hear them within a polyphonic texture that seems to change depending on one's point of musical reference. The reward in learning to play these parts is an experience of African musical time.

The Bell

"Listen to the bell"—that is the continual advice of Ewe teachers. Every act of drumming, singing, and dancing is timed in accordance with the recurring musical phrase played on an iron bell or gong called *gankogui* (pronounced "gahng-*koh*-gu-ee"). On first impression, the part may seem simple, but when set in the rhythmic context of Ewe drumming, it becomes a musical force of great potency. Repetition is key. As the phrase repeats over and over, participants join together in a circling, spiraling world of time.

Seven strokes with a wooden stick on the bell make one pass through the phrase. Music Example 3-1 represents the bell part. As the part repeats in polyrhythmic context, the musical ear groups the bell tones into a variety of patterns. Although the sonic phenomena are unchanging, the part appears different. We experience an aural illusion.

Music Example 3-1
Bell phrase.

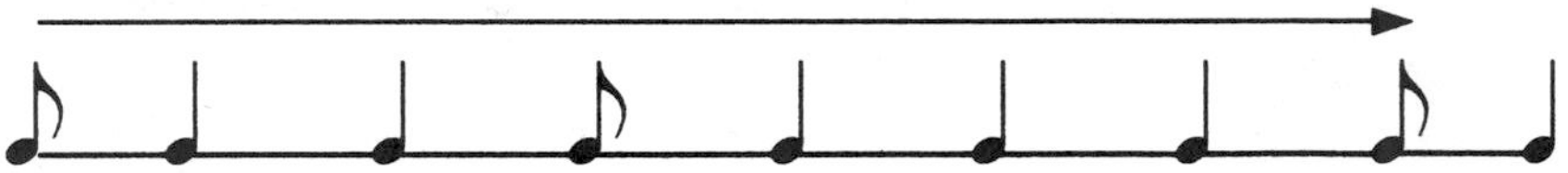

Despite the chameleonlike nature of the bell part, two phrase shapes are more important than others (Music Example 3-2). The note marked with the asterisk may be struck on the lower pitched of the *gankogui*'s two bells, a helpful landmark if one becomes rhythmically disoriented. For analytic clarity, I number the bell tones as shown in Music Example 3-2.

Music Example 3-2
Two shapes of bell phrase.

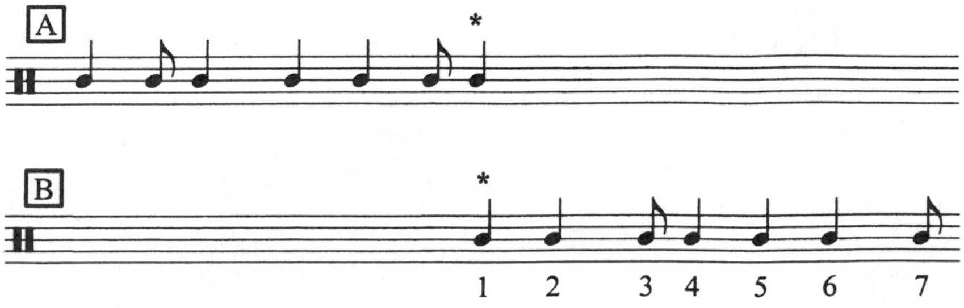

*I have decided not to present the music of the lead drum here. Not only is the material quite complicated, but I believe it best if students approach lead drumming only after a significant period of study, preferably with an Ewe teacher.

Tempo, Pulsation, and Time-Feels

Although many contrasting rhythmic phrases occur simultaneously in the percussion ensemble, competent Ewe musicians unerringly maintain a steady tempo. Rather than confusing players, musical relations among parts help them maintain a consistent time flow.

In my experience, the time-feel (meter) most significant to Ewe performers is what I call the "four-feel." Together with the explicit bell phrase, these four ternary beats (each beat has three quicker units within it) are a constant, implicit foundation for musical perception. When my students first learn a dance step, a drum part, or a song melody, I advise them to lock into the bell phrase and the four-feel beats. Interestingly, this type of groove (often marked by a $\frac{12}{8}$ time signature)* is widespread in African-American music (see Chapter 4).

Godwin Agbeli uses an Ewe children's game to teach the polyrhythm of bell and the four-feel beats (Music Example 3-3). The chant "Matikpo matikpo kple ku dza" means "I will jump, I will jump [to the sound of] 'kple ku dza'"; children leap upward as they say "kple" and land with a hand clap on "dza." I suggest that readers begin to practice the bell and four-beat combination by striking their thighs with open palms. When this is flowing easily, bring out the contrast between the parts by changing one hand to a fist.

To an Ewe musician, these four-feel beats automatically imply a "six-feel" (six quarter notes, or $\frac{6}{4}$ meter). The four- and six-feels are inseparable; they construct musical reality in two ways at once. Using both hands as shown in Music Example 3-4, try playing the bell phrase and the six-feel. The bell part feels different. This is the power of 3:2. After learning the bell and four-feel hand pattern, add a foot tap on the six-feel. Now you have more fully entered the rhythmic world of Ewe music.

Music Example 3-3
Composite: bell and four-feel beats.

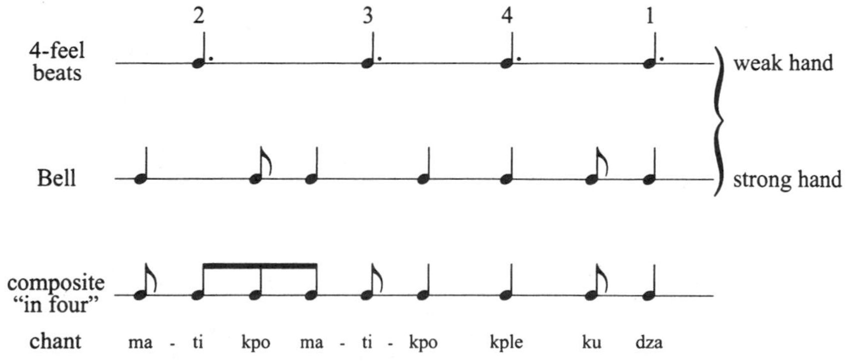

*In this chapter, I use an unconventional "fraction" as the time signature: the numerator shows the number of beats per measure; the note in the denominator shows the type of beat, that is, its internal pulse structure (ternary or binary). All beats in the measure have equal "weight" or metric stress.

Music Example 3-4
Composite: bell and six-feel beats.

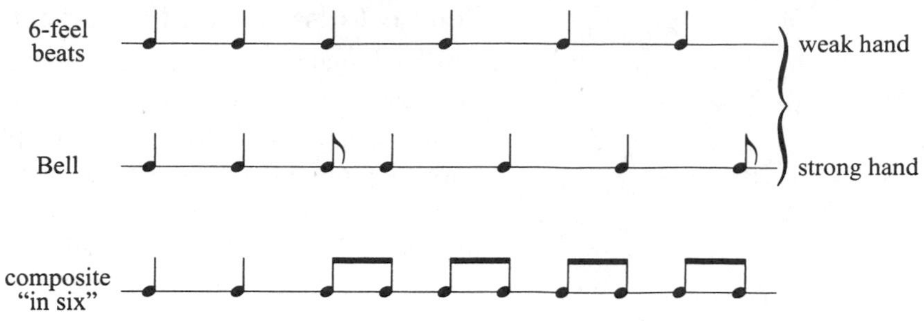

Perhaps some readers are wondering, How does this analytic perspective relate to an Ewe point of view? How do they hear it? These are hard questions to answer. First, we cannot assume that there is just one pervasive Ewe perspective. Second, until recently Ewe musicians had no reason to think about musical structure in terms suited to intercultural education of the kind attempted in *Worlds of Music.* Based on my many years of research, performance, and teaching, I believe that my approach here is co-cultural with the perspective of my Ewe teachers. However, the discovery of ethnographic truth is not my only intent. I also ask practical questions: Does this approach help one hear the music with insight? Does it help people play? Students must answer this question for themselves. I hope the answer is yes!

Music of the Drum Ensemble

The *axatse* (pronounced "ah-*ha*-tseh") is a dried gourd about the size of a cantaloupe covered with a net strung with seeds. In some *Agbekor* groups its role is to sound out the four-feel beats. In another frequently heard phrase, downward strokes on the player's thigh match the *gankogui* while upward strokes against the palm fill in between bell tones. The longer duration of the tone that matches bell stroke 1 gives definition to the shape of the bell phrase; it suggests to the musical ear that the bell phrase begins on stroke 2 and ends on stroke 1 (Music Example 3-5). As the only instrument played by many persons at once, the *axatse* "section" provides a loud, indefinite-pitched sound that is vital to the ensemble's energy.

Music Example 3-5
Axatse phrase.

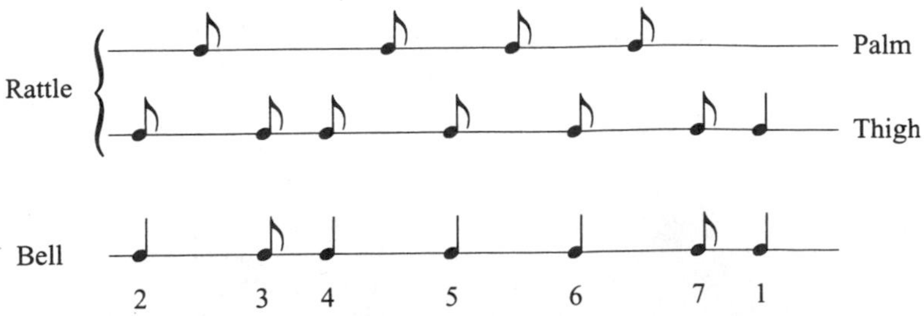

Music Example 3-6
Kaganu phrase.

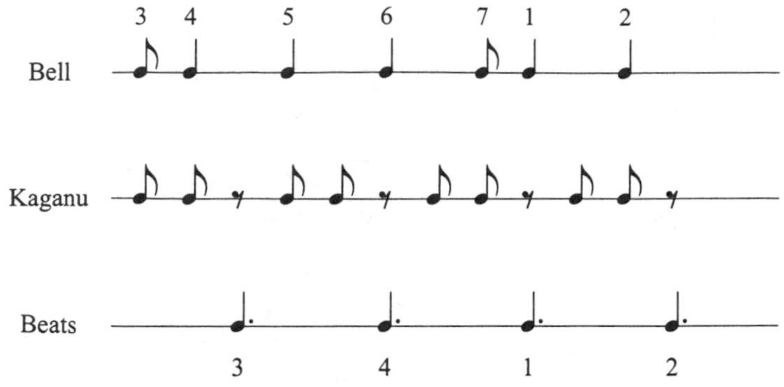

The high pitch and dry timbre of the slender *kaganu* (pronounced "kah-gahng") drum cuts through the more mellow, midrange sounds of the other drums. The *kaganu* part articulates offbeats, that is, moments between the four-feel beats (Music Example 3-6). Although not every *Agbekor* group uses the same phrase, a good one for newcomers to learn marks the second and third pulses within each four-feel beat. Many Ewe teachers advise students to focus on the synchrony between *kaganu* and bell tones 3 and 4; remember—listen to the bell! The late Freeman Donkor, one of my first teachers of Ewe music, said that the rhythm of *kaganu* brings out the flavor of the other parts, like salt in a stew.

The *gankogui, axatse,* and *kaganu* parts create a distinctive quality of musical temporal experience. The long and short tones in the bell phrase sculpt time into asymmetrical proportions. Symmetrical units also are important: The duration of the bell phrase literally is a measure of time; the tones of *axatse* and *kaganu* mark that measure into four equal ternary units. All four beats are strong, but the moments when bell and beat fall together—beats 4 and 1, bell tones 6 and 1—are specially marked in musical awareness; beat 3 is distinctive because it marks the midpoint in the bell phrase. These stable qualities of musical time provide the solid rhythmic foundation for the shifting offbeats found in the songs and lead drumming.

In descending order of relative pitch, the three other drums in the ensemble are *kidi, kloboto,* and *totodzi* (pronounced "*kee*-dee," "*kloh*-boh-toh," and "toh-toh-*dzee*"). Each drum adds its own phrase to *Agbekor*'s unique polyphony. There are two ways of striking a drum skin. Bounce strokes (the stick bounces off the drum skin) have an open ringing sound, whereas press strokes (the stick presses into the drum skin) have a closed muted sound. Bounces make the significant contribution to the group's music; presses keep each player in a groove. The parts discussed below are widespread, but some *Agbekor* groups use slightly different versions.

- In the *kidi* part, three bounces and three presses move at the twelve-unit pulsation rate; the phrase occurs twice within the span of one bell phrase (Music Example 3-7). Polyrhythmic relationships to the time parts help in learning the *kidi:* (a) in each group of

Music Example 3-7
Kidi phrase.

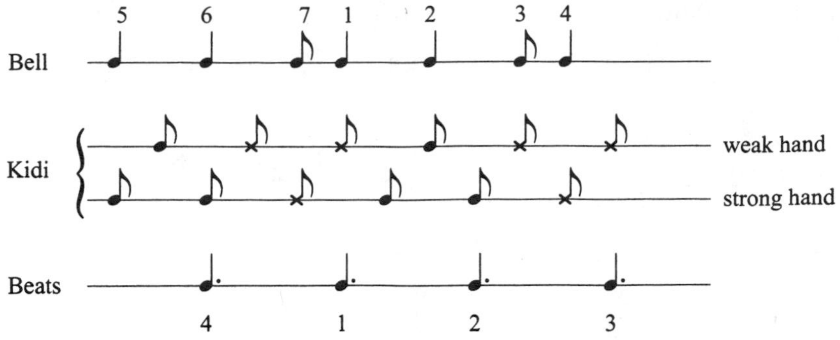

bounces and presses the third stroke is on a beat, (b) bell tones 5 and 6 match open *kidi* tones, and (c) *kidi* closely coincides with *kaganu.*

- The *kloboto* phrase has the same duration as the bell phrase (Music Example 3-8). As if inspired by bell tones 7–1, the part's main idea is a brief bounce-press, offbeat-onbeat figure. *Kloboto*'s insistent accentuation of offbeat moments can reorient a listener into perceiving them as onbeats. This type of implied beat shift (displacement) adds to the multidimensional quality of the music. For example, a person concentrating on *kloboto* may hear the second stroke in each pair of *kaganu* tones to be on the beat. Competent Ewe musicians, however, never lose orientation—they always know the *kloboto* presses are right on the four-feel time.
- The *totodzi* part begins and ends with the *kloboto* (Music Example 3-9). Its two bounce strokes match bell tones 2 and 3, its three press strokes match four-feel beats 3, 4, and 1. Notice the impact of sound quality and body movement on rhythmic shape: The phrase is felt as two strong-hand bounces followed by three weak-hand presses, not according to a three-then-two timing structure.

Let me offer advice for getting into the drumming. Begin by hearing each phrase "in four" and in duet with the bell. Then, stay "in four" but hear ever-larger combinations with other parts. Next, switch to the six-feel.

Music Example 3-8
Kloboto phrase.

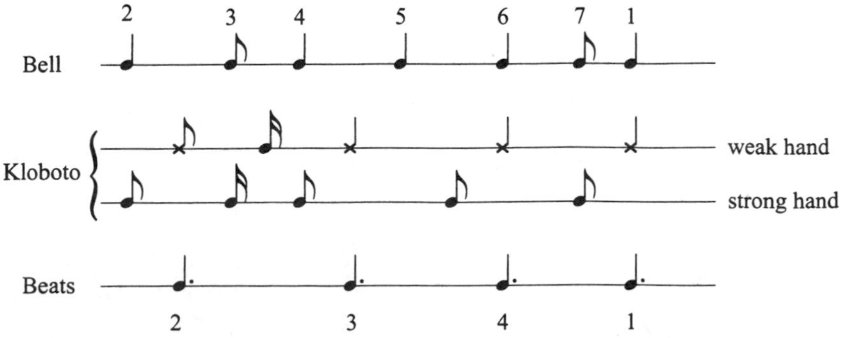

Music Example 3-9
Totodzi phrase.

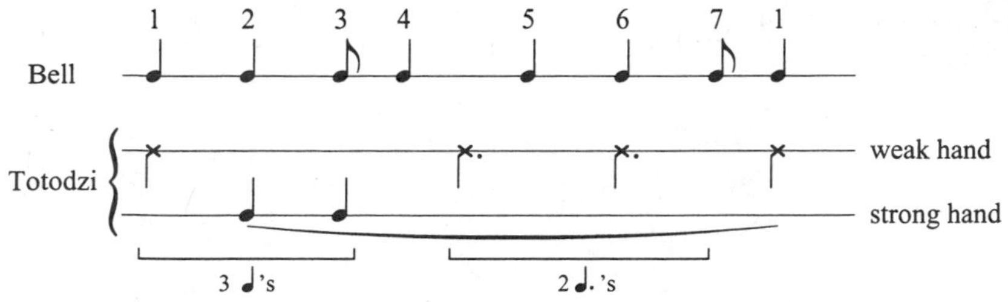

For added fun, try hearing the music "in three" and "in eight." The point is to explore the potency of these phrases, not to create new ones. Stretch your way of hearing, rather than what you are playing. Strive for a cool focus on ensemble relationships, not a hot individual display.

Drum Language

As happens in the instrumental music of many African peoples, Ewe drum phrases often carry unspoken words. Usually, only drummers know the words. Even Ewe speakers cannot understand drum language just by hearing the music—they must be told. Secrecy makes restricted information valuable and powerful. In many parts of Africa "speech must be controlled and contained if silence is to exercise its powers of truth, authenticity, seriousness and healing" (Miller 1990:95).

During my field research, I asked many experts whether they knew drum language for *Agbekor.* Saying he learned them from elders in his hometown of Afiadenyigba, Midawo Alorwoyie shared the following texts with me. His word-for-word and free translations appear beneath the Ewe texts. *Agbekor*'s themes of courage and service are apparent (see also Music Example 3-10).

Drum Language for *Agbekor*

Totodzi	Dzogbe dzi dzi dzi. battlefield/on/on/on We will be on the battlefield.
Kloboto	'Gbe dzi ko mado mado mado. Battlefield/on/only/I will sleep/I will sleep/I will sleep I will die on the battlefield.
Kidi	Kpo afe godzi. Kpo afe godzi. Look/home/side-on. Look/home/side-on. Look back at home. Look back at home.
Kaganu	Miava yi afia. We will come/go/will show We are going to show our bravery.

Music Example 3-10
Agbekor drum language.

Songs

Texts

Agbekor songs engage the subject of war. Many songs celebrate the invincibility of Ewe warriors; others urge courage and loyalty; some reflect on death and express grief. Songs memorialize heroes but do not provide detailed historical information. Unlike the freshly composed songs found in contemporary idioms of Ewe traditional music, *Agbekor* songs are inherited from the past. A song's affective power derives, in part, from its association with the ancestors.

Structural Features

In performance, a song leader and a singing group share the text and melody. As illustrated in the songs that follow, this call-and-response idea supports a variety of subtly different musical forms. The tonal system of *Agbekor* songs has evolved entirely in response to the human singing voice, without being influenced by musical instruments. An ethnomusicologist can identify scales, but in comparison to tuning in South Indian music-culture, for example, an Ewe singers' intonation seems aimed at pitch areas rather than precise pitch points. Melodic motion usually conforms to the rise and fall of speech tones, but Ewe speakers easily understand song lyrics even if the melodic contour contradicts the tonal pattern of the spoken language. Songs add another layer to the rhythm of *Agbekor.* Not surprisingly, a song's polyrhythmic duet with the bell phrase is all-important.

On CD Selection 9 we hear excerpts from my recording of a performance by an *Agbekor* group from the town of Anlo-Afiadenyigba on August 14, 1976. We hear three slow-paced songs, one song in free rhythm, and one fast-paced song.

Slow-Paced Songs

Song #1

Leader:	𝄆	Emiawo miegbona afeawo me. Afegametowo/viwo, midzra nuawo do.	A1
Group:		Repeat lines 1 and 2. 𝄇	A2
Leader:	𝄆	Oo!	B
Group:		Midzra nuawo do. 𝄇	
All:		Repeat lines 1 and 2.	A2
Leader:		We are coming into the homesteads. People/Children of the noble homes, get the things ready.	
Group:		Repeat lines 1 and 2.	
Leader:		Oh!	
Group:		Get the things ready.	

Song #1 announces that people should prepare for the arrival of the *Agbekor* procession. In the A section, the group repeats the leader's text but with a different tune; in the B section, the melodic phrases are shorter, the rhythm of call-and-response more percussive. The song ends with leader and group joining to sing the group's first response. The song's rhythm moves in the three-then-two groove.

Song #2

Leader:	Agbekoviawo, midze aye ee.	A1
Group:	Ada do ee, Kpo nedze ga nu. Ada do!	B1
Leader:	Manyo hawo, midze aye ee.	A2
Group:	Repeat lines 2–4.	B2
Leader:	Agbekor group, be cunning.	
Group:	The day has come. Beat the double bell. The day has come.	
Leader:	Manyo's group, be cunning.	
Group:	Repeat lines 2–4.	

Set at sunrise on the day of battle, song #2 urges Manyo and his warriors to "be cunning." Leader and group divide the text: The leader identifies the actors and the action, and the group evokes the scene. Form, melody, and tonality combine in creating a circular musical effect.

Song #3

Leader:	𝄆	Avu matodzo, Dewoe lawuma?	A1
Group:		Repeat lines 1 and 2. 𝄇	A2

Leader:	‖:	Dewoe?	B^1
Group:		Dewoe lawuma? :‖	B^2
All:		Avu matodzo, Dewoe lawuma?	A^2
Leader:		A hornless dog. Are there any greater than we?	
Group:		Repeat lines 1 and 2.	
Leader:		Any?	
Group:		Greater than we	
All:		Repeat lines 1 and 2.	

Song #3 expresses an important sentiment in *Agbekor* songs: celebrating the singers' power and denigrating the opponent. Here, the enemy is a "hornless dog," that is, an impotent person, and "we" are incomparably great. Ewe composers often make this point by means of rhetorical questions: "Who can trace the footprints of an ant?" that is, Who can defeat us? "Can the pigeon scratch where the fowl scratches?" that is, Can the enemy fight as strongly as we can? "Can a bird cry like the sea?" that is, How can the enemy compare with us? In these playful self-assertions and witty put-downs, we see a parallel with the genres of African-American expressive culture called "signifying" (see Chapter 4 for examples).

CD I
Track 9

Adzo Songs

Rhythmically free songs from the *adzo* section have longer texts than do songs from the slow- and fast-paced portions of an *Agbekor* performance. Like songs #1 and #3, song #4 begins with two sections of leader-group alternation but has a noticeably longer third section sung by the whole group. The issues raised in song #4 are not new to us; this song, however, does make a factual historical reference to Avusu Kpo, an enemy war leader.

Song #4

Leader:	‖:	'Gbekoviwo, xe de ado ahoyo gbe, Be tsawoyo?	A
Group:		Xe ke lado gbe, Gavi tsawoyo? :‖	B
Leader:		Tu nedi!	C^1
Group:		Miahee de alada me.	D
Leader:		Hewo nu,	C^2
Group:		Miahee de alada me.	D
All:		Be la bada fo soshi Ko de alada me. Tu la kaka, Mietsoe da de agboawo dzi	E

		Xe de mado ahoyo gbe ee? Avusu Kpowoe mado lo na xe Be xe nedo dika na alado me. Tsawoyo. Repeat lines 3 and 4.	B
Leader:	‖:	Members of the Agbekor group, can a bird cry like the sea, "Tsawoyo?"	
Group:		Which bird can cry like the sea, "Gavi Tsawoyo?" :‖	
Leader:		Fire the gun!	
Group:		We will turn it aside!	
Leader:		The tips of knives,	
Group:		We will brush them aside!	
All:		A wild animal has found a horsetail switch And put it at his side. The gun broke, We put it on the barricade. Can a bird cry like the sea? Avusu Kpo and his people cannot talk in proverbs to the bird. [unknown] "Tsawoyo." Repeat lines 3 and 4.	

CD 1
Track 9

Fast-Paced Songs

Song #5, like many songs from the fast-paced section, celebrates heroic passion. For example, another song says simply, "Sweet, to put on the war belt is very sweet." Song #5 opens with the vivid image of a confrontation between two war gods (*So*). The Fon from Dahomey and the Anlo are about to fight; the beautiful warriors are preparing; will they have the courage to enter the fray?

Song #5

Leader:	‖:	So kpli So, ne ava va gbedzia Tsyo miado.	A
Group:		Woyawoya Ava va gbedzia, Tsyo miado. :‖	B
Leader:		Oo,	C
Group:		Fowo do gbea, Miayia? Anlowo do gbe.	C
Leader:		Oo,	D
Group:		Anawo do gbea Tsyo miado.	
All:		Repeat lines 3–5.	B

Leader: 𝄆 So and So—if war breaks out on the battlefield
We will have to dress gorgeously.

Group: "Woyowoya"
War breaks out on the battlefield.
We have to dress gorgeously. 𝄇

Leader: Oh,

Group: The Fon are out on the battlefield,
Should we go?
The Anlo are out on the battlefield.

Leader: Oh,

Group: The cowards are out on the battlefield.
Should we go?
The Anlo are out on the battlefield.
Repeat lines 3–5.

Agbekor, as we have seen, is a group effort. Music and dance are a force in cementing social feeling among members of an *Agbekor* society. Other types of African music depend more on the virtuosity and special knowledge of individuals.

A Drummer of Dagbon

CD 1
Track 10

Musicians have had important functions in the political affairs of many African traditional states. We shall turn to the life story of one such person after we look at the music of Dagbon.

On CD Selection 10, we hear singing and drumming of the Dagbamba people (also known as Dagomba) from the southern savannah of western Africa (Ghana). I recorded the music in 1984. The performers are *lunsi* (pronounced "*loon*-see," singular *luna,* pronounced "*loong*-ah"), members of a hereditary clan of drummers. A *luna* fulfills many vital duties in the life of the Dagbamba—verbal artist, genealogist, counselor to royalty, cultural expert, entertainer. The *lunsi* tradition developed in Dagbon, the hierarchical, centralized kingdom of the Dagbamba (Chernoff 1979; DjeDje 1978; and Locke 1990).

The Drums

Lunsi play two kinds of drums—*gungon* (pronounced "goong-*gawng*") and *luna* (Figures 3-3 and 3-4). For both types, a shoulder strap holds the drum in position to receive strokes from a curved wooden stick. The *gungon* is a cylindrical, carved drum with a snare on each of its two heads. The cedar wood of a *luna* is carved into an hourglass shape. By squeezing the leather cords strung between its two drumheads, a player can change the tension of the drumskins and, consequently, the pitch of the drum tones. In the hands of an expert, the drum's sound closely imitates Dagbanli, the spoken

Figure 3.3
Lunsi in performance

Patsy Marshall

language of the Dagbamba. *Lunsi* "talk" and "sing" on their instruments. These musicians are storytellers, chroniclers of the history of their people and their nation.

CD 1
Track 10

A Praise Name Dance

The music we hear on CD Selection 10, called "Nag Biegu" (pronounced "*nah*-oh bee-*ah*-oo"), is one of the many Praise Name Dances (*salima*) of Dagbon. Its title means "ferocious wild bull." This *salima* praises Naa Abdulai, a king of Dagbon in the late 1800s who is remembered for his courage and firm leadership. The "wild bull" refers to a marauding enemy who was killed in combat by Naa Abdulai. As they dance to the drumming, people recall the bravery of the king.

The music has a two-part or verse-chorus form. In the verse, the vocalist and leading *luna* drummers praise Naa Abdulai and allude to events of his chieftaincy; the answering *lunsi* and two *gungon* drummers punctuate the verses with booming, single strokes. The drummed chorus phrase works like a "hook" in a pop song, that is, a catchy, memorable phrase (Music Example 3-11).* The Dagbanli text and an English translation are as follows:

Nag Biegu la to to to,	**It is Nag Biegu,**
Nag Biegu la to to to,	**It is Nag Biegu,**

*The rhythm in measures 5–7 is a standard, if simpler, version of the more exciting phrases heard in Music Example 3-11.

Music Example 3-11
"Nag Biegu" chorus phrases and verse answers. Music transcription by David Locke.

Nag Biegu la to—n nyeo!	It is Nag Biegu—that's him!
Nag Biegu la to,	It is Nag Biegu,
Nag Biegu la to,	It is Nag Biegu,
Nag Biegu la to—kumo!	It is Nag Biegu—kill him!

Life Story: Abubakari Lunna

I have tape-recorded many interviews with my teacher from Dagbon, Abubakari Lunna. When I met him in 1975, he was working as a professional with the Ghana Folkloric Company, a government-sponsored performing arts company based in Accra, the capital of Ghana. In 1988 he retired from government service and returned to northern Ghana, where he served his father, Lun-Naa Wombie, until his father's death. Presently, Mr. Lunna supports his large family as a drummer, farmer, and teacher. The following excerpt from his life story focuses on his teachers.

"My Education in Drumming"

My father's grandfather's name is Abubakari. It is Abubakari who gave birth to Azima and Alidu; Azima was the father of [my teacher] Ngolba and Alidu was father of Wombie, my father. Their old grandfather's name is the one I am carrying, Abubakari. My father never called me "son" until he died; he always called me "grandfather." I acted like their grandfather; we always played like grandson and grandfather.

When I was a young child, my father was not in Dagbon. My father was working as a security guard in the South at Bibiani, the gold town.* I was living with one of my father's teachers, his uncle Lun-Naa Neindoo, the drum chief at Woriboggo, a village near Tolon. When I was six or seven, my mother's father, Tali-Naa Alhassan [a chief of Tolon], took me to his senior brother, a chief of Woriboggo at that time. I was going to be his "shared child." In my drumming tradition, when you give your daughter in marriage and luckily she brings forth children, the husband has to give one to the mother's family. So, I was living in the chief's house.†

---

*There are very significant differences of ecology, history, and culture between what Abubakari calls "the North" and "the South."

†While his father comes from a long line of drummers, Abubakari's mother comes from a royal family.

I was with my mother's uncle for four or five years when he enrolled me in school. They took four of us to Tolon, my mother's home. I lived with my mother's father. We started going to the school. Luckily, in several weeks' time my father came from the South. He called my name, but his uncle told him, "Sorry. The boy's grandfather came and took him to be with the chiefs. Now he is in school." My father said, "What?! Is there any teacher above me? I am also a teacher. How can a teacher give his child to another teacher for training in a different language?" Early in the morning, he walked to Tolon. He held my hand. I was happy because my father had come to take me.

My father spent one month. When he went to the South, he took me with him. Unfortunately, at Bibiani my father didn't have time to teach me. One year when my father came back to Dagbon for the Damba Festival [an annual celebration of the birth of The Holy Prophet Muhammed], he told my grandfather, Lun-Naa Neindoo, "If I keep Abubakari at Bibiani, it will be bad. I want to leave him at home. I don't want him to be a southern boy."

I began learning our drumming talks and the singing. Lun-Naa Neindoo started me with *Dakoli Nye Bii Ba,* the beginning of drumming [i.e., the first repertory learned by young *lunsi*]: "God is the Creator. He can create a tree, He can create grass, He can create a person." You drum all before you say, "A Creator, God, created our grandfather, Bizum [the first *luna*]." The elders have given *Dakoli Nye Bii Ba* to the young ones so that they can practice in the markets. When they know that you are improving, they start you with drumming stories and singing stories. On every market day we, the young drummers, came together and drummed by ourselves.

When the Woriboggo chief made my father *Sampahi-Naa,* the drum chief second to the *Lun-Naa* [the highest rank of drum chief], he could not go back to Bibiani.* My father said, "Now, I am going to work with you on our drumming history talks." He began with the story of Yendi [seat of the paramount chieftaincy of Dagbon]: how Dagbon started, how we traveled from Nigeria and came to Dagbon, how we became drummers, how it happened that our grandfather Bizum made himself a drummer. If he gave me a story today, tomorrow I did it correctly.

I was with my father for a long time, more than five years. My father was hard. I faced difficulty with my father because of his way of teaching. My father would not beat the drum for you. He would sing and you had to do the same thing on *luna.* If you couldn't do it, he would continue until you got it before adding another.

[Later] . . . my father sent me to my teaching-father, Ngolba. He had a good voice, a good hand—every part of drumming, he had it. He had the knowledge, too, and people liked him. When he was drumming, he would make people laugh. People would hire him: "We are having a funeral on this day. Come and help us." I traveled with him, carrying his *luna.* Because of his drumming, Ngolba never sat at home: Every day we went for drumming. That was how people got to know me. Any time I was

---

*Just as the royals of Dagbon have an elaborate hierarchy of chieftaincies, so the *lunsi* have a pyramidlike system of titled positions of authority.

Figure 3.4
Abubakari holding the frame of Mba Ngolba's *luna*.

David Locke

walking, people started calling, "Ngolba, small Ngolba." And with my sweet hand and my quick memory, everyone liked me.

Already I knew something in drumming, so for him to continue with me was not hard. I only had to listen to his story and follow him. When we went to a place and he told stories, I tried to keep it in my mind. When we were resting that night, I asked him, "Oh, my uncle, I heard your talk today. Can you tell me more about it?" There, he would start telling me something. That is how I continued by education with Mba Ngolba.* I was very young to be drumming the deep history rhythms with a sweet hand.

My father called Ngolba and advised him, "I am not feeling happy about all the traveling you and Abubakari are doing. Drummers are bad.

---

*"Mba" means "father" for a *luna* drummer; your teacher becomes your teaching-father.

Somebody might try to spoil your lives. Find something to protect yourself. And protect Abubakari too." Father Ngolba—I can never forget him. Sometimes, when I was sitting at home, he would call me to get something to drink. I couldn't ask him, "Father, what is this?" In Dagbon, you can't ask him—you have to drink it.* My Mba Ngolba did it for me several times.

Another reason why I liked my teacher, my Father Ngolba, is that despite his quick temper, he didn't get angry with me. He loved me. He didn't take even one of his ideas and hide it from me. Even if I asked him about something common that many drummers know, the thing left—he didn't hide it. He would tell me, "I have reserved something. If you bring all your knowledge out in public, some people with quick learning can just collect it."

I respected Ngolba like my father. During farming time I got up early in the morning and went straight to the farm. When he came, he met me there already. If it was not farming time, I would go to his door, kneel down, and say good morning to him. I would stay there, not saying anything until at last he would ask me, "Do you want to go some place?" Only then could I go. Teachers can give you laws like your own father. That is our Dagbamba respect to teachers.

Father Ngolba died in the South. When an old drummer dies, we put a *luna* and a drumstick in the grave. The man who was with Ngolba when he died told me, "Your father said, 'Only bury me with this drumstick—don't add my *luna* to bury me. Give my *luna* to Abubakari.'" I said thank you for that. We finished the funeral back in Dagbon. The second brother to Ngolba spoke to all their family, "Ngolba told me that if it happens he dies, Abubakari should carry on with his duties. He should take his whole inheritance. And Ngolba had nothing other than his *luna*" [see Figure 3-4]. I have his *luna;* it is in my room now.

Conclusion As Discussion

Contrary to the images of chaos and despair conveyed by international mass media, we have encountered African music-cultures of stability, resourcefulness, and self-respect. Abubakari Lunna's life story reveals the rigor of an African musician's education. The erudition, commitment, suffering, and love are profound. Although he says good drumming is "sweet," clearly it is not frivolous or just fun. We could call it "deep." We have also seen that many Africans value the achievements of their ancestors. The Ewe rigorously study *Agbekor* and recreate it with passionate respect in performance.

African music-cultures are strongly humanistic. The human body inspires the construction and playing technique of musical instruments. The spontaneous performances of postal workers (see Chapter 1) point out an important feature of many African music-cultures: Music serves society. As we have experienced, many kinds of African music foster group participation.

*According to Dagbamba etiquette children never question the orders of their father.

Although I encourage African-style musicking, musicians who cross cultural borders need sensitivity to limits and contradictions. To me, nothing approaches the power of time-honored repertory performed in context by born-in-the-tradition culture-bearers. When non-Africans play African music, especially those of us with white skin, the legacy of slavery and colonialism affects how an audience receives the performance. How many enthusiasts for African music love its aesthetic surface but regard spirit possession as superstition?

Music is a joyful yet rigorous discipline. I contend that the hard work of musical analysis yields important benefits. By making clear the sophistication of African musical traditions, analysis promotes an attitude of respect. Analysis helps us understand the inner structure of music; it provides an ear map for appreciative listening and informed performance. In this Chapter I have emphasized musical examples with rhythms based on 3:2. This profound and elemental timing ratio animates many African traditions.

Analysis of musical structure raises big questions that resist simple answers: Can thought be nonverbal? What approach to music yields relevant data and significant explanation? By treating music as an object, does analysis wrongly alienate music from its authentic cultural setting? How can people know each other? Each Chapter in this book benefits from this type of questioning. We seek to know how people understand themselves, but we must acknowledge the impact of our own perspective. Not only does an active involvement in expressive culture provide a wonderful way to learn about other people, but musicking can change a person's own life as well. From this perspective, ethnomusicology helps create new and original music-cultures.

Inquiry into music-culture need not be a passive act of cultural tourism. On the contrary, a cross-cultural encounter can be an active process of self development. When we seek knowledge of African music-cultures, we can also reevaluate our own. As we try our hands at African music, we encounter fresh sonic styles and experience alternative models of social action. Just as African cultures are not static, each student's personal world of music is a work in progress.

References

Appiah, Anthony. 1992. *In My Father's House.* Cambridge, Mass.: Harvard Univ. Press.

Asante, Molefi. 1987. *The Afrocentric Idea.* Philadelphia: Temple Univ. Press.

Chernoff, John. 1979. *African Rhythm and African Sensibility.* Chicago: Univ. of Chicago Press.

Davis, Art. 1994. "Midawo Gideon Foli Alorwoyie: The Life and Music of a West African Drummer." M.A. thesis, Univ. of Illinois at Urbana Champaign.

Djedje, Jacqueline. 1978. "The One-String Fiddle in West Africa." Ph.D. diss., Univ. of California at Los Angeles.

Jones, A. M. 1959. *Studies in African Music.* London: Oxford Univ. Press.

Ladzekpo, Kobla. 1971. "The Social Mechanics of Good Music: A Description of Dance Clubs Among the Anlo Ewe-Speaking People of Ghana." *African Music* 3 (1): 33–42.

Locke, David. 1978. "The Music of Atsiagbekor." Ph.D. diss., Wesleyan Univ.

———. 1990. *Drum Damba.* Tempe, Ariz.: White Cliffs Media.

———. 1992. *Kpegisu: A War Drum of the Ewe.* Tempe, Ariz.: White Cliffs Media.

Miller, Christopher. 1990. *Theories of Africans.* Chicago: Univ. of Chicago Press.

Mphahlele, Ezekiel. 1962. *The African Image.* London: Faber & Faber.

Nketia, J. H. Kwabena. 1964. *Continuity of Traditional Instruction.* Legon, Ghana: Institute of African Studies.

Senghor, Leopold Sedar. 1967. *The Foundations of "Africanite" or "Negritude" and "Arabite."* Trans. Mercer Cook. Paris: Presence Africaine.

Additional Reading

Bebey, Francis. 1975. *African Music: A People's Art.* Trans. J. Bennet. New York: Lawrence Hill.

Bohannan, Paul, and Philip Curtin. 1995. *Africa and Africans.* 4th ed. Prospect Heights, Ill.: Waveland Press.

Brincard, Marie-Therese, ed. 1989. *Sounding Forms: African Musical Instruments.* New York: American Federation of Arts.

Nketia, J. H. Kwabena. 1974. *The Music of Africa.* New York: Norton.

Tucker, Judith Cook. 1986. *Let Your Voice Be Heard! Songs from Ghana and Zimbabwe.* Danbury, Conn.: World Music Press.

Turnbull, Colin. 1961. *The Forest People.* New York: Simon & Schuster.

Additional Listening

Locke, David. *Drum Gahu: Good-time Drumming from the Ewe People of Ghana and Togo.* White Cliffs Media WCM 9494.

Lunna, Abubakari. *Drum Damba featuring Abubakari Lunna, a Master Drummer of Dagbon.* White Cliffs Media WCM 9508.

Additional Viewing

Locke, David, and Godwin Agbeli. 1992. *Kpegisu.* [VHS, video documentary]. Tempe, Ariz.: Distributed by White Cliffs Media Co., ISBN 0-941677-44-3.

CHAPTER

4

North America/Black America/Blues

Jeff Todd Titon

Music of work, music of worship, music of play: the traditional music of African-American people in the United States has a rich and glorious heritage, embracing generations of the black experience. Neither African nor European, it is fully a black-American music, changing through the centuries to give voice to changes in black people's ideas of themselves. Despite the changes, it retains its black-American identity, with a stylistic core of ecstasy and improvisation that transforms the regularity of everyday life into the freedom of expressive artistry. Spirituals, the blues, jazz—to Europeans, these unusual sounds are considered the United States' greatest (some would say her only) contribution to the international musical world. Of course, modern black music does not sound unusual to North Americans, and that is because in this century the black style transformed popular music in America—the music of the theater, movies, radio, and television. Today, country music, rock, pop, and, tellingly, advertising jingles owe a great debt to the black sound. Locate some old 78 rpm records from the early twentieth century; perhaps someone in the neighborhood has a few in the attic, or you may find some in your college or local public library. The music on these old records will sound stilted, square, extravagantly dramatic, unnatural, jerky—not because of the recording process, but because of the influence of grand opera singing and marching band instrumental styles of the period. But in the 1920s, aptly called the Jazz Age, Bessie Smith and other African-American jazz and blues singers revolutionized the craft of singing popular music. Their approach was close to the rhythm and tone of ordinary talk, and this natural way of singing caught on. American popular music was never the same again.

This chapter focuses on the blues. The blues is a familiar music, but its very familiarity presents problems. Chief among them is the misconception that blues is a subset of jazz, that it was a historical phenomenon, a contributing stream that flowed, some time after Bessie Smith died, into the

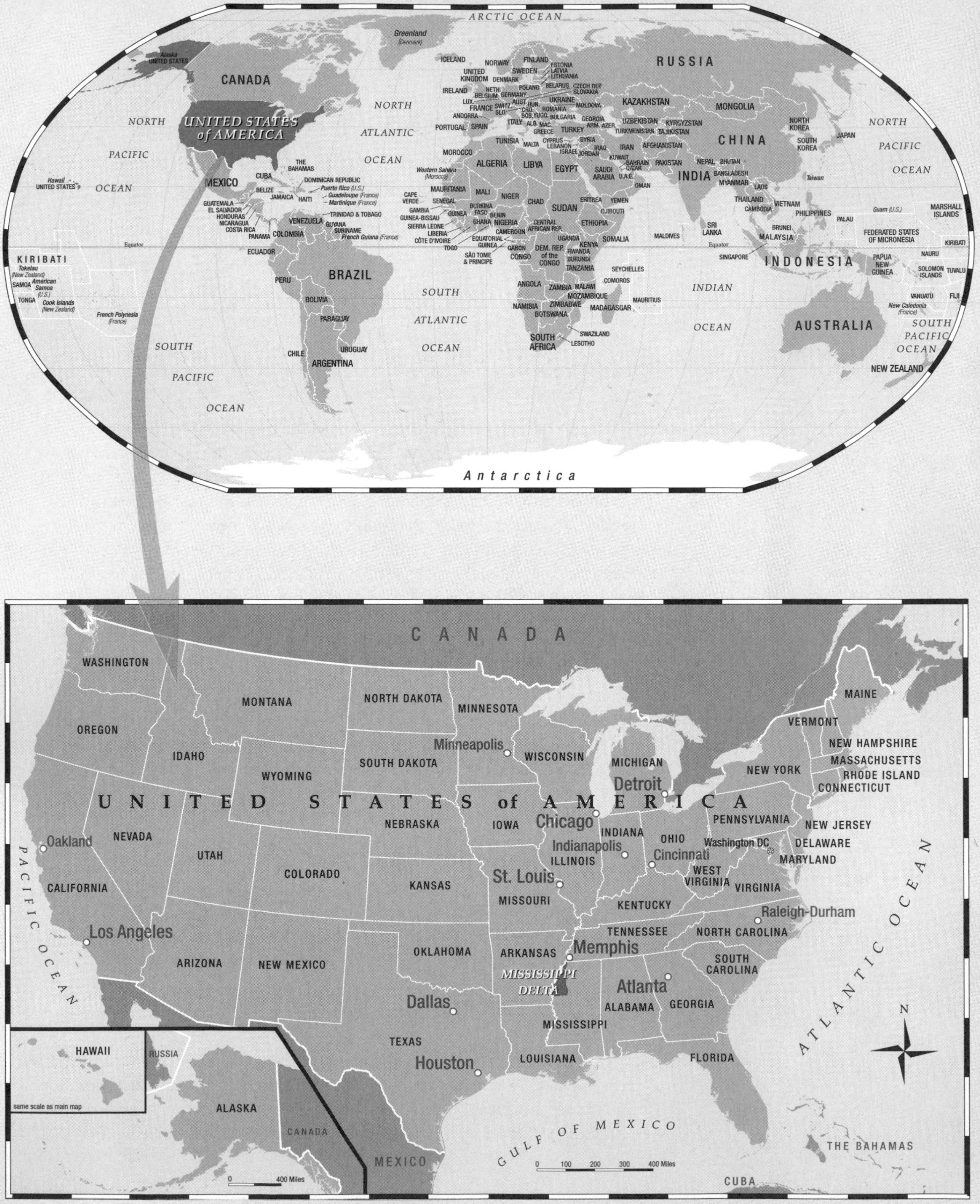
ARCTIC OCEAN
Greenland
(Denmark)
Alaska
UNITED STATES
CANADA
RUSSIA
UNITED STATES of AMERICA
NORTH PACIFIC OCEAN
NORTH ATLANTIC OCEAN
ICELAND
NORWAY
FINLAND
SWEDEN
ESTONIA
LATVIA
LITHUANIA
UNITED KINGDOM
DENMARK
IRELAND
NETH.
BELGIUM
GERMANY
POLAND
BELARUS
CZECH REP.
SLOVAKIA
LUX.
FRANCE
SWITZ.
AUST.
HUN.
UKRAINE
MOLDOVA
ROMANIA
KAZAKHSTAN
MONGOLIA
ANDORRA
SLO.
CRO.
BOS.
YUGO.
BULGARIA
GEORGIA
PORTUGAL
SPAIN
ITALY
ALB.
MAC.
GREECE
TURKEY
ARM.
AZER.
UZBEKISTAN
KYRGYZSTAN
TURKMENISTAN
TAJIKISTAN
NORTH KOREA
JAPAN
SOUTH KOREA
CHINA
TUNISIA
MALTA
CYPRUS
LEBANON
SYRIA
ISRAEL
JORDAN
IRAQ
IRAN
AFGHANISTAN
MOROCCO
KUWAIT
BAHRAIN
QATAR
PAKISTAN
NEPAL
BHUTAN
ALGERIA
LIBYA
EGYPT
SAUDI ARABIA
U.A.E.
INDIA
BANGLADESH
MYANMAR
Taiwan
THE BAHAMAS
Western Sahara
(Morocco)
Hawaii
UNITED STATES
MEXICO
CUBA
DOMINICAN REPUBLIC
Puerto Rico (U.S.)
Guadeloupe (France)
Martinique (France)
BELIZE
JAMAICA
HAITI
GUATEMALA
EL SALVADOR
HONDURAS
NICARAGUA
COSTA RICA
PANAMA
TRINIDAD & TOBAGO
VENEZUELA
GUYANA
SURINAME
French Guiana (France)
COLOMBIA
ECUADOR
CAPE VERDE
MAURITANIA
MALI
NIGER
CHAD
SUDAN
ERITREA
YEMEN
OMAN
SENEGAL
GAMBIA
GUINEA-BISSAU
GUINEA
BURKINA FASO
BENIN
NIGERIA
DJIBOUTI
ETHIOPIA
SIERRA LEONE
LIBERIA
CÔTE D'IVOIRE
GHANA
TOGO
CENTRAL AFRICAN REP.
CAMEROON
EQUATORIAL GUINEA
SÃO TOME & PRINCIPE
GABON
CONGO
DEM. REP. of the CONGO
UGANDA
KENYA
RWANDA
BURUNDI
SOMALIA
TANZANIA
MALDIVES
SRI LANKA
THAILAND
LAOS
VIETNAM
CAMBODIA
PHILIPPINES
PALAU
Guam (U.S.)
MARSHALL ISLANDS
FEDERATED STATES OF MICRONESIA
BRUNEI
MALAYSIA
SINGAPORE
INDONESIA
KIRIBATI
NAURU
PAPUA NEW GUINEA
SOLOMON ISLANDS
TUVALU
Equator
KIRIBATI
Tokelau
(New Zealand)
SAMOA
American Samoa
(U.S.)
TONGA
Cook Islands
(New Zealand)
French Polynesia
(France)
PERU
BRAZIL
BOLIVIA
PARAGUAY
CHILE
URUGUAY
ARGENTINA
SOUTH ATLANTIC OCEAN
SEYCHELLES
COMOROS
ANGOLA
ZAMBIA
MALAWI
MOZAMBIQUE
MAURITIUS
NAMIBIA
ZIMBABWE
BOTSWANA
MADAGASCAR
SOUTH AFRICA
SWAZILAND
LESOTHO
INDIAN OCEAN
AUSTRALIA
VANUATU
FIJI
New Caledonia
(France)
SOUTH PACIFIC OCEAN
NEW ZEALAND
SOUTH PACIFIC OCEAN
NORTH PACIFIC OCEAN
Antarctica
CANADA
WASHINGTON
MONTANA
NORTH DAKOTA
MINNESOTA
MAINE
OREGON
VERMONT
IDAHO
Minneapolis
WISCONSIN
NEW HAMPSHIRE
SOUTH DAKOTA
MICHIGAN
MASSACHUSETTS
WYOMING
NEW YORK
RHODE ISLAND
Detroit
CONNECTICUT
UNITED STATES of AMERICA
NEBRASKA
IOWA
Chicago
PENNSYLVANIA
NEW JERSEY
NEVADA
INDIANA
OHIO
Oakland
Indianapolis
Washington DC
DELAWARE
UTAH
ILLINOIS
Cincinnati
MARYLAND
COLORADO
WEST VIRGINIA
PACIFIC OCEAN
CALIFORNIA
KANSAS
St. Louis
VIRGINIA
MISSOURI
KENTUCKY
Raleigh-Durham
Los Angeles
TENNESSEE
NORTH CAROLINA
OKLAHOMA
ARKANSAS
Memphis
ARIZONA
NEW MEXICO
SOUTH CAROLINA
MISSISSIPPI DELTA
Atlanta
ATLANTIC OCEAN
Dallas
ALABAMA
GEORGIA
MISSISSIPPI
N
HAWAII
RUSSIA
TEXAS
LOUISIANA
FLORIDA
Houston
same scale as main map
ALASKA
CANADA
GULF OF MEXICO
0 100 200 300 400 Miles
THE BAHAMAS
MEXICO
0 400 Miles
CUBA

Figure 4.1
Muddy Waters (McKinley Morganfield), studio photo. Chicago, Illinois, early 1950s.

river of jazz. Nothing could be further from the truth. Blues is best understood as a feeling—"the blues"—and as a specific musical form, whereas jazz is best thought of as a technique, as a *way* of forming. Jazz musicians applied their technique to the blues form, but blues did not lose its identity. Muddy Waters (Figure 4-1), B. B. King, Albert Collins, John Lee Hooker, Koko Taylor, and Buddy Guy, who rose to national prominence as blues singers, came from a vital tradition. Until the 1950s, when desegregation and the Civil Rights Movement changed African-American social and economic conditions, the blues music-culture, with its singers, country juke joints, barrelhouses, city rent parties, street singing, bar scenes, nightclubs, lounges, recordings, and record industry, was a significant part of the black music-culture in the United States. Today the blues music-culture incorporates white as well as black musicians, and its audience is worldwide.

Blues and the Truth

The best entry into the blues is through the words of the songs. It is hard to talk at length about words in songs, and harder still to talk about music. As Charles Seeger, one of the founders of the Society of Ethnomusicology, reminds us, it would be more logical to "music" about music than to talk about it (Seeger 1977:16). In the blues music-culture, when the setting is informal, that is just what happens when one singer responds to another by singing verses of his or her own. Another common response to blues is dancing. Dancers and listeners as a rule have no interest in an articulate body of blues criticism. Speaking of oral literature as a whole, Dennis Tedlock points up the paradox with gentle irony: "Members of primary oral cultures generally limit themselves to brief remarks about performances when they say anything at all, and such remarks are quickly forgotten. There is no such thing as an oral performance of the great critical discourse of the past" (Tedlock 1977:516).

The most common response to blues music is a feeling in the gut, dancing to the beat, nodding assent, a vocalized "that's right, you got it, that's the truth"—not unlike the black Christian's response to a sermon or a gospel song. A good, "deep" blues song leaves you feeling that you have heard the truth, and there is not much more that needs saying. But the words to blues songs are tough. They can stand up to inquiry, to analysis. Because the words pass from one singer to another as a coin goes from hand to hand, they become finely honed and proverbial in their expression: economical, truthful. Response to the words of the songs can be talked about in words. Moreover, blues lyrics have a legitimate claim as serious literature. As literary critics Cleanth Brooks, R. W. B. Lewis, and Robert Penn Warren have written, "In the world of music the recognition of blues as art is well established. But waiving their value as musical art, we may assert that they represent a body of poetic art unique and powerful. . . . No body of folk poetry in America—except, perhaps, the black spirituals—can touch it, and much of the poetry recognized as 'literature,' white or black, seems tepid beside it" (Brooks, Lewis, and Warren 1973:II, 2759).

CD 1
Track 11

We begin by taking an extended look at a single blues performance (CD Selection 11), "Poor Boy Blues," by the Lazy Bill Lucas Blues Band (Figure 4-2). Bill Lucas is the vocalist; he accompanies himself on electric guitar, and he is joined by two other accompanists, one on acoustic guitar and the other on drums. The recording was made in Minneapolis, Minnesota, in 1970. Listen to it now, paying particular attention to the lyrics:

1. I'm just a poor boy; people, I can't even write my name.
   I'm just a poor boy; people, I can't even write my name.
   Every letter in the alphabet to me they look the same.
2. Mother died when I was a baby; father I never seen.
   Mother died when I was a baby; father I never seen.
   When I think how dumb I am, you know it makes me want to scream.
3. Ever since I was the age around eleven or twelve,
   Ever since I was the age around eleven or twelve,
   I just been a poor boy; ain't caught nothing but hell.
4. When I was a child Santa Claus never left one toy.
   When I was a child Santa Claus never left one toy.
   If you have any mercy, please have mercy on poor boy.

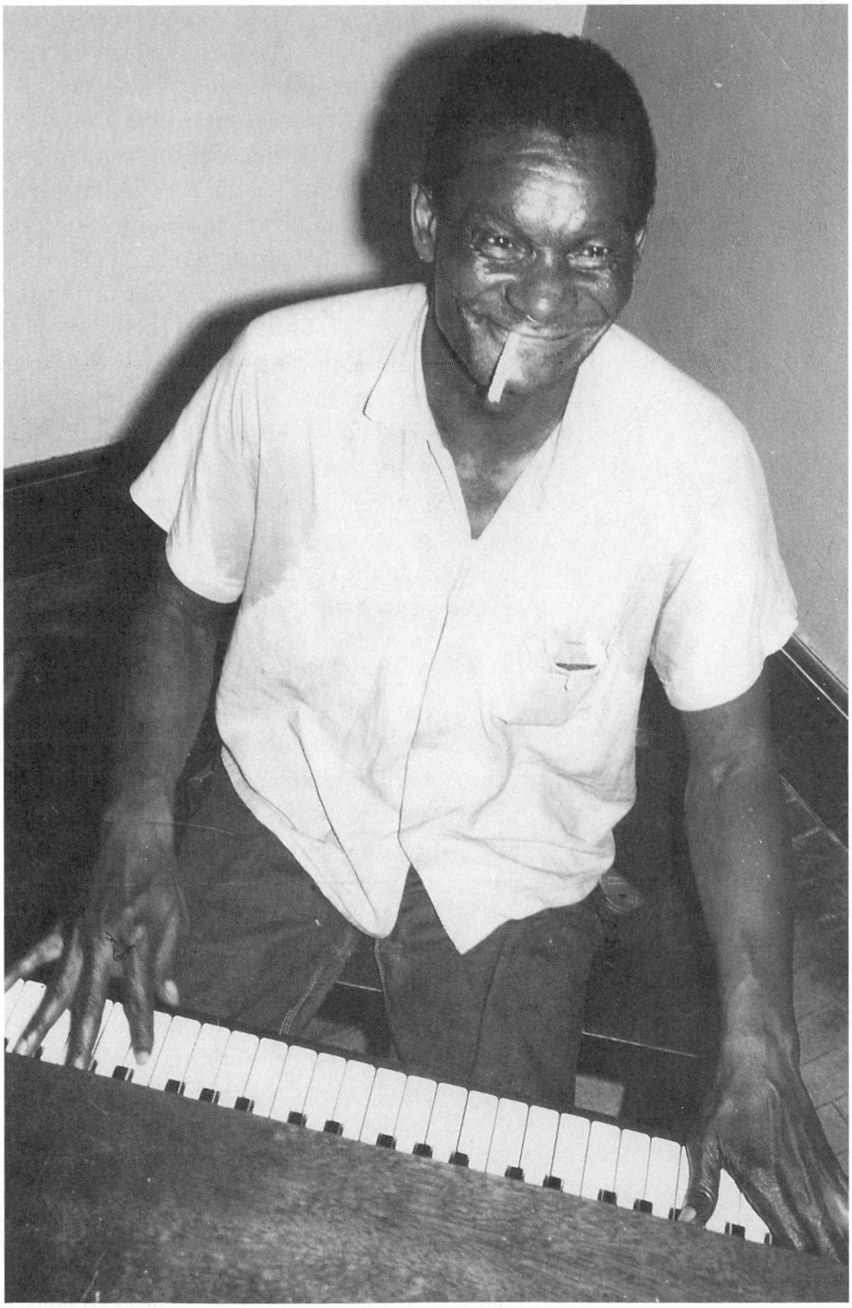

Jeff Todd Titon

Figure 4.2
Lazy Bill Lucas. Minneapolis, Minnesota, 1968.

I did not choose "Poor Boy Blues" because the words were outstanding; they are typical. For me, some of it is good, some not; some of it works, some does not. "I'm just a poor boy; people, I can't even write my name" produces an automatic response of sympathy for the poor boy, but it is not a very deep response. I am sorry for the poor boy's illiteracy, but, heck, everyone has problems. When the line repeats, I am anxious to hear how the stanza will close. "Every letter in the alphabet to me they look the same" brings to my mind's eye a picture of a strange alphabet in which all letters look alike or, rather, in which the differences in their shape have no meaning. The image is clear, it works, and it involves me. This poor boy may be illiterate, but he is perceptive. And not only does the image itself succeed, but the delay of the most important word in the line, *same,* until the end, and the impact of its rhyme with *name,* convinces me I am hearing the truth. Blues singer Eddie "Son" House told me this about how he put his blues stanzas together: "I had enough sense to try to make 'em, rhyme 'em so they'd have have *hits* to 'em with a meaning, some sense to 'em, you know" (Titon 1994:47). The inevitable rightness of the rhyme—you expect it and it rewards you—hits harder than an unrhymed close, particularly because the end rhyme always falls, in blues, on an accented syllable.

I do not respond to "Mother died when I was a baby"; I resist a statement that sounds sentimental. This is not because I think of myself as some kind of tough guy, but because I want the sentiment to be earned. I much prefer the statement at the close of the line: "father I never seen." The effect is in the contrast between the mother who died and the father who might as well be dead. In the image of the father who has never been seen is the mystery of not knowing one's parents. It is not just missing love; for all we know, the poor boy was raised by loving relatives. But a child takes after parents, inherits the biology, so to speak; without knowing your parents you do not fully know yourself. That is the real terror of the poor boy's life. "When I think how dumb I am, you know it makes me want to scream" is a cliché; the rhyme is forced. Okay, scream. Nor do I respond to the third stanza when I hear it, but when I think about it, it seems curious that the poor boy says he began to catch hell from age eleven or twelve. I guess he was catching it all along but did not fully realize it until then. That is a nice point, but a little too subtle to register during a performance. I would have to sing it several times myself to appreciate that aspect of it.

The final stanza takes great risk with sentimentality, calling up Christmas memories, but it succeeds by a matter-of-fact tone—"When I was a child Santa Claus never left one toy"—that dispels the scene's stickiness. Santa Claus never left a toy for anyone, but a child who believes in Santa can enjoy an innocent world where presents reward good little boys and girls. If he could not believe in Santa, I wonder if he ever had any part of the innocent happiness people seem to need early, and in large doses, if they are going to live creative lives. Or it could have been the other way around: He believed in Santa, but Santa, never bringing him a toy, simply did not believe in him.

The song now leads up to its final line, a plea for mercy. "You" are addressed directly: If you have any mercy, show it to the poor boy. Will you? If you heard this from a blind street singer would you put some coins in his cup? Would you be more likely to show mercy to the poor boy than to someone down on his luck who just walks up and asks for spare change? The song will strike some people as sentimental, calling up an easy emotion that is just as quickly forgotten as it is evoked. T. S. Eliot, in a widely influential argument, said that in a work of literature any powerful emotion must have an "objective correlative"; that is, the work itself must demonstrate that there is good reason for the emotion (Eliot [1920] 1964). Has "Poor Boy Blues" given you good reason for mercy? Have you been told the truth, or were you played for a sucker?

Autobiography and the Blues

The effect of "Poor Boy Blues" on a generalized listener can take us only so far, because we have been considering the words in a broad, English-speaking context. What do the words mean to someone in the blues music-culture? What do they mean to Lazy Bill Lucas? As "Poor Boy Blues" is sung in the first person, does the "I" speak for Lucas? What, in short, is the relation of the song and the singer?

More than any other subject, the correspondence between the words to blues songs and the lives of the singers has fascinated people who write about the blues. The blues singer's image as wandering minstrel, blind bard, and untutored genius is idealized, but, according to Samuel Charters, "There is no more romantic figure in popular music than the bluesman, with everything the term involves. And it isn't a false romanticism" (Charters 1977:112). The result is that most books on blues are organized biographically. Some writers have gone so far as to derive the facts of an otherwise obscure blues singer's life and personality from the lyrics of her or his recorded songs. Published life stories of blues singers in their own words, on the other hand, are few (see, for example, Brunoghe 1964; Titon 1974b). If these first-person life stories are read properly, they can be understood as far more reliable expressions of the blues singer's own personality than his song lyrics are, because the lyrics often are borrowed from tradition. Whatever the impulse, most people assume that the lyrics of a blues song do speak for the singer. Paul Oliver wrote, for example, "One of the characteristics of the blues is that it is highly personalized—blues singers nearly always sing about themselves" (Oliver 1974:30). If that is true, then "Poor Boy Blues" should be a reflection of the life and thoughts of Lazy Bill Lucas.

I was a close friend of Bill Lucas's for six years, and played guitar in his blues band for two of them. During our friendship I tape-recorded his recollections of his life for publication first in *Blues Unlimited* (Titon 1969), a British blues research journal, and later in the accompanying notes to his first American LP (Titon 1974a). Let us look, then, at parts of Lucas's life history and see if "Poor Boy Blues" speaks for him.

The Life History of Bill Lucas, Blues Singer*

> I was born in Wynne, Arkansas, on May 29, 1918. I never heard my mother say the exact *time* I was born: she was so upset at the time I guess she wouldn't remember. I have two sisters and three brothers; I was third from my baby sister, the third youngest.

*©1974 by William Lucas and Jeff Titon. A fuller version accompanies Titon 1974a.

Ever since I can remember, I had trouble with my eyesight. Doctors tell me it's the nerves. I can see shapes, I can tell colors, and I know light and dark, but it's hard to focus, and no glasses can help me. An operation might cure it, but there's a chance it could leave me completely blind, and I don't want to take that gamble.

My father was a farmer out in the country from Wynne. He was a sharecropper, farming on the halvers.* In 1922 we moved to Short Bend, Arkansas, but my father wanted to get where there were better living conditions. A lot of his neighbors and friends had come up to Missouri and told him how good it was up there.

About every two or three years we moved from one farm to another. Some places you had good crops, according to the kind of land you had. Some places we had real sandy land, and that wasn't good; but in the places that were swampy, that black land, that was good. You know when you're sharecropping cotton and corn you look for the best location and the best living conditions. And you could move; you didn't have a lease on the place.

So my family moved to Advance, Missouri, in 1924. We moved by night but that doesn't mean we had to slip away. They loaded all our stuff in a wagon and we caught the ten o'clock train. That was my first train ride; I loved the train then. Advance was about twenty-five miles west of the river; it wasn't on the highway, just on the railroad. It was a little town of five hundred; it consisted of two grocery stores and a post office which doubled over into a saloon. We never did go to town much except on Saturdays. In the summertime we'd go in about every week to carry our vegetables to sell in a wagon: watermelons and cabbage and stuff.

My father wanted to own his own farm, but that was impossible. That was a dream. He didn't have enough money to buy it and there weren't any loans like there are nowadays. We owned cattle, we owned pigs. We had about thirteen milk cows, and we had leghorn chickens that gave us bushels of eggs. We were better off than our neighbors because we would sometimes swap our eggs for something we didn't have. We were blessed with eggs and chickens and milk. We were blessed. I tried to, but I never did learn how to milk. I wasn't too much use on the farm. I did a lot of babysitting but not too much else.

There weren't many guitars around, but in 1930 my daddy got me a guitar. I remember so well, just like it was yesterday, he traded a pig for it. Money was scarce down there; we didn't have any money. The boy wanted $7 for it. We didn't have money but we had plenty of pigs. Our neighbors had some boys that played guitar, but they never did take pains and show me how to do it. I would just watch 'em and listen. I learned from sounds. And after they were gone, then I would try to make the guitar sound like I heard them make it sound. It was easier to play single notes than chords. Right now till today I don't use but two fingers to play guitar; I don't play guitar like other people. I wanted the guitar because I liked the noise and it sounded pretty.

---

*A sharecropping arrangement in which the landlord supplied the tenant with a shack, tools, seed, work animals, feed, fuel wood, and half the fertilizer in exchange for half the tenant's crop and labor.

After I got it and come progressing on it, a tune or two here or there, my dad and mama both decided that would be a good way for me to make my living. I knew all the time I wanted to make a career out of it, but after I came progressing on it, well they wanted me to make a career out of it too. But they said I had to be old enough and big enough to take care of it, not to be breaking strings and busting it all up.

My father got me a piano in 1932 for a Christmas present. That was the happiest Christmas I ever had. He didn't trade pigs for that; he paid money for it. Got it at our neighborhood drugstore. It was an upright. It had been a player piano but all the guts had been taken out of it. Well, at the time I knew how to play organ, one of those pump organs; I had played a pump organ we had at home that came about the same time as the guitar. A woman, she was moving, she was breaking up housekeeping, and she gave us the organ. It had two pedals on it and you'd do like riding a bicycle. So it didn't take me long to learn how to bang out a few tunes on the piano.

I didn't know what chords I was making. We got a little scale book that would go behind the keyboard of the piano and tell you all the chords. It was a beginner's book, in big letters. I could see that. You know, a beginner's book is in big letters. And I wanted to learn music, but after I got that far, well, the rest of the music books were so small that I couldn't see the print. And that's why I didn't learn to read music.

I did learn to read the alphabet at home. My parents taught me, and so did the other kids. I used to go to school, but it was just to be with the other kids, and sometimes the kids would teach me. I was just apt; I could pick things up. I had a lot of mother-wit.

So I bumped around on the piano until 1936, when we left the country and came to Cape Girardeau, Missouri. I had to leave my piano; we didn't have room for it. I almost cried. That was when I started playing the guitar on street corners. My dad had day work; that was the idea of him moving to the city, trying to better his living conditions. I forget what he went to work as: I think he worked in a coal yard. We stayed at my sister's house; one of my oldest sisters was married. But we had to go back to Commerce, Missouri. My dad couldn't make it in Cape Girardeau so we went to Commerce. I don't know what he thought he was going to do there because that was a little hick town, wasn't but about three hundred in population there. He didn't farm there; I vaguely can remember what we did now.

At that time I didn't know too much about blues. We had a radio station down there but they all played big band stuff and country and western music. But we didn't call it country and western music back then; we called it hillbilly music. Well, hillbilly music was popular there and so I played hillbilly music on the guitar and sang songs like "She'll be Coming 'round the Mountain" and "It Ain't Gonna Rain No More" and "Wabash Cannonball." The only time I heard any blues was when we'd go to restaurants where a jukebox was and they'd have blues records. And my daddy had a windup phonograph, and we had a few blues records at home by Peetie Wheatstraw and Scrapper Blackwell and Curtis Jones—the old pieces, you know. So I learned a little bit about blues pieces off the records I'd hear around home. I heard Bessie Smith and Daddy Stovepipe and Blind Lemon Jefferson.

At that time I didn't have any knowledge of music. I liked any of it. I even liked those hillbilly songs. And when I heard the blues I liked the blues, but I just liked the music, period. And when I played out on street corners, I'd be playing for white folks mostly, and that was the music they seemed to like better, the hillbilly music. So I played it because I'd been listening to it all the time on the radio and so it wasn't very hard for me to play. The blues didn't *strike* me until I heard Big Bill Broonzy; that's when I wanted to play blues guitar like him.

We lost our mother in 1939. We buried her in Commerce, and we left Commerce after she died. My dad, he went to St. Louis in 1940, still trying to find better living conditions. Later that year he brought me to St. Louis, and that's where I met Big Joe Williams. At that time he wasn't playing in bars or taverns; he was just playing on the street. So he let me join him, and I counted it an honor to be playing with Big Joe Williams because I had heard his blues records while I was still down South. And so we played blues in the street.

But I didn't stay in St. Louis long. My dad and I came to Chicago the day after New Year's in 1941. Sonny Boy Williamson* was the first musician I met with up there. I met him over on Maxwell Street, where they had all their merchandise out on the street, and you could buy anything you wanted on a Sunday, just like you could on a Monday. They had groceries, clothes, hardware, appliances, right out on the street, where people could come to look for bargains. That was a good place to play until the cops made us cut it out. I played a lot with Sonny Boy. Little suburban places around Chicago like Battle Creek, and South Bend. We were playing one-nighters in taverns and parties. Sonny Boy would book himself, and I went around with him. There wasn't much money in it; Sonny Boy paid my expenses and a place to stay with his friends. He was known all up around there. He played with me when he couldn't get nobody else. I didn't have a name at the time.† But I had sense enough to play in time and change chords when he changed; it wasn't but three changes anyhow. We didn't play nothing but the funky blues. He just needed somebody to keep time, back him up on guitar.

Big Bill Broonzy was my idol for guitar, and I'd go sit in on his shows. He'd let me play on the stand between times; I'd play his same songs. Bill knew I couldn't do it as well as he did, so he wasn't mad. In fact he appreciated me for liking his style. I also liked T-Bone Walker, but he made so many chord changes! I was unfortunate to learn changes; I never did know but three changes on the guitar.

I used to play with Little Walter‡ on the street, too, in the black section, where they wanted the blues. I quit playing that hillbilly music when I left St. Louis. In St. Louis I was getting on the blues right smart after I met up with Big Joe Williams. But white folks in Chicago or here in Minneapolis don't like hillbilly music. They tell you right away. "What you think I am? A hillbilly?"

---

*Harmonica player John Lee Williamson (d. 1948).

†He means that the name Bill Lucas was unknown to the blues audiences.

‡Walter Jacobs, generally acknowledged as the finest blues harmonica player after World War II.

I started in my professional career in 1946 when I joined the union. We all joined the union together, me and Willie Mabon and Earl Dranes, two guitars and a piano. We took our first job in 1946 on December 20, in the Tuxedo Lounge, 3119 Indiana, in Chicago. The paid union scale, but scale wasn't much then. The leader didn't get but twelve dollars a night, the sidemen ten dollars. We worked from 9 P.M. until 4 A.M. It was a real nice club. These after-hours clubs always had good crowds because after two o'clock everybody would come in. We had a two-week engagement there, and I thought it was real good money. But then we were kicked back out on the street.

Little Walter and I used to play along with Johnny Young at a place called the Purple Cat—1947. That's where he gave me the name "lazy" at. We'd been there so long Little Walter thought I should go up and turn on the amps, but I never did go up and do that thing, so that's why he started calling me "lazy" Bill, and the name stuck.

In 1948 I started in playing with Homesick James, and sometimes also with Little Hudson. I started out Little Hudson on playing. When I first met him in Chicago around 1945 or 1946 he wasn't playing. Of course he had a guitar, but he wasn't *doing* nothing. I started him and encouraged him and so he'd come and sit in with me and Sonny Boy or me and Willie Mabon or whoever I'd be playing with. He just started like that. And when he got good he was respected. He had a right smart amount of prestige about him, Hudson did. I switched to playing piano in 1950 because they had more guitar players than piano players. But of course I'd been playing piano all along—just not professionally, that's all. Little Hudson needed a piano player for his Red Devils trio. Our first job was at a place called the Plantation, on Thirty-first Street, on the south side of Chicago.

I don't know where he got the idea of the name from, but the drummer had a red devil with pitchforks on the head of his bass drum. And he played in church, too! Would you believe they had to cover up the head of the drum with newspapers? He'd cover the devil up when he'd go to church.

I had a trio, Lazy Bill and the Blue Rhythm, for about three or four months in 1954 (Figure 4-3). We were supposed to do four records a year for Chance, but Art Sheridan went out of business and we never heard about it again. We did one record. Well, I didn't keep my group together long. You know it's kind of hard on a small musician to keep a group together in Chicago very long because they run out of work, and when they don't get work to do, they get with other guys. And there were so many musicians in Chicago that some of 'em were underbidding one another. They'd take a job what I was getting twelve dollars for, they'd take it for eight dollars.

I was doing anything, working with anybody, just so I could make a dime. On a record session, any engagement at all. For a while I was working with a disc jockey on a radio station. He was broadcasting from a dry cleaners and he wanted live music on his broadcast. I did it for the publicity; I didn't get any money for that. Work got so far apart. Every time I'd run out of an engagement, it would be a long time before another one came through. And so Mojo and Jo Jo,* they had come up here to

*George "Mojo" Buford, harmonica player, and Joseph "Jo Jo" Williams, bass player.

Figure 4.3
Lazy Bill and the Blue Rhythm, studio photo. Chicago, Illinois, 1954. L-R: Lazy Bill Lucas, James Bannister, "Miss Hi-Fi," Jo Jo Williams.

Courtesy of Jo Jo Williams

> Minneapolis. They had been working at the Key Club, and they decided they needed a piano player. I wasn't doing anything in Chicago; I was glad to come up here. I had no idea I was doing to stay up here, but I ended up here with a houseful of furniture.

Lazy Bill Lucas and "Poor Boy Blues"

Bill Lucas's account of his life ends in Minneapolis in 1964. The following year I began my graduate studies at the University of Minnesota and met him at a university concert. By that time he had two audiences: the black people on the North Side of the city who still liked the blues, and the white people in the university community. The 1960s was the period of the first so-called blues revival (Groom 1971), during which thousands of blues records from the past four decades were reissued on LPs, dozens of older singers believed dead were "rediscovered" and recorded, and hundreds of younger singers, Bill Lucas among them, found new audiences at university concerts and coffeehouses and festivals. The revival, which attracted a predominantly young, white audience, peaked in the great 1969 and 1970 Ann Arbor (Michigan) Blues Festivals, where the best of three generations of blues singers and blues bands performed for people who had traveled thousands of miles to pitch their tents and attend these three-day events. Bill Lucas was one of the featured performers at the 1970 festival. For his performance he received $400 plus expenses, the most money he ever made for a single job in his musical career.

In the 1960s and 1970s Bill Lucas could not support himself from his musical earnings. A monthly check (roughly a hundred times the minimum hourly wage) from government welfare for the blind supplemented his income. Blues music was in low demand; most of Minneapolis's black community preferred the current black popular music, while others liked jazz or classical music. Some even made a point of disliking blues, either because they were fundamentalist Christians who associate blues with sin or because they viewed blues as the expression of a resignation that is out of touch with modern attitudes toward human rights. Nor was there sufficient work in the university community for Bill. He sang in clubs, bars, and at concerts, but the work was unsteady. When I was in his band (1969–71), our most dependable job was a six-month engagement for two nights each week in the "Grotto Room" of a pizza restaurant. Classified by the musicians' union as a low-level operation, it paid the minimum union scale for an evening's work from nine to one: $23 for Bill, $18 for sidemen (about $60 and $50, respectively, in today's money). On December 11, 1982, Bill Lucas died. A benefit concert to pay his funeral expenses raised nearly $2,000.

His life history not only gives facts about his life but expresses an attitude toward it, and both may be compared with the words of "Poor Boy Blues" to see whether the song speaks personally for Bill Lucas. Some of the facts of the poor boy's life correspond, but others do not. I asked him whether the line about all the letters in the alphabet looking the same held any special meaning for him, and he said it did. Unless letters or numbers were printed very large and thick, he could not make them out. On the other hand, unlike the poor boy in the song who never saw his father, Lucas and his father were very close. Moreover, his experiences of Christmas were happy, and one year he received a piano. What about the attitudes expressed in the song and in the life history? Neither show self-pity. Bill did not have an illustrious career as a blues singer; he scuffled with hard times and took almost any job that was available. Yet he was proud of his accomplishments. "I just sing the funky blues," he said, "and people either like it or they don't."

"Poor Boy Blues" cannot therefore be understood to speak directly for Bill Lucas's personal experience, but it does speak generally for it, as it speaks for tens of thousands of people who have been forced by circumstances into hard times. Thus, in their broad cultural reach, the words of blues songs tell the truth.

Learning the Blues

One question that bears on the relation between Lazy Bill Lucas and "Poor Boy Blues" is the authorship of the song. In fact, Lucas did not compose it; it was put together by St. Louis Jimmy Oden and recorded by him in 1942. Lucas learned the song from the record. Learning someone else's song does not, of course, rule out the possibility that the song speaks for the new singers, for they may be attracted to it precisely because the lyrics suit their experiences and feelings.

In the African-American music-culture almost all blues singers learn songs by imitation, whether in person or from records. There is no such thing as formal lessons. In his life history, Lucas tells how he listened to neighbors play guitar and how he tried to make it sound like they did. After he developed a rudimentary playing technique, he was able to fit accompaniments behind new songs that he learned from others or made up himself. Unquestionably the best way to come to know a song is to make it your own by performing it.

CD 1
Track 11

Listen once again to "Poor Boy Blues" (CD Selection 11), and concentrate first on the instrumental accompaniment. The guitarists and drummer keep a triple rhythm behind Lucas's singing:

When Lucas pauses, the guitar responds with a sequence of single-note triplets (Music Example 4-1). This triplet rhythm is a common way of dividing the beat in slow blues songs. When accented monotonously, as in many rock and roll tunes from the 1950s, it becomes a cliché. Music students familiar with dotted rhythms (from marches and the like) should resist the temptation to hear this as a dotted rhythm. Recordings of white musicians before World War II attempting to play blues and jazz sometimes do not flow or "swing" because the musicians are locked into dotted rhythms.

Now listen to the rhythm of Lucas's vocal, and try to feel both rhythms, vocal and accompaniment, at the same time. You might find this difficult. The reason is that Lucas very seldom sings squarely on the beat. The transcription of his melody (Music Example 4-2) is an oversimplification for the sake of readability, but even here we see a great deal of syncopation, in seemingly delayed entrances or anticipations of the beat. Lucas is not having a hard time *finding* the beat; on the contrary, he deliberately avoids it.

The musical brilliance of "Poor Boy Blues" rests on the difference between vocal and instrumental rhythms. Accents contrast; at times each part has its own meter. The reason is this: While the accompanying instruments stay in triple meter, Lucas sings in alternating duple and triple. In other words, passages of two-against-three polymeter (especially apparent at the outset of measures 1, 5, and 9 in Music Example 4-2) alternate with passages of three-against-three single meter. I have written this example in $\frac{4}{4}$ to bring out the contrast. One feels that Lucas initiates each vocal phrase in triple meter, then quickly shifts to duple, hurrying his phrasing in imitation of speech rhythm.

In Chapter 3 we saw that two-against-three polymeter characterizes black African music. Here we see a deep connection between African and

Music Example 4-1
Rhythmic outline, "Poor Boy Blues."

Music Example 4-2
"Poor Boy Blues," stanza 3, sung by Lazy Bill Lucas, Minneapolis, Minnesota, May, 1970. Recorded and transcribed by Jeff Titon.

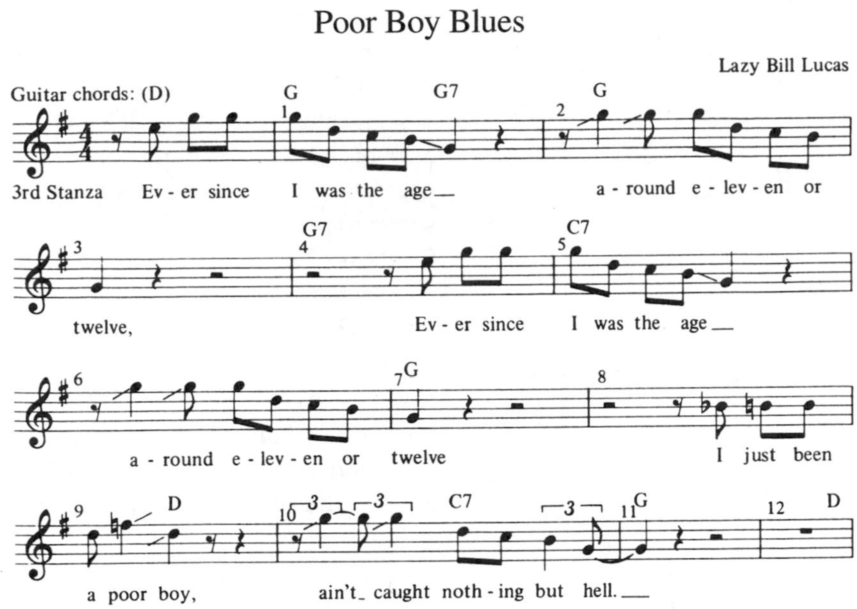

African-American music: rhythmic complexity and polymeter. But our example from the blues is not just an instance of continuous polymeter, as in Africa. Rather, blues music (and jazz, and reggae) *shifts* into and out of polymeter, playfully teasing the boundary. When these shifts occur rapidly, the boundary between single meter and polymeter breaks down. The result is a new sense of time: the graceful forward propulsion we hear as "swing" that makes us feel like moving our whole body in response.

To sing "Poor Boy Blues" as Lucas does, begin by simply *saying* the words to get a feel for the speech rhythms. If you read music, use the transcription (Music Example 4-2) as a guide, but always follow the recording. Listen to the way he slides up to the high G in measures 2, 6, and 10, indicated on the transcription by a solid line just before the note heads. Then hear how he releases "poor" (measure 9) and slides directly afterward into "boy." This sliding and gliding is another type of musical "play," this time with the pitch, not the beat. Finally, listen to him attack the word *twelve* (measures 3 and 7) just ahead of the bar-line rather than as written.

Lucas sings "Poor Boy Blues" in a musical scale I have called the blues scale (Titon 1971). This scale (Music Example 4-3) is uniquely African American, though about fifty years ago it penetrated white pop music in the United States. It typifies blues, jazz, spirituals, gospel tunes, and other

Music Example 4-3
The blues scale (key of G for convenience).

black-American music. It differs significantly from the usual Western diatonic major and minor scales, and it does not correspond to any of the medieval European church modes.

The blues scale's special features are the flatted seventh and the presence of *both* the major and minor third. (Another special feature, seemingly a later development, is the flatted fifth.) A typical use of this double third, sometimes termed the "blue note" by the jazz writers, is shown in measure 8 of Music Example 4-2: Lucas enters on the minor third and proceeds directly to the major third. This is yet another example of "playing" with the pitch in black-American music.

If you are a guitarist, it will be easy to chord along with the record, reading the chord diagrams in Figure 4-4. The transcription shows where the chords begin. Lucas plays "Poor Boy Blues" in the key of G. With the exception of his G and G^7 chords, he employs standard first-position fingering. He prefers the dominant to the dominant seventh (here D instead of D^7) on guitar but the opposite when he plays piano.* Most of his single-note runs are made in the first position, but sometimes he moves up the guitar neck on the first two strings to play the highest notes. If you learn to pick out the accompaniment from the record by ear, you will be learning blues guitar in one of the traditional, time-honored ways.

Figure 4-4
Guitar chord positions, "Poor Boy Blues."

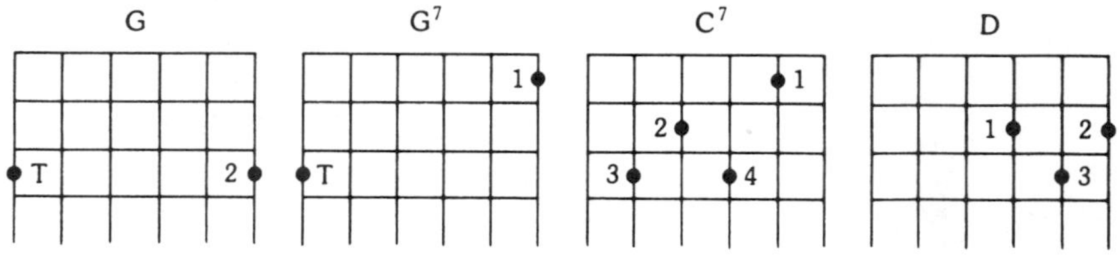

Composing the Blues

Besides learning blues songs from other singers and from records, blues singers make up their own songs. Sometimes they think a song out in advance; sometimes they improvise it during performance. Often a performance is a combination of planning and improvisation. The blues song's first composition unit is the line. If you sing the blues most of your life, blues lines will run through your mind like proverbs, which many indeed are, for instance, "You never miss your water till your well runs dry." A male singer might rhyme it with a line like, "Never miss your woman till she say good-bye." (A female singer's rhyme: "Never miss your good man till he say good-bye.") The singer has just composed the stanza:

You never miss your water till you well runs dry,
No, you never miss your water till your well runs dry,
I never missed my baby till she said good-bye.

*Lucas accompanies himself on piano in another version of "Poor Boy Blues" on *Lazy Bill Lucas,* Philo LP 1007.

It is unusual for a blues singer to "compose" self-consciously. Instead, lines and stanzas seem to "just come," sometimes in a rush but more often one at a time and widely spaced. Blues singer Booker White called the songs he made up "sky songs"; "I have an imaginary mind to do things like that. Didn't have nary a word written down. I just reached up and got 'em" (Evans 1971:253). Another blues singer, Robert Pete Williams, described how his songs came to him: "The atmosphere, the wind blowing carries music along. I don't know if it affects you or not, but it's a sounding that's in the air, you see? And I don't know where it comes from—it could come from the airplanes, or the moaning of automobiles, but anyhow it leaves an air current in the air, you see? That gets in the wind, makes a sounding, you know? And that sounding works up to be a blues" (Wilson 1966:21). Statements like these show the universal aspect of the blues and the singer as an interpreter of the natural world. The sounding airplane, the moaning automobile trace a human pattern in the surrounding atmosphere that "affects" only the gifted interpreter, the translator, the blues singer. When the singer turns it into a song for all to hear, the universal truth is apparent.

If the blues singer plans his stanzas in advance, he memorizes them, sometimes writing them down. As we have seen, the stanzas may or may not speak directly for the personal experience of the singer. St. Louis Jimmy, author of "Poor Boy Blues," said this about another of his songs, "Goin' Down Slow": "My blues came mostly from women. . . . 'Goin' Down Slow' started from a girl, in St. Louis—it wasn't me—I've never been sick a day in my life, but I seen her in the condition she was in—pregnant, tryin' to lose a kid, see. And she looked like she was goin' down slow. And I made that remark to my sister and it came in my mind and I started to writin' it. . . . I looked at other people's troubles and I writes from that, and I writes from my own troubles" (Oliver 1965: 101–2).

Songs that blues singers memorize usually stick to one idea or event. A memorized song, Lucas's "Poor Boy Blues" has four stanzas on the circumstances leading to the poor boy's cry for mercy. But the words in an improvised song seldom show the unity of time, circumstances, or feeling evident in a memorized song. After all, unless you have had lots of practice, it is hard enough to improvise rhymed stanzas, let alone keep to a single subject (compare McLeod and Herndon 1981:59 on improvised Maltese song duels). So an improvising singer usually throws in some memorized, traditional stanzas along with stanzas he or she puts together on the spot.

Social Context and the Meaning of the Blues

The blues song we have taken a close look at, "Poor Boy Blues," is typical and can bring us toward a structural definition of blues as a song form. Textually, blues songs consist of a series of rhymed three-line or quatrain-refrain stanzas, each sung to more or less the same tune. Blues tunes usually consist of twelve-measure (bar) strophes, and they employ a special scale, the blues scale (Music Example 4-3). They are rhythmically complex, employing syncopation and, at times, differing rhythms between singing and instruments. Many other attributes of blues songs—melodic shape, for instance, or the typical raspy timbre—are beyond the scope of this introduction but may be followed up elsewhere (see Titon 1994). But in one respect "Poor Boy Blues" is *not* typical. Most blues lyrics are about lovers, and they fall into a pattern arising from black-American life.

The blues grew and developed when most African-Americans lived as sharecroppers on Southern cotton farms, from late in the nineteenth century until just before World War II, when farm mechanization began to displace the black workers and factory work at high wages in the northern cities attracted them. Down home, young men and women did not marry early; they were needed on the farm. If a young woman became pregnant, she had her baby and brought the child into the household with her parents. She did not lose status in the community, and later she often married the father of her child. When a woman did marry young, her partner often was middle-aged and needed a woman to work and care for his children from a prior marriage. It was good to have plenty of children; when they came of age to work, more hands could go into the cotton and corn fields. Adoption was common; when families broke up, children were farmed out among relatives.

Sociologists and anthropologists, some of them black (such as Charles Johnson), studied this sharecropping culture in the 1920s and 1930s. Interested in patterns of love, marriage, and divorce, the fieldworkers found that partners separated because one could not live with the other's laziness, violence, or adultery. These reasons added up to what they called "mistreatment." A woman was reported as saying her current lover was "nice all right, but I ain't thinking about marrying. Soon as you marry a man he starts mistreating you, and I ain't going to be mistreated no more" (Johnson [1934] 1966:83). Blues songs reflected these attitudes; mistreatment was the most common subject. Once the subject was established, people began to expect mistreatment as the appropriate subject for blues songs, and although many blues were composed about other subjects, the majority have to do with lovers and mistreatment. After World War II the sharecropping culture was less important; the action now took place in the cities where most had gone: Atlanta, New York, Washington, Detroit, Memphis, St. Louis, Chicago, Dallas, Houston, Los Angeles, Oakland. Black family patterns persisted among the lower classes in the urban ghettos, and so did the blues.

Blues lyrics about mistreatment fall into a pattern. The singer casts himself or herself in the role of mistreated victim, introduces an antagonist (usually a mistreating lover), provides incidents that detail the circumstances of the mistreatment, and draws up a bill of indictment. Then, with the listener's tacit approval, the victim becomes the judge, and the drama turns on the verdict: Will he or she accept the mistreatment, try to reform the mistreater, or leave? Resigned acceptance and attempted reform resolve a minority of blues songs. Most often the victim, declaring independence, steps out of the victim's role with an ironic parting shot and leaves. "Dog Me Around," as sung by Howlin' Wolf, is typical in this regard (Figure 4-5).

Figure 4-5
Howlin' Wolf (Chester Burnett).
Ann Arbor Blues Festival, Ann Arbor, Michigan, 1969.

Jeff Todd Titon

Dog Me Around

1. How many more years have I got to let you dog me around?
   How many more years have I got to let you dog me around?
   I'd just as soon rather be dead, sleeping way down in the ground.
2. If I treat you right you wouldn't believe what I've said.
   If I treat you right you wouldn't believe what I've said.
   You think I'm halfway crazy; you think I ought to let you have your way.
3. I'm going upstairs, I'm going to bring back down my clothes.
   I'm going upstairs, I'm going to bring back down my clothes.
   If anybody asks about me, just tell 'em I walked outdoors.

In stanza 1 the singer complains of mistreatment, saying his lover treats him like a dog. "Dog me around" is black-American slang for "treat me like a dog." We learn in stanza 2 that the singer may also be guilty; "If I treat you right" implies mistreatment on both sides of the relationship. (Stanza 2 could be interpreted as dialogue spoken by the singer's mistreating lover; but without an obvious clue like "She said," point of view seldom shifts in blues lyrics.) The singer resolves the drama in stanza 3 when he declares that he will leave his lover. "Just tell 'em I walked outdoors" is an understatement that shows how little the affair means to him.

Blues music in African-American culture helps lovers understand each other and, since the themes are traditional and community-shared, blues songs give listeners community approval for separation in response to mistreatment. The listener who recognizes his or her situation in the lyrics of a blues song is given a nice definition of that situation and shown just what might be done in response. At a Saturday night party, or at home alone, a mistreated lover finds consolation in the blues (Figure 4-6).

The Blues Yesterday

In this chapter we have approached blues as an African-American music. That is historically true: African-Americans invented blues music. But many non-African-American readers of this book already know something about blues because blues today extends well beyond the boundaries of the African-American music-culture. Today more people recognize the name of the British blues singer-guitarist Eric Clapton than they do Muddy Waters and Howlin' Wolf. About thirty-five years ago blues entered mainstream

Figure 4-6
Dancing at a juke joint. Alabama, 1957.

Courtesy of Frederic Ramsey, Jr.

U.S. culture, and in our mass-mediated global village today blues is an attractive commodity. You can hear blues played in Prague, Dar es Salaam, and Tokyo by citizens of Czechoslovakia, Tanzania, and Japan. Today blues is regarded as a universal phenomenon, accessible to all. Yet it is well to remember its history within the African-American communities that nurtured it. The folklorist Alan Lomax believes that blacks were the first Americans to feel the alienation characteristic of the twentieth century, and that blues is the quintessential expression of that alienation.

It is true that African-Americans invented blues, and it is also true that early on people outside the black communities were attracted to it. The white folklorist Howard Odum, for example, collected blues songs in the South prior to 1910. The African-American composer W. C. Handy popularized blues in the 1910s with songs such as "St. Louis Blues," but white singers such as Sophie Tucker recorded blues songs before African-American singers were permitted to do so. African-American blues queens like Bessie Smith made blues the most popular African-American music in the 1920s, and it attracted a small white audience as well as a large black one. The 1920s was also the decade in which downhome blues was first recorded: Blind Blake, the greatest ragtime guitarist; Charley Patton, a songster regarded as the father of Mississippi Delta blues; and a host of others who brought the music out of the local juke joints and house parties and onto recordings that were circulated back into the black communities. Jimmie Rodgers, the first star of country music, whose brief career lasted from 1927 through 1933, sang many blues songs, particularly his "blue yodels." Rodgers, a white Mississippian, learned many of his songs and much of his relaxed singing style from black railroad men. Blues has been an important component within country music ever since. African-American rhythms, jazz instrumental breaks, and the blues scale were critical in the formation of bluegrass, which ironically is usually regarded as one of the purest British-American musical traditions (see Cantwell 1984). The banjo—the quintessential bluegrass instrument—is an African-American invention.

Blues was always a popular form within jazz and remains so today, often regarded there as a "roots" music. Bridging the line between blues and jazz in the 1930s and 1940s were the blues "shouters" such as Jimmy Rushing with Count Basie's orchestra. African-American rhythm and blues of the 1940s followed in the tradition of such blues shouters as Wynonie Harris, Tiny Bradshaw, and Joe Turner, along with crooners such as Charles Brown. In the meantime an urban blues sound arose featuring singers with small bands led by an electric guitar. Aaron "T-Bone" Walker invented urban blues in the 1940s, Riley "B. B." (Blues Boy) King made it immensely popular in the 1950s, and a host of imitators, black and later white, followed. Rock and roll in the 1950s began as a white cover of black rhythm and blues, but by the early 1960s black Americans were able to compete well in that arena, and singers such as Ray Charles and Motown groups like Diana Ross and the Supremes were immensely popular among all young people. Ray Charles's biggest hit, "What'd I Say," was a blues song; blues such as "Maybelline" were among Chuck Berry's best-selling recordings; and it even became possible for downhome singers such as Jimmy Reed, whose "Big Boss Man" climbed high on the pop charts, to cross over.

Blues was crucial in the British rock of the 1960s. Groups such as the Rolling Stones (whose name came from one of Muddy Waters' songs, and whose early albums featured covers of Chicago blues) were part of the British blues revival. Dozens of British blues bands could be found in such cities as London and Liverpool, and talented instrumentalists such as John Mayall and Eric Clapton arose from this ferment in the 1960s. An American blues revival in the same decade gave white musicians Paul Butterfield and Charlie Musselwhite a start, and a new phenomenon appeared: bands whose personnel included a mixture of black and white musicians. Muddy Waters, for example, featured the white harmonica player Paul Oscher and in the 1970s had a white guitarist, Bob Margolin, in his band. Lazy Bill Lucas also led an integrated band.

By the early 1960s blues had become old-fashioned within African-American communities. Outside of strongholds in the Mississippi Delta and Chicago, blues was a marginal music, accounting for a small proportion of jukebox records and receiving little radio airplay. Black intellectuals dismissed blues as a music of resignation, unfit for the contemporary climate of civil rights and black power. Soul music was much more attractive. Yet during this same decade many blues singers revived their careers, finding a new audience. The blues revival of the 1960s brought commercially recorded blues music and black musicians before a largely white public in North America and Europe. Magic Sam, B. B. King, Muddy Waters, and Howlin' Wolf represented the modern electric blues sound, while singers who had made recordings before World War II performed acoustically on the folk music circuit, sounding much as they had decades ago: Roosevelt Sykes, Mississippi John Hurt, Son House, Skip James, John Lee Hooker, Lightnin' Hopkins, Big Joe Williams, and Booker White, to name a few. Buddy Guy, Koko Taylor, and John Lee Hooker, immensely popular today, were active but overshadowed in the 1960s revival.

Blues is a music steeped in tradition. It can alter its appearance to suit changing conditions of the blues music-culture. But despite varied techniques and instrumentation, modern blues has not changed: The blues scale, the twelve-measure form with its characteristic tonic–subdominant–dominant seventh harmonic support, the three-line or quatrain-refrain stanza, and the rhythm crossing between vocal and accompaniment remain. Recorded sound quality aside, some blues recordings made twenty or more years ago sound as if they might have been made today. To hear an example of such a recording, listen to "Sweet Home Chicago" by the Fieldstones, a Memphis-based blues band (CD Selection 12; Figure 4-7).

CD 1
Track 12

Figure 4-7
The Fieldstones.

Sweet Home Chicago

1. Come on, baby don't you want to go;
   Oh come on, baby don't you want to go;
   Back to the same old place, sweet home Chicago.
2. Come on, baby don't you want to go;
   Oh come on, baby don't you want to go;
   Back to the same old place, sweet home Chicago.
3. One and one is two
   Two and two is four,
   Way you love me little girl, you'll
   Never know, crying "Hey,
   Baby don't you want to go
   Back to the same old place, sweet home Chicago.
   [Spoken:] All right, let's go to the windy city, you all.
4. Come on, baby don't you want to go;
   Oh come on, baby don't you want to go;
   Back to the same old place, sweet home Chicago.
5. Two and two is four,
   Four and two is six,
   Way you left me little girl you left me in a
   Heck of a fix, crying "Hey
   Baby don't you want to go
   Back to the same old place, sweet home Chicago.
   Back to the same old place, sweet home Chicago.
   Back to the same old place, sweet home Chicago."

The Fieldstones are Wordie Perkins and Willie Roy Sanders, electric guitars; Lois Brown, electric bass; Bobby Carnes, electric organ; and Joe Hicks, vocal and drums. David Evans, who produced their album (*The Fieldstones: Memphis Blues Today,* High Water LP 1001) and wrote the jacket notes, describes their music as sounding "as low down and funky as the most primitive cotton patch blues and at the same time as polished and contemporary as the latest hit on the radio." Much of this polish results from the band's aesthetic preference for a clean, crisp sound: They keep the drumheads very tight and the electric guitars amplified with only a minimum of distortion. And at the same time, the band is based in tradition. Their repertoire includes blues songs such as "Saddle Up My Pony" and "Dirt Road" that are more than sixty years old, and the guitarists play with their fingers instead of a pick, favoring the key of E like so many traditional Mississippi Delta blues guitarists.

"Sweet Home Chicago" is a blues classic. First recorded by the legendary Delta bluesman Robert Johnson in 1936, it is a staple in the blues repertory and it has been recorded by several prominent rock bands. Although Robert Johnson composed the song, he drew on versions current in oral tradition at the time of his recording; paramount among them was James "Kokomo" Arnold's. Chief among Johnson's numerous original contributions to the piece is its most distinctive feature: the "walking bass line."

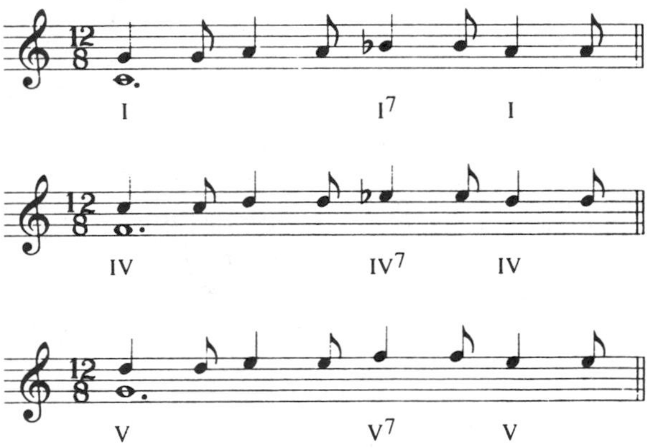

Music Example 4-4
Outline of "walking bass" on guitar, after Robert Johnson. (In key of C for convenience; Johnson usually played it in E.)

To be sure, "walking the basses" was a definitive characteristic of the boogie-woogie, barrelhouse piano style favored by blues pianists in the 1920s and 1930s. But Johnson took the idea of walking bass and adapted a new version of it on the guitar, emphasizing the seventh chord (Music Example 4-4). This small but significant innovation was copied by a host of guitarists and, later, bass players. In the 1950s it became a familiar sound in rhythm and blues and rock and roll. Johnson is also interesting to the blues historian because of his rhythmic innovations and the magnificent poetry of his lyrics. (All but a recently discovered alternate take-one of his original recordings may be heard on the Columbia CD C2K 46222, *Robert Johnson: The Complete Recordings.*)

This walking bass figures prominently in the instrumental introduction to the Fieldstones' version of "Sweet Home Chicago," where it may be heard in the electric bass and second guitar. The bass, guitars, and drums establish a strong triplet rhythm (see the discussion of "Poor Boy Blues" and Music Example 4–1). And, like Lazy Bill Lucas in "Poor Boy Blues," Joe Hicks sings in a duple meter, playfully lagging behind the beat, setting up some intriguing two-against-three polyrhythms in contrast to the instrumental accompaniment. It is almost as if he floats the lyrics atop the pulsating music. To really feel the syncopation, try singing along.

Blues has its share of heroes and heroines who died too young. John Lee (Sonny Boy) Williamson, stabbed to death in Chicago in 1947, was an outstanding singer and blues harmonica player. Robert Johnson, poisoned in his twenties by his girlfriend's jealous husband, would have changed the course of blues history had he lived. As it was, although he had only two recording sessions, his impact on post–World War II Chicago blues was immense.

We turn now to the music of another Mississippi-born, blues singer-guitarist who died before his time: Magic Sam (Sam Maghett, 1937–1969). His first instrument was the diddly-bow. As a young teenager he moved to Chicago with his family. His club and record career began in the 1950s when he was still a teenager. After a stint in the armed services, he returned to the clubs on the west side of Chicago, where his generation of musicians was moving Chicago blues in the direction of soul: the music of James Brown, Otis Redding, Aretha Franklin—the most popular African-American music of the 1960s. Magic Sam recorded three albums for Delmark in Chicago, where he had made a reputation for his soaring vocals and flashy guitar playing. But those who had heard him in the clubs said these studio albums failed to capture the brilliance of his live performances.

Luck changed for Magic Sam abruptly at the 1969 Ann Arbor (Michigan) Blues Festival. B. B. King, Howlin' Wolf, Muddy Waters, Albert King, John Lee Hooker, Freddy King, James Cotton, Big Mama Thornton, Otis Rush, T-Bone Walker, Lightnin' Hopkins—virtually all the major contemporary blues artists performed at this three-day affair. Roosevelt Sykes, Big Joe Williams, Sleepy John Estes, and Son House represented an older generation whose careers had begun before World War II. Luther Allison, Jimmy Dawkins, and Magic Sam were among those representing the future. It was a huge cutting contest, as each artist tried to outdo the others. When the dust settled, in the blues writer John Fishel's words, "if one set [stood] out as surpassing all others in excitement and virtuosity, it [was] Magic Sam's" (1981).

CD 1
Track 13

It was Sunday afternoon, August 3, the last day of the festival, about 3 o'clock—not prime time. Casual in the extreme, Sam arrived a half hour late. He had to borrow a drummer from another band. Somehow in the performance they came together at the highest heat. It was all the more remarkable because of the sparse instrumentation: guitar, bass, and drums. Yet Magic Sam was no ordinary guitarist. On CD Selection 13, "You Don't

Love Me," recorded at the festival from the audience, Sam played his guitar as both a lead and a rhythm instrument, catching a riff that both hearkened back to the deepest blues of the Mississippi Delta and pointed forward to the grooves of the future. Above it all Sam's voice carried effortlessly to the ten thousand in the audience who picked up the groove and as if lifted to their feet by some unseen force danced for the remaining twenty minutes of his set.

Writing about Magic Sam's genius, Dick Shurman viewed him as a postmodern master: "His music had roots in the boogie he loved and in the tension and challenge created by the distraction of a noisy, bustling bar. He was able, *par excellence,* to turn the response of the audience into a foil and a force in the music. Partly because of his reliance on whatever equipment was available (like amps without reverb units and borrowed guitars) and partly because of the loose circumstances and the long nights (usually playing until 4 A.M.), Magic Sam was a world apart from the studio's time limits, structures, and formulas" (1981). Sam's career took off immediately after Ann Arbor. In the next month he toured the European blues clubs, a sure sign that he had arrived. But on December 1, 1969, he died of a heart attack. He was 32 years old.

The Blues Today

Today a blues singer with a large following is Robert Cray. Born in Columbus, Georgia, in 1953, Cray grew up listening to soul music—the Stax/Volt sound of the 1960s, as well as to Ray Charles, Sam Cooke, and, perhaps the most important influence on his singing, Bobby Bland. In 1969 he heard the blues guitarist Albert Collins and modeled his guitar playing after him. Forming a band in 1974, he recorded his first album in 1978, *Who's Been Talkin',* released in 1980. Several albums followed in which Cray fused a new sound, a mixture of blues, funk, and soul that was very much his own. Most of his songs do not follow the twelve-bar blues form, but a few do, and we consider one of them now, "The Score," from *Who's Been Talkin'.*

Cray begins "The Score" by playing his electric guitar, then he sings a verse, responding on guitar in the silences after he sings each line (Music Example 4-5). The rest of the band (piano, electric bass, drums) joins Cray in the second verse. A walking bass line is present like that in "Sweet Home Chicago" (CD Selection 12). Cray's guitar breaks after the verse become more adventurous. The lyrics draw up a familiar blues indictment: The singer's lover is cheating on him, and he says she must leave for good. The first verse is in AB form, the second is quatrain-refrain, and the third doubles the quatrain before the refrain. Even here, in a song that follows standard blues patterns rather closely, Cray chooses to extend the boundaries of the blues verse form.

For our last example of modern blues we turn to a contemporary masterpiece by an older singer, Otis Rush. "Ain't Enough Comin' In"

Music Example 4-5
"The Score." Written by D. Amy. Transcription by Jeff Todd Titon.

You come home look-kin' fun-ky, your clothes all in a mess, and your
stor - y was-n't fit-tin' an-y bet-ter than your dress._ Well all right ba - by _
now I know_ the score. _ Well you bet - ter get to get-tin';
I don't want to see you 'round here an-y - more. _

CD 1
Track 14

(CD Selection 14) was voted the outstanding blues recording of the year 1994 by the readers of *Living Blues* magazine. The song starts with an authoritative drumbeat, and immediately the electric bass sets a heavy rhythmic riff that repeats till the end of the song, changing pitch when the chords change. In its rhythmic constancy the bass provides something like the bell pattern in *Agbekor* (see Chapter 3) that anchors the entire performance. The drummer plays simply but forcefully and unerringly, marking the beat 1–2–3–4, with the accent on 3. A rock drummer would be busier than this and a lot less relentless. The electric bass is louder than the drums, characteristic of black popular music since the 1970s.

Listeners who can recognize the difference between major and minor chords will realize that this is a minor blues, built on the minor i–iv–v chords instead of the major ones. The first chorus is instrumental. Rush plays electric guitar lead above a riffing rhythm section that includes a trumpet and saxophone as well as an organ. The direct, spare playing here sets a somber mood for his powerful vocals that follow. The song features a bridge section ("Now when it's all over . . .") that departs from the usual twelve-bar blues pattern, but you will recognize that otherwise (except for the minor key) the song has a typical blues structure. After the vocals Rush takes the tune twice through with a guitar solo, and this is followed by two choruses in which a saxophone leads, taking some of Rush's ideas and developing them. The bridge returns, followed by two more verses, and Rush takes it out with one more instrumental chorus. Hear how the the guitar sound vibrates at the beginning of the last chorus. This is a tremolo, and Rush is known for getting this effect by pushing his fingers from side to side on the strings (a hand tremolo) rather than using the tremolo bar attached to the electric guitar.

Rush's vocal style is striking. Like many blues singers he hoarsens his voice at times to show great emotion, but he also makes his voice tremble at times, an effect that mirrors his guitar tremolo (and vice versa). Blues writers have called Rush's voice "tortured" with a "frightening intensity" and a "harrowing poetic terror" (Rowe 1979:176) and "tense and oppressive" (Herzhaft 1992:300). There is no denying that Rush has a full, powerful voice. Its vehemence and falling melodic curve may remind you of the Navajo Yeibichai singers (Chapter 2). The lyrics are clever and subtle. Rush wrote them. In the beginning of his career he relied on the professional songwriter Willie Dixon, but after his first hit songs he decided that he could "write one better than that" (Forte 1991:159). When I hear the first line, I think "ain't enough comin' in" refers to money, but in the second line Rush lets me know that I should think of the parallel between love and money: The singer feels that he is giving too much and not getting enough of either in return.

Ain't Enough Comin' In

Oh, I ain't got enough comin' in to take care of what's got to go out.
It ain't enough love or money comin' in, baby, to take care of what's got to go out.
Like a bird I got my wing clipped, my friends; I've got to start all over again.

If the sun ever shine on me again,
Oh lord if the sun ever shine on me again.
Like a bird I got my wing clipped, my friends; I've got to start all over again.

Now when it's all over and said and done, money talks and the fool gets none;
The tough get tough and the tough get goin'; come on baby let me hold you in my arms.

It ain't got enough comin' in to take care of what's got to go out.
Ain't enough love or money comin' in, baby, to take care of what's got to go out.
My friends, I got my wings clipped; I've got to start all over again.

When it's all over and said and done, money talks and the fool gets none;
The tough get tough and the tough get goin'; come on baby let me hold you in my arms.

Ain't got enough comin' in to take care of what's got to go out.
It ain't enough love or money comin' in, baby, to take care of what's got to go out.
Like a bird I got my wings clipped, my friends; I've got to start all over again.

If you don't put nothing' in you can't get nothin' out;
You don't put nothin' in, baby, you can't get nothin' out;
Like a bird I got my wings clipped, my friends; I've got to start all over again.

Who is Otis Rush? Is he the latest singer-guitarist to capitalize on the blues revival of the 1990s? Not at all. Otis Rush has been a blues legend since the 1950s, well known to musicians and serious blues aficionados if not to the general listening public. Stevie Ray Vaughn named his band Double Trouble in honor of Rush's finest song from that decade. Led Zeppelin covered Rush's "I Can't Quit You Baby," with guitarist Jimmy Page lifting Rush's instrumental break note-for-note (Forte 1991:156). Rush's guitar playing turned Eric Clapton into a disciple. When Rush met Clapton in England in 1986 he called Clapton a "great guitar player" and modestly went on, "Everybody plays like somebody. It's good to know that somebody's listening. To me, I'm just a guitar player. I'm not trying to influence nobody, I'm just trying to play, and play well. And hopefully I can sell some records" (Forte 1991: 161).

Figure 4-8
Otis Rush performing at the 1969 Ann Arbor Blues Festival. Note that he plays left-handed.

Jeff Todd Titon

Otis Rush was born in Philadelphia, Mississippi, in 1934 and began playing at age ten. Left-handed, he plays the guitar upside-down, which accounts for some of his uniqueness (see Figure 4-8). Like Bill Lucas, he first sang country music, not blues. It was not until he came to Chicago in the late 1940s and began visiting the blues clubs that he decided to sing and play the blues. Among the musicians who influenced him most strongly were B. B. King, T-Bone Walker, and Magic Sam; but Rush has his own version of modern blues guitar. His style is subtle, spare, cool, the instrumental equivalent of caressing a lover. There is nothing egotistical about it, no showing off. His use of silence is brilliant. Like a fine aged wine at its peak, at its best his music has great presence, neither understated nor flashy: substantial, direct, powerful, and commanding respect.

Rush takes risks on stage and in recordings. Often he would rather try something new than stick with the same old thing, and as a result his performances are uneven. "I know I'm gonna mess up in places, but sometimes I get away with it," he said.

> To me, I'm trying to learn how to play. I'm not ashamed to let people know I'm trying to learn. I'm scuffling, trying to find something new, trying to make it off the ground. I'll be reaching for sounds—right on-stage. I know I'm going to get caught; that's why you hear a lot of bad notes. I can't just play straight. If I hear something, I go after it. Sometimes it works out; then again, you get some bad collisions, so I try to cover it up. Just like a boxer: you get hit, you got to try to recuperate. (Forte 1991:159)

Blues audiences came to feel that Rush never quite reached his potential. Indeed, there are a couple of places in "Ain't Enough Comin' In" where, if you listen closely, you will hear a "bad collision." But in my view the risks are very much worth it, and the album from which this song is taken represents a long overdue turning point in Rush's career. We can hope that in his sixties he can sustain it.

The Blues Music-Culture in the Contemporary World

In this book we have taken an approach in which we seek out music-cultures that correspond more or less to social groups and geographic regions: peoples who form a community and make music together. But this is not the only kind of music-culture. Mass-mediated popular music, presented outside community settings in concerts, recordings, radio, and television, forms communities of listeners and would-be performers that may otherwise have little in common with each other. Until the 1960s the blues music-culture was based in African-American communities; today it embraces people from all over the world. Blues is but one of many local and regional musics that have become immensely popular outside their area of origin; reggae is an obvious example of another. Today world music is presented from the concert stage in many cities in North America and Europe. (What kind of music-culture do the connoisseurs of world music represent?)

We return to the blues to seek answers. Robert Cray has told interviewers that he grew up in an integrated suburb and never experienced the hard times that his predecessors did. He never chopped cotton or plowed and smelled the back end of a mule all day long. He learned to play blues mainly by listening to recordings, not by imitating elder musicians in a local community. Yet there is no doubt that he is a fine blues singer and guitarist, although most of his songs do not follow standard blues forms. He thinks of himself as a blues singer, and he has been promoted as one. Is he? (And who is granted authority to say?) Once a musical genre has been popularized by the mass media, written about, studied, and defined, some of that interpretive activity is carried back to performers, and then people expect the music to conform to those definitions. Record producers, promoters, writers, and lately scholars, few of them raised in African-American communities, are partly responsible for codifying the rules of the genre. How, once standardized, can blues music change and grow but still remain blues? Must singers stay with the old forms, changing only their contents—new wine in old bottles, new lyrics, new instrumentation, in old settings? Must festival promoters choose blues singers on the basis of how well they conform to the genre? Should a folklore police enforce the rules?

In the 1960s, blues, a music that had lost its great popularity among black Americans, captured the hearts of a new audience, young white Americans and Europeans, particularly those who saw in the blues a revolt against stifling middle-class values. In the 1970s the blues revival ebbed as many grew tired of the same old sound. Now, at the beginning of the twenty-first century, we are in the midst of a new blues revival as a new generation of African Americans honors blues as roots music and others discover the music for the first time.

In the house parties and juke joints of the rural South, especially in Texas, Arkansas, and Mississippi, solo singer-guitarists, sometimes with a friend sitting in on guitar or harmonica, continue to sing and play the blues for friends and neighbors. Outside this professional and semiprofessional blues music-culture are countless black blues singers and musicians who no longer perform regularly but who, without a great deal of persuasion,

Figure 4-9
Cicero Blake, vocalist, performing with Mighty Joe Young's Blues Band at Eddie Shaw's Club, Chicago, Illinois, 1977.

Jeff Todd Titon

sing on occasion for family and friends. Today's most active blues music-culture is located in Chicago, a city with a history of great hospitality to the blues (see Figure 4-9). Dozens of blues clubs may also be found in such cities as Houston; St. Louis; Memphis; Clarksdale and other towns in the Mississippi Delta; Oakland–San Francisco; and Detroit. Well-known blues singers such as B. B. King and Buddy Guy tour nationally and, sponsored by the U.S. Department of State, as goodwill ambassadors abroad.

A Few Final Words

Not long ago I was in a club in Chicago and heard a woman blues singer with a powerful voice, backed by a four-piece band. It turned out she had studied voice in preparation for the opera then decided she would have a better career singing blues. Do these historical, economic, and audience changes mean we should abandon our music-culture model (Chapter 1) in the face of real-world complications? No, but we need to keep in mind that it *is* a model, an ideal. Responding to economic, artistic, and interpretive pressures from without as well as within, music-cultures are not isolated entities. Their histories reveal that response to these pressures and that "catching" or defining a music at any one given time comes at the expense of the long view.

References

Brooks, Cleanth, R. W. B. Lewis, and Robert Penn Warren. 1973. *American Literature: The Makers and the Making.* 2 vols. New York: St. Martin's Press.

Brunoghe, Yannick, ed. 1964. *Big Bill Blues.* New York: Oak.

Cantwell, Robert. 1984. *Bluegrass Breakdown.* Urbana: Univ. of Illinois Press.

Charters, Samuel. 1977. *The Legacy of the Blues.* New York: De Capo Press.

Courlander, Harold. 1963. *Negro Folk Music U.S.A.* New York: Columbia Univ. Press.

Cray, Robert. 1980. *Who's Been Talkin'.* Charly CRB 1140.

Eliot, T. S. [1920] 1964. "Hamlet and His Problems." In *The Sacred Wood.* Reprint, New York: Barnes & Noble.

Evans, David. 1971. "Booker White." In *Nothing But the Blues,* edited by Mike Leadbitter. London: Hanover Books.

The Fieldstones. 1983. *The Fieldstones: Memphis Blues Today.* High Water LP 1001.

Fishel, John. 1981. "Magic Sam and the Ann Arbor Blues Festival." Liner notes to Delmark DL-645/646, *Magic Sam Live.*

Forte, Dan. 1991. "Otis Rush." In *Blues Guitar,* ed. Jas Obrecht, 156–62. San Francisco: GPI Books.

Groom, Bob. 1971. *The Blues Revival.* London: Studio Vista.

Herzhaft, Gerard. 1992. *Encyclopedia of the Blues.* Fayetteville: Univ. of Arkansas Press.

Johnson, Charles S. [1934] 1966. *Shadow of the Plantation.* Reprint, Chicago: Univ. of Chicago Press.

Johnson, Robert. 1990. *Robert Johnson: The Complete Recordings.* Columbia CD C2K 46222.

Lucas, William ("Lazy Bill"). 1974. *Lazy Bill Lucas.* Philo LP 1007 (North Ferrisburg, Vt.).

McLeod, Norma, and Marcia Herndon. 1981. *Music as Culture,* 2nd ed. Darby, Pa.: Norwood Editions.

Oliver, Paul. 1965. *Conversation with the Blues.* London: Cassell.

Rowe, Mike. 1979. *Chicago Breakdown.* New York: Da Capo.

Seeger, Charles. 1977. *Studies in Musicology, 1935–1975.* Berkeley: Univ. of California Press.

Shurman, Dick. 1981. "Magic Sam: An Overview." Liner notes to Delmark DL-645/646, *Magic Sam Live.*

Tedlock, Dennis. 1977. "Toward an Oral Poetics." *New Literary History* 8.

Titon, Jeff Todd. 1969. "Calling All Cows." *Blues Unlimited,* nos. 60–63.

———. 1971. "Ethnomusicology of Downhome Blues Phonograph Records, 1926–1930." Ph.D. diss., Univ. of Minnesota.

———, ed. 1974. *From Blues to Pop: The Autobiography of Leonard "Baby Doo" Caston.* Los Angeles: John Edwards Memorial Foundation.

———. 1977. *Early Downhome Blues: A Musical and Cultural Analysis.* Urbana: Univ. of Illinois Press.

———. 1978. "Every Day I Have the Blues: Improvisation and Daily Life." *Southern Folklore Quarterly* 42.

———. 1994. *Early Downhome Blues: A Musical and Cultural Analysis.* Rev. 2nd ed. Chapel Hill: Univ. of North Carolina Press.

Wilson, Al. 1966. "Robert Pete Williams: His Life and Music." *Little Sandy Review* 2 (no. 1).

Additional Reading

Albertson, Chris. 1972. *Bessie.* New York: Stein and Day. [Biography of Bessie Smith.]

Evans, David. 1982. *Big Road Blues.* Berkeley: Univ. of California Press.

Ferris, William. 1978. *Blues from the Delta.* New York: Doubleday.

Finn, Julio. 1992. *The Bluesman.* New York: Interlink.

Floyd, Samuel A., Jr. 1995. *The Power of Black Music.* New York: Oxford Univ. Press.

Franz, Steve. 1996. "The Life and Music of Magic Sam." *Living Blues,* no. 125: 33–44.

George, Nelson. 1988. *The Death of Rhythm and Blues.* New York: Dutton.

Jones, LeRoi. 1963. *Blues People.* New York: Morrow.

Keil, Charles. 1966. *Urban Blues.* Chicago: Univ. of Chicago Press.

King, B. B., with Dave Ritz. 1996. *Blues All Around Me: The Autobiography of B. B. King.* New York: Avon.

Leib, Sandra. 1981. *Mother of the Blues.* Amherst: Univ. of Massachusetts Press. [About Ma Rainey.]

Oliver, Paul. [1972] 1974. *The Story of the Blues.* Reprint, Radnor, Pa.: Chilton Books.

Palmer, Robert. 1981. *Deep Blues.* New York: Viking Press.

Titon, Jeff Todd. 1990. *Downhome Blues Lyrics,* 2nd ed. Urbana: Univ. of Illinois Press. [Anthology of post-WWII lyrics.]

Tooze, Sandra B. 1997. *Muddy Waters: The Mojo Man.* Toronto: ECW Press.

Additional Listening

B. B. King Live at the Regal. ABCS509.

Bessie Smith: The World's Greatest Blues Singer. Columbia GP33.

Blues in the Mississippi Night. Rykodisc RCD 90155.

The Essential Gospel Sampler. Columbia CK 51763.

Let's Get Loose: Folk and Popular Blues Styles. New World NW 290.

Negro Blues and Hollers. Library of Congress AFS L59.

Negro Church Music. Atlantic SD-1351.

Negro Prison Songs. Tradition 1920.

Negro Religious Songs and Services. Library of Congress AFS L10.

One-String Blues. Takoma B 1023. [Diddly-bow]

Religious Music: Congregational and Ceremonial. Library of Congress LBC 1.

Robert Johnson: The Complete Recordings. Columbia C2K 46222.

Roots 'n' Blues: The Retrospective. Columbia C4K 47911.

Roots of the Blues. New World NW 252.

Additional Viewing

The Blues Accordin' to Lightnin' Hopkins. 1979. VHS videotape, 31 min. Color. Directed by Les Blank. El Cerrito, CA: Flower Films.

Bukka White and Son House. 1991. VHS videotape, 60 min. Black and white. Yazoo Video. [Riveting performances of Mississippi Delta blues]

Otis Rush: Mastering Chicago Blues Guitar. 1993. VHS videotape, 90 min. Color. Poundridge, N.Y.: Hot Licks Productions, h.d. ca. [Instruction]

Wild Women Don't Have the Blues. 1989. VHS videotape, 58 min. Color. Dir. Christine Dall. San Francisco: California Newsreel. [A documentary on women blues singers]

CHAPTER

5

Europe/Bosnia

Mark Slobin

This chapter will concentrate on how change has come to local musics, using as a case study a corner of Southeast Europe—Bosnia. We start with the period just after World War II—around 1950—a time when great change came to the region. Communist rule began, lasting through about 1990, replacing a group of slowly industrializing, still heavily rural, capitalist societies with ambitious, managerial, totalitarian governments. Yet old ways continued into new times, as we hear in a song recorded in the early 1950s about the rain, a universal theme for song making. "Paparuda" (CD Selection 15) is sung here by Gypsy children in the countryside of Romania, not far from Bosnia. As American students listen to "Paparuda" and look at the words, they might remember the traditional American song "Rain, Rain, Go Away"; songs about nature can be found around the world.

CD 1
Track 15

Romanian Drought Song, "Paparuda"

Paparuda, ruda (come, little rain, come!), come out and water us with your full buckets over the whole crowd. When you come with the hose, let it flow like water; when you come with the plow, let it run like butter; when you come with the sieve, let it be a barnful. Give me the keys, old woman, that I may open the doors and let the rain come down. Come, little rain, come!

American Children's Song, "Rain, Rain, Go Away"

Rain, rain, go away, little (name of singer) wants to play.
Rain, rain, go away! Come again another day.

The two rain songs share similarities: the type of singer (children) and the subject (a force of nature), but many sharp differences place them in contrast. The American song is a straightforward command chanted by a child who cannot go out and play. The words mean just what they say, and no special costume or equipment is necessary to perform the song. In addition, the text is sung solo and even includes the child's name. Though

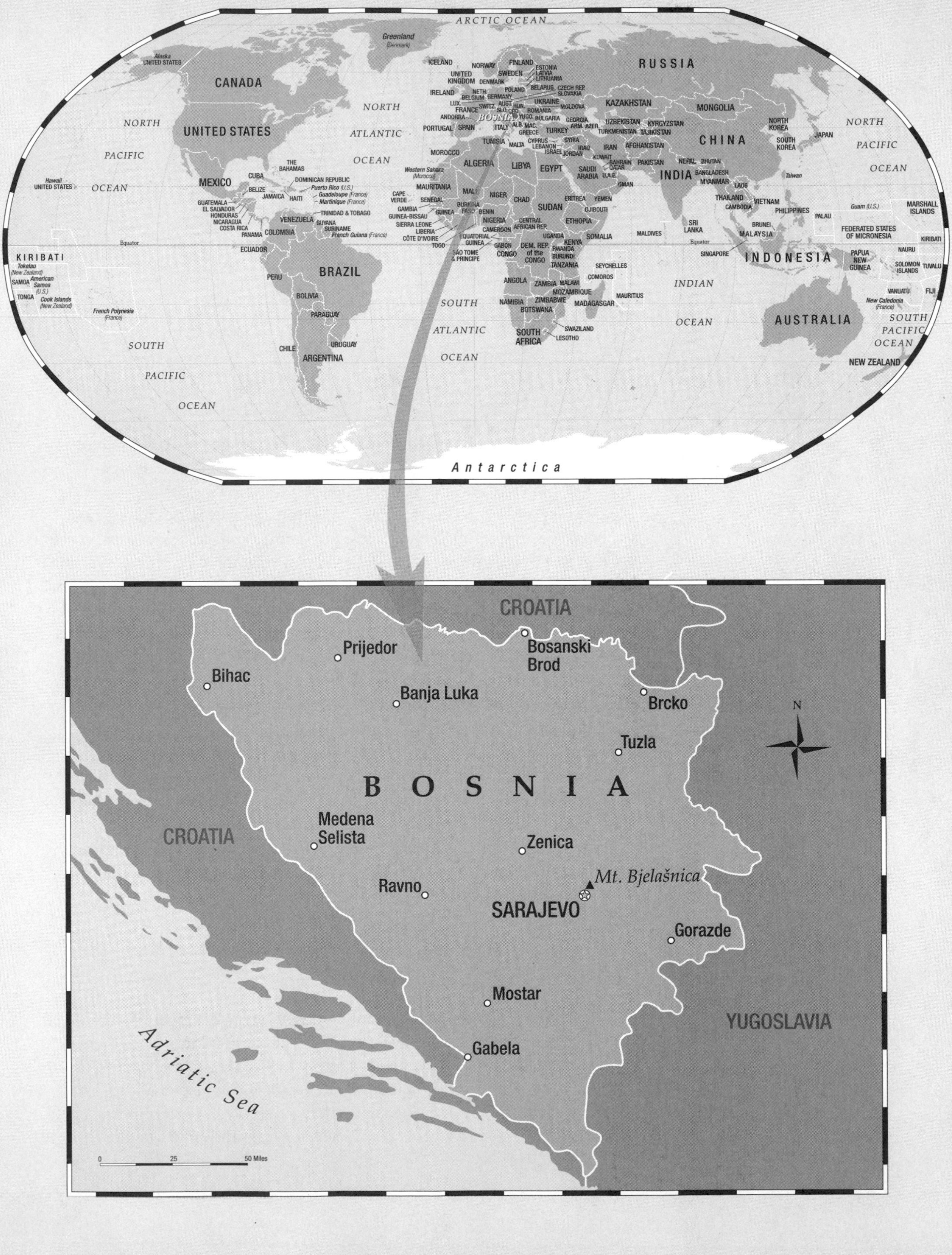

ARCTIC OCEAN
Greenland
(Denmark)
Alaska
UNITED STATES
CANADA
ICELAND
NORWAY
FINLAND
SWEDEN
ESTONIA
LATVIA
LITHUANIA
UNITED KINGDOM
DENMARK
IRELAND
NETH.
BELGIUM
GERMANY
POLAND
BELARUS
CZECH REP.
SLOVAKIA
LUX.
FRANCE
SWITZ.
AUST.
HUN.
UKRAINE
MOLDOVA
ROMANIA
ANDORRA
BOSNIA
YUGO.
BULGARIA
PORTUGAL
SPAIN
ITALY
ALB.
MAC.
GREECE
TURKEY
GEORGIA
ARM.
AZER.
RUSSIA
KAZAKHSTAN
MONGOLIA
UZBEKISTAN
KYRGYZSTAN
TURKMENISTAN
TAJIKISTAN
CHINA
NORTH KOREA
SOUTH KOREA
JAPAN
NORTH
PACIFIC
OCEAN
NORTH
ATLANTIC
OCEAN
UNITED STATES
MEXICO
CUBA
THE BAHAMAS
DOMINICAN REPUBLIC
Puerto Rico (U.S.)
Guadeloupe (France)
Martinique (France)
Hawaii
UNITED STATES
BELIZE
JAMAICA
HAITI
GUATEMALA
EL SALVADOR
HONDURAS
NICARAGUA
COSTA RICA
PANAMA
TRINIDAD & TOBAGO
VENEZUELA
GUYANA
SURINAME
French Guiana (France)
COLOMBIA
ECUADOR
PERU
BRAZIL
BOLIVIA
PARAGUAY
CHILE
ARGENTINA
URUGUAY
MOROCCO
ALGERIA
LIBYA
EGYPT
TUNISIA
MALTA
CYPRUS
LEBANON
ISRAEL
SYRIA
JORDAN
IRAQ
IRAN
KUWAIT
BAHRAIN
QATAR
U.A.E.
SAUDI ARABIA
OMAN
YEMEN
AFGHANISTAN
PAKISTAN
NEPAL
BHUTAN
BANGLADESH
INDIA
MYANMAR
LAOS
THAILAND
CAMBODIA
VIETNAM
PHILIPPINES
Taiwan
Western Sahara (Morocco)
MAURITANIA
MALI
NIGER
CHAD
SUDAN
ERITREA
DJIBOUTI
ETHIOPIA
SOMALIA
CAPE VERDE
SENEGAL
GAMBIA
GUINEA-BISSAU
GUINEA
SIERRA LEONE
LIBERIA
CÔTE D'IVOIRE
TOGO
BURKINA FASO
BENIN
NIGERIA
CAMEROON
CENTRAL AFRICAN REP.
EQUATORIAL GUINEA
GABON
CONGO
SÃO TOME & PRINCIPE
DEM. REP. of the CONGO
UGANDA
KENYA
RWANDA
BURUNDI
TANZANIA
SEYCHELLES
COMOROS
ANGOLA
ZAMBIA
MALAWI
MOZAMBIQUE
NAMIBIA
ZIMBABWE
BOTSWANA
MADAGASCAR
MAURITIUS
SWAZILAND
LESOTHO
SOUTH AFRICA
MALDIVES
SRI LANKA
BRUNEI
MALAYSIA
SINGAPORE
INDONESIA
Equator
KIRIBATI
Tokelau (New Zealand)
SAMOA
American Samoa (U.S.)
TONGA
Cook Islands (New Zealand)
French Polynesia (France)
SOUTH
PACIFIC
OCEAN
SOUTH
ATLANTIC
OCEAN
INDIAN
OCEAN
PALAU
Guam (U.S.)
MARSHALL ISLANDS
FEDERATED STATES OF MICRONESIA
KIRIBATI
NAURU
PAPUA NEW GUINEA
SOLOMON ISLANDS
TUVALU
VANUATU
FIJI
New Caledonia (France)
AUSTRALIA
SOUTH
PACIFIC
OCEAN
NEW ZEALAND
Antarctica
CROATIA
Prijedor
Bosanski Brod
Bihac
Banja Luka
Brcko
Tuzla
N
BOSNIA
Medena Selista
CROATIA
Zenica
Mt. Bjelašnica
Ravno
SARAJEVO
Gorazde
Mostar
YUGOSLAVIA
Gabela
Adriatic Sea
0
25
50 Miles

addressed to the rain, it is meant for the singer. There is no social context for the tune: It does not speak for a group. No special meaning attaches to the rain other than that it gets in the way of fun.

The words to the Romanian song differ drastically. They seek the rain's bounty instead of better weather for playtime. From rain, the text shifts to the image of the plow and butter, calling on the fertility of the earth and the beasts. Instead of denying the course of the seasons, the song impatiently begs nature to continue the cycle of the seasons, from winter to spring—it seeks to continue, rather than stop, action. The song rings with particular urgency because it is sung during times of drought, when the villagers' subsistence is threatened through danger to their crops. In short, the group performance emphasizes a real social context for the song.

In the performance of the Romanian song, no detail seems accidental. The children wear skirts made from flowers that are symbols of spring, and they carry sieves, survival of a rain symbol of the ancient Greek gods. The children themselves, and even the villagers, are probably unaware of the remarkable durability of these symbols over the centuries. The presence of children might stand for the rising generation, associated with the forces of growth (versus decline and death). Growth seems invoked when the adults sprinkle the singing, dancing children with water. The "old woman" who controls the keys to the rain probably is related to the effigy of a hag carried and burned by children in other parts of the region as part of a spring ritual: She stands for winter and must die. Thus a local village musical performance is connected to a network of regional beliefs and musical performances.

The children are Roma (Gypsies), members of an ethnic group often treated throughout the region as outcast from mainstream society yet respected for its music-making talents. The song taps into a subtle sense of status, human values, and roles while the entire performance of "Paparuda" also belongs to the realm of magic and ritual, with the children acting as ambassadors to the forces of nature.

So what seems to be a "simple" song can be seen for what it really is—a complicated cultural package involving props, social organization, deeply held beliefs, and a specific melodic-textual structure crafted for a particular social moment: the time of drought.

What about the musical differences between the two rain songs? The American song needs no special rehearsing, because there is just one melody line and only two notes. Try singing the Romanian song. First, divide your group into two parts. Have one chant the unchanging *hai ploitsa, hai!* line while the other uses words (do it on a syllable like "la"). The singers with words also have different notes to think about: six here, as opposed to only two in the American song. As should be clear from this entire book, just because music comes from a technologically simpler environment, it doesn't mean that it must be musically less complicated—in fact, just the opposite is often true.

The rain song and its evocation of community come from a world of traditional music. That world was always turbulent; peasants in eastern

Europe, as everywhere in agriculturally based societies, were subject to tyrants and greedy landlords, epidemics, natural disasters, and invasions. It was not a timeless, culturally unified zone of unchanging tales and songs. Most people knew at least two languages or dialects, and many were also highly mobile, traveling from place to place or continent to continent for work and trade. Music traveled freely along mountain paths and highways, and in the twentieth century the slow spread of electrical and electronic media—record player, radio, then cassette and television—meant that people anywhere could be swayed by the seductive rhythms of the tango, the hot sound of jazz, or the hard beat of rock. Yet family, local, and national pride and memory ensured continuity. Along with every new layer of music making, older material such as the rain song was being handed down as well, creating a multilayered musical world. Even today, old-style peasant songs play their part as part of identity, or what is now often called "heritage." They coexist with rock, rap, and the latest outside influences.

This chapter focuses on a corner of the world that has undergone extreme change. There was once a multiethnic, federated nation-state called Yugoslavia that disintegrated violently in the early 1990s into its component parts, most of which became new states. Whole regions exchanged or expelled population in a process that involved extreme brutality, leaving thousands dead and millions homeless. The situation in the region remains tense and difficult as of the year 2000. So it is not surprising that along with a selection of stable traditional and contemporary musical styles, this chapter cites three kinds of musical change: dramatic and destructive transformation due to political upheaval, aesthetic and commercial shifts of style, and personal reshaping by musicians who have moved away from their homeland to the United States. We shall concentrate on one region—Bosnia.

Bosnia: From Tradition to Destruction

Our starting point is high in the mountains near the city of Sarajevo, in Bosnia (see Figure 5-1). From 1945 until 1991 Bosnia (and its adjacent area, Herzegovina) formed one of six republics that constituted a federated country called Yugoslavia ("land of the south Slavs"). Sarajevo had grown dramatically after World War II into a city of about a half million as peasants from mountain and lowland villages, as well as from smaller towns and cities, flocked to the newly emerging industries of that ancient town. The city's hosting of the 1984 Olympic Games was a high point in its development as a world-class metropolis. Sadly, the regional war that followed the dissolution of Yugoslavia into new nation-states caused great loss of life and culture in the Sarajevo area, beginning in 1992. The highland villages near the Olympic site, the focus of our first section (see Figure 5-2), had enjoyed long held traditions of folk music and adjusted to newer styles coming in from nearby cities. However, in 1992 the villages were totally destroyed and the population resettled, and so we will be looking at material that suddenly became historic. The fighting has changed not only

William G. Lockwood

Figure 5-1
Hay meadows above the village of Planinica, Bosnia. The village is visible in the upper left corner.

political and ethnic boundaries but music as well. Music has been profoundly affected by this violence and upheaval, particularly after Bosnia was reorganized politically through European and American intervention and occupation over the last few years. For simplicity, we shall keep to the early 1990s.*

We shall first get to know the villagers and then listen to the urban music. Our focus is on the Muslim population, people who have always spoken the same Slavic language (Serbo-Croatian) as their neighbors but who were converted to Islam during the 425-year occupation of the area by the Turkish-led Ottoman Empire (1463–1878).

Music in a Muslim Highlander Village

Mount Bjelašnica (pronounced "Bee-el-*osh*-nitsa"), "the White Mountain," stands as a snow-covered island in the Dinaric mountain range in an area where the mild Mediterranean climate confronts the cold continental weather to the east. Winters are long and harsh, and the soil is not

*I am extremely grateful to Ankica Petrović for first acquainting me with the riches of Bosnian music and to two graduate students from Sarajevo for their materials and expertise (background, translations) in compiling this chapter. Mirjana Laušević granted the use of her field materials in the following description of the Mt. Bjelašnica plateau. Ljerka Vidić Rassmussen contributed her extensive knowledge of the development of Yugoslav popular musics and helped with the difficulties of permissions for recordings that have changed not only owners but countries since their publication. *Note:* I regret the necessary abridgement of some examples due to the time constraints of the accompanying CD package. Deep thanks go to Bill Lockwood for offering his splendid photographs of rural Bosnia.

This chapter is dedicated to all the musicians and musical traditions that, along with their communities, have suffered destruction and displacement in the war that accompanied the collapse of federated Yugoslavia in 1990.

William G. Lockwood

Figure 5-2
The village of Planinica. Note the mosque on the right.

very good for farming. Much of the local highlanders' traditional work involves keeping large flocks of sheep. Women do a lot of the livestock herding and milking and have started to take cheese, milk, and butter to market. In recent years men have supplemented family income by working in industrial jobs in nearby towns and cities. As is common in such isolated environments, a small group of villages shares a common cultural core, and people give themselves a local name, here *planinstaci/planinke* (masculine/feminine), from the word *planina,* mountain. As a local woman puts it, "Everything is almost the same in all fourteen villages." The villagers have a variety of names for other people, groups near and far that they find unlike themselves. Electricity reached this remote plateau only in 1976, and its main musical impact was that it made a much greater variety of music available. This import from the outside world was matched in recent years by an outflow of male villagers to work not just in nearby towns but as far away as Austria and Germany as part of a huge labor migration from the southern to the more prosperous northern regions of Europe. Many returning emigrants built modern houses with all the electronic conveniences, creating a new local social group: urbanized villagers.

As a result, highlander music making offers a good example of musical layering. The older village song styles, which we survey first, are extremely localized. The secular songs do not even contain much Islamic content, which was more fully developed in cities. The main local song genres differ only somewhat from those of neighboring ethnic and religious groups, implying a strong shared regional taste that is at the heart of what we usually call folk music. The three types of local song everyone knows are all polyphonic; that is, they consist of different parts simultaneously sung by a small group of singers, rather than by one person singing alone or by everybody singing the same tune (unison). There are few musical instruments up on Mt. Bjelašnica; voices do the work of communication in the fields and in the village square. The outflow of workers to the cities and the fact that boys no longer do the herding has meant that people have largely forgotten their old handmade instruments, such as shepherd's flutes. For special occasions—fairs, festivals—songs and some electric instruments are joined with voices as accompaniment to dance. Despite all the change and the forgetting of many earlier forms of folklore, such as epic singing about local heroes, for Bosnian Muslims "folksong is perhaps the most viable verbal form of folklore . . . today" (Lockwood 1983:28).

One of the best times to catch a lively song and dance scene is a *mevlud* festival. A *mevlud* is a local version of a widespread ceremony based partly on reading a sacred text that centers on the birth of the Prophet Muhammad. These celebrations can happen at many different times in private to mark personal occasions, but they also are held as large public occasions every weekend in August, when city workers are on vacation and can come home from as far away as Germany to have a good time in their native village. The event has three parts: a religious ceremony, a fair, and an evening gathering. Village girls put on elaborate outfits (see Figure 5-3), while young women who have moved to the city dress in a more urban style. Trucks arriving at the scene of the host village are covered with singing celebrants, with one truck trying to outdo another in song.

During the fair, hundreds of people gather on a meadow, with various groups of singers and musicians competing for space and attention. This is a moment of courtship, when young men and women size each other up, sing about each other, and present themselves the way they want to be

Figure 5-3
Singers of CD Selection 16, the highlander women's ganga song, near the village of Umoljani: Šecira Kadrić, Aiša Kadrić, Enisa Trešnjo.

Mirjana Laušević

understood: rural or urban, available or unavailable, bashful or bold. Girls stick with the singing group they've grown up with, but men move from group to group. Intergroup competition lends an edge to the singing, and everyone evaluates each other's performances. Body posture, song texts, and attitude differ considerably, as we shall hear. Women tend to sing in a well-rehearsed, tight manner meant to show that they have thought things through, are organized, and work hard, characteristics valued in a wife. The songs are complicated, multipart creations that depend on thorough knowledge and long experience, with a leader setting the pace. Only unmarried women sing, so they use the opportunity to enjoy their art during their peak singing years as well as to affirm sisterhood and to display themselves to the whole community, including parents, potential in-laws, and prospective husbands. Songs may praise women's solidarity as well as tease men or comment on the beauties and virtues of highlander life.

Throughout Bosnia and Herzegovina, a popular form of song among several ethnic groups is called *ganga.* Ganga singers meet at an early age (see Figure 5-3) and continue singing together for decades, fine-tuning their sensitivity to each other's sound and skills. Should a woman from a nearby village marry into another village, it might be hard for her to find singing partners even if her style is quite close to the local way of singing. Her new singing companions will immediately notice even the slightest shade of difference in the nuances of local ganga. This highly valued form of singing sounds strange to outsiders, even to others in nearby regions, let alone western European or American listeners, mostly due to the insistence on very close intervals, which "grate" on the unaccustomed ear, and the uncompromising intensity of the delivery. The social organization of the group is reflected in the musical structure: A respected leader sets the tone, literally, and the other singers, usually two, chip in an accompanying pattern called "cutting," "chopping," or "sobbing" that is vocally and emotionally powerful, as you will hear. Music Example 5-1 gives a schematic version of the two ganga songs (CD Selections 16 and 17).

CD 1
Tracks 16, 17

The pauses in the men's ganga are quite long; if you watch them, you might think they are not even about to sing, as they puff on cigarettes and look nonchalant. Just then, they break into coordinated song. A solo voice dominates in the first phrase (A); for the second and third (B, C), the group

Music Example 5-1a
Women's ganga song.

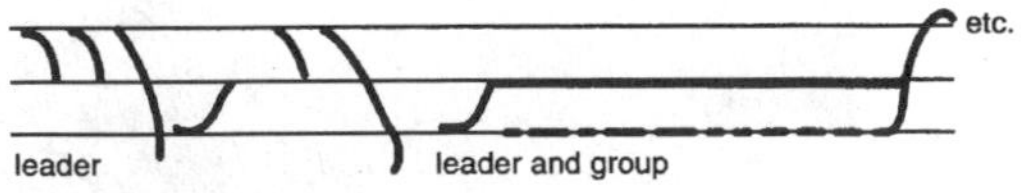

Music Example 5-1b
Men's ganga song.

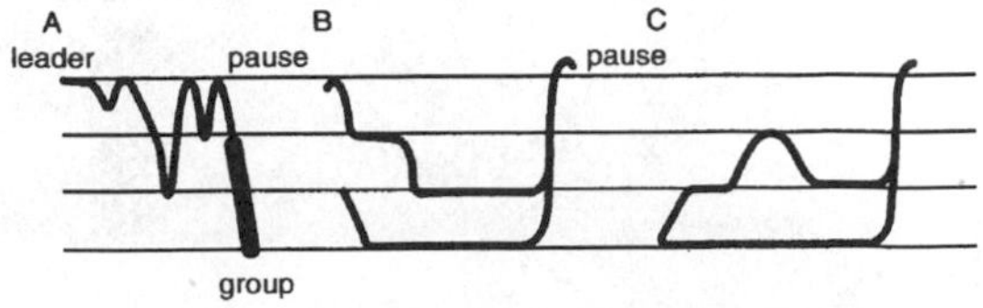

splits into parts that get extremely close and then break into an exuberant rise at the end. As the two lines get closer, the intensity of the effect of blended voices increases as the resonance produces "beats," sharp patterns of acoustic interaction, that are increased by the vocal techniques of the singers.

To experience ganga properly, you should be singing it or listening to friends' songs. Singers are very aware of the acoustic quality they are producing. They perceive their powerful voice production not just physically but sensually. They look forward to the extra resonance that emerges from singing pitches very closely together, enjoying the "cutting edge" of the vibrations. This means that ganga is difficult to record. When the Bosnian ethnomusicologist Ankica Petrović took a group of women into the recording studio, the sound engineers tried to put a microphone on each singer separately to "clarify" the sound as individual tracks, but the women refused. They were used to performing their songs in a tight semicircle, touching shoulders, so they could listen properly to each other and create the right mood. This technique confused the engineers but not the women. They were able to tell the technicians exactly where to place the microphone for the best sound quality.

Ankica Petrović has delved deeply into many sides of the singers' aesthetic, including their feelings about their music. She finds a direct correlation between musical features and this aesthetic: "The melodic range and intervals in this polyphonic singing reflect mutual human relationships within the framework of small interacting communities, while the importance of individual personality is emphasized by individual improvisation. At the end of the ganga, when songs finish on two different tones a major second apart, it is as if different individuals are given the same rights in the community" (Petrović 1977:335). When ganga is sung right, it has a powerful effect on its performers and listeners: "Good performances can move them to tears and 'shudders,' but with a sense of happiness; and they arouse feelings of love and sexual passion among younger people, as well as strong feelings of regional identity among both young and old alike" (Petrović 1977:331).

Let us look at the text of the women's song:

CD 1
Track 16

Sisters, hold on to your chastity like a tear;
The one who kisses you will not take you.

In this lyric, a "tear" is something precious you do not easily let fall. "Take" means marry. So the song is a warning to girls: Do not let yourself be seduced by kisses, because an aggressive young man is probably not the reliable suitor you are looking for.

A typical male song takes a very different angle on boy-girl relations:

CD 1
Track 17

What lifts the heart of a rascal?
A liter of wine and a fine girl.

Young men use the word *baraba* in most songs to describe themselves, which can be translated as rascal, rogue, and hellraiser. Their way of singing is relaxed, self-confident, and boastful, and manhood is the main topic of their songs. However, both men and women also sing songs praising singing itself as a foremost means of expression:

Men's text:

Since we have not sung, brother
The village is unhappy.

Women's text:
I will sing out of spite for my sorrow
So it won't conquer me when it tortures me.

Oh god, what would happen if there were no singing?
What would my heart do with all its burden?

One can alternately compare men's and women's texts to get a sense of the different takes on similar themes. This may seem like a sort of gender duel, through a kind of singing that is also traditional in other Bosnian villages:

Men's:	Enjoy your girlhood, girl, while you are at your mother's Once you're with me, you won't enjoy it.
Women's:	I didn't know, I didn't believe That the fawn (= boyfriend) is dearer than Mom.
Men's:	Come, come, you dark one, it won't be in vain. Let a rascal kiss you just once.
Women's:	If I knew, dear, that I'd be yours You wouldn't be able to count my kisses.
Men's:	Little one, I love your bowlegs More than a crate of Sarajevo beer.
Women's:	My dear, your buddy got the better of you: Instead of you, I love him.
Men's:	Love me or love me not, little one, My hand has caressed you.
Women's:	You can love whomever you want now, You loved me once as well.

This relationship between singing and gender, both performed and closely watched by everyone, can be found around the whole region. For nearby Albanians, Jane Sugarman proposes,

> Singing, rather than merely reflecting notions of gender, also shapes those notions in return. Singing provides Prespارë [the villagers she lived with] with a means of tangibly living out their strongly contrasting notions of femininity and masculinity. Through singing they are temporarily able to model their individual selves into the form of a cultural ideal . . . or they

may use their singing to suggest its revision . . . [Young adults] will experiment increasingly with ways of conveying through song new views of themselves as women and men." (1989:209)

Common to both sexes is a strong sense of place, embodied in many song texts that praise one's own village and ridicule others. But men and women convey differing senses of self in songs and dances. By and large, the highlander male repertory is outwardly oriented and frank, the women's more intimate, poetic, and metaphoric. But in dance and clothing, women can also choose among ways of self-presentation. Mobility and outside musical styles have had their impact on how the sexes regard each other, or at least what ideal of femininity women might choose, urban or rural. Young women express this choice visibly in selecting a dance style.

The village girls want to express their strength and energy through dancing. They lift their legs high and stamp their feet. Those who want to display their urban manners dance closer to the ground, with smaller steps. Those who have lived in the town and cities away from the highlands can choose to identify themselves as more sophisticated, with less stress on their wood-carrying, sheep-herding, and cow-milking skills, underscoring the urban-rural divide that has run through the local scene ever since increased mobility allowed for more lifestyle choices. As one ganga text says, "All honor to the mountain, but I want to go to the valley / Let everyone go where she wants," or, as a girl from the village of Potoci sings, "I wouldn't get married in Potoci; I would rather poison myself," referring to her strong wish to move to the lowlands, to the larger towns and cities of Bosnia. It is to these lowland urban settings that we now turn.

Music of Rural and Urban Lowlands Muslims

In the lowlands are many other forms of singing (see Figure 5-4), as well as more instrumental music than in the highlands. The most typical instrument of the region is the *šargija* (*shar*-ghee-ya), which came originally from the East, from what were Turkish-controlled regions in the old days, and which has become part of Bosnian life, played by Muslims and neighboring Serbs and Croats alike. The *šargija* is a plucked, stringed instrument; over the years the number of strings has been slowly increasing. As happens in many folk music settings, people in recent decades have wanted their instruments to produce more sound, projecting more loudness and richness; eventually, instrument types became electrified and amplified as radio, recordings, and outside influences offered people new ideals of what music "should" sound like.

CD 1
Track 18

In CD Selection 18, you can hear the *šargija.* It once had four strings but now has six (some even have seven) and more frets, to allow for more notes to be played. The tuning is g′-g′-g′-c-f′-g″, where the bass string, c, is surrounded by three drones on g′ and a lower and higher melody string. The text, performed by Skiba and friends, praises the instrument itself:

O *šargija* made of poplar wood
May the one who builds you never get sick.

Figure 5-4
Older styles: a lullaby. Planinica, 1967.

William G. Lockwood

This song combines several musical threads that weave in and out of other examples. Two men sing together, but not mechanically: There is a lot of give-and-take in the way they jointly produce the words and in each man's voice quality and approach to the rhythm and phrasing of the words. This is an example of what ethnomusicologists call *heterophony;* that is, they are doing the "same" thing, but in an individual way, an approach noted above for both men and women's ganga singing.

Another aspect of local musical thinking lies in the sense of rhythm. Notice that you can tap your foot or snap your fingers to some sections of the song but not to others. This fluidity, this elastic sense of time is common to many musical styles of southeastern Europe and nearby areas of the eastern Mediterranean. Yet another interesting quality of this song is the way the *šargija* part is not just one line but projects multiple voices, closely positioned, that might remind one of ganga singing, even including the very close intervals. And each instrumental section is different—again, a flexible approach to detail pervades performance.

All of these sides of the song add up to an aesthetic: a perspective on how musical units should be put together, one that is the basis of a local and regional sound. There is a way of thinking, not just performing, that lies behind traditional music making. As the folk singer Todora Varamezov of Bulgaria said, "Folk songs you can ornament and change as you want. If you change it, then you sing from the heart. It's not like you have learned it lifelessly, as if it's an obligation. Different people sing it different ways." At the same time, there is a limit to variation: "If singers altered the melody too much, they could count on hearing about it from the 'aunts' and 'grannies' who were watching and listening" (Rice 1994:110). Tradition, then, means that both individual variation and collective responsibility coexist in each performance in this type of music making, where people stand face-to-face and ear-to-ear and pay close attention. In music coming from pop recording studios or government-sponsored composers' desks, as we shall see, the musical aesthetic and the social contract about music are tightly intertwined.

One of the important types of song associated with the Bosnian Muslim population is the *sevdalinka.* The root word, *sevda,* comes from Turkish and implies love in terms of passion, and also sadness. Originally, sevdalinkas were adaptations of tunes of *ilahija,* sacred songs. Sevdalinkas can have many different singing and accompaniment styles and topics. Hearing sevdalinkas on the radio and trying to sing them yourself was an early shift away from rural forms like ganga for village girls before more modern forms, like pop and rock styles, became available (Lockwood 1983:35).

CD 1 Track 19

Our example (CD Selection 19), sung by an older man, Himzo Polovina, is about a wedding rather than the more common sevdalinka theme of romantic love. As in all sevdalinkas, symbols and metaphors, rather than straightforward commentary, make the point. To refer to the wedding is to touch upon a key memory of village life. As a researcher from nearby Hungary puts it, "Weddings rank foremost among popular customs: they are a veritable accumulation of ceremonies continuing mythical, religious-ritual, legal, economic, musical, and mimic elements. In some places they became almost festive plays with their chief and supporting characters, supernumeraries, fixed scene, time, music, dances, and audience" (CMPH 1956:689).

Among Bosnian Muslims, weddings can go on for an entire week (see Figure 5-5) and include a great deal of music, which, as for festivals, is gender- and generation-marked, as the folklorist Yvonne Lockwood observed at a 1967 wedding:

> During the day, people came to welcome and see the bride, who sat shyly in the corner. Every night the older men of the village came to the house of the groom's parents where they sat in one room talking and drinking coffee. The maidens, lads, children, and young married men, including the groom, sang and danced in a second room. Behind the closed door of a third room, the women, bride, and young children congregated. Here, secluded from male observation, were some of the best singers and dancers in the village who now only perform at times like this. (Lockwood 1983:20)

The wedding song recorded in an urban radio studio differs dramatically from this traditional village scene. It comes through a radio speaker, not from the lively, charged space of a rural wedding, and is sung and played by professionals, not amateur village musicians. The accompaniment for CD Selection 19 is a *tamburitza* orchestra.

This type of ensemble dates back to about the 1840s, at a time when people in various European countries (notably Italy and Russia) were organizing orchestral ensembles out of older folk stringed instruments. Then, as now, folk music had a romantic aura connected to a preindustrial past imagined to be gentler than the modern world. At the same time,

Figure 5-5
Dancing at a village wedding. Planinica, 1967.

William G. Lockwood

organizers of such groups have always insisted on precise, almost mechanized performance, an aesthetic deeply opposed to the more informal village way of music making. It is not accidental that this new aesthetic arose with urbanization and the onset of a regimented work force in urban industrial contexts. As time went on, these folk orchestras also became connected to national pride and local identity. In the period of cultural control by the Communist Party, national identity and artistic expression were both tightly organized by the state. This approach was tried out first in what was the Soviet Union, the world's largest multiethnic country for nearly seventy-five years (1917–91) and the first nation-state to have a system completely based on socialist principles. Culture was under the control of a complex bureaucracy made of many organizations, and all the media—print and electronic, news and entertainment—were run by the government with no private enterprise allowed.

This state-managed cultural system spread to several eastern European countries from 1945 until around 1990, when they were under the direct influence of Soviet power as implemented by local regimes. This "east bloc" included Poland, Czechoslovakia (now the Czech Republic and Slovakia), Hungary, Rumania, and Bulgaria. Bosnia was part of Yugoslavia, whose leader, Tito, had broken away from Soviet control in 1948 but who maintained a comparable system of communist party-led government. The state acted as the main patron and police of all artistic—including musical—activity, deciding what could or could not be published, listened to, or supported. As we shall see, the Yugoslav system was freer than that of its neighbors, producing some maverick musical results, but in the case of a radio orchestra such as the one that accompanies this sevdalinka, the goal is an official, not an informal or folk sound. CD Selection 19 is very tightly arranged for voice and folk orchestra. This type of arrangement is a good example of managed traditionalism. You can hear the careful professionalism of "official culture" in the precisely orchestrated instruments and the somewhat reined-in voice of the singer. In fact, the directors of this ensemble prided themselves on working out the "sloppiness" of folk musicians (interview, Laušević 1994). This attitude combines the precommunist, bourgeois love for "updating" folk music with the socialist approach to "disciplining" national culture.

In the lyrics of the sevdalinka song the figure of the golden thread from heaven that enwraps the bride, groom, and wedding party is an old image, a stock figure that appears in many songs:

Trepetljika trepetala

That which trembles is full of pearls.
These white castles [=homes] of ours are full of joy
All the kinfolk are in the castle.
The mother is celebrating the wedding of the son.
Everyone is happy, but the mother most of all.
They brought her the [flower name]-smelling maiden
The golden thread stretched from the clear sky
And wrapped around the groom's fez
From the fez, it stretched around the bride's veil.

The idea of folk ensembles like the *tamburitza* orchestra traveled well to places to which eastern Europeans emigrated, such as the United States. There, a Pittsburgh-based folksong and dance ensemble called the Tamburitzans has been in existence since 1936 (see Forry 1978) and continues to charm audiences not only in the United States but elsewhere on tour. Their publicity characterizes the group as "a spirited troupe" that has "captivated audiences throughout the Americas, the former Soviet Union and Europe with its joyful performances. . . . Wearing colorful native folk costumes, the Tammies offer a trip into some of the most fascinating parts of the Balkans and other lands with their lively village dances and vibrant songs" (World Music Institute brochure, 1994). Words like *colorful, native, folk,* and *vibrant,* coupled with *village, fascinating,* and *Balkans,* evoke a concert experience that will be comfortably exotic, historical, and ethnographic, but also familiar (note the Americanized nickname, the "Tammies") and, above all, highly professional.

The same New York concert series the Tammies performed for in 1994 also featured the first American tour of an old folk-based troupe from Slovakia, a country in eastern Europe, that promised "dazzling folkdances, music and songs of a country which lies in the heart of Europe . . . highlighted by breathtaking acrobatic dances expressing the poetry, lyricism and passion of the Slovak people, their history and culture." Note the connection between the adjectives stressing showcraft—*dazzling, acrobatic*—and those underscoring soulfulness—*poetry, lyricism, passion.* This approach to marketing goes back to the original purposes of professional folk ensembles: the projection of a local sensibility and history culled from peasant sources into an arena of modern theatricalized performance by nonpeasants who "clean up" and "perfect" the expressive culture of ordinary villagers. This impulse began in intellectual circles over a hundred years ago, flourished under the state patronage of communist regimes, and continues in emigration and in postcommunist life as an expression of identity and as a vehicle for cross-cultural presentation and arts marketing. The idea has spread around the world, from the national dance troupes of African countries to the recently created folk ensemble of aboriginal peoples of Taiwan.

At the same time, the particular styles of music presented in this chapter have had a significant, long-term impact on less formal amateur song and dance activity in the United States (as well as western Europe), where for about fifty years informal "Balkan" groups have been a feature of the cultural landscape in college towns and cities across the United States. There is something about the infectious dance rhythms and soulful singing of the region that cuts across many social and geographic boundaries.

Popular Music Styles: "Newly Composed Folk Music" and Rock

One of the bureaucratically defined styles of music that emerged in Yugoslavia's last decades (1960s–1980s) was called "newly composed folk music." Ordinarily we think of folk music as something handed down from generation to generation. Yet with millions of Yugoslav villagers moving to big cities, the lifestyle of much of the population was "newly composed" beginning in the 1950s (see Figure 5-6). Similar seismic shifts of populations and musical styles happened in many countries of the world in this period, including (just a little earlier, in the 1930s and 1940s) the United States, where masses of black and white southerners moved to the big cities of the north, creating the urban blues (Chapter 4) and parallel

Figure 5-6
Villagers from Planinica going to the town of Bugojno, 1967.

William G. Lockwood

styles such as honky-tonk country music. In Peru, Mexico, India, and elsewhere, musics based loosely on elements drawn from earlier rural styles but "juiced up" in the city became the norm for a majority of the world's peoples. Yugoslavia was no exception.

The difference in eastern Europe was that the state, rather than a group of local entrepreneurs, monitored this development. Allowing some star performers to develop, the government nevertheless held on to control of record-pressing plants, the airwaves, and the types of taxation placed on different kinds of music. For a long time in Yugoslavia, musics considered "useful" to social engineering were not taxed, while those considered distracting or "vulgar" were taxed to show disapproval and to help subsidize the "right" kinds of music. Nevertheless, "newly composed folk music" took over the consciousness of most Yugoslavs, who identified with the combination of roots sounds and big-city topics, voices, and instrumentation.

CD I
Track 20

Our example of "newly composed folk music" (CD Selection 20) comes from the work of Lepa Brena, the stage name of a young Bosnian Muslim woman from the city of Brčko. This fiery young singer hit the top of the pop charts early in Yugoslavia and starred in music video–like films. A distinctive feature of the Yugoslav music-culture was the fact that the bureaucracy and Communist Party were perfectly willing to allow such stardom, even with its money-making potential, to flourish within a socialist state.

The musical makeup of the song seems to come mostly from the nearby region of Macedonia, once part of Yugoslavia and now a separate nation. The rhythm can be beaten out as 2 + 2 + 2 + 3, or an overall pattern of 9, and is partly played on the Macedonian *darabuka* drum. This type of rhythm is common to the southeastern corner of Europe and adjacent Turkey. Locally, it is called a *čoček* ("chaw-check") dance. In the local sensibility, it is felt as "eastern," or "oriental," as are aspects of the voice quality and text delivery Lepa Brena offers here. In a sense, this sort of sound signals "exotic" to the mainstream listener, providing a kind of local color that, although not exactly Bosnian, works in this song as part of the Bosnian boosterism the text declares:

Mani zemlju koja Bosnu nema

1. I've been in eternal Rome, I've seen the Greek sea,
   But there's no better place than my Brčko
   Chorus: Don't bother with a country that doesn't have Bosnia
   Or with a man who dozes when next to a woman.
2. There, where those highlands are, where the world is brighter
   I've seen a lot of the world, but Bosnia's the dearest to me.
   [Chorus]
3. Whoever wants to understand Bosnia has to be born there;
   We Bosnians really know how to live life.
   [Chorus]

Lyrics (translated) "Mani zemlju koja Bosnu nema" by Lepa Brena, from the album *Lepa Brena & Slatki Greh,* 1984, used by permission of PGP RTS.

Here the highlands we started our survey with stand unmistakably for the heart of Bosnian life. This is very like the nostalgic appeal in U.S. country music to "the old mountain home." The pairing of sexual love with love of homeland is common enough in many world pop musics, the erotic often being a metaphor (in literature, music, or film) for nationalism, but also a way of selling songs.

Though newly composed folk was an urban form, it was not the only new sound in the cities. Rock, first a direct imitation of British and U.S. groups, genres, and styles, slowly became domesticated in all the European countries, finding its niche in the welter of local musics. In Bosnia, as elsewhere, it was largely educated, middle-class youth that took up this world style. In the socialist system, the children of bureaucrats, managers, and arts professionals had a higher status and a different outlook than the children of former peasants did. Many rock songs spoke to the concerns of rock worldwide—urban alienation, the generation gap, problems of love—but these had a more political edge in a controlling system such as communism.

CD 1
Track 21

As an example of rock-oriented music, you will be listening to a folk-based song in tune with our topic, rather than the more philosophical, literary rock of singer-songwriters. "Da zna zora" (CD Selection 21), released in 1989, quotes a *varoška,* or small-town, song that has roots in the earlier twentieth century. It is by Željko Bebek, also the lead singer of the most famous Sarajevo band, Bijelo Dugme ("White Button"). Their leader, Bregović, used to say that "all of us are peasants three times removed" (in Glavan and Vrdoljak 1981). That distance is reflected in the very attenuated folk presence in this song; references to the folk tradition would probably be understood somewhat ironically by a hip, young, city rock fan. The guest singer on "Da zna zora" is a popular singer of the style Lepa Brena represents, so this song is a fusion of urban subcultures: the more intellectual, British and U.S.-influenced rock, and the more pop, folk-based "newly composed" style.

This mixture is apparent in the song's elements. It takes from tradition an old folk-style melody, a slow introduction to an up-tempo danceable tune, and some country sounds. From the rock world it takes the simple chord changes, the beat, the electric guitars with their tentative heavy-metal licks, and the weary vocal style. The lyrics are pretty straightforward:

Da zna zora

If the dawn knew how strongly I love
Oh, the dawn wouldn't break for a year.

Day and night, night and day, I drink deep red wine;
Oh, just before dawn I go home drunk.

If the dawn knew which sweetheart I love
The rosy dawn would never break.

"Da zna zora." Željko Bebek and Halid Beslić. From the album *Bebek: Niko više ne sanja,* 1989, used by permission of Croatia Records.

As of the spring of 1992, neither the erotic localism of Lepa Brena nor the rock romanticism of Bebek could speak to what befell Bosnia. As part of the dissolution of the country of Yugoslavia and the declaring of new nation-states, Bosnia became a battleground as soon as it declared itself a sovereign state in 1992. Not only did neighbors—Serbia and Croatia—engage their forces, but the multiethnic Bosnian population of Serbs, Croats, and Muslims split into warring camps and coalitions. Through 1995, thousands were killed, millions became refugees, and vast stretches of town and countryside were devastated by fierce fighting. The villages on Mt. Bjelašnica described earlier were destroyed by Bosnian Serbs, as was 85 percent of Lepa Brena's and Mensur Hatićs (see later) town, Brčko. Sarajevo, the capital of Bosnia, remained under Bosnian Serb siege for over three years—a particularly bitter turn of fate, since in that multiethnic city, ethnic and religious distinctions had seemed to dissolve into a congenial cosmopolitan culture between 1945 and 1990, most people's memory span. Music has also become a battleground, as pop and rock stars have emigrated or have taken sides in the conflict, causing reorientation of their audience. Lepa Brena, for example, chose to become a star for the Serbian side. Songs, genres, and bands that were once national became identified with the various warring factions, who all turned to music videos to promote their cause.

Such scenes have occurred elsewhere in the world, causing severe dislocation and disjuncture. The musical life of such war-torn countries as Afghanistan or of the former Soviet lands Armenia, Georgia, and Tajikistan have been changed irrevocably. Even in relatively peaceful places, economic need and incentives have caused a huge world labor force to move from home, a phenomenon for which the too-bureaucratic-sounding term *deterritorialization* has been coined. Uprooted from familiar surroundings, often traumatized by memory, these world wanderers always find music to be an important lifeline connecting them to their past and to their loved ones far away. So it seems fitting to include in our short survey two musicians who are not living in Bosnia, but come from it and who carry Bosnian traditions to the United States, in very different circumstances: Mensur Hatić and Flory Jagoda.

Two Bosnian Musicians Abroad

Mensur Hatić: Versatile Musical Traveler

Mensur Hatić (pronounced "*Ha*-titch") was born in Bjelijna, halfway between the Bosnian towns of Brčko and Tuzla, in 1961 and grew up in Brčko, the predominantly Muslim city celebrated in the song by Lepa Brena, his compatriot cited earlier (CD Selection 22). He now lives in Detroit, where he makes his living repairing accordions (see Figure 5-7) and was interviewed in 1994 by Mark Slobin for this chapter. Quite musical from an early age, he was exposed to a variety of musics, taking advantage of both a network of public classical music school opportunities, particularly stressed in socialist countries, and the local ethnic and popular styles.

Mirjana Laušević

Figure 5-7
Mensur Hatić (accordion) and Youri Younakov (clarinet) of Ivo Papazov's band Trakiya, playing at Ramblewood, a Balkan summer music camp at Darlington, Maryland, 1994. The Balkan music scholar Carol Silverman is at center.

His father, an accomplished singer-accordionist who knew a great many *sevdalinka,* taught them to Mensur and encouraged him on the accordion. After high school, the army, and a year of college he began to play professionally, touring and making commercial recordings. Because of Yugoslavia's location and the presence of many Yugoslav workers abroad, he and his band could leave on Friday, play in Germany, and be back home on Monday.

Mensur's life through 1990 was richly layered in musical experience and travel. As a versatile musician, he quickly adapted himself to a continentwide network of Yugoslav touring groups and audiences, catering to the hundreds of thousands of expatriates scattered around western Europe. He enhanced his earning power by apprenticing in instrument building and repairing in major factories in Italy and Germany and by certifying himself as a music teacher in his hometown. With a secure base in Brčko, where he built himself a house complete with an elaborate stereo system, Mensur was both traditionalist and postmodernist, deeply Bosnian but internationalist in outlook, looking for the chance to use his skills, as musicians always have, to gain a foothold in a very dynamic, insecure local economy and intercultural atmosphere. While other musicians in exile have failed to find a foothold, lost outside the environment of their particular audience, Mensur's flexibility has served him well.

Just before the onset of war in then-Yugoslavia, Mensur left for the United States, apparently anticipating and thus avoiding the conflagration that would engulf his town and country. Now he lives in Detroit in a neighborhood of older, reasonably priced housing with a large eastern European immigrant population set in a sea of ethnic diversity. Not surprisingly, he has found that his musical skills fit right in, and he plays for parties of former Yugoslavs and in local multiethnic clubs.

CD 1
Track 22

Now listen to a piece Mensur wrote himself, inspired by living near a train station (CD Selection 22). He takes the sound of the train and improvises on it in quite an original fashion. This sort of piece is, as Mensur says, a kind of universal language; wherever trains have played an important part in people's lives, musicians have written train pieces.

The piece has four distinct components: (1) a slowly accelerating theme at the beginning (A); (2) train whistle sounds; (3) a short, insistent repeated melody (B); and (4) a one-time improvised tune over steady bass (C). These combine in the pattern ABCBA, with the train whistle interjections providing an overall framework. The speeding-up of A at the beginning is matched by a slowing-down reprise of A at the end to make the whole piece cyclical:

Music Example 5-2
Components of "Train Piece" by Mensur Hatić. Transcription by Mark Slobin.

In terms of style, two of Mensur's approaches are worth noting. One is the melodic structure of A. It is actually made up of two segments we can call a and b. Mensur plays ab, but then b itself repeats in its own extended form, b′. This freely expanding sense of melody is part of the improvisational aesthetic of folk music. The second place this can be heard is in the accompaniment to the B and C sections, played on the accordion buttons (the melody is played on the keys). Using the basic interval of a fourth (transcribed here as e-a), Mensur creates a steady bass line that moves against the melody, again in a free, shifting pattern of small melodic units.

Flory Jagoda: Keeper of the Sephardic Jewish Tradition of Bosnia

Before 1940, the twelve thousand Jews of Sarajevo made up about 10 percent of the city's population and acted as lively, long-term contributors to the local culture and music. Tunes were shared by Jews, Muslims, Croats, and Serbs, each community adapting melodies to their own ritual or social needs. The Bosnian Jews were mostly of Sephardic background. This means that their ancestors were part of a wave of immigration from Spain after 1492, when the Christian rulers who reconquered Spain from the Muslims forcibly exiled the Jews and Muslims. The Jews, who had developed a long, collaborative cultural relationship with the Muslims, fled to Muslim-controlled areas of southeastern Europe, the eastern Mediterranean, and north Africa. These Spanish Jews, or Sephardim, had strong traditions of poetry and song that dated back to the Middle Ages and that they took with them to their new homes. Learning local languages, they also kept on speaking their own vernacular, a Spanish-based language called Ladino, or Judeo-Spanish.

During World War II the Bosnian Jews suffered the fate of some six million Jews across Europe, being deported to death camps by Nazi occupiers. Less than a thousand survived, now a vanishingly small percentage of the nearly half-million population of the newly swollen Sarajevo. This small postwar remnant kept up its culture, and during the early stages of the Yugoslav war of the 1990s the Jews, as onlookers, helped as mediators. But by the mid-1990s very few Jews were left in Bosnia to carry on their centuries-old traditions, most having emigrated to Israel, the United States, or elsewhere.

Flory Jagoda (see Figure 5-8) was born in Sarajevo in 1923 to a Sephardic family, Altarac, known for its singers and musicians. She escaped from the region during World War II and emigrated to the United States, becoming the sole survivor of her family. By managing to escape her community's destruction, she was able to preserve the heritage of her childhood. Today she enhances her tradition by making her own arrangements of folk materials, performing with other family members in an ensemble that has recorded and toured widely. Here is what Flory Jagoda says about her childhood and what she learned from her *nona,* her grandmother:

> In my Nona's kitchen there was a drawer that was magic to us children. It contained sheets upon sheets of paper written in Hebrew script which we could not decipher, but those words, when sung by my Nona, we understood. These Ladino songs had been learned from her mother, and her mother before her, and so on for generations. . . . I am trying . . . to again open my Nona's drawer and pass on a taste of the talent and way of life which produced the Altarac family, that it might live on, both in the songs I remember and in my own musical memories of that now-disappeared time. (Jagoda 1989)

For Flory Jagoda, then, the music provides cultural continuity. When she escaped from the German occupation, she took her accordion with her,

Figure 5-8
Flory Jagoda, a Bosnian Sephardic Jewish singer who lives in the United States.

Courtsey of Flory Jagoda

though she had to leave her grandmother's book of songs behind. Now she says, "Those songs my Nona sang and the accordion that saved my life were the only things I brought with me to America, the only things that were left from my childhood" (interview with M. Laušević, 1992).

Individual musicians, such as Mensur Hatić, can be strongly interested in keeping their ears open for new sounds, which they enjoy assimilating both for the sheer pleasure of learning and for economic viability. Whole communities, like the Sephardic Jews of Sarajevo, can also be musically adaptable and selective out of a survival sense of accommodation, because they have a variegated history of environments in which they have lived, or also just for the sheer aesthetic satisfaction of singing and playing across the full range of surrounding musical resources.

CD I
Track 23

The song selected here from Flory Jagoda's ample storehouse (CD Selection 23) is about Sarajevo, about the men of the family, who can hardly wait for the end of the Sabbath so they can go out and party:

Klaro del dija

The roosters are starting to crow;
It's time to get up,
Let's not wait; the sun and the day
Start up the happy crowd.
From Havdalah to the Šadrvan*
When the girls dance and sing.
Until tomorrow, at dawn,
The crowd disperses.

---

*Havdalah is the Jewish ceremony that marks the transition from the Sabbath to the weekday world, on Saturday at sunset. The Šadrvan was a well-known Sarajevo café in the old days, located near the Jewish neighborhood.

Lyrics (translated), Sephardic Jewish song "Klaro del dija" from Sarajevo, sung by Flory Jagoda. From *Kanikas Diminona,* Global Village Music CD C139, 1989. Used with permission.

She sings with her family group, who provide guitar and vocal backup, their contribution to the further transmission of their great-grandmother's songbook. To round out the complexity of such traveling transmission, in the late 1980s Flory Jagoda returned to Sarajevo to give a concert, and later some of her songs were played on the local television station, probably the first time Jewish songs were publicly aired. These songs were greeted enthusiastically by the remaining Jewish community, which had lost its tradition through the radical disjuncture of war and postwar cultural assimilation. So through the channel of Jagoda's visit, this Sephardic music went back into circulation after a fifty-year absence.

Between them, Mensur Hatić and Flory Jagoda represent two common but contrasting versions of musical diaspora, meaning music of a population that feels far away from home. Both have felt disjuncture and cultural loss through warfare. For the Sephardic Jews, the loss is total, as Sarajevo is unlikely to have a significant Jewish population in any foreseeable future. Flory Jagoda's adaptation to these conditions has been to embark on a personal quest for preservation and arrangement as a monument to a bygone culture and for her own sense of continuity. For the much younger Hatić, who feels the effect of a current war, flexibility and resourcefulness are the keys to economic survival in the music business while he keeps a watchful eye on events back home to determine where his future lies. Both musicians use music as a lifeline in turbulent cultural waters, an impulse shared by countless millions of deterritorialized and migrant peoples at the end of the twentieth century.

References

CMPH (Corpus Musicae Popularis Hungaricae). 1956. Vol. III/B *Lakodalom,* ed. L. Kiss. Hungarian Academy of Sciences.

Forry, Mark. 1978. "Becar Music in the Serbian Community of Los Angeles: Evolution and Transformation." In *Selected Reports in Ethnomusicology* 3/1, ed. J. Porter.

Glavan, Darko, and Dražen Vrdoljak. 1981. *Ništa mudro.* Zagreb: Polet Rock.

Jagoda, Flory. 1991. Liner notes to *Kantikas di mi nona.* Global Village C139.

Laušević, Mirjana. 1993. "Rascals and Shepherdesses: Music and Gender on a Bosnian Mountain." M.A. thesis, Wesleyan Univ.

Lockwood, Yvonne. 1983. *Text and Context: Folksong in a Bosnian Muslim Village.* Columbus, Ohio: Slavica.

Petrović, Ankica. 1977. "Ganga, a Form of Traditional Rural Singing in Yugoslavia." Ph.D. diss., Queen's Univ., Belfast.

Rice, Timothy. 1994. *May It Fill Your Soul: Experiencing Bulgarian Music.* Chicago: Univ. of Chicago Press.

Sugarman, Jane. 1989. "The Nightingale and the Partridge: Singing and Gender Among Prespa Albanians." *Ethnomusicology* 33 (2): 191–215.

Additional Reading

Bartók, Béla. 1931. *Hungarian Folk Music.* [Reprinted twice in English]

Kligman, Gail. 1981. *Calus: Symbolic Transformation in Rumanian Ritual.* Chicago: Univ. of Chicago Press.

———. 1988. *The Wedding of the Dead.* Berkeley: Univ. of California Press. Both Kligman works provide good examples of work on southeastern European peasant ritual.

Kodály, Zoltán. 1960. *Folk Music of Hungary.* Budapest: Corvina.

Lockwood, William G. 1975. *European Moslems: Economy and Ethnicity in Western Bosnia.* New York: Academic Press.

Petrović, Ankica. 1977. "Ganga: A Form of Traditional Rural Singing in Yugoslavia." Ph.D. diss., Queen's Univ., Belfast.

Ramet, S., ed. 1994. *Rocking the State: Rock Music and Politics in Eastern Europe and Russia.* Boulder, Colo.: Westview Press. General history of rock music.

Ryback, T. 1990. *Rock around the Bloc.* London: Oxford Univ. Press. General history of rock music through 1990.

Rice, Timothy. 1994. *May It Fill Your Soul: Experiencing Bulgarian Music.* Chicago: Univ. of Chicago Press. Best single introduction to Bosnia; includes an ample CD of music selections.

Sarosi, Balint. 1978. *Gypsy Music.* Budapest: Corvina.

———. 1986. *Folk Music: Hungarian Musical Idiom.* Budapest: Corvina.

Slobin, Mark. 1996. *Retuning Culture: Music and Change in Eastern Europe.* Durham, N.C.: Duke Univ. Press. Survey of questions raised by numerous authors, including those concerning many other countries of central and eastern Europe that have undergone some of the changes that Bosnia has.

Additional Listening

Since the onset of the war in the 1990s, it is difficult to keep track of shifting ownership of record labels and availability of locally produced albums for most of former Yugoslavia. Flory Jagoda has three albums on the Global Village label. The most available albums are popular or "official" ensembles, with older, more traditional sounds being hard to find. Newer evolutions of folk sounds can be heard in recordings by such bands as Hungary's

Muzikas or Bulgaria's Ivo Papazov. Here are some currently available recordings for the regions covered in this chapter:

Bulgaria Compilation. Elektra/Nonesuch 79195.

Bosnia: Echoes of an Endangered World. Smithsonian Folkways CD SF 4047.

Folk Music from Szatmari Region. Hungaroton 18192. [Hungary]

Macedonia: Songs and Dances. Elektra/Nonesuch 72038. [Bulgaria]

Marta Sebestyen: Apocrypha. Rykodisc 1368. [Hungary; a more experimental folk-based album]

Two Girls Started to Sing. Rounder 1055. [Bulgaria]

Vocal and Instrumental Polyphony. Chant du Monde LDY 274897. [Albania]

CHAPTER

6

India/South India

David B. Reck

Imagine in your mind's eye being dropped into the thriving city of Madras in South India. Under the burning tropical sun framed by large white clouds in a brilliant blue sky, beneath rising dust that hangs mistlike over the asphalt streets, palm trees, and whitewashed concrete buildings, you would be faced with a bewildering confusion of elements: The traffic, seemingly chaotic, pits colorful trucks, buses, taxis, and automobiles against a kaleidoscopic array of bicycles, mopeds, handcarts, motorcycles, and three-wheeled motor rickshaws (see Figures 6-1, 6-2). Streams of people, a human river, pour out from the sidewalks and onto the streets. The pungent odor of curries drifts through the air from restaurants and food stalls. Sidewalk vendors sit by their symmetrical arrangements of wristwatches, cutlery, and plastic toys. Others carry bananas,

Figure 6-1
Mount Road, one of the busiest commercial streets in Madras.

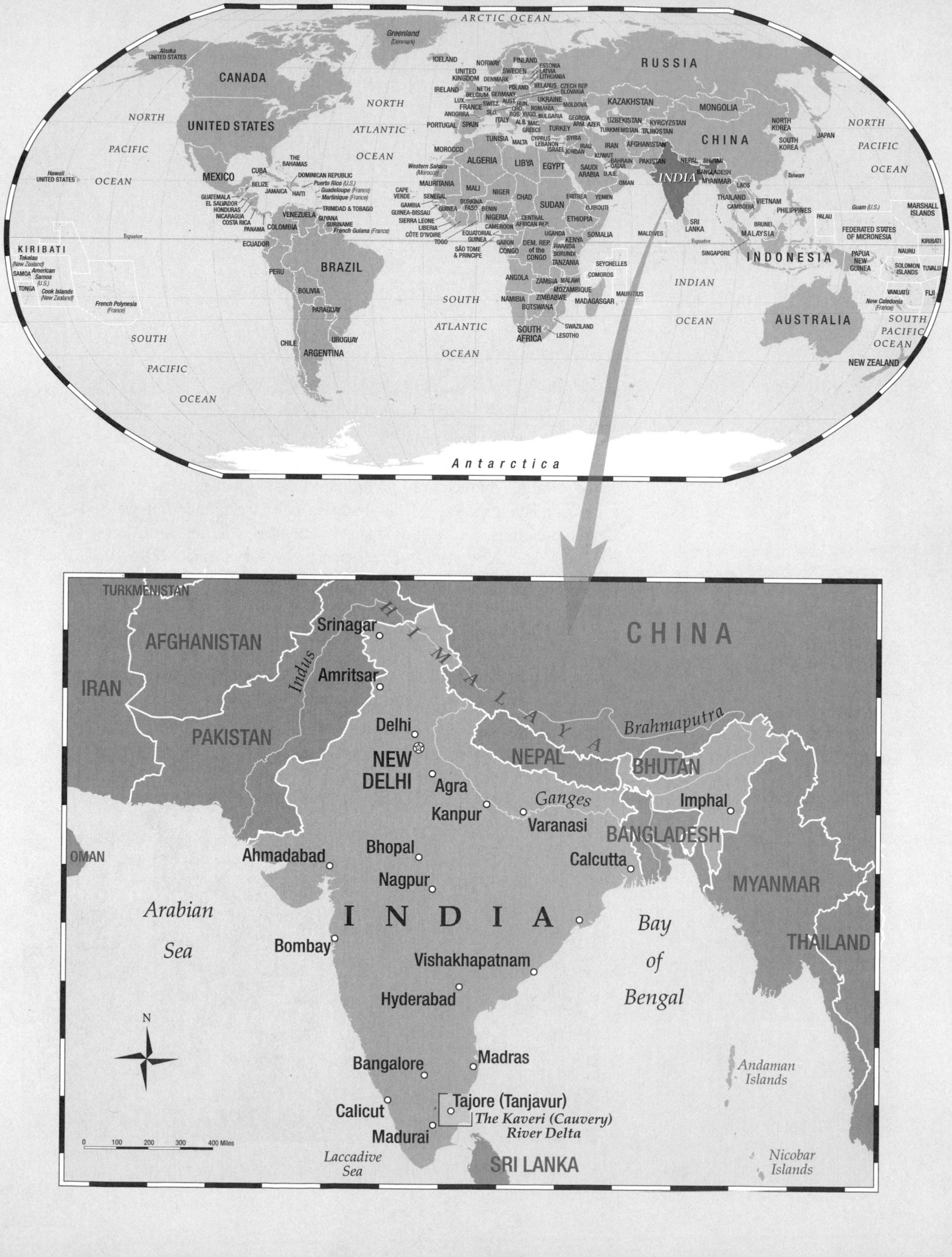
ARCTIC OCEAN
Greenland
RUSSIA
CANADA
UNITED STATES
NORTH ATLANTIC OCEAN
NORTH PACIFIC OCEAN
MEXICO
CHINA
INDIA
KAZAKHSTAN
MONGOLIA
ALGERIA
LIBYA
EGYPT
SUDAN
BRAZIL
PERU
ARGENTINA
SOUTH ATLANTIC OCEAN
SOUTH PACIFIC OCEAN
INDIAN OCEAN
INDONESIA
AUSTRALIA
NEW ZEALAND
SOUTH AFRICA
KIRIBATI
Antarctica
TURKMENISTAN
AFGHANISTAN
IRAN
PAKISTAN
OMAN
Indus
HIMALAYA
CHINA
Srinagar
Amritsar
Delhi
NEW DELHI
Agra
Kanpur
Varanasi
Ganges
Brahmaputra
NEPAL
BHUTAN
Imphal
BANGLADESH
Calcutta
MYANMAR
THAILAND
Bhopal
Ahmadabad
Nagpur
INDIA
Arabian Sea
Bay of Bengal
Bombay
Vishakhapatnam
Hyderabad
N
Bangalore
Madras
Tajore (Tanjavur)
The Kaveri (Cauvery) River Delta
Calicut
Madurai
0 100 200 300 400 Miles
Laccadive Sea
SRI LANKA
Andaman Islands
Nicobar Islands

Figure 6-2
Bunder Street in Georgetown, a section of Madras that grew up around the offices, warehouses, and fort of the British East India Company.

flowers, or rolls of brilliantly colored cloth in baskets on their heads. A roadside astrologer sits under a tree. A few feet down the street (under the next tree) might be a cobbler or a bicycle repairman.

Modern skyscrapers and high-rise apartments abut mud-and-thatch village-style huts. Spacious air-conditioned movie theaters and showrooms for silks, motorcycles, refrigerators, and television sets border crowded bazaars with tiny shops selling jewelry, perfumes, rugs, and spices. Massive mills and factories producing everything from computers to automobiles contrast with the humble establishments of traditional craftsmen working with the tools and methods of generations past.

There are other jarring juxtapositions. A bullock cart with massive wheels creaks under the weight of its load, an electrical transformer. A loin-clothed laborer, a turban protecting his head from the sun, stands momentarily next to a businessman holding a briefcase and dressed in fashionable Madison Avenue suit and tie. Hindu religious rites thousands of years old dedicate a nuclear power generator. The old and the new, the indigenous and the transplanted, coexist. It is almost as if the layers of four thousand years of history have been frozen—in people, objects, beliefs, lifestyles, buildings—to exist simultaneously in an inexplicable present.

The Environment of Indian Musics

History, Culture, Politics

The facts about India are staggering. Its population of over 700 million (one-fifth of the world's population) exists in an area less than half the size of the United States. There are fifteen major languages (most with different alphabets) and dozens of dialects. India's history is a continuous thread going back to the great cities of the Indus Valley civilization (3000–1500 B.C.E.).

Owing perhaps to its geography—a peninsula cut off from neighboring lands by jungles, deserts, and the towering Himalaya mountains—India has developed forms of culture and lifeways that are distinctly its own. Yet its size and its variety of terrain have also produced great regional differences.

The largest such division is between the Hindi-related language groups of the North and the Dravidian-speaking peoples of the South, a division that is paralleled in the two styles of "classical" music: the northern *hindusthani* style and the southern *karnataka* tradition.

Numerous influences have come into India, the earliest being the immigration of Aryan people from central Asia (beginning in the second millennium B.C.E.), whose Indo-European language was related to the languages of Europe. Perhaps the most important later influences came from the Islamic conquests (beginning in the twelfth century C.E.) and the British, who made India "the jewel of their colonies" (seventeenth to twentieth centuries). Cultural ideas, along with technology, came with each group, but a characteristic pattern has emerged each time: The new ideas (and people) were absorbed, assimilated, and digested, emerging finally in a new and undeniably Indian synthesis.

In music this synthesis and transformation can be seen in the relationship between the *ragas* (music/expressive modes)* and forms of India and those of Iran and the Middle East (the Islamic influence), as well as in the adaptation of the European violin, clarinet, and harmonium—all played in a distinctly Indian manner—from the English.

The arts, along with the sciences and philosophical and religious thought, have flourished in India from the earliest times. Great kings and great dynasties built thousands of magnificent palaces, temples, forts, towers, tombs, and cities. Indian sculpture in stone, wood, or bronze and Indian painting (notably the book-sized miniatures) rank among the greatest masterpieces of world art. Traditional literature is dominated by the two major epics—the *Ramayana* and the *Mahabharata* (written down between 400 B.C.E. and 400 C.E. but believed to exist in oral traditions much earlier). There have been dozens of major Indian authors, poets, and playwrights, however; the most famous was Kalidasa, who lived in the fourth and fifth centuries. There are numerous collections of stories and fables.

Indian soil has also been the locus of great religious development. The four *Vedas* (believed to have crystalized as early as 1200 B.C.E.) and the later *Upanishads* contain religious and abstract philosophical thought of such logic and beauty that they have fascinated Western thinkers such as Thoreau and scientists such as Robert Oppenheimer. The *Puranas* (first century C.E. to the present) are filled with the myths of the gods and goddesses of popular Hinduism. Thinkers such as Shankara (?788–829) rank

*An English equivalent follows the italicized word here and, where appropriate, throughout this chapter.

among the great philosophers of the world. The ancient physical and mental disciplines of yoga are now practiced by millions of Americans and Europeans and taught in universities and meditation centers, and even on television. In recent times, activist saints such as Mahatma Gandhi (1869–1948) have preached nonviolence combined with radical social action to a world addicted to military power, violence, and exploitation.

Excellence in the arts continues today in many areas. Musicians such as Ali Akbar Khan or Ravi Shankar are as well known in the West as rock and pop stars. Satyajit Ray was one of the acknowledged masters of contemporary cinema; R. K. Narayan's and Salman Rushdie's novels, written in English, have won widespread critical acclaim. And there are hundreds of poets, musicians, painters, authors, filmmakers, and thinkers of great depth and skill whose work is not known abroad. Finally, there are the many humble crafters, carrying out centuries-old traditions in weaving, fabric painting, embroidery, metalwork, wood carving, jewelry, basketry, and other crafts, who support an export trade of fine handmade goods admired throughout the world.

The problems of modern India are immense. Successive governments have attacked but not completely solved serious problems of overpopulation, terrorism, social order, and an agriculture dependent on monsoon rains, which may either bring famine if they fail or devastating floods and hurricanes if they are too heavy.

The political system, based on British parliamentary rule, is democratic, though it can appear chaotic to an outsider. Change is occurring in the face

Figure 6-3
The traditional wedding of a young couple is laced with ancient ritual and music. Note the garlanded images of Hindu deities on the wall.

of the apparent immovable inertia of age-old traditions. There are, therefore, steel mills and locomotive factories and nuclear power plants; there are soft drinks, modern airline and railway systems, computers everywhere, well-equipped armed forces, and a growing and prosperous middle class with world-class competence and brilliance particularly in the sciences, technology, and business. There are subways, skyscrapers, discos, and jazz bars. At the same time there is the juxtaposition of the new with the archaic—in customs, lifeways, ways of seeing, and ways of doing. The old, traditional ways survive through all the changes of time and history (see Figure 6-3). This coexistence is part of the amazement and fascination of India—and perhaps also part of its strength.

Many Musics

Imagine strolling through one of the more traditional neighborhoods of Madras, such as the section of Mylapore, where we come into contact with many forms of music. The music that we hear would reflect many levels of folk or popular or classical art and many layers of society. It may be built on ancient traditions passed down by generations, or new ones; it may have sprouted and grown on Indian soil, or it may be an exotic transplant, undergoing a process that, unless stopped by outright rejection, will ultimately metamorphose it into an Indian synthesis (see Figure 6-4).

CD I Track 24

The predominant music here and elsewhere in South India, blasting out of house radios or loudspeakers mounted at the front doors of shops and tea-stalls, is the sound of "cine music." Listen to the recording of "Engal kalyanam" ("Our Wedding"; CD Selection 24). Indian pop music is called "cine music" or "film music" because almost all the songs come from hit movies in Hindi, Tamil, or other regional languages. Virtually all movies are musicals. Cine music is a curious and sometimes bizarre blend of East and West: choppy and hyperactive melodies, often in "oriental" scales, are belted out by nasal singers over Latin rhythms and an eclectic accompaniment that may include trap set, electric organs and guitars, violins, xylophones, celeste, bongos, *sitar, tabla,* or bamboo flute. More recently some genres of Indian pop music have been crafted to sound exactly like their Western pop counterparts, with only their lyrics in Indian languages making them distinguishable from the latest hit tune. The lyrics of cine songs tend to focus on the eternal trivia and complications of love and romance. "Engal kalyanam" takes a light-hearted look at the commotion and excitement of an Indian wedding, with the ever-present relatives and the joyful feelings of the happy couple.

Engal kalyanam

Our marriage is a confusion/commotion marriage!
  Sons-in-law spend for the marriage
    and the father-in-law puts up the *pandal*[1]
      to receive gifts.

Morning is the wedding, and evening is the wedding night.

Enliven! Love marriage.[2]
Tomorrow won't the marriage altar give the garlands?[3]
Won't the drums drum with the pipes?

The lovers' story is performed in the eyes.
How much struggle: to perform in the eyes!
A colorful chariot is running beside me;
Heaven is coming to us!

Mother-in-law is putting on eye makeup
And the sons-in-law are staring at the mirror;
Processions wind along the streets with firecrackers,
And all are giving their blessings.

Shall we have ten to sixteen children?
Shall the trimness of the body be lost?
You hated men,
(Yet) you gave desire!
I am the God of Love!
You are the reason!

Your cheeks are inviting me;
The thoughts are asking for one.
Eyes are like bright lightning;
What are the pleasures we haven't experienced?

He [father-in-law] had prayed to the God of Tirupati[4]
To perform the marriage in Tirupati
So that they [the bride and groom] might live
prosperous lives.

Sons-in-law should come home
and give a send-off to the father-in-law
so that he can take up *sanyasin*![5]

—translation from the Tamil by S. B. Rajeswari

1. *Pandal:* a temporary wedding canopy of bamboo and palm leaves.

2. A "love marriage" is contrasted with a marriage arranged by parents, often with pragmatic objectives.

3. The bride and groom exchange garlands at an important part of the ceremony.

4. Tirupati is the site of the great temple to Lord Venkateswara, the most popular shrine in South India.

5. That is, the new son-in-law should take over the responsibilities of his wife's father, who can then retire and take up a religious life (*sanyasin*).

The same musical characteristics hold for many of the forms of folk music and street entertainments: for snake charmers piping on their *punjis* (a kind of gourd-and-reed bagpipe), for mendicants playing small gongs or the conchshell *shanku,* for musicians accompanying acrobats and dancers or street theater.

Figure 6-4
A poster advertises *Thillana Mohanambal*, a popular Tamil movie adapted from a famous novel about the romance and marriage of a dancer and a musician.

Often forms of music are connected with forms of worship. Each large temple has its musicians: singers of ritual songs, performers of *harikatha bhagavatham* (a kind of storytelling and sermon interspersed with classical and religious song) or the religious ensemble of double-reed *nagaswaram* and drums, which provide music for temple and household ceremonies, processions, and weddings.

There may also be unmodified transplants. Student rock bands play hits from England and the United States; Westernized clubs may have a dance combo or jazz band; Christian churches sing hymns or mount a Christmas production of Handel's *Messiah.* And there is the curious hybrid from the British military bands of the colonial era: the street bands, which—sometimes elaborately uniformed—play Western band instruments (bass and snare drums, cymbals, trumpets, trombones, clarinets, saxophones, and so on). These groups blast mostly unison melodies from the pop music repertoire to claphammer percussion as they march in wedding, temple, and political processions.

We might also hear more traditional types of music. Minstrels carrying simple instruments like the one-stringed gourd and bamboo *ektara* or the washtub bass–like *kudam* (literally "clay pot") sing from door to door hoping for a few *paisa* (pennies) or a gift of rice.

Finally, echoing from concert halls, from temples, from *nagaswaram* piping ensembles, and from radios we would hear *karnataka sangeeta* (both words are accented on the second syllable), the classical music of South India. We call it classical not because it is necessarily more complicated or polished or difficult to perform than many of the folk traditions, but because it has a status as a cultivated high art form in India similar to that of "classical," or "art," or "serious" music in the West. This status is today shared by the classical dance traditions such as *bharata natyam, kathak,* or *odissi.*

Listen to the example of *karnataka* music on the CD (CD Selection 25), or to any of the recordings recommended in the discography. Try to become familiar with the sound and style of *karnataka sangeeta* so that you can form a background for the explorations and analysis that follow later in this chapter. Make a list of some of the characteristics of the music. Try humming or singing along with the slower passages. Best of all, try listening to *karnataka* music intensively over several days or a week, even while you read, talk, daydream, or do chores. Try to absorb as much of the music as you can.

Karnataka Sangeeta, The Classical Music of South India

The tradition of the flutist T. Viswanathan and drummer Ramnad V. Raghavan, who play the classical music example in the recorded selection, is called *karnataka sangeeta,* music of the Carnatic, the southern plateau. Its roots lie in the distant past. The earliest extant theoretical work is the *Natya shastra* by Bharata, a treatise on theater, dance, and music dating from between the second century B.C.E. to the fifth century C.E.

But the actual sound and practice of Indian classical music, as it grew and developed through generation after generation of musicians working in the courts of kings or in the immense temple complexes, has been lost. One of the characteristics of an oral tradition such as that in Indian music is that it lives day to day in performance, in human beings, the musicians.

From about the thirteenth century scholars began to notice a difference in India between the classical style of the North (today called *hindusthani* music) and of the South (*karnataka sangeeta,* or Carnatic music). While both styles use *ragas* (melodic modes) and *talas* (metric cycles) and have many similarities, the systems also differ considerably. We might say (simplifying tremendously) that the northern style and its instruments (like the *sitar, sarod,* and *tabla*) have been more greatly influenced by Persian and other elements of Islamic culture. In *hindusthani* music seemingly timeless broad improvisations eventually evolve into sections of brilliant virtuosity. By contrast the *karnataka* style of the more orthodox Hindu South is built around an immense repertoire of precomposed songs. The musical texture tends to sound more busy and active, more consistently ornamented.

Karnataka sangeeta began to stabilize into its present shape in the sixteenth century. Purandara Dasa (1484–1564), sometimes called the father of *karnataka* music, composed not only many songs but also the standard lessons and exercises that are still memorized by every music student today. A "golden age" occurred between about 1750 and 1850 when the forms and performance style that have continued to the present day were set. Thousands of new *kritis* (compositions) were composed, new *ragas* were invented, and the conceptual forms of older *ragas* expanded. Three great saint-composers dominate this period and the *karnataka sangeeta* tradition as a whole: Syama Sastri (1762–1827), Tyagaraja (1767–1847), and Muttuswamy Dikshitar (1776–1836) (Figure 6-5). A clever South-Indian proverb compares the music of the *trimurthy,* the "three deities." Dikshitar is said to have written music that is like a coconut: The "hard shell" of his brilliantly

Figure 6-5
Three great saint-composers (left to right): Muttuswamy Dikshitar, Tyagaraja, and Syama Sastri, as seen in contemporary prints.

intellectual musical structures and complex, scholarly, and sometimes esoteric texts "must be broken to taste the sweet nut and milk inside." By contrast, Syama Sastri's music is said to be like a banana: "The fruit is not so difficult to get to, but still one must peel off the bitter skin"—Sastri's complicated rhythms and *talas* (cycles) of five and seven beats—"before enjoying its flavor." But Tyagaraja's songs are said to be like fresh, ripe grapes; both poetry and melody are immediately accessible: "To enjoy it one needs merely to bite into it. Even the skin is soft and sweet." It is no wonder, then, that Tyagaraja's extraordinarily beautiful songs dominate the repertoire, loved and held like precious gems in the hearts and memory of musicians and music lovers alike (Isaac 1967: 23–24).

A Performance Segment: The Sound World

Now that we have become familiar with the sound and style—and some of the background—of *karnataka* music,* we can begin to explore the music itself, how it is put together and shaped in performance. What we might call a "performance segment" is a unit in a concert that is built by the musician around the central core of a precomposed piece, a song. This unit may include various types of improvisation in the same *raga* and *tala* as the core piece. A concert is made up of a series of such performance segments (as many as twelve or fourteen), each in a different *raga* and based on a different composition.

The individual South-Indian musician can exercise great flexibility in the shaping of each performance segment. That is, he or she can select from various options and procedures. We shall look into some of these possibilities later. First, listen to the performance built on "Ivaraku jucinadi," a short but beautiful song by the great poet and composer Tyagaraja (CD Selection 25). The performers are T. Viswanathan, who plays the bamboo flute, and Ramnad V. Raghavan, who accompanies on the *mridangam* (pronounced "mm-ree-*dun*-gum") drum (Figure 6-6). Both musicians come from celebrated musical families and have concertized extensively in India and throughout the world.

CD 2
Track 1

*Though women excel in many areas of *karnatak* music—voice, violin, flute, and *veena,* for example—and many of the most famous *karnatak* concert artists are women, drumming and percussion artists have tended to be exclusively male.

Figure 6-6
T. Viswanathan, flute; Ramnad V. Raghavan, *mridangam.*

Courtesy of T. Viswanathany

Instruments

Viswanathan's instrument is a side-blown flute made of hollowed-out bamboo, a little less than a foot and a half in length. The mouth hole and seven (sometimes eight) finger holes are burned into the bamboo with a hot metal rod. Since only a single *raga* scale of seven tones to the octave naturally occurs with the placement of the holes (*raga harikambhoji,* equivalent in Western music to a major scale with a flat seventh), the musician must achieve the tuning of the other seventy-one *melakarta* scales—as well as the subtle intonation and ornaments of each of hundreds of *ragas*—with intricate variances of fingering (partially covering some holes) and embouchure (changing the angle of the breath in the mouth hole to flatten or sharpen the pitch). Thus, while the South-Indian bamboo flute itself is perhaps one of the world's simplest instruments, its playing technique is extraordinarily complex.

Raghavan's instrument, the barrel-shaped double-headed *mridangam,* is the principal drum of South-Indian classical music. Its body is made from a hollowed-out log of jackwood. The leather skins of the two drumheads are held by leather strapping buttressed by movable pegs jammed beneath to aid in tuning. Both heads are made from multiple layers of leather, the outer layers cut with circular holes in the middle. The lower (untuned) left-hand head has a blob of wet wheat paste applied in the center to give it a booming sound. The center of the right-hand head (which is tuned to the tonic note, the *sruti,* of the soloist, in this case the flute) has a hard, metallic black spot made from many finely polished layers of rice paste and other ingredients. The sophistication of these drumheads, combined with the hand and finger techniques of the drummer, makes possible up to fifteen or more distinct sounds (many at different pitches). The use of the fingers as miniature drumsticks allows the drummer to play passages of incredible speed and complexity. The mridangam is propped horizontally in front of the player, resting between knee and ankle, as he sits on a mat on the floor.

The Ensemble

One way of looking at the music of India is to divide the musical texture (and the instruments) into functional layers. On the recording, you may have noticed that the *sruti*-box plays drone notes (to be discussed next) and the flute plays melody notes. There is no harmony, that is, not in the way that we in the West are used to. When the *mridangam* enters, a new functional layer appears: the rhythmic. Thus we might draw a picture using symbols for each functional layer (Figure 6-7).

Figure 6-7
The three layers of the musical texture.

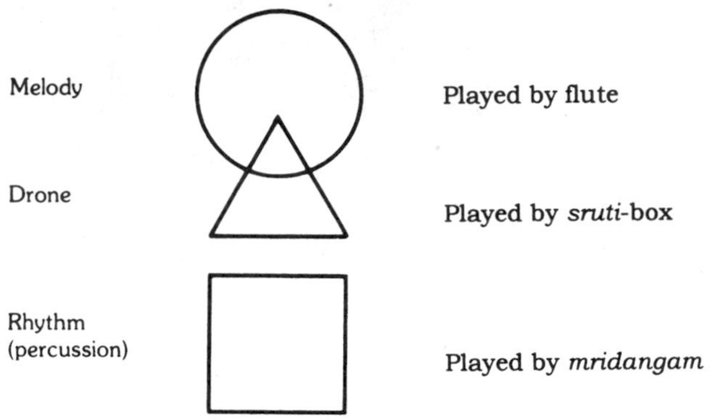

In our recording, two musicians on only two instruments, the bamboo flute and *mridangam,* with the background drone provided by an electronic *sruti*-box, can take care of all the functions necessary for the texture of *karnataka* music. But one of the marvels of the tradition is that instruments and musicians can be added to each functional layer. One could in a large ensemble have as many as ten musicians working within the three functional layers (see Figure 6-8). Because each layer is strictly defined by function and because within each layer there are traditionally accepted ways of doing things, ways for the musicians to relate to each other, there is never any confusion. There is not even (among professionals) a need for rehearsals. Musicians simply appear for a concert, sit down, and play.

Sruti (The Drone)

Central to the texture of much of India's music, folk and classical, is the idea of the drone, an unchanging tone or group of tones against which the melody moves. (We in the West are familiar with drone notes in bagpiping, five-string banjo playing, fiddling, and the mountain dulcimer.) The drone,

Figure 6-8
Layers of the musical texture with added instruments.

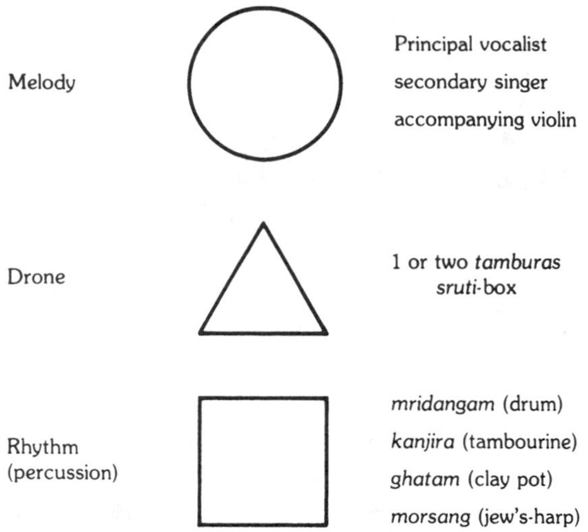

or *sruti* (pronounced "*shroo*-ti"), marks the tonal center—the center of gravity—for the melody and its *raga.* Unobtrusive, calm, quiet, static, the drone is like the earth from which the melodies of the musicians fly, from which they start and to which they return.

CD 2
Track 1

In our recording you may have noticed that the sound of the *sruti*-box is the first thing heard, before the entrance of the flute, providing a constant background for the performance. In *karnataka* music the notes used for the drone are the tonal center and a perfect fifth above it. Indian musicians may choose whatever tonal center is convenient for their instrument or their vocal range. For simplicity we have written our notation in concert C, although the *sruti,* the tonic or tonal center, is not fixed but can be transposed to any pitch (Music Example 6-1). Each note of a *raga* relates to drone notes in varying degrees of consonance and dissonance. The dissonant notes tend to "pull" (almost as if in a gravitational field) toward tones that blend with the drone.

Music Example 6-1
The tonal center and perfect fifth as drone notes.

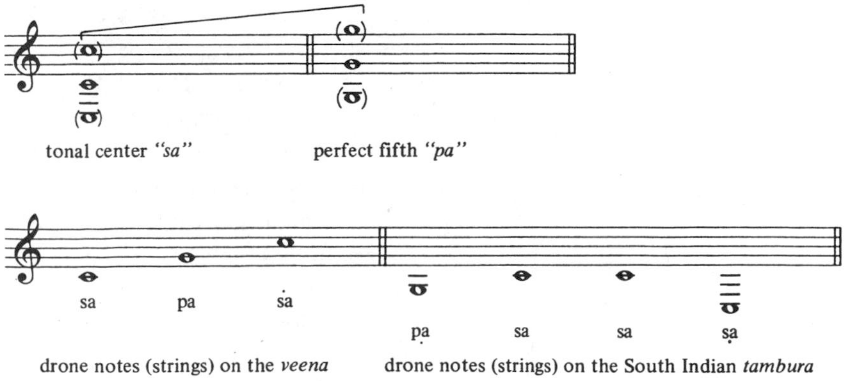

Raga (The Expressive Mode)

CD 2
Track 1

Listen again to the first three minutes of the performance by T. Viswanathan (CD Selection 25). Use a stopwatch or a wristwatch (with hour, minute, and second hands starting at twelve o'clock) to help identify sections in our analysis.

The flute begins alone (without the drum) in a kind of free-flowing melodic improvisation called *alapana.* The melody evolves gradually, without a sense of beat or time cycles. Pauses between musical phrases are filled in with drone notes. There are slides and tremolos, trills, bends, barely heard grace notes, and vibratos—a whole range of *gamaka* (ornamentation). In many *ragas* the tones are sharper or flatter than those we are used to in Western classical musical, particularly on the fixed-pitch tuning of the piano. And the intervals of the scale might be quite different. But in this case—*raga sankarabharanam* (pronounced "*shan*-ka-ra-*bha*-ra-nam")—the basic unornamented scale (if we were to hear it) is the same as the Western major scale. Try to observe the many ways in which the *raga sankarabharanam* in performance is made to sound different from the major scale.

The ancient texts define a *raga* as "that which colors the mind." In fact, in Sanskrit the primary meaning of the word *raga* is "coloring, dyeing, tingeing." This connection with generating feelings and emotions in human beings, "coloring the mind," is important because a *raga* is much more than what we in the West call a scale. A *raga* is in some ways a mystical expressive force with a musical personality all its own. This "musical personality" is, in part, technical—a collection of notes, scale, intonations, ornaments, characteristic melodic phrases, and so on. Each *raga* has its rules and moves, something like the game of chess. While some of the facts about *ragas* can be verbalized and written down, a musician does not memorize a *raga* or learn it from a book. (*Ragas* are too elusive for that!) Rather, one gets to know a *raga* gradually—by contact with it, hearing it performed by others, performing it oneself—almost as one gets to know a friend by his or her face, clothes, voice, and personality.

Traditionally *ragas* are said to have "musical-psychological resemblances." A particular *raga* may be associated with certain human emotions, specific colors, various Hindu deities, a season of the year, a time of day, or certain magical properties. Contemporary South-Indian musicians are not overly concerned with these associations, but they are aware of the expressive force of *ragas,* their power, and their capability to create deep feelings in the human heart.

T. Viswanathan's *alapana* uses the scale, melodic phrases, intonation, and ornaments that mark the *raga* as *sankarabharanam,* the *raga* set by the composed song that forms the core of the performance segment. *Sankara* (lit. "auspicious") is one of the names of the great god Shiva, and *bharanam* means "upholding, supporting, preserving." This ancient and powerful *raga* is considered to be exceedingly complex, a major *raga* whose many facets may be explored by a musician in lengthy *alapanas* or other forms of improvisation. Though serious in tone, it also has a sweetness to it; and it is perhaps this pleasing quality that makes it one of the most popular *ragas* in the *karnataka* tradition.

Scale, *Raga sankarabharanam*

The *sankarabharanam* scale is shown in Music Example 6–2 both in plain notation and ornamented as it might be sung by a South-Indian musician. It has the same seven notes in both the ascending and descending scales. Almost all the notes may be decorated with appropriate oscillations, slides, bends, flickering turns, and sliding glissandos: a network of *gamakas* that also give *sankarabharanam* its personality. The subtlety of these ornaments cannot be shown precisely in notation, but they may be heard if you listen closely.

Music Example 6-2
Raga sankarabharanam, scale plain and with *gamaka* (ornamentation). Transcription by David B. Reck.

CD 2
Track 1

Try singing or humming along with the opening passages of the *alpana* (CD Selection 25). You can notice two things from this example (and from the recording). First, a "note" in *karnataka* music is not necessarily a single tone (as in one piano key); rather, it can be a whole constellation of tones, a miniature universe of sound. Second, movement between tones tends not to be in discrete steps like a staircase (as in a piano keyboard), but continuous, with portamentos and glissandos (Figure 6-9).

Certain notes in *raga sankarabharanam* seem to be stable places of rest. Melodic phrases may come to closure on these tones, center on them, emphasize them, and extend them into notes of longer duration. We might call these centering notes "pillar tones" (Music Example 6-3).

Finally, there are special note groups, melody bits, and musical phrases that are typical of *raga sankarabharanam.* These are like the face and physical features of a person; to a musician they are the most obvious features of the *raga.*

Viswanathan's *alapana* exposition of *raga sankarabharanam* is relatively brief, about three minutes in length (CD Selection 25), and shows careful planning of its proportions. Using a stopwatch or wristwatch you can trace

Figure 6-9
Notes and melodic movement, compared with piano.

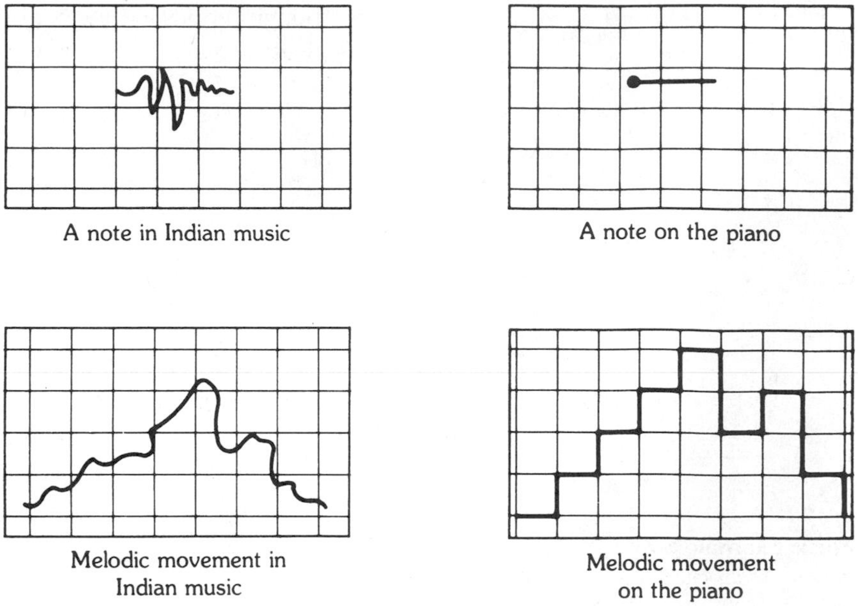

Music Example 6-3
"Pillar tones" in *raga sankarabharanam.*

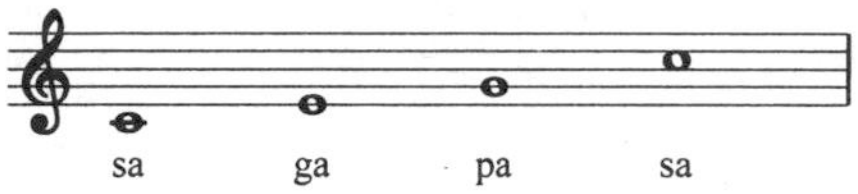

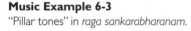

the commentary that follows. Beginning on the phrase *ga, ri, sa, sa* (E, D, C, C), he begins his exploration of the lower octave, centering on *sa* (middle C). At about :15 he moves down to a centering on lower *pa* (G), playing beautiful phrases in the lower register of the flute. At 1:00 he plays a long note on *sa* (middle C) and begins the next stage of the *alapana:* the ascent through the middle range to the upper octave. After a brief centering on *ga* (E), he moves up to *pa* (G) as his pillar tone, and the phrases gain more speed and energy. At 2:00 he reaches high *sa* (c′) and the third stage of the *alapana*—exploration of the highest octave and virtuosic sweeps through the full range of the instrument. Reaching up to high *ri* and *ga* (d′ and e′) he breaks into *brikkas,* lightning-fast phrases that bring the improvisation to a climax. Finally at about 2:45 he begins (as he likes to put it) his "return home," the final descent to a coming-to-rest on *sa* (middle C) at 3:00. Viswanathan's improvisation, though brief, is in fact an encapsulated form of *alapanas* that may be up to twenty minutes long. As he notes in his classic scholarly work on the form (Viswanathan 1975), the basic plan, with minor variants, remains the same.

Tala (The Time Cycle)

Immediately after the *alapana* comes the rendition of the *kriti* ("composition"). The *kriti* "Ivaraku jucinadi" is of course in the same *raga* as the *alapana,* since the core piece sets the *raga* for the entire performance segment. But a new element has been added along with the drum: a *tala,* or time cycle.

The *tala* in this case is *Adi,* a time cycle of eight beats subdivided 4 + 2 + 2. *Adi tala* may also be counted with the hands, as shown in Figure 6-10. The *tala* cycle, once it has entered along with the *mridangam* drum, will continue now until the end of the performance segment. Try counting the *tala* along with the recording. Many *tala* cycles also occur in slow tempo. In this case one would add an extra pulse, an "and" between each beat, as in Figure 6-11.

Figure 6-10
Counting in *Adi tala.*

Adi tala: 4 + 2 + 2 = 8 beats

1 2 3 4 /5 6 /7 8 //

Clap ⏟ Clap Clap

Finger Count* Wave Wave

*2nd beat = little finger and thumb.
3rd beat = ring finger and thumb.
4th beat = middle finger and thumb.

Figure 6-11
Counting in slow tempo with added pulses (compare with Figure 6-10).

Adi tala (slow tempo)

1 . 2 . 3 . 4 . /5 . 6 . /7 . 8 . //
(&) (&) (&) (&) (&) (&) (&) (&)

Clap ⏟ Clap Clap

Finger count Wave Wave

The *tala* cycles of *karnataka* music differ from the meters of Western music (time signatures of 4/4, 3/4, 2/4, 6/8, and so on) in a significant way. *Talas* may be built from uneven groupings of beats (4 + 2 + 2, 1 + 2, and so on). These groupings are marked by hand claps. Even *talas* with the same total number of beats may sound different because of the different accents created by the beat groupings and by the hand claps.

Musical Structure: Improvisation

The classical music of India—North and South—has two facets: *kalpita sangeeta,* or precomposed music, and *manodharma sangeeta,* improvised music. We have seen that in a typical concert there is a balance between the tasteful and beautiful rendering of the composition of the great composers and the contemporary musicians' exploration of their own creative imagination and skill. These balances work through an intricate framework of procedures and possibilities, and the musician's improvisation itself works within the limits of a kind of "musical tool kit" handed down by his tradition.

There are four major types of improvisation found in *karnataka* music:

1. 1. *Alapana* is a free-flowing gradual exposition and exploration of the *raga,* its facets, characteristic *gamaka,* and moods. Its phrases evolve in proselike "breath rhythms." It is improvised before a composition and introduces the *raga* of the composition.

   The *alapana* follows a general plan set both by the tradition as a whole and by the individual improvisational habits of the musician. Both combine to make the musician's tool kit. *Alapanas* are often shaped by a centering on "pillar tones" that progress higher and by a gradual climb in pitch to the highest range of the instrument or voice. There is then a quick descent back down to the middle register, with an ending on the tonal center. The slower phrases are occasionally broken by quick virtuoso bursts of *brikkas.*

2. *Tanam* is a more rhythmic exposition of the *raga,* a lively and strongly articulated working through of combinations of note groups. Although *tanam* is not restricted by the cycles of any *tala,* it does have a strong "beat sense." Its highly rhythmic phrases tend to fall within constantly changing patterns of twos and threes (♫'s and ♫♪'s), setting up melodic and rhythmic units of asymmetrical length. *Tanam* is shaped like an *alapana,* moving from low phrases to a high peak, followed by a descent. *Tanam* occurs after the *alapana* and before the composition. Viswanathan chooses not to use this form in his performance (CD Selection 25).

3. *Niraval* is an improvised variation on one melody line, or phrase, of the song. It takes the words and their rhythmic setting as a basis, spinning out gradually more and more elaborate and virtuosic melodic variations. (In an instrumental performance, the words are thought of by the performer, though they are not, of course, "heard" by the audience.) Because the same words appear over and over again in different melodic settings, an almost mystical transformation occurs: New meanings take shape and disappear, hidden associations emerge, and subtle nuances come into focus.

   Niraval occurs within the composition, following the melody line on which it is based. It fits within the *tala* cycle of the piece (as well as the *raga* mode). Viswanathan also opts to skip this form in his performance.

4. *Svara kalpana* ("imagined notes") occurs after *niraval*—that is, in the middle of a composition—or after a complete run-through of the song. It fits into both the *raga* and the *tala* of the composition. *Svara kalpana* is without a text; instead, it is sung to the names of the notes: *sa, ri, ga, ma,* and so on. The improvised sections return again and again to the "island" of a theme taken from the composition. *Svara kalpana* improvisations increase in length gradually from a few notes (before the theme) to extended passages many cycles in length and full of complicated rhythmic and melodic invention and

clever calculation. In some respects *svara kalpana,* especially when sung, is similar in sound to the "scat singing" of jazz.

Musical Structure: The Kriti

All compositions in *karnataka* music are songs, melodies with words. The composer is also a poet (although his poetry may be free verse), and the text—even when it deals with love—is usually of a religious nature. The thousands of songs of the tradition have been passed down from generation to generation like jewels on a string. But because they are not precisely notated, but instead taught and learned orally, there is no definitive version of a song (in the sense that a symphony or sonata by Beethoven or Mozart exists in an "original," which has been written and can be printed on paper). As it passes through different lines of teachers and disciples, *gurus* and *sishyas,* on its journey from the composer to the present, the same composition may take different shapes. Yet a composition, a song, remains itself—different versions coexist—just as a jazz tune remains itself despite the many interpretations of different singers and musicians over the years.

The *kriti* (composition) is the major form of South-Indian concert performance.* It is amazingly flexible, almost liquid in its structure and expressive potential; some *kritis* are tiny, while others are massive pieces extending ten or fifteen minutes in length. Most of the major composers—such as the "big three" of Tyagaraja, Dikshitar, and Sastri—have concentrated on *kritis* for the expression of their musical and poetic thought. Each treats the form in his own way, with his own touch. The *kriti* may be performed alone on a concert program, for its own intrinsic beauty, or it may serve as the core piece for improvisations that are woven before, in the middle of, or after it.

The *kriti* has three sections:

1. *Pallavi* ("the sprouting," "blossoming"): the opening section. The name of the *kriti* comes from the first several words of the *pallavi*—*Ivaraku jucinadi* in the *kriti* of Viswanathan's performance. The *pallavi*—both melody and words—is extremely important because part of it recurs (rondolike) after the next two sections. Its size is often expanded through *sangati* (variations) on its melody lines.
2. *Anupallavi* ("after the sprouting, blossoming"): a secondary, contrasting section, often pushing to a kind of climax before a return to the *pallavi* theme. It also may be expanded through composed *sangati* on its melody lines. In some *kritis* there is a recapitulation of the tune of the *anupallavi* (but not its words) to form the last part of the next section, the *charanam.*
3. *Charanam* ("verse" or "foot"): usually a more relaxed, tranquil section. Occasionally it is a series of energetic "verses" that alternate

*Other forms are the *varnam,* a kind of "concert etude"; the slow and stately *padam* and the lively *tillana* and *javali* (all three adapted from the dance tradition); the *bhajana,* a devotational song; and the *pallavi,* a single melodic phrase expanded through manipulation and improvisation.

with the *pallavi* theme. As noted, the latter half of the *charanam* may incorporate all or part of the melody of the *anupallavi,* giving the impression of a kind of recapitulation. There is a rondolike return to the *pallavi* theme at the very end.

There may be an additional section, lively and highly rhythmic, called a *chitta svaram* if it has no words or a *svara sahityam* if it has a text. It may be interposed after the *anupallavi,* the *charanam,* or both, before the reprise of the *pallavi* theme. Often this section will be added by a later composer or musician.

We can map out the form of the *kriti* as shown in Figure 6-12. There are, of course, any number of diversions from this scheme. But many of the *kritis* of the *karnataka* music tradition can fit into or otherwise relate to our map. The three major sections are set off in performance by a pause, during which the drummer comes to the forefront with cadential rhythmic patterns.

All in all, the *kriti* as a composition is a magnificent form, balancing repetition, reprises, and melodic recapitulation of larger units with variation and new and unexpected material. Its poetic text gives it an extra dimension, as does the *raga,* the "mysical expressive force" from which its melodies are spun.

Figure 6-12
Structure of the *kriti.*

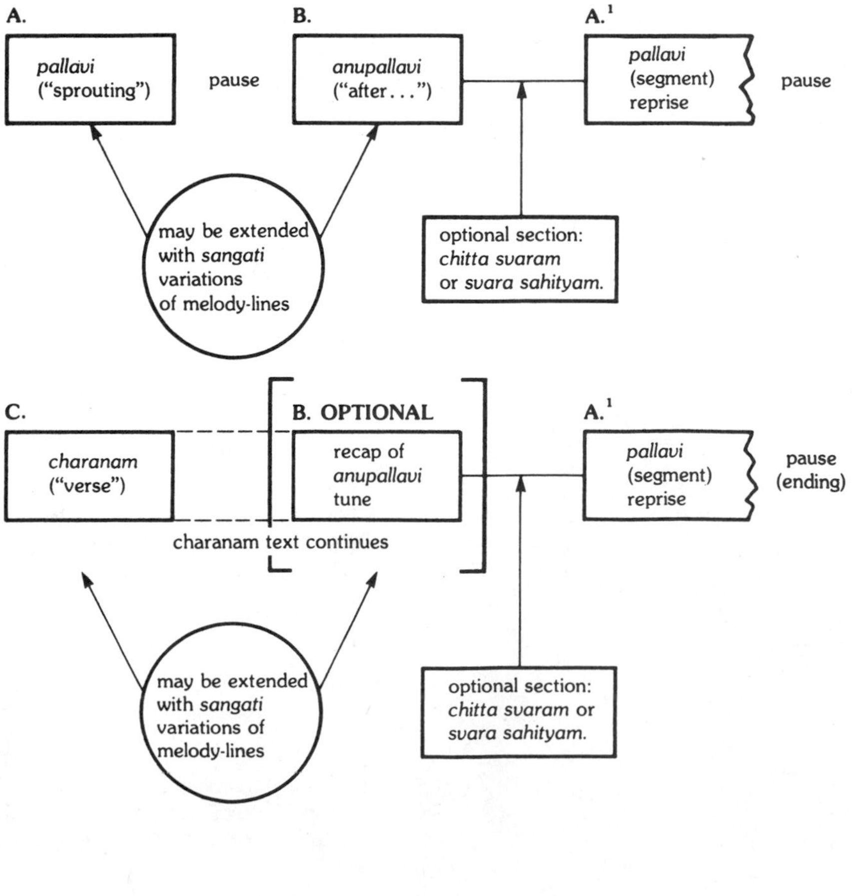

CD 2
Track 1

A transcription of Viswanathan's notation of his version of "Ivaraku jucinadi" is given in Music Example 6-4. All melodic lines in this *kriti* begin 1½ beats after the first pulse of the *tala* cycle (their ending overlapping into the first 1½ beats of the next *tala* cycle).

Music Example 6-4

Kriti "Ivaraku jucinadi" in notation. Transcription by David B. Reck.

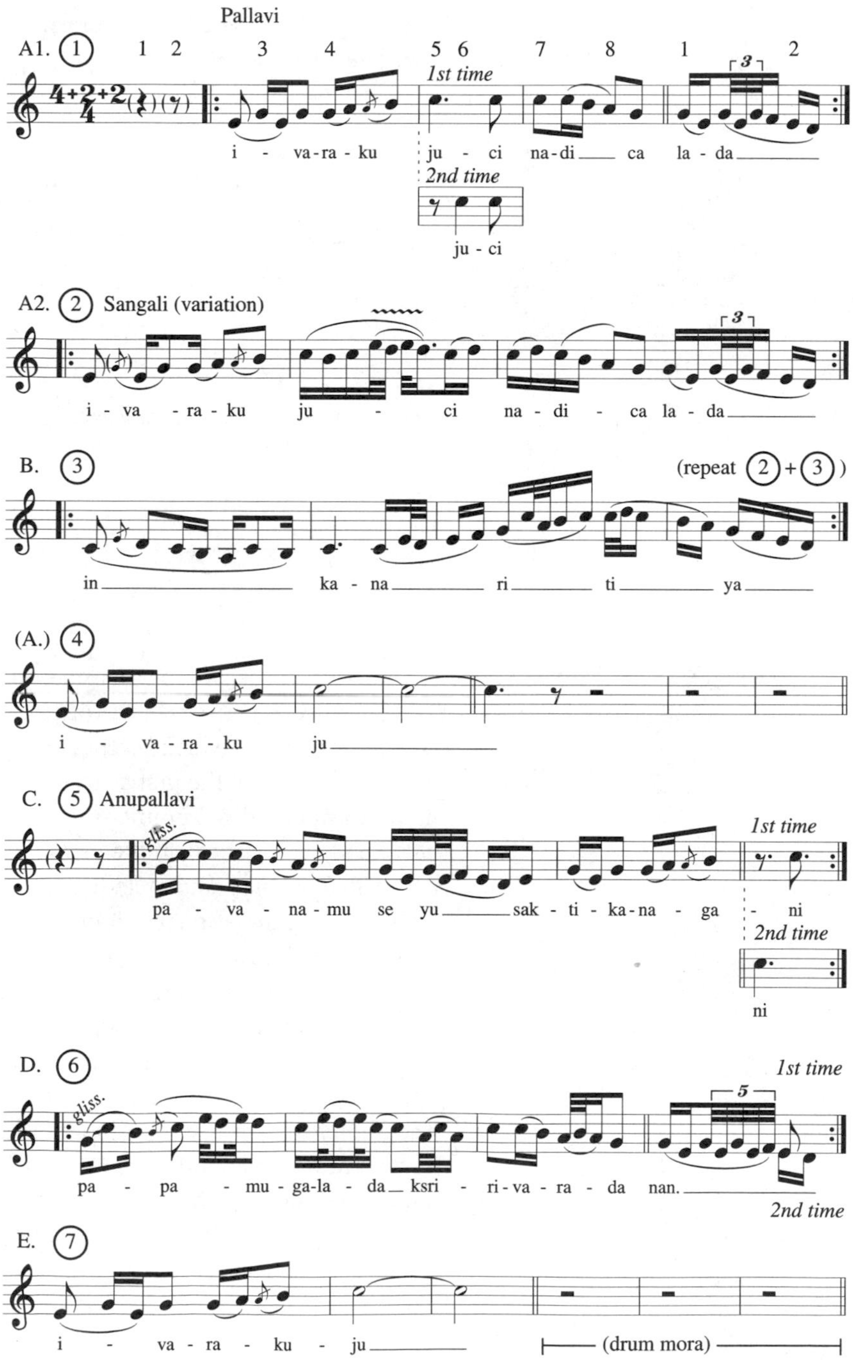

(continued)

Music Example 6-4
(continued)

CD 2
Track 1

The *pallavi* section begins at about 3 minutes and 5 seconds into the performance. It consists of the opening melody line (1), which is repeated, and its *sangati* (2), which is repeated in alternation with a new melody line (3). A repetition of the first phrase of melody line 1 closes out the section. In performance the drummer marks this closure with a thrice-repeated *mora* pattern occurring in the extra *tala* cycle.

The first *anupallavi* melody begins at about 3:50. It contrasts sharply with the ascent/descent contour of the *pallavi* tunes, centering on high *sa* (c′), descending, and then climbing up again. Both melody lines, (5) and (6), are repeated. A return to the opening melodic phrase of the *kriti* (1) and a second drum *mora* closes out the section.

The *charanam,* with its centering on *pa* (G), begins at about 4:25. It is more static and relaxed. Typical of the composer Tyagaraja, the last part of the *charanam* comprises a recapitulation of the melodies of the *anupallavi.* A final return to melody line (1), which by now is heard as a kind of refrain, and a third drum *mora* close out the rendition of the *kriti,* ending at about 5:12 on the stopwatch. The song is finished, but in Viswanathan's performance (CD Selection 25) it is time for further improvisation.

The Song Text

Tyagaraja's "Ivaraku jucinadi," the core piece of the performance segment, is like most *kritis* a devotional song whose text is addressed to one of the deities of Hinduism. In this case the god is Vishnu, the preserver of the universe, with several subtle references to his earthly incarnations as the handsome and heroic god-kings Krishna and Rama. The language of the song text is Telugu with a literal translation by T. Viswanathan and a free translation by C. Ramanujachari (1966):

Ivaraku jucinadi

Pallavi:	ivaruku	Thus far
	jucinadi	(lit. seeing) witnessed, waited
	inkanaritiya?	still, should it be so?
Anupallavi:	pavananu seyu	(You) who have the power to purify everything
	saktikanagani	which cannot be controlled (destroyed)
	papamugalada?	is there any sin?
	ksrivarada	dark boon-giver (Rama, Krishna, Vishnu)
	nan	mine.
Caranam 3:	nagasana	O rider of Garuda!
	sadagamna	(I who am) always pleading,
	ghruna sagara	Compassion-Ocean,
	ninnuvina	other than yourself
	evaru?	who is there?
	nive	(believing) you alone (are my)
	gatiyani	savior,
	vevega	urgently (lit, fast)
	moralanidu	(who is) beseeching,
	tyagarajuni	Tyagaraja,
	ragarahita	O one without attachment,
	nan.	me.

Is not what You have so long witnessed enough?
Should You continue to be so?
Is there any sin which cannot be destroyed by Your all-purifying power?
Without worshipping Your lotus feet, through greed I have become more and more tangled in the bondage of *samsara* (the eternal cycle of birth and death),
And I have been unable to bear the consequent distress.

Who is there for me except You?
Taking You to be my only savior,
I have been submitting my plaintive prayers to You

Of course, in an instrumental performance the words are not audible, as they would be in a vocal performance. Yet both the musicians and the more sophisticated members of the audience will know the song text (much as we may reflect upon the lyrics of a tune performed in an instrumental arrangement). In fact, some traditional *veena* players may sing at times as they play, and in concerts T. Viswanathan often puts aside his flute to sing certain passages.

CD 2
Track 1

Svara kalpana in the Performance

After the performance of the complete *kriti* (about 5:12 on the stopwatch), Viswanathan begins playing *svara kalpana* improvisations. (If there were a violin accompanist or another melodic soloist, the musicians would alternate solos.) The improvised *svaras* always return to a phrase from the song, which forms a kind of fixed island in the ever-changing sea of improvisation. This island is called the *idam* (lit. "place"), and it has two aspects: (1) the *raga* note on which the phrase starts and (2) the place in the *tala* cycle where it begins.

In Viswanathan's performance "the place" is the opening phrase from the song (melody line 1), which begins on the note *ga* (E) 1½ beats after the beginning of the *tala* cycle (Music Example 6-5). The musician must shape the improvisation so that the svaras lead smoothly back to the *idam.*

Music Example 6-5
Opening phrase (*idam*) of "Ivaraku jucinadi."

Svara kalpana may occur in two degrees of speed. In the first speed the predominant movement is two articulated notes per beat (there may also be some notes held longer). In the second speed, the predominant movement shifts to a double time of four articulated notes per beat (Music Example 6-6).

Music Example 6-6
The *svara kalpana.*

The svara kalpana begins in the first *kala,* or, the first degree of speed. This means that the predominant movement is in eighth notes (two to a beat):

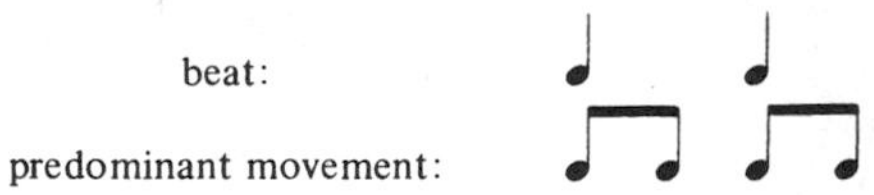

Notice how the improvisations keep returning to the "island" of the theme taken from the charanam ("verse"):

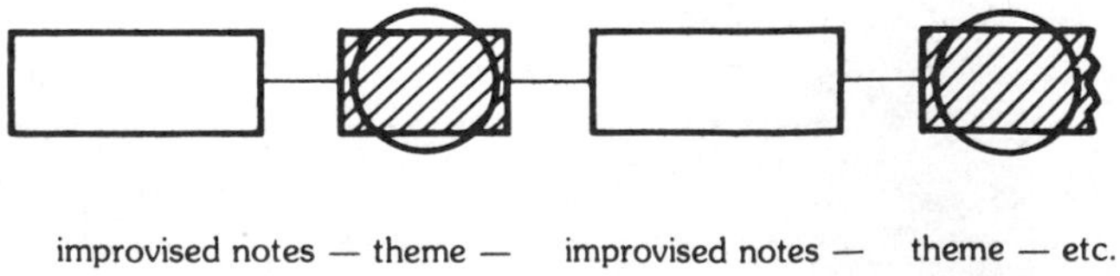

The *svara kalpana* improvisations shift gears and move into double-time. In this "second *kala,*" or second degree of speed, the predominant movement as in sixteenth notes (four to a beat):

CD 2
Track 1

Viswanathan's *svara kalpana* improvisations begin in slow speed, first *kala* (at about 5:12 on the stopwatch), immediately after the drum *mora.* After several short improvisations, each leading to the "place," he builds a longer passage beginning with an exploration of the low register and working up to a climax in the upper octave (at 6:00). There is a sudden shift to double time—second *kala*—at 6:12. Again the improvisations begin with short passages (each resolving on the *idam*) and a buildup to improvisations of greater and greater length. The final passage culminates with a shift of the "place" to the first beat of the *tala* cycle and the note *pa* (G).

At this point (about 7:10) a process called *koraippu* (lit. "shortening") begins. The musician first fills two cycles of the *tala* with increasingly complex and rhythmically inventive passages. A relatively fixed group of five notes leads to the resolution. Then the improvised passages are progressively compressed to one *tala* cycle (8 beats), ½ cycle (4 beats), ¼ cycle (2 beats), and finally one beat or less. Notice how Raghavan supports the process with his drum rhythms.

The *svara kalpana* section ends with final passage leading up to a rhythmic and melodic *mora,* a precomposed, thrice-repeated closing pattern (at about 8:33). Viswanathan in this performance plays notes in the *raga* to the rhythmic structure in Music Example 6-7.

Music Example 6-7
Rhythmic outline of T. Viswanathan's *mora* that brings his *svara kalpana* to a close.

South-Indian musicians take great pleasure in complicated in *svara kalpana.* It is part and parcel of the performer's tool kit. In a sense, the cerebral nature of this aspect of musical thinking balances another highly prized quality: *bhava,* or pure emotional expression.

The Drummer's Art

Until now we have concentrated on the melodic aspect of *karnataka* music. But drumming in India is not only important in the texture of performance but fascinating, complicated, and exciting in itself as well. The *mridangam* drummer and other percussionists play in an improvisatory style based on hundreds or thousands of rhythmic patterns that they have memorized, absorbed, and stored in the memory of their brains and hands. In the heat of a performance the percussionist may use precomposed patterns, arranging them like an artist of collage in predictable or unpredictable groupings. Or he may create entirely new groupings or patterns, spontaneous, yet within the limits and grammar of his rhythmic language (see Figure 6-13).

At the basis of the *mridangam* drummer's art are between fifteen and seventeen drum strokes—distinctive individual tones produced on different parts of the drumheads by different finger combinations or parts of the hands. These strokes, individually and when put together into rhythmic patterns, can be expressed in *solkattu,* spoken syllables that imitate the sound of the drum stroke and precisely duplicate each rhythmic pattern. Normally, spoken *solkattus* are used only in learning and practice, but there is also a tradition in South India to recite *solkattu* as part of a concert performance.

Figure 6-13
Drummers in a religious procession in Madras. Even folk musicians such as these play patterns of great complexity.

CD 2
Track 1

Now listen one more time to the performance segment (CD Selection 25). This time focus on Ramnad V. Raghavan's drumming. Like the melodic soloist, the South-Indian drummer (and his accompanying percussionists, if any) follows a kind of "map" of procedures. At times he may simply keep time, keep *tala.* Or he may "shadow" or reflect the subtle rhythms and phrases of the melodic soloist. A good drummer knows the repertoire of songs in the *karnataka* tradition, knows their flow and feeling, and shapes his accompaniment to the "rhythmic essence" of each song.

The drummer emerges from the background during pauses or long-held notes in the melody; he also emerges at cadential points, marking the endings and "joints" of sections (as we have seen) with his formulaic *mora* (ending) or cadential patterns with their threefold repetitions. If an improvising melodic soloist pops into a formulaic pattern, an alert drummer is quick to recognize the pattern, duplicate it with an ornamental drum version, and carry it to the end.

It is important to remember that South-Indian percussionists (like melodic soloists) do not merely "play off the top of their heads." Through years of training and study and listening, their brains are, in a sense, programmed with hundreds of building blocks, formulas, and possibilities of larger combinations. They are also calculating constantly, like a mathematician, how these formulas and patterns of asymmetrical lengths will fit into or against the *tala* cycles, how they will come out right at the end (on the downbeat of the *tala* cycle or the beginning of a song melody line).

But drummers are much more than a manipulator, merely shifting around and arranging pieces of an invisible rhythmic jigsaw puzzle. Rather, they are creating within a system. And in the process they may compose variations, superimpose sometimes startling juxtapositions, flow from easy time keeping to mind-boggling complicated patterns or sections, stop for meaningful pauses and start again, support a melodic soloist or work cleverly against him or her, or stamp out the identity of cadences—the "joints" and endings of sections of compositions.

Though we have only touched the surface of the drummer's art, we can begin to appreciate what must be a rhythmic system as complicated as any in the world, a system that balances beautifully with the complexities of melody seen in the *ragas.* As an old Sanskrit verse says:

श्रुतिर्माता लयः पिता

Sruti marta layah pita
"Melody is the mother, rhythm is the father."
(after P. Sambamoorthy)

The final section of the performance (at about 8:50 on CD Selection 25) is a drum solo, a *tani avartanam.* Though brief, barely two minutes long, it contains many of the features of an extended drum solo (ten to fifteen minutes long) that one might hear in a concert. At times, as the scholar David Nelson has observed, the drummer may merely be marking time. Then he will proceed into a complex rhythmic composition—composed not on paper but in the drummer's head. These compositions usually involve permutations of rhythmic ideas, or repetitions of a lengthy pattern in different degrees of speed (while the beat of the *tala* remains constant). At about 9:15 on the stopwatch Raghavan, for instance, moves into a section in *tisram;* that is, instead of the rhythmic flow moving in beat divisions of 2s, 4s, or 8s, each beat is now divided into triplets—3s and 6s. Thirty seconds later the pulse shifts back to duple and a cascade of drum timbres and lightning-fast drum strokes build to the climactic thrice-repeated final *korvai* (beginning at 10:18).

On the resolution of the *korvai* the flute reenters with the opening phrase of the song and the performance segment is concluded.

An Ear Map

CD 2
Track 1

In their brief performance (CD Selection 25; Figure 6-14) T. Viswanathan and Ramnad V. Raghavan have encapsulated many of the elements that in a concert performance segment might be stretched to last as long as forty-five minutes. The relative proportions of the improvisations and song would remain much the same, though the musical development would occur at a much more leisurely pace.

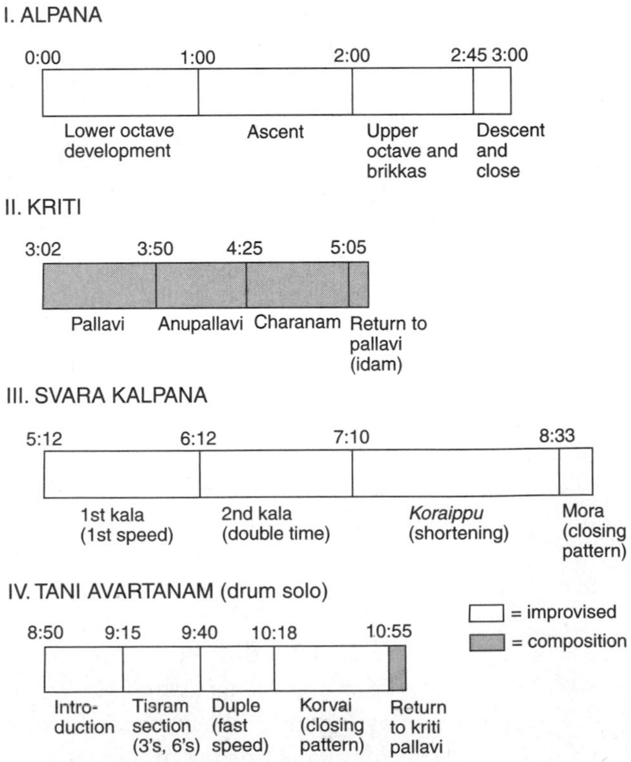

Figure 6-14
Ear map of "Ivaraku jucinadi" (CD Selection 25).

On another occasion, at another performance, the musicians might decide—using the same *kriti* as a core piece—to choose another set of balances. Because the soloist draws from his musical tool kit—the procedures and ideas and performance habits stored in his memory, as well as his conceptual image of the *raga*—much in his successive performances might be the same. But much, sparked by the creative instinct, would be new or different. That is one of the wonders of the *karnataka* music tradition.

Indian Music and the West

India's culture has long been able to assimilate outside influences. Common classical instruments such as the *sitar* and *tabla* have musical lineages that can be traced through Iran and central Asia as far east as northern Africa. Three and a half centuries of British colonial rule also left its mark, as has an increasing awareness in the late twentieth century of European and American pop and classical music brought by radio and cable television, CDs, and cassettes. As early as the nineteenth century, Indian composers wrote "exotic" pieces (in a genre known as "English notes") that parodied the choppy, unornamented tunes and four-square rhythms of British waltzes and military marches. The great composer and poet Dikshitar even set Sanskrit lyrics to such well-known tunes as "God Save the Queen."

The nature of Indian "cine music" (sometimes described as a musical *masala,* a spicy soup that can include almost anything) has contributed to a culture in which the violin, clarinet, mandolin, guitar, saxophone, synthesizer, and banjo have been used and accepted in Indian classical performance. And since the 1970s Indian musicians have been quick to recognize that the improvisational nature of jazz might relate well to *raga* improvisation in Indian music, and the genre known in India as "fusion" continues to attract a younger generation.

In addition, more than ever before Indians are studying, working, and living abroad. Cohesive communities of Indian immigrants, many trained in music, are now found in almost every major city or university town on earth. The children of first-generation immigrants especially often find themselves in a bicultural world where the "Indianness" of their home and family must be balanced with the pervasive dominance of the mainstream cultural environment. The result has been a development of various Indo-pop styles such as "bhangra" in England or "tassa-beat soca" in Trinidad, which combine drones, scales, and sometimes the instruments of Indian folk and classical traditions with the beat and electric sound of mainstream rock and pop styles.

Indian music has also infiltrated the West through the interest of European and American musicians. Beginning in the 1950s the *sitar* virtuoso Ravi Shankar was and continues to be a seminal figure. Having spent years in Paris as a boy with the dance troupe of his brother, Uday Shankar, he was able to move with sophisticated ease in the elite worlds of Western classical and pop music. By the 1960s his *sitar* performances with the *tabla* master Alla Rakha at venues as varied as the Edinburgh Music Festival and the Monterey Pop Festival eventually gave him superstar status. At the same time his activities varied from writing film scores (Satyajit Ray's *Apu* trilogy) to more experimental work.

Shankar has over the years released several collaborative recordings—all of them "west meets east" musical dialogues—with famous Western musicians, among them the concert violinst Yehudi Menuhin, the French flute virtuoso Pierre Rampal, the jazz musician Paul Horn, and the minimalist composer Philip Glass. In the album *East Greets East* he performs with traditional Japanese musicians, and his *Shankar Family and Friends,* an early 1970s album made in San Francisco with several dozen Western and Indian musicians (including one listed enigmatically as "Harris Georgeson"), includes Indo-pop instrumentals and a ballet score. In addition Shankar has composed two concertos for *sitar* and symphony orchestra.

In the mid-1960s Shankar acquired the most famous of his students, George Harrison of the Beatles. Harrison's interest in Indian classical music and religious philosophy (the Beatles, along with other celebrities, for a time followed guru Maharishi Mahesh Yogi) resulted in a finely crafted series of Indian-based songs ranging from "Love Me Too" to the philosophical "The Inner Light," the latter recorded in Bombay. Many of John Lennon's compositions in this period also had an Indian influence, though the synthesis was more opaque. For example, in "Tomorrow Never Knows" drones, exotic riffs, and Indian instruments float in a complex hallucinogenic texture of backward tapes and sound effects (described by one writer as "a stampeding herd of elephants gone mad") to evoke the otherworldly dream state of the lyrics, themselves inspired by the *Tibetan Book of the Dead* as interpreted by the LSD guru Timothy Leary.

In "Love Me Too," from the 1966 album *Revolver,* the *sitar* begins with a brief introduction of the notes of the *raga*-like scale in unmeasured time, a hint of *alapana.* A background drone of *tambura* and bass guitar continues throughout. The *tabla* drumbeat enters, establishing a driving metrical pulse of the *tala*-like cycles. Harrison's vocal line is sung in flat tones and ends with a descending melisma of distinct Indian vocal sound. In the chorus the repetitive riffs alternating between *sitar* and voice are reminiscent of the "question and answer" interplay among Indian musicians in performance. An improvisatory *sitar* and *tabla* interlude with *tala*-like metrical cycles of seven beats, later changing to five- and three-beat cycles, leads to the final rendition of chorus and verse. The instrumental postlude in faster tempo corresponds to the ending climactic sections of *hindusthani* music performance. All of this in a three-minute song!

Collaborations between Western pop and Indian musicians have continued to the present. The English jazz guitarist John McLaughlin in his groups the Mahavishnu Orchestra and Shakti turned to South-Indian musicians such as L. Shankar, violin; Ramnad V. Raghavan, *mridangam;* and Vinayakram, *ghatum* to create a *raga*-based improvisatory fusion music. And groups such as the Canadian percussion ensemble Nexus regularly use Indian instruments and such musicians as the Toronto-based *mridangam* virtuoso Trichy Sankaran.

Indo-pop music has flourished especially in England, where large immigrant communities from former colonies continue to generate new forms and sounds. The singer and composer Sheila Chandra, born to Indian parents in 1965, has treated diverse musical influences East and West with intelligence, wit, and sensitivity. A former child television star, in the 1980s she joined with Steve Coe and Martin Smith to form an innovative band, Monsoon, dedicated to the creation of a new popular music based on an English/Indian fusion. In her more recent work Chandra has focused on the unique qualities of her voice—often set simply against electronic and acoustic drones—and explored the synthesis of world vocal music traditions from the British Isles, Spain, India, and North Africa.

In South India the composer and songwriter Ilaiyaraja is a superstar, a musical genius with a celebrity compared to that reserved in the United States for a Michael Jordan, a Madonna, or a Harrison Ford. Born in a small village in 1943 to a family in the lowest stratum of the Indian caste system (*harijan,* or untouchable), Ilaiyaraja left high school to join an itinerant family band formed by his stepbrother to provide entertainment at political rallies and village festivals. Seeking his musical fortune in Madras, he apprenticed himself to "Master" Dhanaraj, a film and pop song composer for one of the big film studios. The eccentric "Master" proved to be the catalyst for the development of his young student's talent, teaching him not only the techniques of scoring Indian films but also the *karnataka* classical tradition, Western music notation, and the music of Mozart, Bach, and Beethoven. Ilaiyaraja supported himself by playing guitar in various studio orchestras. In his spare time he arranged Western pop songs by Paul Simon, the Beatles, and others.

Ilaiyaraja's big break came in 1976 when he was hired to provide the songs and background music for the hit film *Annakkili.* In contrast to the glitzy, shallow, urban Indian pop songs of that day, Ilaiyaraja echoed the earthy rural theme of the film by drawing upon South India's folk song tradition. His vibrant folklike melodies, backed by driving rhythms and an orchestra of folk instruments, took the country by storm, blaring from radios and marketplace loudspeakers, sung by homemakers, children, taxi drivers, and minstrels alike. In the ensuing years Ilaiyaraja was to write songs and the background music for nearly seven hundred films. Much of his music has drawn on his knowledge of the traditional *karnataka raga* system, as well as his skill at adapting Western concepts of harmony, counterpoint, and orchestration into the Indian context. He has become so famous that his name precedes those of the movie stars in posters and titles. Today he heads a large music production company, with a state-of-the-art recording studio and a large staff of musicians, producers, and technicians. A highly disciplined artist, each day he disappears into his studio in the early morning hours to compose, emerging in the afternoon for recording sessions that may last well into the night.

References

The Beatles. 1966. *Revolver.* Parlophone CD CDP 7 464412.

Chandra, Sheila. 1971. *Silk.* Shanachie CD 64035.

———. 1992. *Weaving My Ancestor's Voices.* Caroline CD CAROL 2322-2.

Ilaiyaraja. n.d. *How to Name It.* Oriental Records CD ORI/AAMS CD-115.

Isaac, L. 1967. *Theory of Indian Music.* Madras, India: L. Isaac.

McLaughlin, John. n.d. *Best of Mahavishnu.* Columbia PCT-36394.

———. n.d. *Shakti.* Columbia Jazz Contemporary Masters CD CK-46868.

Ramanujachari, C. 1966. *The Spiritual Heritage of Tyagaraja* [Translations of song text by Tyagaraja]. Madras, India. Sri Ramakrishna Math.

Ravi Shankar. 1974. *Shankar Family and Friends.* Dark Horse SP-22002.

———. 1978. *East Greets East.* Deutsche Grammophone 2531-381.

———. 1971. *Concerto for Sitar and Orchestra.* Angel SPD 36806.

———. n.d. *Ragamala: Concerto for Sitar and Orchestra No. 2.* Angel DS 37935.

———. n.d. *West Meets East.* (with Yehudi Menuhin) I–III. Angel S-36418, S-36026, SQ-37200.

Viswanathan, T. 1975. "Raga alapana in South Indian Music." Ph.D. diss., Wesleyan Univ.

Classroom Resources

Kumar, Kanthimathi, and Jean Stackhouse. 1988. *Classical Music of South India: Karnatic Tradition in Western Notation.* Stuyvesant, N.Y.: Pendragon Press. [Beginning lessons and simple songs with free translations of song texts]

Nelson, David. 1989. *Madras Music Videos.* Available from D. Nelson, 340 Westhampton Road, Northampton, Mass. 01060. [Videotapes of concert performances of South Indian music]

Additional Reading

Basham, A. L. 1959. *The Wonder That Was India.* New York: Grove Press.

Brown, Robert E. 1971. "India's Music." In *Readings in Ethnomusicology,* edited by David P. McAllester, 192–329. New York: Johnson Reprint.

Edwardes, Michael. 1970. *A History of India.* New York: Universal Library.

Lanmoy, Richard. 1971. *The Speaking Tree: A Study of Indian Culture and Society.* New York: Oxford Univ. Press.

Mohan, Anuradha. 1994. "Ilaiyaraja: Composer As Phenomenon in Tamil Film Culture." M.A. thesis, Wesleyan Univ.

Raghavan, Ramnad V. 1971. Personal communication, drumming lessons.

Rajeswari, S. B. 1989. Personal communication, song translation.

Reck, David. 1985. "Beatles Orientalis: Influences from Asia in a Popular Song Tradition." Asian Music 16 (1): 83–149.

———. 1983. "A Musician's Toolkit: A Study of Five Performances by Thirugokarnam Ramachandra Iyer." Ph.D. diss., Wesleyan Univ.

Sambamoorthy, P. 1963. *South Indian Music,* book 4. Madras: Indian Music Publishing House.

———. 1964. *South Indian Music,* book 3. Madras: Indian Music Publishing House.

Shankar, Ravi. 1968. *My Music, My Life.* New York: Simon and Schuster.

Wade, Bonnie. 1988. *Music of India: The Classical Traditions.* Riverdale, Md.: Riverdale.

Additional Listening

The website http://www.medieval.org/music/world/carnatic/cblsup.html has an annotated list of CDs, each with commentary, plus relevant information on South-Indian (Carnatic) music, composers, performers, and musical style. In particular, you might want to look for the following CDs.

An Anthology of South Indian Classical Music. Ocora 5900001/2/3/4 (4 CDs).

Gopinath, Kadri. *A Tribute to Adolphe Sax.* Oriental 230/231. [saxophone]

Iyer, Semmangudi Srinivasa. *The Doyen of Carnatic Music.* Oriental 140. [vocal]

Jayaraman, Lalgudi J. *Violin Virtuoso: Lalgudi J. Jayaraman.* Oriental AAMS-125.

Krishnan, T.N. *The Vibrant Violin of "Sangita Kalanidhi."* Oriental 140.

Mahalingam, T. R. ("Mali"). *Divine Sounds of the Bamboo Flute.* Oriental 183/184 (2CDs).

Moulana, Sheik Chinna. *Nadhasvaram.* Wergo SM-1507. [*nagaswaram.*]

Music for Bharata Natyam. Oriental 176. [South-Indian dance music]

Narayanaswamy, K. V. *Guru Padam.* Koel 063. [vocal]

Padmanabhan, Rajeswari. *Surabi.* SonicSoul Acoustics (no number; released in 1998). [*veena*]

Ramani, N. *Lotus Signatures.* MOW CDT-141. [flute]

Ranganayaki Rajagopalan. Makar 029. [*veena*]

Sankaran, Trichy. *The Language of Rhythm.* MOW 150. [*mridangam*]

Subbulakshmi, M. S. *M. S. Subbulakshmi: Live at Carnegie Hall.* EMI India 147808/809 (2CDs). [vocal]

———. *M. S. Subbulakshmi: Radio Recitals.* EMI India CDNF 147764/65 (2CDs). [vocal]

Viswanathan, T. *Classical Flute of South India.* JVC VICG-5453.

Major Sources for Recordings

Music of the World (MOW label). P. O. Box 3620, Chapel Hill, N.C. 27515, phone: (888) 264-6689. http://www.rootsworld.com/rw/motw/indexx2.html

Oriental Records. P. O. Box 387, Williston Park, N.Y. 11596. http://www.orientalrecords.com

Raag Music. Los Angeles, Cal., phone: (310) 479-5225. http://www.webcom.com/raag/ca-v-art.html

SonicSoul Acoustics. 15183 Dane Lane, Portland, Oreg. 97229, phone: (503) 531-0270. E-mail: kartha1@aol.com

CHAPTER

7

Asia/Indonesia

R. Anderson Sutton

Indonesia is a country justly proud of its great cultural diversity. Nowhere is this diversity more evident than in the stunning variety of musical and related performing arts found throughout its several thousand populated islands. Known formerly as the Dutch East Indies, Indonesia is one of many modern nations whose boundaries were formed during the centuries of European colonial domination, placing peoples with contrasting languages, arts, systems of belief, and conceptions of the world under a single rule. The adoption of a national language in the early twentieth century was a crucial step in building the unity necessary to win a revolution against the Dutch (1945–49). More recently, a pan-Indonesian popular culture is contributing to an increased sense of national unity, particularly among the younger generation. Nevertheless, though we can identify some general cultural traits, including musical ones, shared by many peoples of Indonesia, it is problematic to speak of an "Indonesian" culture, or an "Indonesian" style of music. Regional diversity is still very much in evidence, contributing to the economic and political turmoil that has kept Indonesia in the news in the past few years.

Most Indonesians' first language is not the national language (Indonesian) but one of the more than two hundred separate languages found throughout this vast archipelago. And though many Indonesians are familiar with the sounds of Indonesian pop music and such Western stars as Mariah Carey and the Backstreet Boys, they also know, to a greater or lesser extent, their own regional musical traditions. Many kinds of music exist side by side in Indonesia, in a complex pluralism that reflects both the diversity of the native population and the receptiveness of that population to centuries of outside influence. Indonesia is, then, a country that can truly be said to be home to worlds of music.

What sort of impressions might you first have of this country? You would probably arrive in the nation's capital, Jakarta, a teeming metropolis of about nine million people—some very wealthy, most rather poor. Jakarta is near the western end of the north coast of Java, Indonesia's most heavily

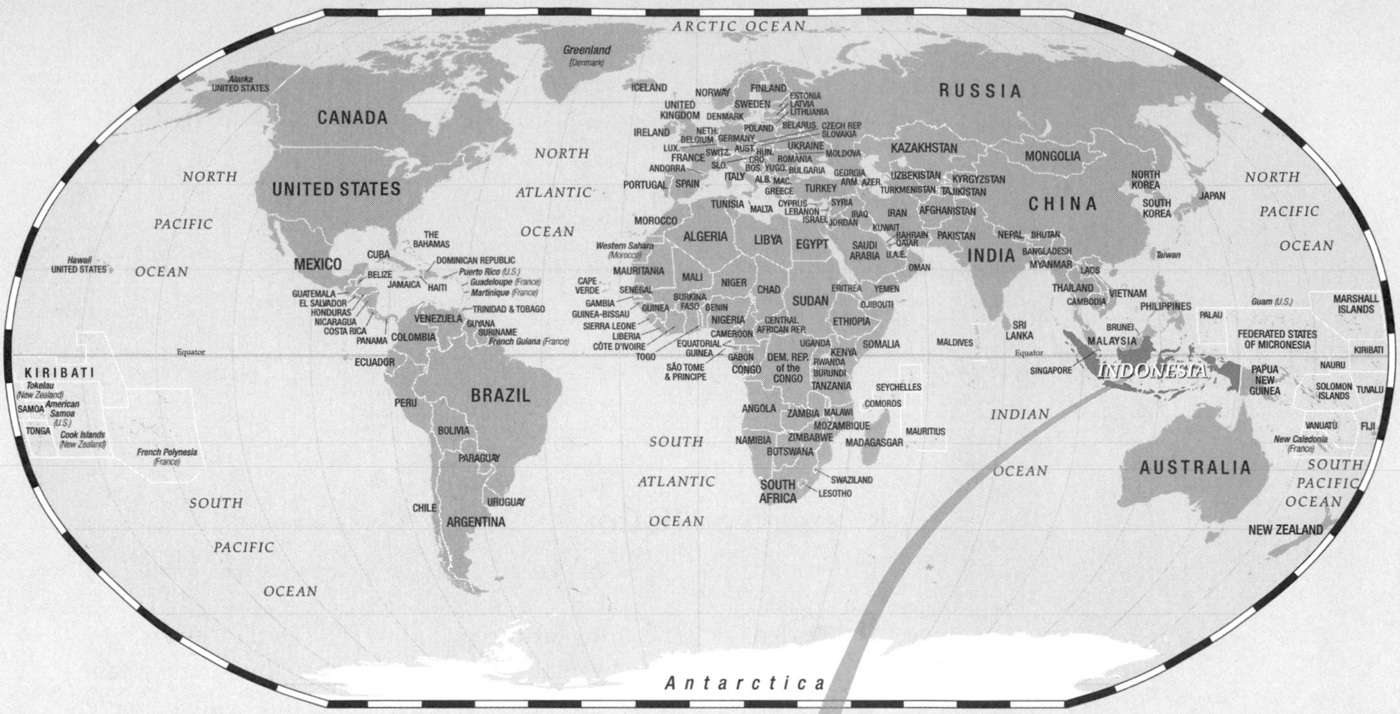
ARCTIC OCEAN
Greenland
(Denmark)
Alaska
UNITED STATES
CANADA
UNITED STATES
NORTH
PACIFIC
OCEAN
Hawaii
UNITED STATES
MEXICO
CUBA
THE BAHAMAS
DOMINICAN REPUBLIC
Puerto Rico (U.S.)
Guadeloupe (France)
Martinique (France)
BELIZE
JAMAICA
HAITI
GUATEMALA
EL SALVADOR
HONDURAS
NICARAGUA
COSTA RICA
PANAMA
TRINIDAD & TOBAGO
VENEZUELA
GUYANA
SURINAME
French Guiana (France)
COLOMBIA
ECUADOR
PERU
BRAZIL
BOLIVIA
PARAGUAY
CHILE
URUGUAY
ARGENTINA
KIRIBATI
Tokelau
(New Zealand)
SAMOA
American Samoa
(U.S.)
TONGA
Cook Islands
(New Zealand)
French Polynesia
(France)
Equator
SOUTH
PACIFIC
OCEAN
NORTH
ATLANTIC
OCEAN
SOUTH
ATLANTIC
OCEAN
ICELAND
NORWAY
FINLAND
SWEDEN
ESTONIA
LATVIA
LITHUANIA
UNITED KINGDOM
DENMARK
IRELAND
NETH.
BELGIUM
GERMANY
POLAND
BELARUS
CZECH REP.
SLOVAKIA
LUX.
FRANCE
SWITZ.
AUST.
HUN.
UKRAINE
MOLDOVA
ANDORRA
SLO.
CRO.
BOS.
YUGO.
ROMANIA
BULGARIA
PORTUGAL
SPAIN
ITALY
ALB.
MAC.
GREECE
TURKEY
GEORGIA
ARM.
AZER.
RUSSIA
KAZAKHSTAN
UZBEKISTAN
KYRGYZSTAN
TURKMENISTAN
TAJIKISTAN
MONGOLIA
NORTH KOREA
SOUTH KOREA
JAPAN
CHINA
AFGHANISTAN
PAKISTAN
NEPAL
BHUTAN
BANGLADESH
INDIA
MYANMAR
LAOS
THAILAND
CAMBODIA
VIETNAM
PHILIPPINES
Taiwan
MOROCCO
TUNISIA
MALTA
CYPRUS
LEBANON
ISRAEL
SYRIA
IRAQ
IRAN
JORDAN
KUWAIT
BAHRAIN
QATAR
U.A.E.
OMAN
SAUDI ARABIA
YEMEN
Western Sahara
(Morocco)
ALGERIA
LIBYA
EGYPT
MAURITANIA
MALI
NIGER
CHAD
SUDAN
ERITREA
DJIBOUTI
ETHIOPIA
SOMALIA
CAPE VERDE
SENEGAL
GAMBIA
GUINEA-BISSAU
GUINEA
SIERRA LEONE
LIBERIA
CÔTE D'IVOIRE
BURKINA FASO
BENIN
TOGO
NIGERIA
CAMEROON
CENTRAL AFRICAN REP.
EQUATORIAL GUINEA
GABON
SÃO TOME & PRINCIPE
CONGO
DEM. REP. of the CONGO
UGANDA
KENYA
RWANDA
BURUNDI
TANZANIA
SEYCHELLES
COMOROS
MALAWI
ZAMBIA
ANGOLA
MOZAMBIQUE
ZIMBABWE
NAMIBIA
BOTSWANA
MADAGASCAR
MAURITIUS
SWAZILAND
LESOTHO
SOUTH AFRICA
MALDIVES
SRI LANKA
Equator
SINGAPORE
MALAYSIA
BRUNEI
INDONESIA
INDIAN
OCEAN
PALAU
Guam (U.S.)
MARSHALL ISLANDS
FEDERATED STATES OF MICRONESIA
KIRIBATI
NAURU
PAPUA NEW GUINEA
SOLOMON ISLANDS
TUVALU
VANUATU
FIJI
New Caledonia
(France)
AUSTRALIA
NEW ZEALAND
NORTH
PACIFIC
OCEAN
SOUTH
PACIFIC
OCEAN
Antarctica

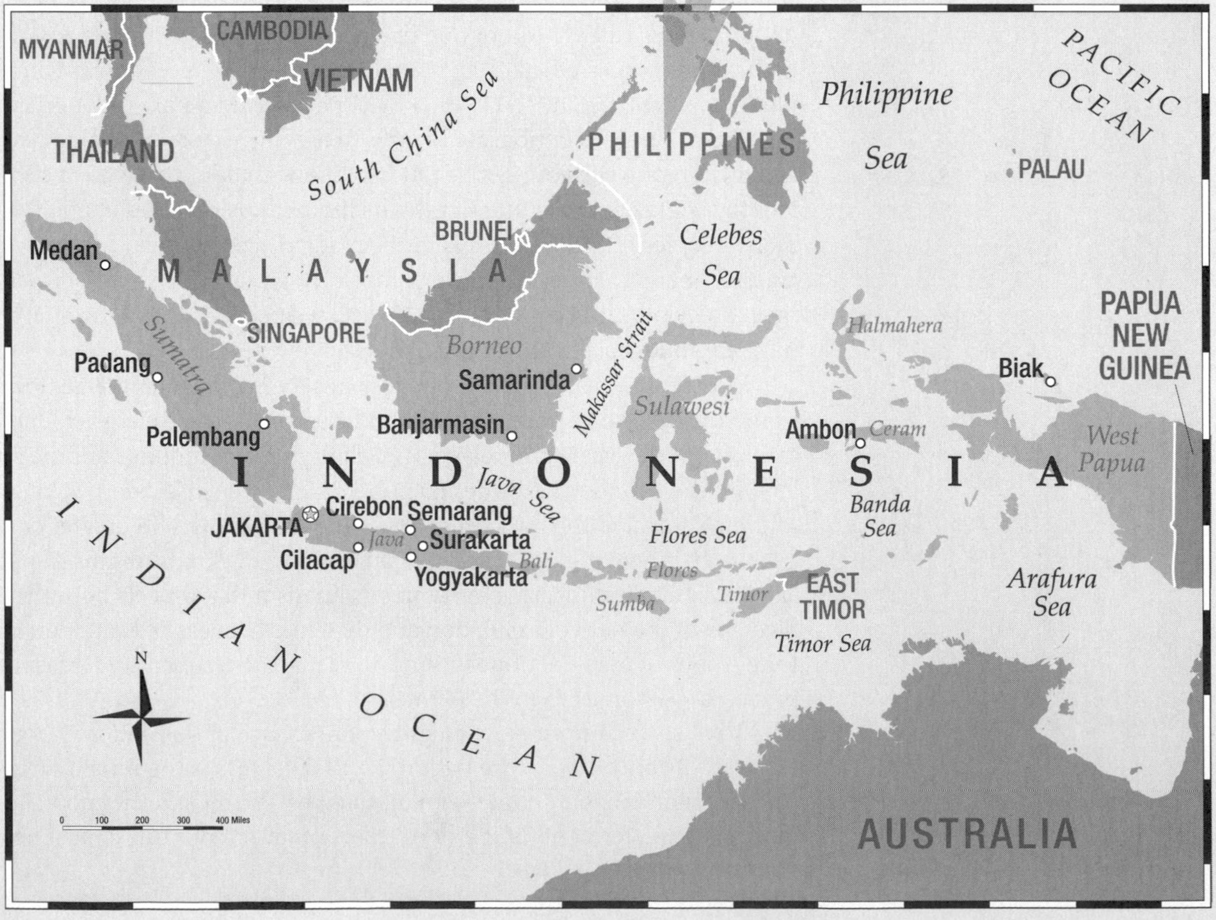
MYANMAR
CAMBODIA
VIETNAM
THAILAND
South China Sea
PHILIPPINES
Philippine
Sea
PACIFIC
OCEAN
PALAU
BRUNEI
MALAYSIA
Medan
Celebes
Sea
SINGAPORE
Sumatra
Borneo
Padang
Samarinda
Makassar Strait
Halmahera
PAPUA
NEW
GUINEA
Biak
Palembang
Banjarmasin
Sulawesi
Ambon
Ceram
West
Papua
INDONESIA
Java
Sea
Cirebon
Semarang
JAKARTA
Java
Surakarta
Cilacap
Yogyakarta
Bali
Flores Sea
Banda
Sea
Flores
Sumba
Timor
EAST
TIMOR
Arafura
Sea
Timor Sea
INDIAN
OCEAN
N
0
100
200
300
400 Miles
AUSTRALIA

populated (but not largest) island. The mix of Indonesia's many cultures is nowhere more fully realized than in this special city. Many kinds of music are heard here. Western-style night clubs and discos do a lively business until the early hours of the morning. Javanese *gamelan* (percussion ensemble) music accompanies nightly performances of *wayang orang* theatre (an elaborate type of dance-drama from central Java). You might also run across Jakarta's own *gambang-kromong* (small percussion ensemble), and perhaps a troupe from Bali, Sumatra, or any of the many other islands performing traditional music and dance at the Jakarta arts center Taman Ismael Marzuki. Once you get your bearings, learn to bargain for taxis or pedicabs, and develop a taste for highly seasoned food, you can get a sense of Indonesia's many cultures by roaming this complex city. But much of what you encounter here has strong roots in the various regions from which it has been derived.

Central Java

Java is an island of just less than 50,000 square miles—very nearly the size of New York State and slightly smaller than Nepal. With close to 100 million people, it is one of the most densely populated regions in the world. (Indonesia's total population is about 208 million.) Most of the central and eastern two thirds of the island is inhabited by Indonesia's largest ethnic group, the Javanese, 70 million people who share a common language and other cultural traits, including music, though some local differences persist. In the western third of the island live the Sundanese, whose language and arts are distinct from those of the Javanese. Despite its dense population, Java remains mostly a farming society, with wet-rice agriculture as the predominant source of livelihood. While most Javanese profess to be Muslim, only a small percentage follow orthodox practice. More adhere to a blend of Islam with Hinduism and Buddhism (introduced in Java over one thousand years ago), and with what most scholars believe to be a still earlier layer of belief in benevolent and mischievous spirits and in ancestor veneration. The worldview that embraces these many layers of belief is often referred to as *kejawèn*—literally, *Javanese,* or *Javaneseness,* a term that indicates its importance in Javanese self-conception.

From Jakarta a twelve-hour ride on bus or train through shimmering wet-rice fields, set in the plains between gracefully sloping volcanic mountains, leads to Yogyakarta (often abbreviated to "Yogya" and pronounced "Jogja"), one of two court cities in the cultural heartland of central Java. The other, less than fifty miles to the northeast, is Surakarta (usually known as "Solo"). Most Javanese point to these two cities as the cultural centers where traditional *gamelan* music and related performing arts have flourished in their most elaborate and refined forms. These courtly developments are contrasted with the rougher styles associated with the villages and outlying districts.

Yogya is a sprawling city with a population of close to 400,000. It has few buildings taller than four stories. Away from the several major streets lined with stores flashing neon signs and blaring popular music, Yogya is in many ways like a dense collection of villages. Yet at its center is one of Java's two major royal courts (*kraton*), official home of the tenth sultan (His Highness Hamengku Buwana X). Unlike any Western palace or court, the *kraton* is a complex of small buildings and open pavilions, appropriate for the warm, tropical climate. Its design is not merely for comfort, however. The *kraton* is endowed with mystical significance as an earthly symbol of the macrocosmos, the ordered universe, with orientation to the cardinal directions. And the ruler, whose residence is located at the very center of the *kraton,* is imbued with divine powers, like the Hindu-Javanese kings of many centuries ago.

In many of these pavilions the court *gamelan* ensembles are kept. Some date back many centuries and are used only for rare ritual occasions; others were built or augmented more recently and are used more frequently. Most of these, like other treasured heirlooms belonging to the court, are believed to contain special powers and are shown respect and given offerings. Also kept in the palace are numerous sets of finely carved and painted *wayang kulit* (shadow puppets made of water buffalo hide) used in all-night performances of highly sophisticated and entertaining shadow plays. Classical Javanese dance, with *gamelan* accompaniment, is rehearsed regularly and performed for special palace functions.

Though the *kraton* is still regarded as a cultural center, it is far less active now than it was prior to World War II (during which the Japanese occupied Indonesia). Much activity in the traditional Javanese arts is to be found outside the court, sponsored by private individuals and also by such modern institutions as the national radio station and public schools and colleges. In the rural villages, which long served as a source and inspiration for the more refined courtly arts, a variety of musical and related performing arts continue to play a vital role in Javanese life.

Gamelan

The word *gamelan* refers to a set of instruments unified by their tuning and often by their decorative carving and painting (see Figure 7-1). Most *gamelans* consist of several kinds of metal slab instruments (similar in some ways to the Western vibraphone) and tuned knobbed gongs. The word *gong* itself is one of the very few English words derived from Indonesian languages. (Two others are *ketchup* and *amok.*) In English, *gong* may refer to any variety of percussion instrument whose sound-producing vibrations are concentrated in the center of the instrument, rather than the edge like a bell. In Javanese it refers specifically to the larger hanging knobbed gongs in *gamelan* ensembles and is part of a family of words relating to largeness, greatness, and grandeur—*agung* (great, kingly), *ageng* (large), and *gunung* (mountain). In addition to gongs and other metal instruments, a *gamelan* ensemble normally has at least one drum and may have other kinds of instruments: winds, strings, and wooden percussion instruments (xylophones).

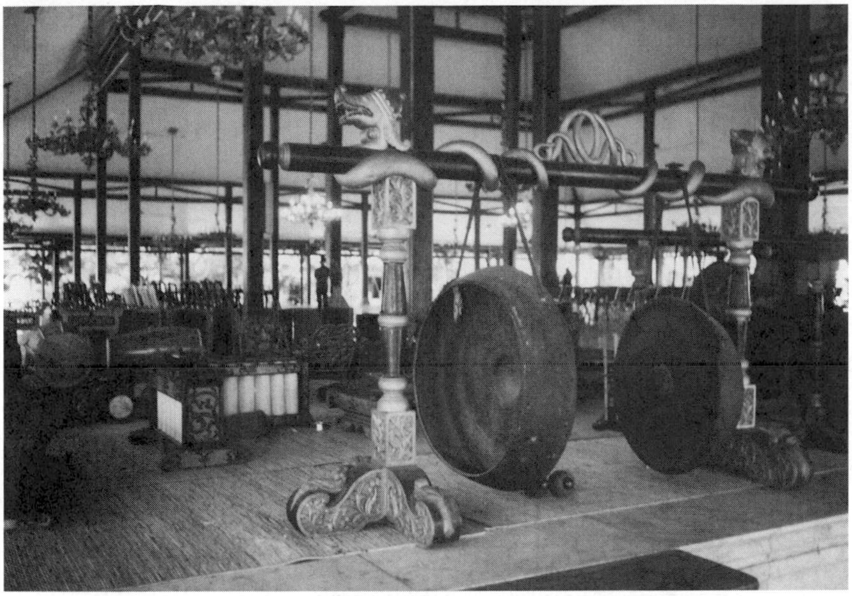

Figure 7-1
The *gamelan* Kyai Kanyut Mèsem ("Tempted to Smile") in the Mangkunegaran palace, Surakarta, Central Java. In foreground: *gong ageng* and *gong siyem.*

Arthur Durkee, Earth Visions Photographics

Some ancient ceremonial *gamelans* have only a few knobbed gongs and one or two drums. The kind of *gamelan* most often used in central Java today is a large set, comprising instruments ranging from deep booming gongs three feet in diameter to sets of high-pitched tuned gongs (gong-chimes) and slab instruments, with three drums, several bamboo flutes, zithers, xylophones, and a two-stringed fiddle.

Instruments in the present-day *gamelan* are tuned to one of two scale systems: *sléndro,* a five-tone system made up of nearly equidistant intervals, normally notated with the numerals 1, 2, 3, 5, and 6 (no 4); and *pélog,* a seven-tone system made up of large and small intervals, normally notated 1, 2, 3, 4, 5, 6, and 7. Some *gamelans* are entirely *sléndro,* others entirely *pélog,* but many are actually double ensembles, combining a full set of instruments for each system. The scale systems are incompatible and only in a few rare cases are they played simultaneously. Neither of these scale systems can be played on a Western piano. Music Example 7-1 shows the Western major scale in comparison with sample intervals for one instance

Music Example 7-1
Western scale and representative *pélog* and *sléndro* scales. Based on measurements of *gamelan* Mardiswara (Surjodiningrat, Sudarjana, and Susanto 1972:51–53).

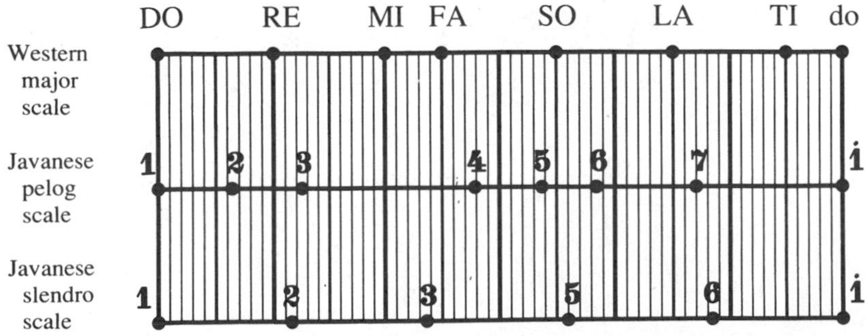

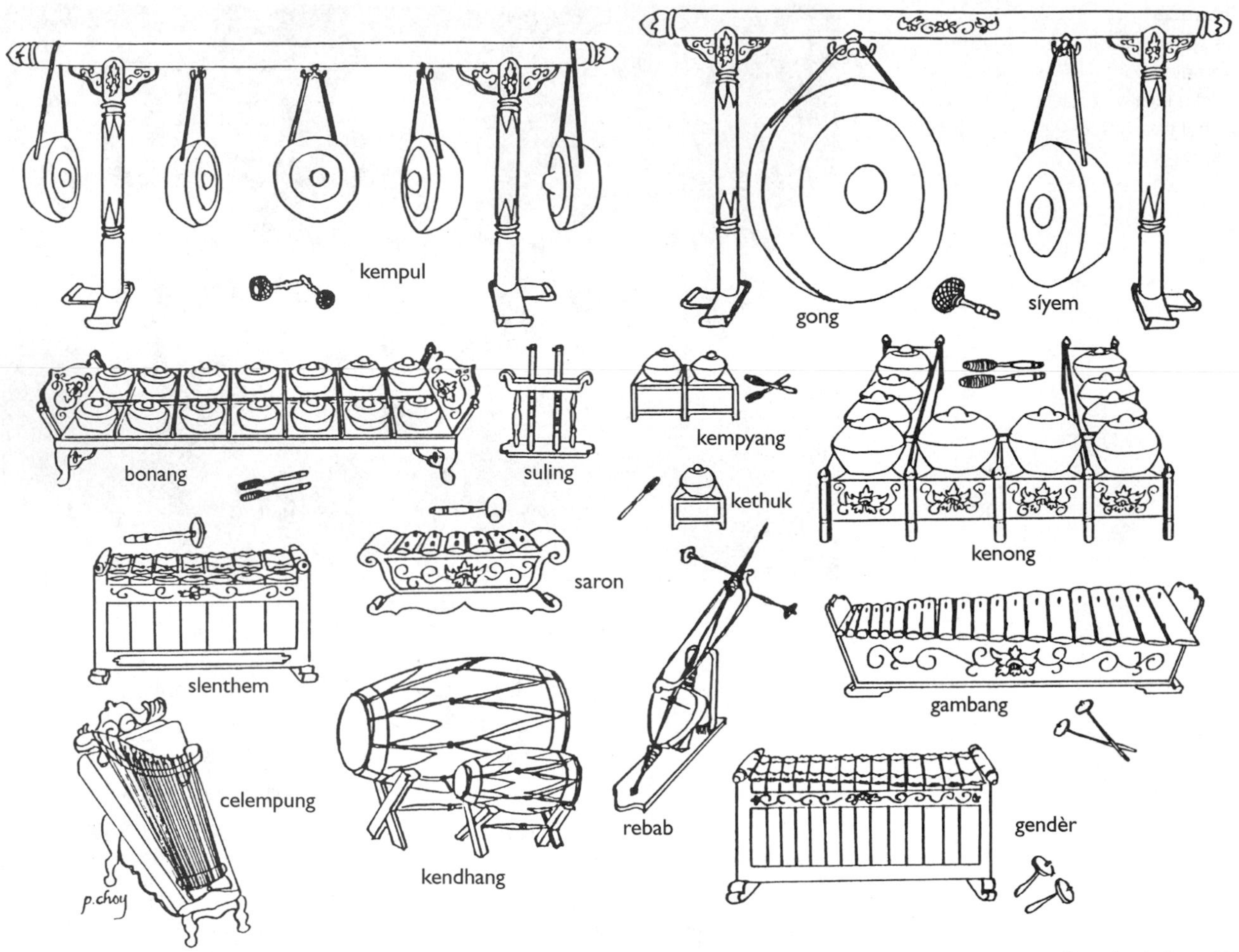

Illustration by Peggy Choy

Figure 7-2
Central Javanese *gamelan* instruments.

of *sléndro* and one of *pélog* (these are not entirely standardized, as I shall explain).

The instrumentation of a full *sléndro-pélog gamelan* varies slightly but usually includes all or most of the instruments given in the following list. Most of these are illustrated in Figure 7-2.

Knobbed Gong Instruments

GONG AGENG	Largest of the hanging gongs, suspended vertically from a wooden frame; one or two in each *gamelan*; often simply called *gong;* played with a round, padded beater
SIYEM	Middle-sized hanging gong; usually from one to four in each *gamelan;* also called gong suwukan; played with a round, padded beater
KEMPUL	Smallest hanging gong; from two to ten per *gamelan;* played with a round, padded beater

KENONG	Largest of the kettle gongs, resting horizontally in a wooden frame; from two to twelve per *gamelan;* played with a padded stick beater
KETHUK	Small kettle gong; one for each scale system; played with a padded stick beater
KEMPYANG	Set of two kettle gongs, smaller than *kethuk;* used only for *pélog;* played with two padded stick beaters
BONANG BARUNG	Set of ten, twelve, or fourteen kettle gongs resting horizontally in two parallel rows in a wooden frame; one set for each scale system; often simply called *bonang;* played with two padded stick beaters
BONANG PANERUS	Smaller member of the *bonang* family; same as *bonang barung* but tuned an octave higher; one for each scale system

Metal Keyed Instruments

SARON DEMUNG	Largest member of the *saron* (single-octave metallophone) family; six or seven thick metal keys resting over a trough resonator; usually one or two for each scale system; often simply called *demung;* played with a wooden mallet
SARON BARUNG	Like *saron demung,* but an octave higher; usually from two to four for each scale system; often simply called *saron*
SARON PEKING	Like *saron barung,* but an octave higher; often simply called *peking*
GENDÈR SLENTHEM	Six or seven thin metal keys suspended by strings over cylindrical resonators made of bamboo or metal; one for each scale system; often simply called *slenthem;* played with a padded disc beater
GENDÈR BARUNG	Thirteen or fourteen thin metal keys, suspended over cylindrical resonators; one for *sléndro,* two for *pélog: bem* (with tones 1, 2, 3, 5, and 6 in each octave) and *barang* (with tones 2, 3, 5, 6, and 7 in each octave); often simply called *gendèr;* played with two padded disc beaters
GENDÈR PANERUS	Like *gendèr barung,* but an octave higher

Other Melodic Instruments

GAMBANG	Seventeen to twenty-three wooden keys resting over a trough resonator; one for *sléndro;* one or two for *pélog* (if two, like *gendèr barung* and *gendèr panerus;* if only one, exchange keys enable player to arrange instrument for *bem*—with 1s—or for *barang*—with 7s); played with two padded disc beaters

CELEMPUNG	Zither, usually supported at about a thirty-degree angle by four legs, with twenty to twenty-six strings arranged in ten to thirteen "double courses" (as on a twelve-string guitar); one for *sléndro,* one or two for *pélog* (cf. *gambang*); plucked with thumbnails
SITER	Smaller zither, resting on floor or in horizontal frame, with from ten to twenty-six strings in single or double courses, one for *sléndro,* one or two for *pélog* (cf. *gambang* and *celempung*); plucked with thumbnails
SULING	End-blown bamboo flute; one for *sléndro,* one or two for *pélog*
REBAB	Two-stringed fiddle; one or two per *gamelan*

Drums

KENDHANG GENDHING	Largest of the hand drums; two leather heads, laced onto a barrel-shaped shell; one per *gamelan*
KENDHANG CIBLON	Middle-sized hand drum, like *kendhang gendhing;* often simply called *ciblon*
KENDHANG KETIPUNG	Smallest hand drum, often simply called *ketipung*
BEDHUG	Large stick-beaten drum; two leather heads, tacked onto a cylindrical shell; one per *gamelan*

There is no standard arrangement of these instruments in the performance space, though almost without exception they are placed at right angles to one another, reflecting the Javanese concern with the cardinal directions (see Figure 7-3). Generally the larger gong instruments are in the back, with the *saron* family immediately in front of them, *bonang* family and *bedhug* drum to the sides, other melodic instruments in front, and the *kendhang* drums in the center. The placement of the instruments reflects their relative loudness and their function in the performance of pieces, which I will discuss shortly.

The *gamelan* instruments are normally complemented by singers: a small male chorus (*gérong*) and female soloists (*pesindhèn*). Java also supports a highly developed tradition of unaccompanied vocal music (*tembang*), which serves as a major vehicle for Javanese poetry. In fact, the word *tembang* is best translated into English as "sung poetry." Although Javanese have recorded their *tembang* in several writing systems for over one thousand years, these are normally neither read silently nor read aloud in a speaking voice, but sung. Even important letters between members of the nobility were, until this century, composed as *tembang* and delivered as song. Though the postal system has eliminated this practice, vocal music, whether with *gamelan* or unaccompanied, enjoys great popularity in Java today.

Arthur Durkee, Earth Visions Photographics

Figure 7-3
Gamelan musicians in the Kraton Kasunanan (royal palace) in Surakarta, Central Java. In foreground, *bonang* (left) and *slenthem* (right).

The relation between vocal and instrumental orientations in *gamelan* music is reflected in the two major groupings of instruments in the present-day Javanese *gamelan:* "loud-playing" and "soft-playing." History suggests that these two groupings were once separate ensembles and were combined as recently as the sixteenth or early seventeenth centuries. Loud-playing ensembles were associated with festivals, processions, and other noisy outdoor events and were strictly instrumental. Soft-playing ensembles were intended for more intimate gatherings, often indoors, and involved singing. Even today, performance style distinguishes these two groupings. In loud-playing style, only the drums and louder metal instruments are used, as listed in the following left-hand column. In soft-playing style, these instruments, or most of them, are played softly, and the voices and instruments listed in the following right-hand column are featured.

Loud-Playing Instruments	Soft-Playing Instruments
gong ageng	*gendèr barung*
siyem	*gendèr panerus*
kempul	*gambang*
kenong	*celempung*
kethuk	*siter*
kempyang	*suling*
bonang family	*rebab*
saron family	
slenthem	
kendhang family	
bedhug	

Gamelan Construction

Bronze is the preferred metal for *gamelan* manufacture, owing both to its durability and to its rich, sweet sound quality. Brass and iron are also used, especially in rural areas. They are considerably cheaper than bronze, easier to tune, but less sonorous. Bronze *gamelan* instruments are forged (some cast in their basic shapes and then forged) in a long and difficult process. Though the metal worker in many societies occupies a low status, in Java he has traditionally been held in high regard. The act of forging bronze instruments not only requires great skill but is also imbued with mystical significance. Working with metals, transforming molten copper and tin (the metals that make bronze alloy) into sound-producing instruments, is believed to make one especially vulnerable to dangerous forces in the spirit world. For this reason the smiths make ritual preparation and may actually assume mythical identities during the forging process. The chief smith is ritually transformed into Panji, a powerful Javanese mythical hero, and the smith's assistants become Panji's family and servants (see Becker 1988; Kunst 1973:138).

The largest gongs may require a full month of labor and a truckload of coal for the forge that heats the metal. Only after appropriate meditation, prayer, fasting, and preparation of offerings does a smith undertake to make a large gong. The molten bronze is pounded, reheated, pounded, reheated, and gradually shaped into a large knobbed gong that may measure three feet or more in diameter. A false hit at any stage can crack the gong, and the process must begin all over.

Gamelan Identity

A *gamelan*, particularly a bronze set with one or two fine large gongs, is often held in great respect, given a proper name, and given offerings on Thursday evenings (the beginning of the Muslim holy day). Though *gamelan* makers have recently begun to duplicate precise tuning and decorative designs, generally each *gamelan* is a unique set, whose instruments would both look and sound out of place in another ensemble. Formerly, attempting even to copy the tuning and design of palace *gamelan* instruments was forbidden, as these were reserved for the ruler and were directly associated with his power.

The variability in tuning from one *gamelan* to another is certainly not the result of a casual sense of pitch among Javanese musicians and *gamelan* makers. On the contrary, great care is taken in the making and in the occasional retuning of *gamelan* sets to arrive at a pleasing tuning—one that is seen to fit the particular physical condition of the instruments and the tastes of the individual owner. I spent one month with a tuner, his two assistants, and an expert musician as they gradually reached consensus on an agreeable tuning and then altered the tuning of the many bronze gong and metal slab instruments through a long process of hammering and filing—all by hand. Bronze has the curious property of changing tuning—

rather markedly during the first few years after forging, and more subtly over a period of twenty to thirty years, until it is finally "settled." It might seem that the lack of a standard tuning would cause musical chaos, but the actual latitude is small.

Gamelan Performance Contexts

Despite the changes wrought by modern institutions (formal musical instruction in schools and dissemination through the mass media) in the contexts of music making and the ways music is understood, Javanese music is more closely interrelated with other performing arts and more intimately bound to other aspects of life than are the arts in the West (Figure 7-4). "Concerts" of *gamelan* music simply do not occur, at least not in anything like the circumstances of a concert of Western classical music. The closest thing to a *gamelan* "concert" in Java is *uyon-uyon* (or *klenèngan*), but these are better understood as social events that involve *gamelan* music. They are usually held to commemorate a day of ritual importance, such as a birth, circumcision, or wedding. Normally a family sponsors such an event and invites neighbors and relatives, while others are welcome to look on and listen. The invited guests are served food and are expected to socialize freely through the duration of the event. No one expects the guests to be quiet during the performance of pieces or to pay rapt attention to them the way an audience does at a Western concert. Rather, the music, carefully played though it may be, is seen to contribute to the festiveness of the larger social event, helping to make it *ramé* (lively, busy in a positive way). Connoisseurs among the guests will ask for a favorite piece and may pay close attention to the way the ensemble or a particular singer or

Figure 7-4
Musicians playing the *gamelan* Kyai Kanyut Mèsem. Mangkunegaran palace, Surakarta, Central Java. In foreground: *Sarons, kempul,* and *gongs* on left; *saron peking* and *bonangs* on right.

Arthur Durkee, Earth Visions Photographics

instrumentalist performs, but not to the exclusion of friendly interaction with the hosts and other guests. While the music is intended to entertain those present (without dance or drama), it also serves a ritual function, helping to maintain balance at important transitional points in the life of a person or community.

More often, *gamelan* music is performed as accompaniment for dance or theater—a refined female ensemble dance (*srimpi* or *bedhaya;* see Figures 7-5, 7-6), a flirtatious female solo dance; a vigorous, martial lance dance; or an evening of drama based on Javanese legendary history, for example. A list of traditional genres currently performed in central Java with *gamelan* accompaniment would be long. Some are presented primarily

Figure 7-5
Dancers at Pujokusuman in Yogyarkarta perform a *srimpi*, a female court dance.

Courtesy of Peggy Choy

Durkee, Earth Visions Photographics

Figure 7-6
Dancers at Pakualaman Palace in Yogyakarta perform a *bedhaya*, a female court dance (here with innovative costumes).

in commercial settings, with an audience buying tickets. Others are more often part of a ritual ceremony.

The genre held in the highest esteem by most Javanese, and nearly always reserved for ritual ceremony, is the shadow puppet theatre (*wayang kulit*), which dates back a thousand years. Beginning with an overture played on the *gamelan* during the early evening, shadow puppet perfor mances normally last until dawn. With a screen stretched before him,* lamp overhead, and puppets to both sides, one master puppeteer (*dhalang*) operates all the puppets, performs all the narration and dialogue, sings mood songs, and directs the musicians for a period of about eight hours, with no intermission.

The musicians do not play constantly throughout the evening, but they must be ever ready to respond to a signal from the puppeteer. He leads the musicians and accents the action of the drama through a variety of percussion patterns that he plays by hitting against the wooden puppet chest to his left and by clanging metal plates suspended from the rim of the chest. If he is holding puppets in both hands, he uses his foot to sound these signals. He must be highly skilled as a manipulator, director, singer, and storyteller.

What the puppeteer delivers is not a fixed play written by a known playwright, but rather his own rendition of a basic story—usually closely related to versions performed by other puppeteers, but never exactly the same. It might be a well-known episode from the *Ramayana* or *Mahabharata,* epics of Indian origin that have been adapted and transformed in many parts of Southeast Asia and have been known in Java for a thousand

*Almost all Javanese puppeteers are male.

years. The music is drawn from a large repertory of pieces, none specific to a single play and many of which are played in other contexts as well.

A good musician knows many hundreds of pieces, but the pieces, like the shadow plays, are generally not uniform. Many regional and individual variants exist for some pieces. More important, the very conception of what constitutes a "*gamelan* piece" or "*gamelan* composition" (in Javanese: *gendhing*) is different from the Western notion of a musical piece, particularly as that notion has developed in the Western art music or "classical" tradition.

Gamelan Music: A Javanese *Gendhing* in Performance

CD 2 Track 2

We can best begin to understand what a Javanese *gendhing* is by considering one in some detail—how it is conceived and how it is realized in performance. Listen to "Bubaran Kembang Pacar" (CD Selection 26). This is from a recording I made in Yogyakarta with some of the most highly regarded senior musicians associated with the court. It was played on a bronze *gamelan* at the house of one of Yogyakarta's best known dancers and choreographers, Dr. Soedarsono, who founded the National Dance Academy (ASTI) in Yogyakarta and recently retired from serving as rector of the Indonesian Arts Institute there. You will note that it is an example of loud-playing style throughout. And you might have guessed that it is in the *pélog* scale system, with small and large intervals. It uses the *pélog bem* scale—tones 1, 2, 3, 5, and 6, with an occasional 4, but no 7. But what about its structure: How are the sounds organized in this piece—or, more precisely, this performance of this piece?

Unless they are connected directly to a previous piece in a medley sequence, Javanese *gendhings* begin with a solo introduction, played on one instrument or sung by a solo singer. Here a short introduction is played on the *bonang barung* by Pak Sastrapustaka, a well-known teacher and musician (1913–1991). During the latter portion, this *bonang* is joined by the two drums *kendhang gendhing* and *ketipung,* played (as is customary) by one drummer—in this case, the court musician Pak Kawindro. The drummer in the Javanese *gamelan* acts as a conductor, controlling the tempo and the dynamics (the relative levels of loudness and softness). He or she need not be visible to other musicians, since the "conducting" is accomplished purely through sound signals. He or she does not stand in front of the ensemble but sits unobtrusively in the midst of it.

Although we discussed the choice of "Bubaran Kembang Pacar" at this recording session, experienced musicians recognize the identity of the *gendhing* from the introduction and do not need to be told what piece is about to be performed. The *bonang* player (or other musician providing an introduction) may simply play the introduction to an appropriate piece and expect the other musicians to follow. At the end of the introduction, most of the rest of the ensemble joins in, the large gong sounds, and the main body of the *gendhing* begins.

The structure of this main body is based on principles of balance, divisions and subdivisions, and cycles that repeat. The basic time and melodic unit in *gendhing* is the *gongan,* a phrase marked off by the sound of either the largest gong (*gong ageng*) or the slightly smaller gong *siyem.* For most *gendhings,* these phrases are of regular length as measured in beats of the *balungan,* the melodic part usually played on the *slenthem* and the *saron* family—almost always some factor of two: 8 beats, 16 beats, 32 beats, 64 beats, 128 beats, 256 beats. (In the genre of pieces that serve as the staple for accompanying dramatic action, as we shall see, *gongans* are of irregular length and the regular unit is marked instead by the smaller gong *kempul.*) A *gongan* is subdivided into two or four shorter phrases by the *kenong,* and these further subdivided by *kempul, kethuk,* and in some lengthier pieces by *kempyang.*

The result is a pattern of interlocking percussion that repeats until a sound signal from the drummer or one of the lead melodic instruments (*bonang* in loud-playing style, *rebab* in soft-playing) directs the performers to end or to proceed to a different piece. Whereas in Western music composers provide explicit directions for performers to repeat a section, in Javanese *gamelan* performance repetition is assumed.

As we speak of "phrases" in describing music, Javanese liken the *gongan* to a sentence and conceive of the subdividing parts as "punctuation." For "Bubaran Kembang Pacar," after the gong stroke at the end of the introduction, the pattern of gong punctuation shown in Music Example 7-2 is repeated throughout.

Music Example 7-2
Interlocking punctuation pattern in "Bubaran Kembang Pacar."

```
.  .  .  .  .  .  .  .  .  .  .  .  .  .  .  .
t  w  t  N  t  P  t  N  t  P  t  N  t  P  t  N
                                             G
         t = kethuk
         N = kenong
         P = kempul
         G = gong or siyem
         w = rest
         . = one beat in balungan melody
```

The time distribution of the gong's punctuating beats is even, but the degree of stress or weight is not (even though no beat is played more loudly than any other on any single instrument). Javanese listeners feel the progression of stress levels indicated in Music Example 7-3, based on the levels of subdivision.

Music Example 7-3
Stress levels in punctuation pattern of "Bubaran Kembang Pacar."

```
SUBDIVISIONS
full gongan:                                                        G
1st level:                N              N              N           N
2nd level:     w                 P              P              P
3rd level:  t       t       t       t       t       t       t       t
           ------------------------------------------------------------
           wk  md  wk  str wk  md  wk  str wk  md  wk  str wk  md  wk  xstr

beat no.    1   2   3   4   5   6   7   8   9  10  11  12  13  14  15  16

              (wk = weak; md = medium; str = strong; xstr = very strong)
```

The strongest beat is the one coinciding with the largest and deepest sounding phrase marker, the *gong* (G), and with the *kenong* (N)—at the end of the phrase. Javanese would count this as one, *two,* three, **four,** etc., with the strongest beat being the sixteenth. This is the only beat where two punctuating gong instruments coincide. It is this "coincidence" that gives a sense of repose, a release of the rhythmic tension that builds through the course of the *gongan.*

Although in the West one may dismiss events as "mere coincidence," in Java the simultaneous occurrence of several events, the alignment of days of the week and dates (like our Friday the 13th), can be profoundly meaningful. It is not uncommon to determine a suitable day for a wedding, or for moving house, based on the coincidence of a certain day in the seven-day week with a certain day in the Javanese five-day market week, and this in turn within a certain Javanese month (in the lunar calendar rather than the solar calendar used in the West). And the simultaneous occurrence of what to Westerners would seem to be unrelated (and therefore meaningless) events—such as the sounding of a certain bird while in the course of carrying out a particular activity—can be interpreted in Java as an important omen.

This deep-seated view of the workings of the natural world is reflected in the structure of *gamelan* music, where coincidence is central to the coherence of the music. The sounding of the *gong* with the *kenong* marks the musical instant of greatest weight and is the only point at which a *gendhing* may end. Yet other lesser points of coincidence also carry weight. If we consider the piece from the perspective of the *balungan* melody, it is at the coincidence of the *balungan* with the *kenong* strokes that the next strongest stress is felt. And in pieces with longer *gongans* (e.g., 32, 64, or 128 beats), where there are many more *saron* beats and therefore many of them do not coincide with any punctuating gong, each *kenong* stroke and even each *kethuk* stroke may be an instance of emphasis and temporary repose.

The ethnomusicologist Judith Becker and her former student Stanley Hoffman have found it useful to represent the cyclic structure of *gendhings* by mapping patterns onto a circle, relating the flow of musical time to the recurring course traced by the hands on a clock. The pattern used in "Bubaran Kembang Pacar," then, can be notated as shown in Music Example 7-4. Becker has argued convincingly that the cyclic structure of Javanese *gendhings* reflects the persistence of Hindu-Buddhist conceptions of time introduced to Java during the first millennium C.E. and not wholly eliminated by the subsequent adoption of Islam. (For an elaboration of this theory, see Hoffman 1978, Becker 1979, and especially Becker 1981.)

Today the players of most of the punctuating instruments have a choice of pitch in performance of many pieces. Their choice is normally determined by the *balungan* melody tone played simultaneously, or the one about to be emphasized in the following phrase. However, when performing pieces in loud-playing style it is not unusual to use a single pitch throughout, reflecting earlier practice, when only one *kempul* and one or two *kenongs* were made for each *gamelan.* Here the musicians opt for this

Music Example 7-4
Punctuation pattern in "Bubaran Kembang Pacar" represented as a circle.

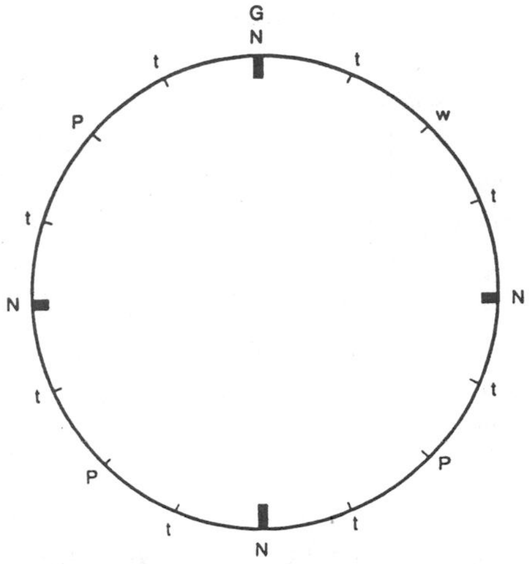

older practice; they use *kempul* tone 6 throughout and a special *kenong* tuned to tone 5 in the octave below the other *kenong.* The *kethuk,* as is customary in Yogya, is tuned to tone 2. The *gong* player chooses to sound the *gong ageng* only for the first and last *gong* strokes; otherwise he plays the smaller *gong siyem,* tuned to tone 2.

The punctuation pattern and its relation to the *balungan* melody is indicated in the first word of the full name of a *gendhing.* In fact, the way Javanese refer to *gendhings* normally includes their formal structure (in this case *bubaran*—sixteen beats per *gongan,* four *kenong* beats per *gongan*), the name of a particular melody (in this case "Kembang Pacar"—a kind of red flower), the scale system (*pélog*), and the modal category (*pathet nem*).

CD 2
Track 2

Let us now consider the *balungan* melody of this piece, notated as performed on the *saron demung, saron barung,* and *slenthem* (Music Example 7-5). The system used here and elsewhere in this chapter is the cipher (number) notation system now widely used throughout central and eastern Java. Dots in place of numerals indicate a rest—or, more correctly, the sustaining of the previous tone. Dots below numerals indicate the lower octave, and dots above indicate the higher octave. An extra space or two is often given after groups of four beats as a means of demarcating a "measure"—though in Java the stress is on the *last* beat, not the first. Today many Javanese musicians refer to notation to learn or to recall particular pieces, but they do not generally read from notation in performance. And

Music Example 7-5
Introduction and *balungan* melody for "Bubaran Kembang Pacar."

Introduction (on bonang): 5 3 5 . 2 3 5 6 2 4 5 4 2 15555 (G N over the final 5)

Main Body

punctuation (same each gongan):	t w t N	t P t N	t P t N	t P t N (G)
1st gongan:	3 6 3 5	3 6 3 5	3 6 3 5	6 5 3 2
2nd gongan:	6 5 3 2	6 5 3 2	6 5 3 2	5 3 5 6
3rd gongan:	2 1 2 6	2 1 2 6	2 1 2 6	3 5 3 2
4th gongan:	5 3 5 .	2 3 5 6	2 4 5 4	2 1 6 5

what is notated is usually only the *balungan* melody and introduction; the parts played on other instruments are recreated in relation to the *balungan* melody and are open to some degree of personal interpretation.

The piece consists of four *gongans* (each, of course, with the same *bubaran* structure), played one after the other. Each of the first three begins with a measure that is played three times in succession and ends on the same tone as the previous gong tone. This kind of regularity enhances the balanced symmetry provided by the punctuation structure. The fourth *gongan,* which stands out with its one rest (fourth beat) and lack of internal repetition, is melodically quite similar to the introduction and leads right back into the first.

The whole main body can be repeated as many times as the drummer desires, or as is appropriate to the context in which it is performed. Pieces in *bubaran* form usually are played at the end of performances—*bubar* means "to disperse." The guests or audience are expected to leave during the playing of the piece; thus the number of repetitions may depend on the length of time it takes those in attendance to get up to leave.

Already we have a fairly good understanding of the structure of this piece as performed. Let us focus our attention now on the part played by the drummer, using the smallest and largest drums in combination. Throughout the piece he plays a pattern specific not to this particular piece, but, like the punctuating pattern, generic to the *bubaran* form. That is, the drumming for any of the forty or so other pieces in this form would be the same: a particular introductory pattern, several variant patterns for the main body, and a special contrasting pattern reserved only for the playing of the final *gongan* and which, together with the slowing of tempo, acts to signal the ending. The patterns are made up of a vocabulary of drum strokes, each with a name that imitates onomatopoetically the actual drum sound (Music Example 7-6).

Music Example 7-6
Drum patterns for "Bubaran Kembang Pacar."

```
Introduction:                                                  N/G
 5   3   5   .    2   3   5   6    2   4   5   4    2   1 5 5 5 5
                                   T   T   d   D    T   d   d   .

Main Body:
            t   w   t   N    t   P   t   N    t   P   t   N    t   P   t   N/G
  (e.g.)    3   6   3   5    3   6   3   5    3   6   3   5    6   5   3   2
  A:        d   d   d D .    d   d   d D .    d   d   d D .  d D d D   d D .
                                       (played in 1st, 2nd, & 4th gongan)

            2   1   2   6    2   1   2   6    2   1   2   6    3   5   3   2
  B:      T d D . T d D .  T d D . T d D .  T d D . T d D .  d D d D   d D .
                                       (played in 3rd gongan)

            5   3   5   .    2   3   5   6    2   4   5   4    2   1   6   5
  Ending:   T d d   d   D    T d d D T d D    d D T d T d T  D d   D   d d .
                                       (played in 4th gongan, last time)
```

d = dung (a high, resonant sound produced by one or two fingers striking the larger head of the ketipung)
T = Tak (a short, crisp sound produced by slapping the smaller head of the of the ketipung with the palm)
D = Dang (a deep sound, produced by hitting the larger head of the kendhang gendhing, often in combination with Tak on the ketipung)

It is the drummer who first begins to play faster, thereby signaling the ensemble to speed up at the end of the second time through the large cycle of four *gongans.* As warning that he or she intends to end, he or she alters the last few strokes in the penultimate *gongan* (from dDdD .dD. to dDdD .TdD). This way the other musicians all know they are to slacken the tempo, though the precise rate is determined by the drummer. The playing of the ending pattern through the last *gongan* confirms his or her intentions.

We have seen how the punctuating gong parts and the drumming fit with the *balungan* in "Bubaran Kembang Pacar." We can now turn to the elaborating melodic instruments—here the *bonang barung* and *bonang panerus*—which normally play at a faster rate, subdividing the *balungan* part and providing variations based on the *balungan* melody. In pieces with *balungan* played at slower tempos, the *saron peking* also provides a limited degree of melodic elaboration, but in Yogyanese court style the instrument is sometimes omitted (as it is here).

I mentioned earlier that the only part normally notated is the *balungan.* Other melodic parts are derived through processes generally understood by practicing musicians. Ideally all musicians can play all the parts. In reality this is true only in the best professional groups, but most musicians have at least a passive knowledge of all the instruments and know how to respond to various signals and subtler nuances.

The two *bonangs* here perform in a style called "walking," usually alternating left and right hands in sounding combinations of tones derived from the *balungan.* The *bonang barung* part played the first time through the four *gongans* is notated in Music Example 7-7. The arrangement of kettle gongs on the instrument is given in the upper portion of the figure, and the notation below (with the same cipher system used to notate the *balungan*).

Music Example 7-7
Bonang barung part played in "Bubaran Kembang Pacar."

```
                      4̇    6̇    5̇    3̇    2̇    1̇    7̇
Kettles on bonang:
                      1    7    2    3    5    6    4

Bonang Playing in Bubaran Kembang Pacar:

balungan:     3   6   3   5    3   6   3   5    3   6   3   5    6   5   3   2

bonang:     3 6 3 6 3 5 3 5  3 6 3 6 3 5 3 5  3 6 3 6 3 5 3 5  6 5 3 5 6 . 6 .
                                                                       2   2

balungan:     6   5   3   2    6   5   3   2    6   5   3   2    5   3   5   6

bonang:     6 5 3 5 6 . 6 .  6 5 3 5 6 . 6 .  6 5 3 5 6 . 6 .  5 3 5 3 6 6 6̇ .
                    2   2            2   2            2   2                6

balungan:     2   1   2   6    2   1   2   6    2   1   2   6    3   5   3   2

bonang:     2̇ 1̇ 2̇ 1̇ 5 6 1̇ 6  2̇ 1̇ 2̇ 1̇ 5 6 1̇ 6  2̇ 1̇ 2̇ 1̇ 6 6 6̇ .  3 3 3̇ . 2 2 2̇ .
                                                          6       3       2

balungan:     5   3   5   .    2   3   5   6    2   4   5   4    2   1   6   5

bonang:     5̇ 3̇ 5̇ 3̇ 5 5 5̇ .  2̇ 3̇ 2̇ 3̇ 5̇ 6̇ 5̇ 6̇  2̇ 4̇ 2̇ 4̇ 5̇ 4̇ 5̇ 4̇  2̇ 1̇ 2̇ 1̇ 6 5 3 5
                        5
```

In later repetitions the *bonang barung* part remains similar, the variations reflecting the sensibilities of the player, who both adjusts to tempo changes and alters patterns purely for the aesthetic enjoyment of variation. The player has not learned a particular *bonang* part or set of variations, note for note, for this one piece. Rather, he or she has thoroughly internalized a vocabulary of traditional patterns known to fit with certain phrases of *balungan.* What a player usually will have learned about the particular piece, other than its *balungan,* is the octave register in which to play personal variations (e.g., 3 6 3 6 rather than 3̇ 6̇ 3̇ 6̇).

The *bonang panerus* plays similar sorts of variations of the *balungan* melody, but at twice the rate of the *bonang barung.* Music Example 7-8 gives *balungan, bonang barung,* and *panang panerus* for the first *gongan.* The arrangement of kettles is identical to that of *bonang barung,* though each is tuned an octave higher than the corresponding *bonang barung* kettle. You can see in this figure how the two *bonangs* vary by repetition: 3 6 in the *balungan* becomes 3 6 3 6 in the *bonang barung* part and 363.3636 in the *bonang panerus* part—all heard simultaneously.

Music Example 7-8
Bonang barung and *panerus* parts for "Bubaran Kembang Pacar," first *gongan.*

```
balungan:     3   6   3   5    3   6   3   5    3   6   3   5    6   5   3   2

bon. bar.:  3 6 3 6 3 5 3 5  3 6 3 6 3 5 3 5  3 6 3 6 3 5 3 5  6 5 3 5 6 . 6 .
                                                                        2   2

bon. pnr.: 363.3636353.3535 363.3636353.3535 363.3636353.3535 656.6535626.626.
```

Yet it is not simply a matter of mechanical replication throughout, for alternate tones can be substituted (e.g., 6 5 3 5 instead of 6 5 6 5) and other choices can be made. Still, we can understand why the Javanese refer to the *saron* and *slenthem* melody as *balungan:* the term literally means "outline" or "skeleton." And it provides just that for the elaborating instruments and, in soft-playing style, for the voices as well. The degree to which the *saron* and *slenthem* part actually sounds like an outline depends on its tempo and the resulting levels at which it is subdivided by the elaborating instruments.

Irama Level

In this performance of "Bubaran Kembang Pacar," the *bonang barung* plays at twice the density of the *balungan,* subdividing it by two. This ratio defines one of five possible levels of *balungan* subdivision, known as the *irama* level. If the tempo had slowed sufficiently the *bonang barung* would double its ratio with the *balungan,* subdividing each beat by four. Ward Keeler aptly likens the process to a car shifting gears, in this case down-shifting as it goes up a steep grade (Keeler 1987:225). And the *bonang panerus,* in order to maintain its relationship with the *bonang barung,* would double as well, resulting in an eight-to-one ratio with the *balungan.* At the slowest *balungan* tempo, the *bonang barung* would have a ratio of sixteen beats to one *balungan* beat, and the *bonang panerus,* along with several of the soft instruments, would play a full thirty-two beats for each *balungan* beat!

Performing Your Own *Gamelan* Music

To get the feeling of *gamelan* ensemble performance, all you need is a group of seven or eight people. They can use any percussion instruments available, such as Orff instruments, or simply use their voices. Start by assigning each punctuating instrument to one person. The gong player can simply say "gong" (in a low, booming voice), the *kempul* player "pul" (middle voice) the *kenong* player "nong" (long and high) and the *kethuk* player "tuk" (short and low). Another can be assigned to play the drum pattern (saying the syllables given in the patterns in Music Example 7-6). Then the remaining performers can divide among themselves the *balungan* melody and, if they are inclined, some *bonang* elaboration. With a larger group, people can double up on all instruments except the drum.

Try the piece we have listened to, since the tune is familiar. The "drummer" should control the tempo and play the ending pattern, slowing down to end. Try different versions with different numbers of repetitions. You can end at any gong tone; it does not have to be at the end of the fourth *gongan.*

Gamelan Music and Shadow Puppetry

Now we consider some of the music most closely associated with shadow puppet performance (Figure 7-7). The piece we have studied is seldom played for dance or dramatic accompaniment. The musical staples of the shadow puppet repertory are pieces with dense *kenong* and *kempul* playing, and *gongans* of varying length—pieces that generate a level of excitement, partly because of the dense gong punctuation. For each *pathet* there are at least three of these staple pieces: relatively calm (*ayak-ayakan*), somewhat

Figure 7-7
Puppeteer Ki Gondo Darman performing *wayang kulit* at the ASKI Performing Arts Academy in Surakarta.

Arthur Durkee, Earth Visions Photographics

excited (*srepegan, playon*) and very excited (*sampak*). The *gong* punctuation is densest in the very excited pieces and less so in the calm pieces. Which piece is to be played is determined by the puppeteer, who must be just as thoroughly at home with the *gamelan* music as he is with the many hundreds of characters and stories that make up this tradition.

CD 2
Tracks 3, 4

We are going to listen to two versions of one of these pieces, the Yogyanese "Playon Lasem" *sléndro pathet nem* (CD Selections 27 and 28). Depending on the mood the puppeteer wishes to establish, the piece can be played in loud-playing or in soft-playing style, or switched at any point. (*Ayak-ayakan,* the calmest of the three, is usually in soft-playing style; and *sampak,* the most excited, is always performed in loud-playing style). Also, the length of the piece can be radically tailored to suit the needs of the dramatic moment. Sometimes it may go on, through repetition of a central section, for five or ten minutes. The first instance we shall hear takes a little over a minute, only beginning to repeat when the puppeteer signals the playing of a special ending phrase. All the musicians must know one or two of these ending phrases for each *gong* tone and be ready to tag the appropriate one onto any *gongan* if the signal comes.

Music Example 7-9 gives *balungan* notation for the entire piece. The *gong ageng* or *siyem* sound at the end of each line, as written. The *kenong* plays on every *balungan* beat, the *kempul* every second beat (except where the *gong* sounds), and the *kethuk* between the beats. Notice that here the frequency of "coincidence" between *gong* punctuators is very high: every second beat! To Javanese, this makes for exciting music, appropriate for scenes charged with emotion, even for fights. Quick rapping on the puppet chest signals the musicians to play. The drummer, playing the middle-sized drum (*ciblon*), and sometimes the *kenong* player as well, enter just before the rest of the ensemble.

Music Example 7-9
"Playon Lasem," *sléndro pathet nem.*

```
Introductory portion:      (signal....)  5                 Length of Gongan
                      6 5  6 5 6 5  2 3 5 6                   10 beats
                 1 6 5 6  2 3 5 3  2 1 2 1                   12 beats
                 2 1 2 1  6 5 3 5  2 3 5 6                   12 beats
                 1 6 5 6  5 3 2 3  1 2 3 2**                 12 beats

Repeated portion:
    [: 5 6 5 3  5 6 5 3  6 5 2 6  5 2 3 5*                   16 beats
                         3 2 3 2  6 5 2 3                     8 beats
       5 3 5 3  5 2 3 5  1 6 5 3  2 1 3 2                    16 beats
                         6 6 1 2  3 5 6 5                     8 beats
                2 1 2 1  2 1 3 2  5 6 1 6                    12 beats
                         3 2 5 3  6 5 3 2 :]                  8 beats
  Endings:
   *  from gong tone 5 (first rendition):   2 1  3 2 1 6
   ** from gong tone 2 (second rendition):  5 3  2 1 2 6
```

- -

```
Punctuation Pattern for playon/srepegan form:

   kempul & gong:        P  (repeat x ?)    G        e.g.:   P   P   P   P   G
   kenong & kethuk:   tNtN  (repeat x ?) tNtN             tNtNtNtNtNtNtNtNtNtN
   balungan:             . .  (etc.)      . .              6 5 6 5 6 5 2 3 5 6
```

During the course of the all-night performance at which I recorded these examples, the puppeteer (Ki Suparman) signaled this piece to be played eighteen times—all, of course, within the *pathet nem* section of the night, which lasted from about 9:00 A.M. until about 1:30 A.M.

CD 2 Track 3

The first rendition you hear (CD Selection 27) begins in soft style but speeds and gets loud by the end of the first *gongan.* It then proceeds through the entire melody, begins to repeat the main section, and ends, on signal, after the first *gongan.*

CD 2 Track 4

In the second rendition (CD Selection 28), entirely in loud-playing style, the musicians never even reach the "main" section. To add variety to this rendition, played quite late during the *pathet nem* section (about 12:30 A.M.), the *saron* players play variant phrases for some of the passages notated in Music Example 7-9, though the *slenthem* player holds to the previous version.

Even without such change, we can see that this one piece has the potential for a great variety of renditions, through changes in tempo, instrumentation, and ending points. This is the essence of shadow puppet music—a very well known piece, played over and over, but uniquely tailored each time to fit precisely with the dramatic intentions of the puppeteer and kept fresh by the inventiveness of the instrumentalists and singers, who constantly add subtle variations.

Bali

Lying just east of Java, separated by a narrow strait, is the island of Bali, whose unique culture and spectacular natural beauty have fascinated scholars, artists, and tourists from around the world. It is also a place where almost everyone takes part in some activity we would call artistic: music, dance, carving, painting. And while the Balinese demonstrate abilities that often strike the Westerner as spectacular, they maintain that such activities are a normal part of life. The exquisite masked dancer by night may well be a rice farmer by day, and the player of lightning-fast interlocking musical passages accompanying him may manage a small eating stall.

Most of the several million people inhabiting this small island adhere not to Islam, Indonesia's majority religion, but to a blend of Hinduism and Buddhism resembling that which flourished in Java prior to the spread of Islam (fifteenth to sixteenth centuries C.E.). Though it would be a mistake to believe that what exists in Bali today represents a living museum of Javanese Hindu-Buddhist culture, the Balinese and Javanese share elements of a common cultural heritage. As in Java, we find percussion ensembles known as *gamelan* (or *gambelan*), with metal slab instruments and knobbed gong instruments that look and sound very similar to those of the Javanese *gamelan.* Some of the names are the same (*gendèr, gong, gambang, saron, suling, rebab*) or similar (*kempur, kemong*). Most ensembles employ some version of the *pélog* scale system (some with all seven tones, others with five or six). The accompaniment for Balinese shadow puppetry, as in Java, employs the *sléndro* scale system, although the instruments used consist only of a quartet of *gendèrs* (augmented by a few other instruments for *Ramayana* stories). Many Balinese pieces employ gong punctuating patterns similar in principle to those of Java. The Balinese play *gamelan* for ritual observances, as in Java, though usually at temple festivals, or in procession to or from them rather than at someone's residence.

Nevertheless the music of these two neighboring cultures is not the same. One fundamental difference is that the Balinese maintain a variety of ensembles, each with its distinct instrumentation and associated with certain occasions and functions. There is no single large ensemble that one can simply call the Balinese *gamelan.* Still, the style of music one hears performed on most ensembles in Bali (1) is strictly instrumental, (2) is characterized by changes in tempo and loudness (often abrupt), and (3) requires a dazzling technique by many of the musicians, who play fast interlocking rhythms, often consisting of asymmetrical groupings of two or three very fast beats. People often comment that Balinese music is exciting and dynamic compared with other Indonesian musics, exploiting contrasts in the manner of Western art music.

Listeners also comment on the shimmery quality of the many varieties of bronze ensembles. This quality is obtained by tuning instruments in pairs, with one instrument intentionally tuned slightly higher in pitch than its partner. When sounded together, they produce very fast vibrations. In the West, piano tuners rely on these same vibrations, called "beats," to "temper" the tuning, though on a piano it is intervals that are made intentionally "out of tune," rather than identical strings sounding the same tone. Of course, the intentionally "out-of-tune" pairs of metallophones are perceived to be "in tune" (i.e., culturally correct) in Bali, just as the piano is in our culture.

The most popular ensemble in Bali today is the *gamelan gong kebyar,* which developed during the early twentieth century, along with the virtuosic dance it often accompanies (also called *kebyar*—literally "flash," "dazzle"). *Kebyar* music is indeed flashy, requiring not only great virtuosity of the players but also a consummate sense of ensemble—the ability of many to play as one. This music can be heard on any of a number of commercially available recordings (see the list at the end of this chapter).

Rarer today, though making something of a comeback in modified form after its near extinction seventy years ago with the decline of the Balinese courts, is the *gamelan semar pegulingan* (Figure 7-8). The name has been rendered in English as "*gamelan* of the love god." It was formerly played for the king's pleasure within the court during the late afternoon and evening and with slight modification became the favored ensemble to accompany the famous *lègong* (an intricate dance performed by three young girls). It is a rather delicate-sounding ensemble, yet unmistakably Balinese. It is this ensemble that the late composer and scholar of Balinese music Colin McPhee heard by chance on early recordings and that enticed him to travel in 1931 to Bali, where he stayed to study Balinese music for nearly ten years.

Figure 7-8
The *gamelan semar pegulingan* of Teges, Kanginan, Peliatan, Bali.

Richard Wallis

CD 2
Track 5

Listen to "Tabuh Gari" (CD Selection 29), which serves in Bali as a closing piece, a counterpart to the *bubaran* pieces in Java. "Tabuh Gari" begins with an introduction (*pengawit*) in two sections. The first starts in free rhythm (without steady pulse) on the *trompong,* a set of fourteen kettle gongs, like the Javanese *bonang,* but in a single row. The second section (*penyumu*) begins at the first sound of the *kempur*—the largest gong in the ensemble, similar to the Javanese *siyem*—and other instruments join and establish a pulse.

At the next sound of the *kempur* (32 beats after the first), the full ensemble plays the main section (*pengawak*). The main body, which resembles the Javanese *balungan* in its regular, even rhythm, is played on single-octave gendèr-type instruments known as *jublags* (or *calungs*). Every fourth tone is stressed by the *jegogans,* which are like the *jublags,* but an octave lower. Delicate and skillful interlocking is performed on higher-pitched instruments of the *gendèr* family (*kantilans* and *gangsas*). Four bamboo flutes (*sulings*) double the faster instrumental parts. Other percussion instruments provide secondary punctuation and emphasis. The *pengawak* stops momentarily at the next *kempur* stroke, only to start up again and repeat. A second pause leads on to the final, livelier section, the *pengecèt,* which is played over and over. The tempo is controlled throughout all sections but the first by the interlocking patterns of two drummers, each playing a double-headed cylindrical drum (*kendhang*).

The Balinese have long used a system of notation for recording the melodies of their most sacred pieces, though they do not use notation in performance. The system is based on contrasting vowel sounds, naming tones *dong, déng, dung, dang,* and *ding* (with variants for six- and seven-tone melodies). Since you have already had to learn one new notation system in this chapter, and since it is readily applicable to Balinese as well as Javanese *pélog,* I have decided on notation in Javanese cipher for the main melody (*jublag* part) in the *penyumu, pengawak,* and *pengecèt* sections (Music Example 7-10). This may not sound like the "main" melody at first hearing, since the faster-moving and more rhythmically varied elaborations of this melody are more audible throughout. The tempo is roughly forty-eight beats per minute in the *penyumu,* thirty-six beats per minute in the *pengawak,* and sixty-six beats per minute for most of the *pengecèt* (speeding toward the end).

Music Example 7-10
"Tabuh Gari," played on the *gamelan semar pegulingan.*

```
Introduction (on trompong):                  . . . 5P        P = kempur

Penyemu:        1 3 6 3  1 3 1 5  2 5 2 6  5 6 3 6
                5 6 2 3  5 2 3 5  6 5 3 2  5 3 2 6P

Pengawak:       5 6 1 2 *3 2 5 6  5 6 1 2  3 5 3 5         _  = jegogan
                6 5 3 5  2 3 5 6  5 6 3 5  3 6 5 3
                1 2 3 2  5 6 5 3  5 3 1 2  1 6 5 3
                5.3 5 6  5 6 3 5  6 5 3 6  5 3 1 2
                6 1 5 3  2 6 1 2P  (1st time: . . . 2, return to *3, above)
                                   (2nd time: . 5 . 2P, move on to pengecèt)

Pengecèt:       3 5 3 2P 3 5 3 2P  1 6 3 2P 1 6 3 2P  (repeat many times)
```

Even in this piece, representing a style of considerable age and what might be called the quieter side of Balinese music, you can hear the shimmering metallic filigree, the asymmetrical rhythms, and the changes in tempo so important to Balinese music. I hope this one brief example has whetted your appetite to explore the incredible variety of Balinese music, which, more than any other Indonesian tradition, is well represented on records commercially available in Europe and North America.

Indonesian Popular Music

Most of the music Indonesians would identify as "popular" is, like most popular music anywhere in the world, characterized by the use of at least some Western instruments and Western harmony (see Hatch 1989). It is disseminated through the mass media, performed by recognized stars, and is essentially a "commercial" genre. Without going into the interesting history of Western-influenced music in Indonesia, which has primarily been in the popular vein, I would like to introduce one variety of contemporary popular music and consider one key representative superstar. This is a genre sometimes known as *pop berat* (literally "heavy pop"; see Hatch 1989) or sometimes as *pop kreatif* ("creative pop"), represented by Guruh Sukarnoputra. Guruh is of the elite; he is the youngest living son of the founding father of the Republic of Indonesia, President Sukarno. Born in 1953, Guruh was raised in the presidential palace in Jakarta, college educated, and formally trained not only in piano but also in traditional Javanese and Balinese *gamelan.* Like his father, Guruh feels an intense patriotism that at times seems to blind him to the glaring inequities in contemporary Indonesian society. And, again like his father, Guruh is far from orthodox Islam and sees Indonesia's culture as pluralistic and inescapably mixed with influences from the West. But where President Sukarno wielded power like a latter-day god-king with a matchless gift of oratory, Guruh does so through his music.

After his father's death in 1970 Guruh began his musical career, playing first with a pop music group in Jakarta. After several years of architectural study in Holland, he formed his innovative and highly acclaimed Guruh Gipsy group. In early 1977 he released the *Guruh Gipsy* cassette, which one critic later called the most important Indonesian cassette of the 1970s. Here Guruh demonstrates musically his penchant for unusual juxtapositions and superimpositions of Western and Indonesian elements. He also demonstrates a worldly musical sophistication, with arrangements drawing on a full spectrum of U.S. popular styles from circus music to Motown soul music, 1930s crooning to 1990s heavy metal. The music of Guruh Gipsy sounds radically different from one cut to the next and often even within one single piece. It is a music for listening, not for casual social dancing.

CD 2
Track 6

Listen to the several excerpts from a lengthy (sixteen-minute) piece entitled "Indonesia Maharddhika," which translates as "Indonesia [is] Free," using an intentionally archaic word for "free": the Sanskrit-sounding *maharddhika,* rather than the modern Indonesian *merdeka* (CD Selection 30). The first excerpt combines acid rock, a gapped scale closely resembling *pélog,* and Old Javanese poetry. The second presents a combination of interlocking Balinese metallophones (*gangsas*) with electric guitar and synthesizer, and the third an optimistic, patriotic text with episodic breaks.

Excerpts from "Indonesia Maharddhika"

A: (In Old Javanese language)
Om awighnam astu
DINGaryan ring sasi karo
ROhinikanta padem
NIcitha redite prathama . . .

B: Instrumental (Balinese gamelan with electric guitars and synthesizer)

C: (In Indonesian language)

Cerah gilang gemilang	Clear and bright
Harapan masa datang	The hope for the coming era
Rukun damai mulia	Harmonious, peaceful, glorious
Indonesia tercinta	Beloved Indonesia
Selamat sejahtera	Safe and prosperous
GUnung langit samudra	Mountain, sky, ocean
RUH semesta memuja.	The whole spirit worships.

Traditional Javanese court poets often incorporated their names within their poems by means of a device known as *sandhi asma* (literally "hidden name"), whereby the first syllable of each line was part of the author's name. Guruh uses the device, constructing the lines of poetry so that the first syllables or first letters conceal the first names of members of Guruh Gipsy: Oding, Roni, Chris, and Guruh.

Since the release of this important cassette, Guruh's music has become increasingly less experimental, but it remains both sophisticated and eclectic. More recent cassettes show influences from driving disco music, sassy Broadway musicals, soft Brazilian sambas, stirring Sousa marches, late Romantic opera, and even the dissonant orchestral sonorities of twentieth-century Western concert music. He has mounted many spectacular performances that combine such blatant signs of patriotism as red and white costumes (the national colors) and incessant flag-waving on stage, with music performed by a variety of popular stars. These shows have been fantastically expensive by Indonesian standards, some costing over $100,000, with tickets priced far beyond the reach of any but the most wealthy. Guruh's musical expressions of patriotism have drawn considerable criticism from the press, who have labeled it both "elitist" and "naive."

Guruh is but one of several hundred pop stars in Indonesia today. His musical sound can begin to give you an idea of the complexity of Indonesia's popular music—still mostly unexplored by research scholars. The idea of combining *gamelan* music with pop music, explored by Guruh since the 1970s, has become a major trend in the late 1990s. Alongside this synthesis, Western styles of pop (from easy listening and country, to ska and reggae, to heavy metal and rap) created and performed by Indonesian musicians is widely heard at live concerts and on cassettes, radio, and television, including MTV shows produced in Indonesia. For a taste of Indonesia's popular style known as *dangdut,* which incorporates Indian film music (as we have heard in CD 1-24, "Engal kalyanam, in Chapter 6), sample Rhoma Irama's "Begadang II" on *Indonesian Popular Music* (Smithsonian Folkways CD SF 40056).

Guruh's public personality is enigmatic, even meek. His tastes in songwriting and stage production, combined with his direct descent from a leader of mythical stature give him a powerful and mysterious presence. Guruh's lyrics are complex. He often chooses obscure words and unusual musical instruments. His music has had to build its own following, mostly among urban elite youth on Java. Guruh has also drawn on Indonesia's religious traditions, and he has aspired to use his music to do more than entertain. He offers spiritual guidance to his listeners and followers. He sees himself as a spokesman for the past glory and future hopes of the nation.

Other pop music stars represent different beliefs. Throughout this chapter we have experienced some of the great diversity within Indonesia's music. In popular as well as other types of music we glimpse that diversity and find that it applies not only to traditional regional culture but also to popular music disseminated nationally.

In June 1999, Indonesia experienced its first free elections in more than forty years, with a staggering forty-eight political parties vying for seats in the people's consultative assembly (a new diversity based more on political philosophy and religion than on regional or ethnic identity). This new openness has already begun to affect Indonesian music by engendering an outpouring of political songs on commercial cassettes and a new celebration of street singers accompanying their urgent and impassioned songs with guitars and shouts of "Reformasi!" ("Reformation!").

References

Becker, Judith. 1979. "Time and Tune in Java." In *The Imagination of Reality: Essays in Southeast Asian Coherence Systems,* edited by A. L. Becker and Aram A. Yengoyan, 197–210. Norwood, N.J.: Ablex.

———. 1981. "Hindu-Buddhist Time in Javanese Gamelan Music." In *The Study of Time,* vol. 4, edited by J. F. Fraser. New York: Springer-Verlag.

———. 1988. "Earth, Fire, *Sakti,* and the Javanese Gamelan." *Ethnomusicology* 32 (3): 385–91.

Guruh Gipsy. 1976. PT Dela Rahita, Jakarta.

Hatch, Martin. 1989. "Popular Music in Indonesia (1983)." In *World Music, Politics and Social Change,* edited by Simon Frith, 47–67. Manchester, England: Univ. Press.

Hoffman, Stanley B. 1978. "Epistemology and Music: A Javanese Example." *Ethnomusicology* 22 (1): 69–88.

Indonesian Popular Music: Kroncong, Dangdut, and Langgam Jawa. Music of Indonesia 2. Compiled and annotated by Philip Yampolsky. Smithsonian Folkways CD SF 40056.

Keeler, Ward. 1987. *Javanese Shadow Plays, Javanese Selves.* Princeton, N.J.: Princeton Univ. Press.

Kunst, Jaap. 1973. *Music in Java: Its History, Its Theory, and Its Technique.* 2 vols. 3rd rev. ed. by Ernst Heins. The Hague: Martinus Nijhoff.

Surjodiningrat, Wasisto, P. J. Sudarjana, and Adhi Susanto. 1972. *Tone Measurements of Outstanding Javanese Gamelans in Jogjakarta and Surakarta.* Yogyakarta: Gadjah Mada Univ. Press.

Additional Reading

On Music:

Becker, Judith. 1980. *Traditional Music in Modern Java: Gamelan in a Changing Society.* Honolulu: Univ. Press of Hawaii.

Becker, Judith, and Alan Feinstein, eds. 1984, 1987, and 1988. *Karawitan: Source Readings in Javanese Gamelan and Vocal Music.* 3 vols. Ann Arbor: Univ. of Michigan Center for South and Southeast Asian Studies.

Brinner, Ben. 1995. *Knowing Music, Making Music.* Chicago: Univ. of Chicago Press.

Hood, Mantle. 1954. *The Nuclear Theme as a Determinant of Paṭet in Javanese Music.* Groningen, Netherlands: J. B. Wolters.

Hood, Mantle, and Hardja Susilo. 1967. *Music of the Venerable Dark Cloud: Introduction, Commentary, and Analysis.* Los Angeles: Univ. of California Press.

Lindsay, Jennifer. 1992. *Javanese Gamelan: Traditional Orchestra of Indonesia,* 2nd ed. New York: Oxford Univ. Press.

Manuel, Peter. 1988. *Popular Musics of the Non-Western World: An Introductory Survey* (esp. pp. 205–20). New York: Oxford Univ. Press.

McPhee, Colin. 1966. *Music in Bali.* New Haven, Conn.: Yale Univ. Press.

Sumarsam. 1995. *Gamelan: Cultural Interaction and Musical Development in Central Java.* Chicago: Univ. of Chicago Press.

Sutton, R. Anderson. 1991. *Traditions of Gamelan Music in Java: Musical Pluralism and Regional Identity.* Cambridge: Cambridge Univ. Press.

Tenzer, Michael. 1991. *Balinese Music.* Berkeley, Calif., and Singapore: Periplus.

Additional Listening

Java:

Bedhaya Duradasih, Court of Music of Kraton Surakarta II. King Record KICC 5193.

Chamber Music of Central Java. King Record KICC 5152.

Court Music of Kraton Surakarta. King Music KICC 5151.

The Gamelan of Cirebon. World Music Library KICC 5130.

Java: "Langen Mandra Wanara," Opéra de Danuredjo VII. Musiques traditionelles vivantes III. Ocora 558 507/9.

Java: Palais Royal de Yogyakarta, Volume 4: La musique de concert. Ocora (Radio France) C 560087.

Javanese Court Gamelan. Elektra/Nonesuch Explorer Series 972044-2.

Klenengan Session of Solonese Gamelan I. King Record KICC 5185.

Langendriyan, Music of Mangkunegaran Solo II. King Record KICC 5194.

Music of Mangkunegaran Solo I. King Record KICC 5184.

Music from the Outskirts of Jakarta: Gambang Kromong. Smithsonian Folkways SF 40057.

The Music of K. R. T. Wasitodiningrat. CMP Records CD 3007.

Sangkala. Icon 5501 (Distributed by Elektra/Asylum).

Shadow Music of Java. Rounder CD 5060.

Songs before Dawn: Gandrung Banyuwangi. Smithsonian Folkways SF 40055.

The Sultan's Pleasure: Javanese Gamelan and Vocal Music from the Palace of Yogyakarta. Music of the World CDT-116.

Bali:

Bali: Gamelan and Kecak. Elektra Nonesuch Explorer Series CD 979204-4.

Gamelan Gong Kebyar, Bali. Elektra Nonesuch CD 79280-2.

Gamelan Music of Bali. Lyrichord LYRCD–7179.

Golden rain: Gong Kebyar of Gunung Sari, Bali. Elektra Nonesuch CD 79219-2.

Kecak from Bali. Kecak Ganda Sari. Bridge BCD 9019.

Music of Bali: Gamelan Semar Pegulingan from the Village of Ketewel. Lyrichord LYRCD 7408.

Music of the Gamelan Gong Kebyar, Bali. Vital Records 401-2 (2 discs).

Additional Viewing

The JVC Video Anthology of World Music and Dance (videorecording), 1990. Edited by Fujii Tomoaki, with assistant editors Omori Yasuhiro and Sakurai Tetsuo; in collaboration with the National Museum of Ethnology (Osaka); produced by Ichikawa Katsumori, directed by Nakagawa Kunihiko and Ichihashi Yuji. Victor Company of Japan, Ltd., in collaboration with Smithsonian Folkways Recordings. Distributed by Rounder Records, Cambridge, MA 02140. 30 videocassettes + guide.

Volume 9 contains footage of Javanese shadow puppetry (poor quality), along with studio footage of Balinese *kecak* ("monkey chant") and Sundanese music (recorded in Japan).

Volume 10 contains a variety of Balinese examples, recorded in Bali, mostly employing a *gamelan semar pegulingan* (even for contexts in which this ensemble is not appropriate).

Bali:

Bali Beyond the Postcard (16mm film and VHS videorecording), 1991. Produced and directed by Nancy Dine, Peggy Stern, and David Dawkins. Distributed by Filmakers Library, New York, and by "Outside in July," 59 Barrow Street, New York, NY 10014. *Gamelan* and dance in four generations of a Balinese family.

Releasing the Spirits: A Village Cremation in Bali (VHS videorecording), 1991 [1981]. Directed by Patsy Asch, Linda Connor, *et al.* Distributed by Documentary Educational Resources, Watertown, MA. Cremation rituals in a central Balinese village.

Java:

Traditional Dances of Indonesia, Dances of Jogjakarta, Central Java: Langen Mandra Wanara (videorecording), 1990 [from 16mm film made in 1975]. Directed and produced by William Heick. Distributed by University of California Extension Media Center, 2176 Shattuck Ave., Berkeley, CA 94704. Dance-opera presenting an episode from the *Ramayana.*

Traditional Dances of Indonesia, Dances of Surakarta, Central Java: Srimpi Anglir Mendung (videorecording), 1990 [from 16mm film made in 1976]. Directed and produced by William Heick. Distributed by University of California Extension Media Center, 2176 Shattuck Ave., Berkeley, CA 94704. Refined female court dance.

(Ten additional videorecordings from the same distributor present additional dances from Java, as well as dances from Bali and West Sumatra.)

CHAPTER

8

East Asia/Japan

Linda K. Fujie

Present-day Japan impresses the first-time visitor as an intense, fascinating, and sometimes confusing combination of old and new, of Eastern and Western and things beyond categorization. Strolling through the Ginza area of Tokyo, for example, you find many colorful remnants of an earlier age sprinkled among the gigantic department stores and elegant boutiques. You also find the ubiquitous McDonald's (*Makudonarudosu*). Tiny noodle shops and old stores selling kimono material or fine china carry the atmosphere of a past era. Looming over a central boulevard, in the midst of modern office buildings, is the Kabuki-za, a large, impressive theater built in the traditional style.

As the visitor begins to sense from the streets of Japan's capital, many aspects of Japanese life today—from architecture to social attitudes to music—are an intriguing mix of the traditional and the foreign. Japan has absorbed outside cultural influences for centuries, many of which originate in other parts of Asia. The writing system comes from China, and one of the major religions, Buddhism, is from India, through Korea and China. Connections with Chinese and Korean music and musical instruments are a fundamental part of the history of traditional music in Japan.* In the late nineteenth and twentieth centuries, European and American ideas and objects have also had a major impact on Japanese culture.

Although cultural borrowing has clearly been important in Japanese history, the stereotype of the Japanese as "mere imitators" must also be laid aside. The Japanese have developed a unique culture, both through their own creativity and by imaginatively adapting foreign elements into their own culture. Historically, geographical and political circumstances have isolated Japan to the extent that such independent creativity and adaptation were necessary. A group of islands separated from the Asian continent by an often treacherous sea, Japan set itself apart for several centuries. This

*In this chapter, "traditional music" in relation to Japan will refer to those musical genres developed mainly in pre-Meiji Japan—that is, before 1868 and the beginning of a period of strong Western influence on Japanese music.

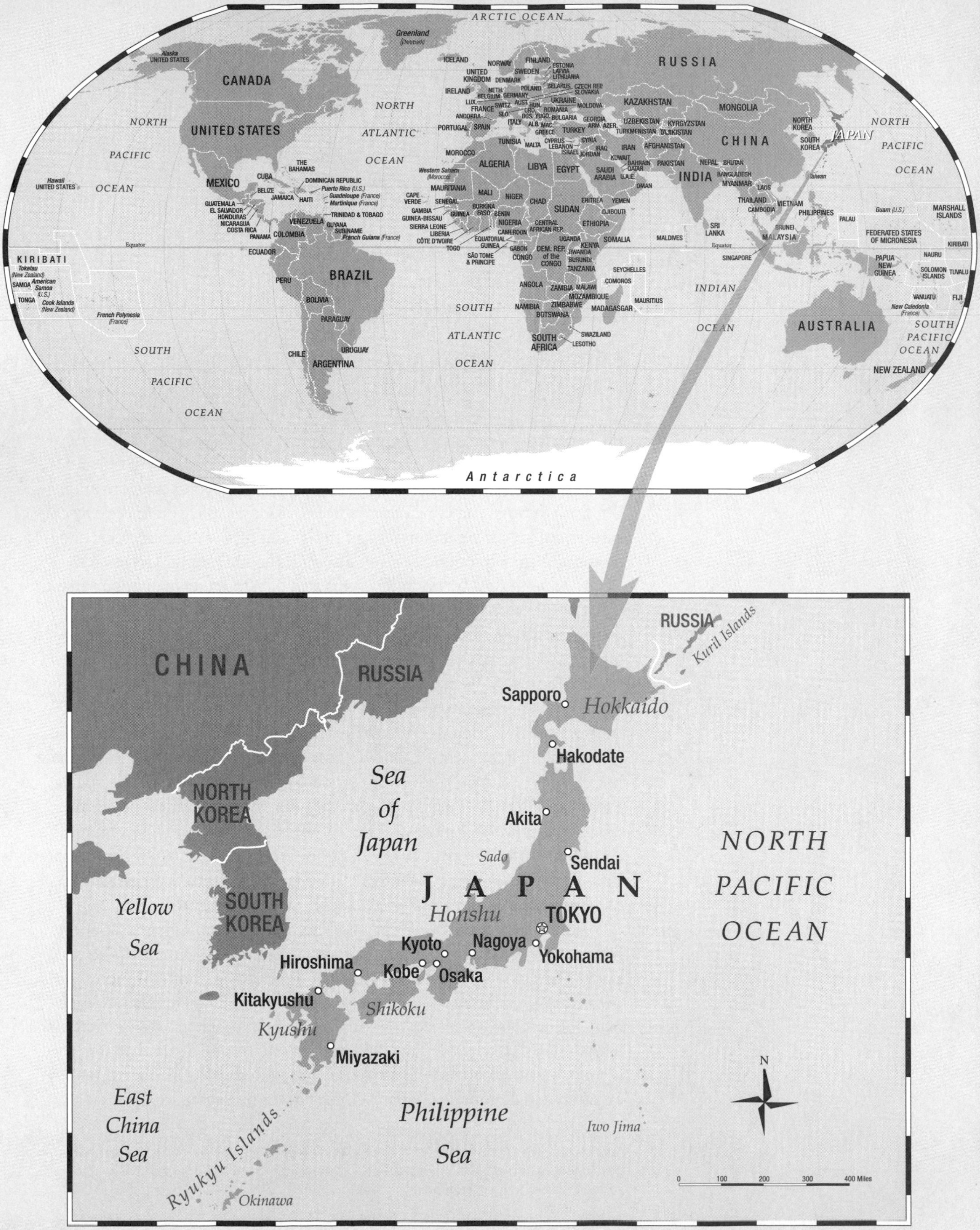

ARCTIC OCEAN
Greenland
(Denmark)
Alaska
UNITED STATES
CANADA
ICELAND
NORWAY
FINLAND
SWEDEN
ESTONIA
LATVIA
LITHUANIA
UNITED KINGDOM
DENMARK
IRELAND
NETH.
BELGIUM
GERMANY
POLAND
BELARUS
CZECH REP.
SLOVAKIA
LUX.
FRANCE
SWITZ.
AUST.
HUN.
UKRAINE
MOLDOVA
ROMANIA
ANDORRA
SLO.
CRO.
BOS.
YUGO.
BULGARIA
PORTUGAL
SPAIN
ITALY
ALB.
MAC.
GREECE
TURKEY
GEORGIA
ARM.
AZER.
RUSSIA
KAZAKHSTAN
MONGOLIA
UZBEKISTAN
KYRGYZSTAN
TURKMENISTAN
TAJIKISTAN
NORTH KOREA
SOUTH KOREA
JAPAN
CHINA
NORTH
PACIFIC
OCEAN
UNITED STATES
NORTH
ATLANTIC
OCEAN
TUNISIA
MALTA
CYPRUS
LEBANON
SYRIA
ISRAEL
JORDAN
IRAQ
IRAN
AFGHANISTAN
KUWAIT
BAHRAIN
QATAR
PAKISTAN
NEPAL
BHUTAN
BANGLADESH
MOROCCO
ALGERIA
LIBYA
EGYPT
SAUDI ARABIA
U.A.E.
OMAN
INDIA
MYANMAR
LAOS
Taiwan
Western Sahara
(Morocco)
THE BAHAMAS
Hawaii
UNITED STATES
MEXICO
CUBA
DOMINICAN REPUBLIC
Puerto Rico (U.S.)
Guadeloupe (France)
Martinique (France)
BELIZE
JAMAICA
HAITI
GUATEMALA
EL SALVADOR
HONDURAS
NICARAGUA
COSTA RICA
PANAMA
TRINIDAD & TOBAGO
VENEZUELA
GUYANA
SURINAME
French Guiana (France)
COLOMBIA
ECUADOR
MAURITANIA
CAPE VERDE
SENEGAL
GAMBIA
GUINEA-BISSAU
GUINEA
SIERRA LEONE
LIBERIA
CÔTE D'IVOIRE
TOGO
MALI
NIGER
BURKINA FASO
BENIN
NIGERIA
CHAD
SUDAN
ERITREA
YEMEN
DJIBOUTI
ETHIOPIA
SOMALIA
CENTRAL AFRICAN REP.
CAMEROON
EQUATORIAL GUINEA
GABON
CONGO
SÃO TOME & PRINCIPE
DEM. REP. of the CONGO
UGANDA
KENYA
RWANDA
BURUNDI
TANZANIA
THAILAND
CAMBODIA
VIETNAM
PHILIPPINES
PALAU
Guam (U.S.)
MARSHALL ISLANDS
FEDERATED STATES OF MICRONESIA
KIRIBATI
SRI LANKA
MALDIVES
BRUNEI
MALAYSIA
SINGAPORE
Equator
KIRIBATI
Tokelau
(New Zealand)
SAMOA
American Samoa
(U.S.)
TONGA
Cook Islands
(New Zealand)
French Polynesia
(France)
PERU
BRAZIL
BOLIVIA
PARAGUAY
CHILE
ARGENTINA
URUGUAY
SOUTH
PACIFIC
OCEAN
SOUTH
ATLANTIC
OCEAN
ANGOLA
ZAMBIA
MALAWI
MOZAMBIQUE
NAMIBIA
ZIMBABWE
BOTSWANA
MADAGASCAR
SOUTH AFRICA
SWAZILAND
LESOTHO
SEYCHELLES
COMOROS
MAURITIUS
INDIAN
OCEAN
PAPUA NEW GUINEA
NAURU
SOLOMON ISLANDS
TUVALU
VANUATU
FIJI
New Caledonia
(France)
AUSTRALIA
SOUTH
PACIFIC
OCEAN
NEW ZEALAND
Antarctica
CHINA
RUSSIA
RUSSIA
Kuril Islands
Sapporo
Hokkaido
Hakodate
Sea
of
Japan
NORTH KOREA
Akita
Sado
Sendai
NORTH
PACIFIC
OCEAN
JAPAN
Yellow
Sea
SOUTH KOREA
Honshu
TOKYO
Kyoto
Nagoya
Yokohama
Hiroshima
Kobe
Osaka
Kitakyushu
Shikoku
Kyushu
Miyazaki
N
East
China
Sea
Philippine
Sea
Iwo Jima
Ryukyu Islands
Okinawa
0
100
200
300
400 Miles

isolation reached its height in the Tokugawa, or Edo, period (1600–1867), when Japan's borders were mostly closed to the outside world. Many customs and ideas considered "traditionally Japanese" were developed during this period. Most traditional music presented in this chapter, for instance, dates from the Tokugawa period, though its roots may go back farther.

On the whole, Japan's culture combines a deep respect for tradition with creativity and flexibility. Many layers of culture, musical and otherwise, exist side by side, different yet harmonious. One sign of this diversity lies in the music the Japanese listen to today.

Japanese Traditional Music

In the last hundred years, the Japanese have become more involved with new music, devoting less time to traditional music. Since the Meiji period (1868–1911) Western music has been influential, and its spread has been officially encouraged through the educational system. Despite the overwhelming influence of music from outside Japan, however, traditional music remains viable. The *kabuki* and *bunraku* theaters in the larger cities are still well attended, as are concerts of traditional instrumental and vocal music. Teachers of instruments such as the *shakuhachi* and the *shamisen* still find many interested pupils of all ages, and televised instruction for such instruments in recent years has helped bolster their popularity. Perhaps the large amount of Western influence has made young people more appreciative of the different beauty of Japanese music and its special relationship to Japanese history and culture.

To begin to understand traditional Japanese music we may find it helpful to examine its genreal characteristics. There are exceptions to these generalizations, but they should be used as a point of reference for the musical examples that follow.

Pitch/Scales

Like Western music, Japanese music divides the octave into twelve tones. The Japanese tonal system is based on the Chinese system, which in turn developed in a way similar to the Pythagorian system of the West. These notes, when put in pitch sequence, represent an untempered chromatic scale of 12 semitones. While equal temperament has strongly influenced contemporary performers, the exact intervals between notes still differ in traditional music according to genre, school, the piece performed, and the individual performer (Koizumi 1974:73). No single set of pitches is used by all musicians. For example, the mode system used in *gagaku* (orchestra music derived from T'ang China) differs from that used in music for the *koto* (a thirteen-stringed zither). The *gagaku* modal system is linked to Chinese systems, while the *koto* system developed several centuries later in Japan.

Considering this diversity in scale systems, it is not surprising that music historians have developed a wide range of theories to describe them. According to one traditional theory, much Japanese music (excluding older genres such as *gagaku* and Buddhist chanting) is based on two pentatonic scales, either with or without semitones. A more recent theory holds that the traditional concept of the pentatonic scale (such as the *in* and *yo* scales) does not adequately explain what is found in the music itself. Instead, it is more useful to interpret Japanese music on the basis of "nuclear tones," located a fourth apart, and the main notes that appear between them (Koizumi 1974:76). In fact, much melodic movement tends to emphasize this interval (e.g., the use of *miyako-bushi* nuclear tones in "Hakusen no," CD Selection 32).

Timbre

The Japanese aesthetic sense favors the use of a broad range of sounds and tone qualities in their music. In particular, "unpitched" sounds are commonly heard in the middle of instrumental melodies. When we hear a sound wave with a stable frequency, it is easy for us to distinguish pitch. But if the frequency varies too quickly, we do not hear a pitch. A cymbal, for example, is unpitched compared with an oboe. In Japanese music, examples of unpitched sound include the very breathy sound made on the *shakuhachi* bamboo flute or the hard twang produced when the plectrum strikes the *shamisen* lute. Just as Japanese poetry is full of appreciation for unpitched sounds of nature such as water flowing or trees whispering in the wind, Japanese music recreates such sounds for the enjoyment of their listeners. (An example of this characteristic can be heard in CD Selection 31, "Tsuru no sugomori.")

Melody/Harmony

The diversity of Japanese melodies makes generalization difficult—the melodies of folk songs differ greatly in rhythm, pitch, and structure from those of *shakuhachi* music, for example. Japanese melodies often contain short motifs that are repeated, in part or in their entirety, throughout a piece. (See, for example, CD Selection 32, "Hakusen no," in which segments of phrases are repeated and varied.) Complete repetition of phrases sometimes occurs at the beginning and end of a piece, such as in the *shamisen* accompaniment to "Hakusen no," thereby lending an air of finality to the conclusion.

In the *shakuhachi* piece (CD Selection 31) the pitch movement in the melody strikes the non-Japanese listener as extremely slow; in fact, the dynamic and timbre changes give the melody its life, rather than rapid changes in pitch. In contrast to this, much vocal music contains elaborate vocal ornamentation, as heard in CD Selections 32 and 33.

Only Western-influenced Japanese music uses Western harmony. His most common when two or more instruments (or voice and instrument) play together is a heterophonic texture, in which both or all parts play basically the same melody but in slightly different versions.

Rhythm

One distinctive characteristic of Japanese music lies in the flexibility of pulse in many pieces. In Western music, pulses almost always occur at regular time intervals (forming "beats") and are arranged most commonly in groups of two, three, four, or six (creating a "meter"). Music can also have irregular intervals between the pulses, however, and this is sometimes called "beatless" or "flexible" or "free" rhythm. Those accustomed to Western music may have difficulty at first listening to music that lacks a steady beat, because it seems hard to follow without the firm rhythmic structure they expect. But this music conveys a powerful expression of feeling because of its freedom and flexibility. Such beatless rhythm is found in many kinds of Japanese music, from folk song to music of the *shakuhachi.*

Even when a steady beat is present, there can be a sense of flexibility to it, as in the festival music example presented later. When there is a sense of beat in Japanese music, those beats usually occur in groups of two, four, or eight.

Japanese music uses a wide variety of tempos, from very slow to very fast. Often, in music associated with the theater, the tempo accelerates as excitement and drama build in the play.

Musical Form

The most common musical form in Japanese music is called *jo-ha-kyu* and is based mainly on rhythmic rather than melodic changes. *Jo* means "introduction" and is the slow beginning section: *ha* is literally "breaking apart," and here the tempo builds; finally, *kyū,* or "rushing," finds the tempo reaching its peak, only to slow before the piece ends. As a loose form, this tripartite structure applies in some cases to entire pieces as well as to sections of those pieces and individual phrases.

In the following sections, several different kinds of Japanese music will be explained, illustrating some of the colorful diversity of musical life in that country today. The history of each instrument or musical genre provides a fascinating look into the rich, vibrant life of traditional Japanese cities and villages during the times of the *samurai,* wandering Buddhist priests, and *geisha.*

The *shakuhachi* flute is linked to the social turbulence of early Tokugawa times, as well as to Zen philosophy and aesthetics. A *shakuhachi* piece provides an example of free rhythm, one of the most important characteristics of Japanese music. The *geisha* and O-Yo, a female composer of the late Tokugawa period, were important in the development of the short *kouta* songs. These songs, sung to the accompaniment of the *shamisen,* exemplify heterophonic texture in Japanese music.

These kinds of music are generally labeled "art" or "classical" music. In comparison to "folk" music, art music has stricter guild systems, more regulation over skill level, and more professionalism. The terms *art* and *folk* are imported from the West, however, and the dividing line between the two categories has become blurred today as folk musicians become more professionalized and form their own guild systems.

Later in the chapter we shall look at folk songs from northern Japan, described in its contemporary contexts to show how traditional music is faring in modern Japan. Finally, we shall explore present-day Japanese popular music, which shows musical features of both East and West, and the world of *karaoke* singing, in which live singing and technology are mixed in a unique way.

Shakuhachi

Considering its range of tones from soft and ethereal to rough and violent, the *shakuhachi* appears surprisingly simple in construction. This flute is made of a length of bamboo from the bottom part of a bamboo stalk, including part of the root. The name *shakuhachi* derives from the length of the standard instrument. Shaku signifies a traditional unit of measure (equivalent to about 30 cm) and *hachi* stands for 8, together meaning 1.8 *shaku,* or about 54 cm. The standard *shakuhachi* has four holes in the front of the instrument and one in the back for the thumb of the left hand.

The *shakuhachi*'s versatility in pitch and tone production is due to its construction. Held vertically, the flute has a mouthpiece at the top that is cut obliquely on the side away from the player. By partially covering the finger holes and changing the angle of the lips to the mouthpiece, a player can produce a wide variety of pitches and tone qualities. Not only does the *shakuhachi* easily produce microtones, but it also generates tones ranging from "pure" (with few overtones) to very breathy, sounding almost like white noise.

Solo *shakuhachi* performance flourished during the Tokugawa period (1600–1867). This was a golden age in Japanese cultural life. It was a time of peace, during which the *shōgun* living in Tokyo ruled over a united country, while the Kyoto emperor held only nominal power. After centuries of violent struggles between different factions of aristocrats and military leaders, Japan welcomed peace and prospered under it.

During this period, a group of priests called *komusō* (literally "emptiness monks") wandered the countryside, playing the *shakuhachi.* The *honkyoku,* or main solo repertoire for the instrument, derives from the pieces played by the *komusō.* All of these pieces, the most spiritual and meditative of the present-day *shakuhachi* repertoire, have a free rhythm; that is, they lack a regular beat.

Komusō were organized into the Fuke sect of Buddhism, which propagated a Zen basis for *shakuhachi* playing. Zen Buddhism, a philosophy that has spread throughout much of Asia and the world in various forms, is based on the idea that intellect is not needed in the pursuit of truth. We can search to know *about* things, but we do not really *know* them. To know them, we must throw away our notions of scientific investigation and logical reasoning and instead rely on a heightened awareness and intuition about life.

Various means for reaching that state of heightened awareness of enlightenment (*satori* in Japanese) have been proposed. These include pondering *kōan,* or paradoxical riddles (the most famous being, "What is the sound of one hand clapping?") and the practice of *zazen,* sitting in silent meditation. In the Fuke sect, playing the *shakuhachi* also was regarded as a means of reaching enlightenment. For this reason, the *shakuhachi* was not called a musical instrument by its performers but a *hōki,* or "spiritual tool." The spiritual approach to the playing of the instrument is called *suizen,* or "blowing Zen."

According to *suizen,* the goal of *shakuhachi* coincides with the goal of Zen: to reach enlightenment, proceeding into unlimited "knowing." How this is done is not formulated precisely (as it cannot be, from the Zen perspective), but one common notion is called *ichōon jōbutsu,* or "enlightenment in a single note." According to this theory, one could reach enlightenment suddenly when blowing a single tone.

Breathing is crucial in *shakuhachi* playing and its connection with Zen. The exhaling of breath is heard in the dynamic level and tone quality of a pitch; at the same time, it carries with it the possibility of instant spiritual enlightenment. Thus, each moment of "performance," whether the intake of breath or its slow release, whether the subtle, delicate shading of a tone or the explosion of air through the instrument, can be interpreted in the context of a larger spiritual life.

The breathing pattern is important in learning to play the *shakuhachi.* Each phrase takes one full breath, with dramatic shifts in dynamic level according to how quickly the air is expelled. The typical phrase in *shakuhachi honkyoku* music follows the natural breathing pattern, the sound growing fainter toward the end of the phrase as the air in the lungs runs out. When this dynamic pattern is broken by a gradual or sudden increase in volume, it makes a pronounced impression on the listener.

CD 2
Track 7

The performer of the *shakuhachi* piece in CD Selection 31, Kawase Junsuke,* is one of the best known *shakuhachi* musicians in Japan and the head of a stylistic school of playing (Figure 8-1). This piece, a part of the *honkyoku* (solo) repertory of the Kinko style of performance, is called "Tsuru no sugomori," or "Nesting Cranes." The version recorded here is performed in the *kabuki* theater and therefore is accompanied by *shamisen* (Figure 8-2); this part is not notated in the following transcription. The music describes a winter scene during which cranes make their nests. The fast trills in the *shakuhachi* imitate the bird's fluttering wings. "Tsuru no sugomori" is performed in one of the most famous *kabuki* plays, *Kanadehon chushingura,* or Treasury of Local Retainers, during a scene when parting lovers suddenly notice the scene outdoors.

---

*Japanese names are given in the Japanese order; family name followed by given name.

Figure 8-1
Kawase Junsuke playing the *shakuhachi.*

Linda Fujie

The first time one listens to this piece, it is best just to sit back and relax, appreciating the overall mood. For later listening, the transcription in Music Example 8-1 shows in Western notation the general outline of the piece. Western notation is limiting in conveying uneven rhythms, and so the transcription here is only approximate in time values. Phrases—defined by points at which a breath is taken by the musician—are numbered for reference.

After listening to this piece a few times, you may sense that certain phrases are repeated; in fact, this short piece has many repetitions of melodic material. For example, phrase 1 is heard again (with some modifications) in phrases 6, 9, 17, and 24. The group of phrases numbered 1 to 5 are repeated in phrases 9 to 13, and most of the other phrases are variations on previous melodic material. There is also a clear climax to the piece, created by changes in pitch and dynamics.

One of the most obvious characteristics of this piece is that almost every phrase increases or decreases in volume; in many cases the musician increases the volume on one long note and decreases it on the next one.

Music Example 8-1
"Tsuru no sugomori." Transcription by Linda Fujie.

, = breath taken ↑↓ = pitch goes up/down by quarter tone

This careful breath control must be learned and practiced over years to prevent running out of breath too soon and to maintain constant control over tone quality.

A knowledge of some of the techniques used to play *shakuhachi* will help explain how some of the tones in this performance are produced. Sometimes the player flattens or sharpens a pitch by changing the angle of the lips to the mouthpiece. This is called *meri* when the pitch is lowered, producing a soft tone, and *kari* when the pitch is raised. (Occasionally the pitch is lowered and again raised, as at the end of phrase 22.)

The musician changes pitch also through finger techniques, depending on the effect desired. A finger can slowly open or close a hole, it can quickly tap a hole (creating an accent), or cover only a portion of a hole. These techniques are necessary because tonguing is not used to separate notes in *shakuhachi* playing.

Different techniques of breath release into the flute also create interesting effects such as *muraiki,* an explosion of breath into the instrument. In addition, *shakuhachi* players use flutter tonguing, finger tremolos, and vibrato—all of which can be heard in the first few phrases of "Tsuru no sugomori." One common technique of producing vibrato is to shake the head while blowing into the instrument, either from side to side or up and down.

This piece shows both a variety of timbres within one piece and flexibility of pulse, basic characteristics of Japanese music. Some notes have a thin sound, while others have rich, full tone. Some notes sound "purer" to our ears; others are breathier. The *shakuhachi* player expresses the music through such changes in timbre. With the exception perhaps of contemporary music, this variety of tone quality is rarely found within a single piece written for a Western wind instrument. In terms of Japanese musical aesthetics, however, this contrast of timbres is important to the texture and expression of the piece.

The lack of a regular pulse means that learning a piece requires a good ear and an excellent sense of timing on the part of the student. Most forms of musical notation convey the time durations of notes easily if the music has a steady pulse. But without such a pulse, the original time values are difficult to communicate in a written score. Perhaps this is one reason that musical notation never developed into an important teaching tool in most forms of traditional Japanese music. Because Japanese musicians could not rely on scores to teach them the rhythm of a piece, they used them more as a device to help them remember how the piece should sound. First, of course, performers must acquire this memory by listening to their teacher (and perhaps other students) many times.

The idea of *ma* (literally "space" or "interval") is linked to both rhythm and to the Zen background of *shakuhachi* playing. Ma refers to the overall timing of a piece—not just the pauses and rests, but also the relationship between sound and silence on which all music is fundamentally based. It embraces the idea that sound enhances silence and silence enhances

Figure 8-2
Geisha performing at a party. The woman on the right holds a *shamisen.*

Linda Fujie

sound. This emphasis on silence conforms with Zen ideas concerning the importance of emptiness and space. The player who is aware of *ma* begins his or her notes with an instinctive care for the length and quality of the silences before and after. This concept applies particularly to music with a beatless rhythm, because the sounds and silences fall at irregular points and the player is more active in creating those moments.

Performers often link the concept of *ma* to the quality of a musical performance. Musicians speak of "good *ma*" or "bad *ma*," referring to the quality of the sounds and silences and their proportion to one another. When this proportion is deemed appropriate—a subjective judgment that is learned only from years of experience—then the performance has been successful.

Though the Fuke sect priests have long disappeared from the roads of Japan, many players keep the *shakuhachi* tradition alive today, both in Japan and abroad. Because of the instrument's versatility of pitch and timbre, composers and performers like to use it in various contemporary genres, such as jazz, fusion, and New Age music. At the same time, the meditative, spiritual nature of the *honkyoku* is continually reaffirmed through performances given by several active *shakuhachi* master players.

Kouta

Another of the well-loved Japanese traditional instruments is the *shamisen,* a three-stringed long-necked lute (see Figure 8-2). In contrast to the *shakuhachi,* which has associations with austere spirituality and meditation, the *shamisen* is often used to convey an outpouring of emotion and drama. For this reason it is considered an excellent instrument for the theater, expressing highly dramatic situations in the *bunraku* puppet theater to great effect. It is also used in another major theatrical form, *kabuki,* and sometimes to accompany folk song, as in CD Selection 33. In a more intimate setting, the *shamisen* also accompanies short, evocative songs called *kouta* (literally, "short song").

The present-day *shamisen* is a descendent of a long line of related instruments stretching back to the *sanshin* of Okinawa, the *san-hsien* of China, and perhaps further back to the Middle East or Central Asia.* While the Okinawan *sanshin* is covered with snakeskin, on the Japanese mainland the instrument is traditionally covered with cat skin or sometimes dog skin. (As these are now expensive, however, plastic is commonly found on *shamisen* used for practice.) There are different kinds of *shamisen,* varying in shape, weight, material, and overall size; the type used depends on the musical genre played.

The body of the *shamisen* is made of a wooden box roughly square in shape, covered on both sides with skin or plastic. A long piece of wood, forming the unfretted neck, is inserted into this box. Pegs at the top of the neck hold the three strings, each string of a different thickness. In some kinds of music, a large plectrum is used for striking and plucking the instrument. Sometimes in *kouta,* however, the bare fingers or fingernails pluck the strings, producing a lighter, less percussive sound.

A rather unusual sound in the *shamisen* confirms the importance of unpitched sounds in Japanese music. This is a special buzz or hum called *sawari* (literally, "touch"), which is purposefully added to the instrument when it is made. The lowest string does not rest on the upper bridge but resonates against a special cavity made near the top of the instrument's neck. This string sets a noise in motion, to which the other strings can contribute in sympathetic vibration. The result is a pitchless buzzing sound that is essential to the tonal flavor of the *shamisen.* Japanese instrument makers intentionally build these timbres into their instruments. Buzzing is also deliberately built into many African instruments, such as the *axatse,* (Chapter 3).

The *kouta* is a song form that evokes many images and allusions in a short (generally, one- to three-minute) time. *Kouta* as we know it today dates from the mid-nineteenth century, though the same name was used to describe another kind of song in earlier centuries (Kurada 1982:894–95).

The development of the present-day *kouta* is closely linked to the participation of women in Japanese traditional music. One of the earliest composers of *kouta* was O-Yo (1840–1901). The daughter of the head master of *kiyomoto* (a style of *shamisen* music used in *kabuki*), O-Yo was an excellent musician. As a woman, she was not allowed to take over her father's position after his death; instead she married a man who then inherited his title. But O-Yo took up most of his duties.

---

*Theories that the Chinese *san-hsien* derived from Egyptian or Persian sources are summarized in Kikkawa 1981:157–58.

O-Yo was not allowed to play the *shamisen* on the *kabuki* stage because only men appeared there. She was nevertheless an active performer at private parties in teahouses and restaurants. For such private gatherings she probably composed *kouta* such as "Saru wa uki," thought to be the first *kouta* ever composed (Kikkawa 1981:350). Although women were banned from participating in many of the elite forms of musical performance in Japan, they played a key role in teaching that music to generations of male performers. O-Yo herself was an important transmitter of the *kiyomoto* tradition of her father, teaching it to many people from all parts of Japan.

O-Yo's musical world and her involvement with both an older form of music (*kiyomoto*) and a new form (*kouta*) can best be understood in the context of the *iemoto* guild system. This system, active also in O-Yo's time, is a powerful influence on the traditional arts—music, dance, flower arranging, the tea ceremony, and many other artistic areas. The guild is the transmitter of knowledge and the legitimizer of teachers and performers in each art form.

In music, several different guilds may be involved with one type of music (for example, music for the *shakuhachi* or for the *nō* theater), but each guild will have its own slightly different performance style and repertoire. By illustration, one who wishes to become a *shakuhachi* performer must decide which style he or she wants to learn, then become affiliated with the guild that follows that style. Often this affiliation lasts as long as the individual performs on the *shakuhachi.*

Guilds not only transmit knowledge; they also control quality. Each guild sets the standards for teachers and pupils. If an individual works diligently, he or she may be given a license to teach and an artistic name from the guild. The *iemoto* system thus provides a structure through which the arts have been taught, performed, and preserved for hundreds of years in Japan. It has contributed positively to maintaining the artistic level in traditional Japanese music. Its strict regulation of performance standards has preserved musical traditions that could otherwise have changed drastically or even died out through the years.

According to the rules of this system, new composition in many genres of music was discouraged or even forbidden. This conservatism is linked to a reverence for tradition in the arts that is still prevalent among Japanese musicians today. Many believe that the "classic" body of music has been handed down with painstaking precision for decades or centuries through the toil of countless musicians. The composition of a new piece of music by an individual was for years considered "arrogant self-expression." If a new piece were composed and proved to have merit, it had to be ascribed to the leader of the guild, who in turn might attribute it to an earlier *iemoto* leader. This reluctance to accept new compositions meant that if they were written, they often had no official recognition. For this reason, when someone like O-Yo composed new music, it was in a new genre such as *kouta.* Because there was no *iemoto* associated yet with that kind of music, the restrictions that would otherwise apply toward composition did not exist.

By the end of the Tokugawa period, the *kouta* was linked to the *geisha* of the city of Edo (which became known as Tokyo in 1868) and the life of the teahouses. For many people today, the lively, intense world of Edo during the Tokugawa period epitomizes the Japanese spirit. Though the official Japanese capital was Kyoto, where the emperor resided, Edo was the actual seat of government where the *shōgun* held state in his castle. It was also the most populous city in Japan as well as one of the largest in the world. The influx of people from all over the country, crowded into tenements and wildly pursuing wealth, pleasure, or both, spurred the coining of the phrase "Edo wa tenka no hakidamari" (Edo is the nation's rubbish heap).

The streets teemed with *chōnin,* townspeople who were members of either the merchant or the artisan classes. With the expansion of the economy during the peaceful Tokugawa period, some *chōnin* became wealthy and powerful. They patronized the theaters, teahouses, and brothels, making their increasingly sophisticated mark on the aesthetics of the drama, music, and dance of the period: a sense of style that combines wit, sensuousness, and restraint. The Edo pursuit of momentary pleasure represents the epitome of the *ukiyo,* or "floating world."

The *kouta,* as sung by the *geisha* of such licensed quarters as the Yoshiwara area of Edo, reflects their world of beauty and style. The songs' lyrics often convey romantic or erotic themes, but such references are subtle. Puns, double-entendres and poetic devices appear frequently in *kouta* lyrics, and sometimes even a Japanese will miss their suggestive undertones.

CD 2
Track 8

In the *kouta* example found in CD Selection 32, entitled "Hakusen no" ("A White Fan"), both the image of a white fan and the beauty of nature are used as metaphors for romantic commitment. This particular song shows little of the whimsical side of *kouta;* it is considered suitable for performance at wedding banquets or private parties. At the wedding banquet, this song would be sung to the honored couple.

Though declining in numbers, *geisha* are still trained in Japan to entertain at such occasions. The traditional musical instrument of the *geisha* is the *shamisen,* which is used often to accompany vocal music such as the *kouta.* This recording was made by a *geisha* in the 1960s who lived near the former Yoshiwara quarter of Tokyo. Here we show the lyrics of the *kouta* and an English translation. (The letters on the left-hand side refer to melodic material and will be explained later.)

Hakusen no

A	Hakusen no	A white fan
B	sue hirogari no	spreading out
C	sue kakete	lasting forever
B	kataki chigiri no	the firm pledges
(A)	gin kaname	like the silver node of the fan
(B)	kagayaku kage ni	shimmering in shadows
D	matsu ga e no	the boughs of pine trees
E	ha-iro mo masaru	the splendid leafy color of
(B)	fukamidori	a deep green
E	tachiyoru niwa no	the clearness of the pond

(E)	ike sumite	in the garden approached
(B)	nami kaze tatanu	undisturbed by waves of wind,
C	mizu no omo	the surface of the water
B	urayamashii de	What an enviable life,
(B)	wa nai ka na.	don't you think?

Lyrics "Hakusen no." Shitaya Kotsuru. Denon/Nippon Columbia Co. Ltd. WK-170.

Traditional Japanese poetry arranges lines according to their syllabic content, favoring lines with five and seven syllables. The lyrics of "Hakusen no" contain alternating lines of five and seven syllables. (Extended vowels and the letter *n* at the end of a syllable count as separate syllables.) A poetic device known as *kakekotoba,* or "pivot word," is found on the sixth line: the word *kagayaku* ("shimmering") can be interpreted as both referring to the silver node of the fan (the pin holding the fan together at the bottom) and to the pine tree boughs, "shimmering" in the shadows. Such pivot words are often found in Japanese poetry and are made possible by the flexibility of Japanese grammar.

Several auspicious symbols appear in the text. The pine tree has a special symbolism for the Japanese as a tree of special beauty and longevity. A clear pond, "undisturbed by waves or wind," also presents a peaceful, auspicious image of the future life of a couple. The words *sue hirogari* literally refer to the unfolding of a fan, but can also mean to enjoy increasing prosperity as time goes on.

Music Example 8-2 is a transcription of "Hakusen no." As in the *shakuhachi* example, the difficulties of conveying uneven time values in Western notation are apparent. The vocal part has been inserted rhythmically in relation to the steady beat of the *shamisen,* which is the easiest part to follow.

Music Example 8-2
"Hakusen no." Transcription by Linda Fujie.

(continues)

Music Example 8-2
(continued)

This transcription shows only the vocal and *shamisen* parts; in the recording, we also hear an accompanying ensemble made up of the *ko-tsuzumi* and *otsuzumi* drums and the *nōkan* flute. These instruments, typical of the *nō* theater, were added to the commercial recording of this song; *geisha* also sing "Hakusen no" with the *shamisen* alone. Another sound not transcribed are the calls known as *kakegoe,* which help to cue the ensemble as well as add to the atmosphere of the song.

A heterophonic relationship between two or more parts is typical of Japanese ensemble music. In CD Selection 32 such a heterophony characterizes the voice and *shamisen.* Rather than sounding simultaneously on the same beat, the two parts tend to weave in and out; sometimes the voice precedes the *shamisen* in presenting the melody and sometimes the *shamisen* plays the notes first. The result of this constant staggering and shifting is a duet in which the melody is shared and enhanced by both voice and instrument. An example of this heterophony can be found in the third line, as the *shamisen* anticipates several of the sung notes. Listening carefully to the entire song, try to find other such examples. Are there also times when the voice anticipates what the *shamisen* will play?

One of the most interesting aspects of the vocal part is the flexibility of beat, which contrasts to the even beat of the *shamisen.* See, for example, how the rhythm of the vocal and *shamisen* parts fit together in the line beginning "tachiyoru . . ."; just as the listener thinks a predictable pattern has been established, the rhythm shifts. The sophistication of this kind of rhythmic contrast has appealed for centuries to the Japanese ear. Together, melodic and rhythmic variety in Japanese ensemble music create a complex, often exciting musical texture.

The vocal melody contains several thematic phrases that repeat in slightly varied forms. The letters next to the lyrics show one way of interpreting these phrases. Repeating letters indicate phrases that are repeated exactly or nearly exactly, while letters in parentheses signify more modified repetitions. For example, the seven different "B" phrases have in common long, repeated notes followed by a descending interval, highly ornamented, of a third to a sixth, or some part of this combination.

The *shamisen* part opens and closes the song with the same rhythmically emphasized theme, and it occasionally plays a short solo phrase between lines of text. Sometimes small motifs are repeated; one that occurs several times is shown in Music Example 8-3.

Music Example 8-3
Motif in *shamisen* part, "Hakusen no."

This and other similar motifs in the *shamisen* part stress the notes D and G. The scale used in "Hakusen no" is the *in* scale, based on D. However, there are constant shifts to the same scale based on G, which is closely related to the D scale. A prominent difference between the two scales lies in the A flat found in the G scale, whereas the D scale contains an A natural. Another scale shift takes place in the line "kagayaku. . . ," which stresses the notes G, D♭, C, denoting a temporary change to the C-based *in* scale. Such rapid changes from one scale to another are common in Japanese music even in short songs like *kouta.* Hearing this song, the listener is drawn into the refined yet playful atmosphere of the Tokugawa teahouses.

The next music that we will examine, folk song, traditionally belonged to the farming class or the poorer merchants in the cities. But people from many levels of society, in Tokugawa times as now, know this music. Folk music is still found in many everyday locations: in the streets, in the fields, and at social occasions of both the city and the countryside.

Folk Song

In traditional Japan, people sang folk songs, or *minyo,* while they planted the rice in spring, threw their nets into the sea, wove cloth, and pounded grain. Folk songs accompanied many daily activities—to relieve boredom, to provide a steady beat for some activity, as encouragement for a group working at some task, as individual expression, or as a combination of these.

While the everyday uses of folk song have not entirely disappeared from Japan, fewer contemporary Japanese are finding them relevant to their lives. Still, based on a recent survey of musical preferences, *minyō* is one of the most popular forms of music in Japan today (NHK Hōsō 1982:68).

The continuing popularity of folk songs is tied to their identification with the countryside and a sometimes romanticized vision of rural life on the part of city dwellers. Folk songs evoke a past thought to be simpler and more natural, and this appeals to many Japanese today.

In addition to an association with rural life, many Japanese folk songs connect to a specific region of the country. This is the case in "Nikata-bushi," in CD Selection 33, from the region of Akita, in northwestern Japan. With the growth of industry in the years after World War II, many Japanese left the rural areas to find work in the cities, and today people from a particular region—or their descendants—gather in many of these urban areas and sing folk songs as reminders of the villagers from which they came.

Japanese not only listen to folk songs but usually learn to sing a few as well, either from family and friends or in elementary school. Often they sing them at parties, when they are called on to sing a favorite song. Real enthusiasts take lessons with a good singer and attend folk song clubs or other gatherings where they can perform in front of other enthusiasts. Amateur folk song contests have become a regular feature on Japanese television, presenting folk singers from around the country. In these contests, singers give their renditions of folk songs, which are then evaluated by a board of "experts," who might tell the singer that his or her vibrato is too broad or hand gestures too dramatic for that particular song.

Folk song preservation societies have sprung up around the country (Groemer 1994). These societies are formed by amateurs who aim to "preserve" a particular local song and style of performing that song. The activities of these clubs help foster pride and a sense of identity among the dwellers of a village or a neighborhood within a city (Hughes 1981, 1990–91).

Folk song performance has become more professional and standardized in recent years owing to televised *minyō* and the changing tastes of the public. Training to sing folk song at a professional level demands years of study. In recent years, folk song has developed its own *iemoto*-like system, modeled after that found in traditional art music. For example, Asano Sanae, the singer on CD Selection 33, has been a pupil of the *shamisen* player Asano Umewaka for several years . In the manner of the *iemoto* system, she received her artistic name from him, including her teacher's last name. As a teenager, she moved from Osaka to Akita to become his apprentice, and she now participates regularly in concerts and competitions. Her teacher, in his seventies at the time of this recording, grew up in the Akita area and spent most of his life as a farmer, while slowly gaining a local and then a national reputation as a fine player of the Tsugaru *shamisen,* a type of *shamisen* used for virtuoso accompaniment of folk song. His former students live throughout Japan and teach his style of *shamisen* playing and singing.

CD 2
Track 9

Listening to CD Selection 33, we hear first the sound of the *shamisen* but with a stronger tone than we heard in the *kouta* example. This *shamisen* is indeed different in construction, with a larger body, longer neck, and thicker skin. The first notes sound on the open strings, allowing the player

Figure 8-3
Folk singer of Akita. The woman on the right is Asano Sanae, who sings CD Selection 33. Another apprentice, Asano Yoshie, stands in the middle. This picture was taken in 1986 at the Folklife Festival of the Smithsonian Institution, Washington, D.C.

Linda Fujie

to tune the instrument before beginning the piece. (You can hear the pitch change slightly as the player adjusts the strings.) The same "tuning" occurs later, in the instrumental interlude between verses.

The song text is composed of two verses, each set in the syllabic pattern typical of folk song: 7–7–7–5. The text of each verse is set to almost identical music, even down to the ornamentation used. Similarly, the patterns heard in the *shamisen* part between the two verses almost repeat the patterns played in the introduction.

Nikata-bushi

Nikata tera-machi	The temple town Nikata
no hana baasama	a woman selling flowers
hana mo urazu ni	she doesn't sell them
abura uru.	but enjoys herself instead.
Takai o-yama no	On a high mountain
goten no sakura	a cherry blossom tree at a mansion
eda wa nana eda	has seven branches
yae ni saku.	and blossoms abundantly.

As in the *kouta* example, the instrument plays a more or less steady pulse while the voice has a flexible rhythm. Look, for example, at the long notes and elaborate ornamentation in the vocal part, as seen in this transcription of the beginning of the second verse (Music Example 8-4). In the transcription a time line underneath follows the regular beats of the *shamisen* part, so that the vocal part can be seen in relation to a steady unit of time.

Music Example 8-4
"Nikata-bushi." Transcription by Linda Fujie.

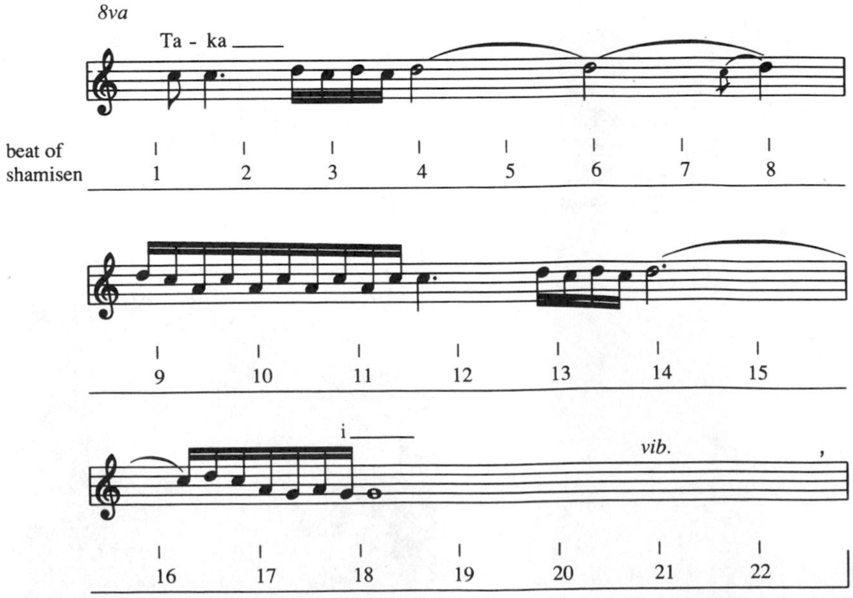

(continues)

Music Example 8-4
(continued)

The perfect fourth and perfect fifth are important intervals in many Japanese folk songs. In the transcribed section, for example, the longest notes are D″, G′ and D′, and these tones are the pivotal notes throughout the song. Both the *yo* scale and *minyō* tetrachords can be discerned here. Just before the voice enters with each verse, the *shamisen* player makes an exclamation that sounds like "huh!" This is another example of *kakegoe,* as first heard in the *kouta* selection.

Sanae's elderly teacher might be considered a "true," old-fashioned folk singer and *shamisen* player in this Tsugaru style, having learned it from childhood in his own native area. On the other hand, Sanae has studied purposefully to become a professional folk singer. This training is reflected in many ways in her performance, such as her ornamentation, precision, clarity of voice, and general presentation. Her singing of *minyō* interests us, however, because Japanese increasingly value these qualities in a *minyō* singer.

Popular Music

The traditional music genres described up to now had been conveyed from performer to audience without electronic media for many centuries. At a single performance the audience of these traditional genres was relatively small, and establishing rapport with that audience was crucial to success. Today, music performances are regularly presented on radio, television, and other media. A single recorded performance may be heard by millions of people who are unseen to the musicians.

In addition to changing the ways traditional music is played and perceived, mass media and technology have also stimulated the growth of a new kind of music in Japan, which we shall call here "popular music."* Since 1907, when the first commercial music recording was released in Japan, the composition, performance, and appreciation of music has changed dramatically. Music recorded specifically for commercial release in Japan, with the aim of appealing to the mass audience, exhibits several characteristics:

1. Performance within a set time limit (generally three to five minutes)
2. A focus on themes that appeal to a broad public (though regional or specialty audiences are also sometimes targeted)
3. Stanza form and a steady beat, making the music more accessible to the Japanese who have become more accustomed to Western music
4. Performers who aim to reproduce the recorded version of the music in live performance so as to fulfill audience expectations
5. Dramatic rise and fall in popularity over time

This "Top 40" mentality was novel to the Japanese; in their previous experience it was common for many kinds of music dating from different eras in Japanese history to survive side by side as vital elements of the country's musical life. Now, through the association of songs with a specific point in time, generations have begun to identify with "their" songs, with the result that music can be used as an age marker.

Through the mass media, music performed by "others" (particularly professionals) became more available to more people than ever before. Today, there is scarcely a home in Japan without a radio, television set, or stereo, and many have all three. As people listen to the same recordings and to the same performance of a song, they are united by a common musical experience; they also develop certain expectations as to what music should sound like. Of course, a similar process has occurred worldwide as popular music has penetrated all corners of the globe. In Japan, the spread of music through records, tapes, and compact discs has advanced very rapidly.

Historical Background

The types of popular music found in today's Japan developed as the modern Japanese state emerged. Interestingly the current music scene has become exceedingly diverse in a country known in the past for its high degree of cultural homogeneity. The rise of this contemporary hetero-

*Popular music is defined here as music primarily created for and transmitted by the various mass media. While some genres of so-called popular song that flourished among the masses in pre-Meiji Japan also have exerted an impact on the popular music of today, only those genres particularly linked to contemporary popular genres are discussed here.

geneous music-culture and specifically "Japanese" popular music can be traced to the latter half of the nineteenth century. At this time, wide-ranging reforms were introduced to Japanese society to enable the country to deal with Western powers. The government introduced a constitutional monarchy and made many structural changes in the society to allow a mercantile and industrial economy to flourish.

After their long era of isolation, the Japanese felt it necessary to "modernize" life around them, which for a while meant adopting Western models. Leaders rapidly installed a system of compulsory education and decided that Japan also needed compulsory singing in its schools. In the late 1870s Izawa Shuji, a Japanese school principal who had studied in Massachusetts, and Luther Whiting Mason, an American who was director of music for the Boston primary schools, developed a plan for music instruction in Japanese public schools.

In the following years *shōka* songs were introduced to meet a goal of teaching songs that blended Japanese and Western elements. The newly composed songs used melodies based on a traditional Japanese scale within the structure of a stanza form and a regular meter. Other songs introduced in the schools contained Western melodies such as "Auld Lang Syne" and "Swanee River" set with Japanese texts. Through songs like these, both *shōka* and Western songs, the Japanese masses were introduced to Western musical structure, scale, and rhythm.

In the 1880s a new kind of song became popular. Called *enka,* it represented a blend of Western and Japanese music. At first, *enka* lyrics were topical, expressing attitudes toward contemporary social and political movements. But these deeply political songs were transformed through the decades to become comic and, finally, after World War II sentimental songs full of nostalgia and longing. In any case their influence on the development of Japanese popular song as a whole is unmistakable.

One might imagine that the older generation would be the one most likely to appreciate such nostalgic expressions of sadness. Indeed, to many younger people who grew up with rock music, *enka* sounds too old-fashioned and sentimental. By the mid-1970s the audiences for *enka* were growing older, and the genre did not seem to hold much appeal for younger listeners. But then a new phenomenon called *karaoke* appeared on the scene, reinvigorating the *enka* and bringing it to a new, younger audience.

Popular Music Today

In *karaoke* (ka-ra-oh-kay), or "empty orchestra" anyone with the proper equipment can sing his or her favorite songs to a full orchestral accompaniment. A typical set-up includes a cassette tape player, a tape of the musical accompaniment to a favorite song, and one or two microphones for amplifying the voice as the amateur sings the melodic line.

Enka were, and continue to be, the songs of choice for most karaoke users. Other kinds of music found on *karaoke* tapes include Japanese folk and contemporary "pop" songs, as well as Western popular songs. A *karaoke* singer may sing the lyrics of these songs either from memory or by consulting a book containing the lyrics to hundreds of songs.

In Japan a large variety of *karaoke* machines are produced, ranging in price from about $200 to $5,000 but averaging about $2,000. The difference in price is determined by the machine's features. The more expensive models are used in restaurants, bars, wedding halls, and special *karaoke* singing centers. At these places, customers or guests sing songs of their choice from a wide selection available on tape, singing either alone or in couples. Models priced in the middle range are often installed in smaller bars as well as on touring buses and trains so that Japanese traveling in groups can sing to each other on long trips. The inexpensive models are designed for home use, so that users can practice for these public performances. There are even battery-powered models for outdoor use.

The *karaoke* technology made available to the consumer was developed to support and enhance his or her voice as much as possible. One can adjust the volume of the vocal part in relation to the instrumental background, and even switch on an echo device when desired (to add a kind of "singing-in-the-shower" effect). Some equipment is digitized, permitting singers to change the key of the original accompaniment tape to one in their own register. Even the musical accompaniment is designed to be helpful to the singer; the orchestra stays in the background to avoid stealing the show from the singer, but one instrument reinforces the melodic line, in case the singer becomes lost.

This equipment has reinforced the traditional Japanese custom of group singing. Japanese feel that singing helps to establish a relaxed atmosphere and feeling of closeness with others. Social groups—based on professional, school, familial, or community relationships—are important in Japanese life, and the Japanese put much effort into harmonious relationships within these groups. For example, to improve relations among company employees, management organizes special activities such as group tours to spas and drinking parties. On these occasions, *karaoke* is used to break down the social barriers created by the company hierarchy. For this purpose, mere conversation, even when mixed with drinking, does not suffice, because it is based on knowledge and wit. *Karaoke* is a different kind of socializing, through which the most sentimental, nostalgic ideas can be expressed—and are even encouraged—when sung through the *karaoke* machine.

Karaoke singing also reinforces group harmony through the expectation that each member of a group will participate by singing in front of the group. Even if someone feels embarrassed and wants to refuse, he or she usually gives in and sings at least one song in order to maintain the spirit of group harmony. In recent years, *karaoke* has become popular around the world; one can find "*karaoke* bars" in South America, Europe, and the United States, for example. However, public *karaoke* singing in these continents does not influence and control group social dynamics to the same degree as in Japan and other Asian countries.

Karaoke technology works also as an outlet for stress. For instance, the echo feature gives singers a sense of removal from their everyday identity.

One Japanese living in the United States stated, "It's great to hear your own voice, resounding throughout the room. You feel all your tension disappear." Some businessmen in Japan enjoy going to *karaoke* bars after work just for that purpose: to relieve the accumulated stress from a day of work by belting down a few drinks and belting out a few songs. One survey shows that *karaoke* is most popular among male, white-collar workers between the ages of twenty and forty-nine; the same survey also found that, within any age group, those who enjoyed *karaoke* the most were "those who like to sing" and "those who like to drink" (NHK Hōsō 1982:24–25).

Japanese businessmen living abroad find *karaoke* bars in which they can spend their afterhours. In New York City, for example, where a large population of Japanese businessmen work, a fierce competition had broken out among the many *karaoke* bars to install the latest technological developments. One such development is the laser disc video machine, which shows a series of videotaped scenes to accompany each song. Besides adding visual stimulation, this apparatus also allows singers to look up at their listeners and at the screen instead of having their heads buried in the lyric book.

While the content of the music is quite different, there is an interesting similarity in the way *enka* songs (as sung over *karaoke* machines) and traditional music are learned. Both involve aural skills—listening very carefully to an "original" version (of the recording in the case of *enka,* and of the teacher in traditional music) and imitating it as skillfully as possible. These days, some notation can also be involved. Real *karaoke* enthusiasts can even study with a teacher for pointers or technique but, for the most part, singers become familiar with the melody and interpretation of a song by listening to a recorded professional version many times.

At the top level of performance, though, *karaoke* performances are expected to produce more than exact imitations of another's performance. For example, some expensive models of *karaoke* machines can automatically score a performer on a scale of 1 to 100. One enthusiast told me that in his experience "exact" reproduction of a song in its original interpretation might bring you a score of 98 or 99, but not 100. For the highest score, an element of "personal expressiveness" is necessary, while at the same time one must completely reproduce the original version. In the traditional music genres described earlier, we have seen this same standardization of music performance among the lower-ranking performers, with expectations for more personal creativity at the highest level.

Enka composers have adapted their songs to the tastes of the younger generation. Background accompaniment ranges from the earlier simple guitar accompaniment to sophisticated orchestral arrangements and heavier, rock-type beats. More "upbeat" *enka* have been issued, with faster tempos and more optimistic lyrics, though these are still in the minority. Finally, vocal ornamentation, so emphasized in earlier *enka,* is toned down in the newer versions because the youth are more accustomed to hearing Western-style vocalization.

CD 2
Track 10

The *enka* song found in CD Selection 34 ("Naite Nagasaki," or "Crying Nagasaki") is typical of the more old-fashioned variety of *enka* meant for a middle-aged audience. Recorded in 1988 by a *geisha,* the mournfully romantic theme of the song, its orchestral background, and its vocal style appeal to people who visit a bar with a *karaoke* machine after a long day at work and want to indulge in a little emotionalism. The text describes a woman alone in her room as she contemplates the departure of her lover.

Naite Nagasaki ("Crying Nagasaki")

Saka no mukō ni	On the other side of the hill
yogisha ga mieru	I can see the night train.
Anata noseteku	Taking you away,
nobori no ressha	the northbound train.
Okuritai kedo	I want to send you off
okureba tsurai	but if I do it will be painful.
Heya no mado kara	From the window of my room
te o furu watashi	I wave good-bye to you.
Naite naite naite	Crying, crying, crying,
Nagasaki	Nagasaki,
Ame ni narisō, ne.	It looks like rain, doesn't it?
Wakarenakereba	That you were someone
naranaihito to	with whom I'd have to part—
shitte inagara	although I knew this,
moyashita inochi	a burning fate,
sugaritsukitai	wanting to cling to you,
Maruyamadōri	along the Maruyamadōri [street name]
jitto koraete	with steady endurance,
aruita watashi	I walked:
Naite naite naite	Crying, crying, crying,
Nagasaki	Nagasaki,
Ame ni narisō, ne.	It looks like rain, doesn't it?
Minato yokaze	The night wind from the port
fukikomu kabe ni	blows against the wall
furete setsunai	making flutter
anata no heyagi	your robe hanging there.
nigai o-sake o	I drown myself
abiteru watashi	in bitter *sake.*
Naite naite naite	Crying, crying, crying,
Nagasaki	Nagasaki,
Ame ni narisō, ne.	It looks like rain, doesn't it?

Lyrics "Naite Nagasaki." Kanda Fukumaru. Denon/Nippon Columbia Co. Ltd.

Several images brought out in the song are common to many *enka* songs. The setting of the port town of Nagasaki conjures up romantic associations and particularly the sadness of lovers parting. The scenes of drowning oneself in sake, crying in the windy night, and—on top of all that—rain are also found in hundreds of other *enka* songs. For such themes, the Japanese prefer to use a natural minor scale, sometimes with the sharped seventh added. At times, the melody too emphasizes the sad mood, for example in the setting of the words "Naite, naite . . . ," as though the singer were sobbing (Music Example 8-5).

The form of the song is also typical of *enka*—a simple strophe with a refrain. It opens and closes with instrumental sections, which also recur

Music Example 8-5
"Naite Nagasaki" (first verse). Transcription by Linda Fujie.

between strophes. As soon as the voice enters, the background accompaniment becomes minimal, consisting mainly of a bass guitar playing a bass line and other orchestral and electronic instruments filling in the harmony. This accompaniment begins to expand towards the end of the stanza as the vocal part reaches the climax at "Naite, naite . . ."

Harmonically, *enka* tend to use a conservative progression of chords, like most Western popular music. There is a brief modulation to the relative major (on the last "Nagasaki"), but otherwise the main movement is between the tonic, subdominant, and dominant of A minor.

"Naite Nagasaki" contains complicated orchestration, the use of background singers, and other elements indicative of Western popular music influence. However, the occasional use of vocal ornamentation reflects Japanese taste in vocal quality. Examples can be found in the slight tremolo heard in the voice in the line "nobori no ressha," the occasional use of vibrato before the end of a stanza, and the final ornamented fall from the B to the A at the end of the transcribed stanza.

The large Japanese music industry produces many other kinds of popular music in addition to *enka.* Some are strongly influenced by Western genres, and some show connections to Japanese musical traditions. The term *kayōkyoku* describes Japanese popular song as a whole, and particularly the songs (including *enka*) that mix Western and Japanese musical elements. This combination is usually a blend of Japanese melodies made from pentatonic scales with Western harmonic progressions and metrical organization. Since the mid-1970s, however, many of the contemporary songs have been written in Western scales, especially major modes, conforming to the imported music listened to by Japanese youth.

In Japan today, popular music includes easy listening, rock, punk, and other musics based on Western models although sometimes deviating from them in interesting ways. In addition, Japanese identify four other types of popular song. *Gunka* (literally, "military songs") are concerned with war. *Fōku songu* ("folk songs") refer to what people in North America call the products of singer-songwriters (such as Bob Dylan), while the lyrics, sung in Japanese by their composers, usually refer to Japanese social or political issues. *Nyū myūshiku* ("new music") developed out of *fōku songu,* but here the lyrics convey an introverted, personal point of view, and the melody is more important than a strong beat. Finally, *pops* is a young teenage music, in which the recording industry plays a major role in developing the teenage singers' musical skills and their images of youth and innocence. Television exposure is critical, and *pops* singers' careers rise and fall rapidly. The music sounds Western and, to add a touch of sophistication, often includes a few words of English.

Final Words

We have reviewed a small sample of the wide variety of music heard in Japan today. This sample contains many examples of the mixture of native with foreign elements in the evolution of new musical forms.

The *shakuhachi* was developed from an instrument of Chinese origin that entered Japan around the eighth century. The Zen philosophy that underlay the instrument's use in meditation also originated in China. The prototype of the *shamisen,* used to play *kouta* and music of the puppet theater and to accompany traditional folk song, can be traced to Okinawa, China, and beyond. Finally, popular music as a whole is based in form, rhythmic and harmonic structure, and instrumental accompaniment on Western music; only the melodic component and the lyric content in some cases reflect Japanese traditions.

Of course, one can question the concept itself of "tradition" or the "traditional culture" of a nation or people, especially in terms of "purity" of origin. What culture in the world has not borrowed cultural elements from another, with the roots of that borrowing going so far back that few think of the idea or custom as borrowed?

We find, in examining the Japanese music-culture, the expression of some aspects of the varied Japanese character. For instance, popular nonsense songs find their roots in a certain outlandish sense of humor that the Japanese sometimes indulge in. (Anyone who has watched Japanese television for any length of time, particularly game shows, can attest to this.) On a more sober note, the idea of emptying one's soul and reaching a state of selflessness as preparation for the performance of *shakuhachi* reflects the strong underlying influence of Zen thought in Japanese culture. This influence touches many other areas of Japanese daily life, in regard to not only mental preparation for a future task, but also self-control and self-discipline. Finally, the indulgence in pathos and extreme emotional anguish, as expressed in *enka* songs, reveals another side of the Japanese character. Listening to Japanese music and learning about its connections to past and present society, we become aware of the richness of Japanese life.

References

Hughes, David. 1981. "Japanese Folk Song Preservation Societies: Their History and Nature." In *International Symposium on the Conservation and Restoration of Cultural Property,* edited by the Organizing Committee of ISCRCP. Tokyo: Tokyo National Research Institute of Cultural Properties.

———. 1990–91. "Japanese 'New Folk Songs,' Old and New." *Asian Music* 22 (1): 1–49.

Kikkawa Eishi. 1981. *Nihon ongaku no rekishi* [The History of Japanese Music]. Osaka: Sōgensha.

Koizumi Fumio. 1974. *Nihon no ongaku* [Japanese Music]. Tokyo: National Theater of Japan.

Kurada Yoshihiro. 1982. "Kouta." In *Ongaku daijiten* [Encyclopedia Musica], edited by Shitanaka Kunihiko. Tokyo: Heibonsha.

NHK Hōsō Seron Chōsajo, eds. 1982. *Gendaijin to ongaku* [Contemporary People and Music]. Tokyo: Nippon Hōsō Shuppan Kyōkai.

Additional Reading

Adachi, Barbara. 1985. *Backstage at Bunraku: A Behind-the-Scenes Look at Japan's Traditional Puppet Theater.* New York: Weatherhill.

Adriaansz, Willem. 1973. *The Kumiuta and Danmono Traditions of Japanese Koto Music.* Berkeley: Univ. of California Press.

Blasdel, Christopher Yohmei. 1988. *The Shakuhachi: A Manual for Learning.* Tokyo: Ongaku no Tomo Sha.

Crihfield, Liza. 1979. *Kouta: "Little Songs" of the Geisha World.* Rutland, Vt.: Charles E. Tuttle.

Dalby, Liza Crihfield. 1983. *Geisha.* Berkeley: Univ. of California Press.

Fujie, Linda. 1986. "The Process of Oral Transmission in Japanese Performing Arts: The Teaching of *Matsuri-bayashi* in Tokyo." In *The Oral and the Literate in Music,* edited by Yoshihiko Tokumaru and Osamu Yamaguti. Tokyo: Academia Music.

Groemer, Gerald. 1994. "Fifteen Years of Folk Song Collection in Japan: Reports and Recordings of the 'Emergency Folk Song Survey.'" *Asian Folklore Studies* 53 (2): 199–225.

Gutzwiller, Andreas, and Gerald Bennett. 1991. "The World of a Single Sound: Basic Structure of the Music of the Japanese Flute Shakuhachi." *Musica Asiatica* 6:36–59.

Herd, Judith Ann. 1984. "Play it again, Isamu!" *Mainichi Daily News,* 9 July 1984, 9.

Hughes, David. 1990–91. "Japanese 'New Folk Songs,' Old and New." *Asian Music* 22 (1): 1–49.

Kishibe Shigeo. 1984. *The Traditional Music of Japan.* Tokyo: Ongaku no Tomo Sha.

Malm, William. 1959. *Japanese Music and Musical Instruments.* Rutland, Vt.: Charles E. Tuttle.

———. 1971. *Modern Music of Meiji Japan.* In *Tradition and Modernization in Japanese Culture,* edited by Donald H. Shirley. Princeton, N.J.: Princeton Univ. Press.

Mitsui Toru. 1984. "Japan in Japan: Notes on an Aspect of the Popular Music Record Industry in Japan." *Popular Music* 3:107–20.

Okada Maki. 1991. "Musical Characteristics of *Enka*." *Popular Music* 10 (3): 283–303.

Additional Listening

"Nihon no dentô ongaku" [Japanese Traditional Music]. CD Series. King Record Co. (2-12-13 Ottowa, Bunkyo-ku, Tokyo 112).

Vol. 1: *Gagaku.* KICH 2001.

Vol. 2: *Nôgaku.* KICH 2002.

Vol. 3: *Kabuki.* KICH 2003.

Vol. 4: *Biwa.* KICH 2004.

Vol. 5: *Shakuhachi.* KICH 2005.

Vol. 6: *Sô.* KICH 2006.

Vol. 7: *Sankyoku.* KICH 2007.

Vol. 8: *Shamisen. I.* KICH 2008.

Vol. 9: *Shamisen. II.* KICH 2009.

Vol. 10: *Percussion.* KICH 2010.

"Music of Japanese People." CD Series. King Record Co. (2-12-13 Ottowa, Bunkyo-ku, Tokyo 112).

Vol. 1: *Harmony of Japanese Music.* KICH 2021.
Vol. 2: *Japanese Dance Music.* KICH 2022.
Vol. 3: *Japanese Work Songs.* KICH 2023.
Vol. 4: *Jam Session of Tsugaru-Shamisen.* KICH 2024.
Vol. 5: *Music of Okinawa.* KICH 2025.
Vol. 6: *Music of Yaeyama and Miyako.* KICH 2026.
Vol. 7: *Music of Amami.* KICH 2027.
Vol. 8: *Music of Japanese Festivals.* KICH 2028.
Vol. 9: *Soundscape of Japan.* KICH 2029.
Vol. 10: *A Collection of Unique Musical Instruments.* KICH 2030.

CHAPTER 9

Latin America/Ecuador

John M. Schechter

Latin America is a region of many regions. It is a continent and a half with more than twenty different countries in which Spanish, Portuguese, French, and dozens of Native-American languages in hundreds of dialects are spoken. It is at once the majestic Andes mountains, the endless emptiness of the Peruvian-Chilean desert, and the lush rain forests of the huge Amazon basin. Latin American cultures are also enormously diverse, yet most share a common heritage of Spanish or Portuguese colonialism and American and European cultural influences. Several ports in Colombia and Brazil were major colonial centers for the importation of black slaves; Latin America remains a rich repository of African and African-American music-cultural traditions, including rituals, musical forms and practices, and types of musical instruments. Native-American cultures that were not eradicated by European diseases have in many cases retained distinctive languages, dress, musical forms, and music rituals.

In Latin American culture, mixture is the norm, not the exception. When you walk through the countryside of Ecuador, for example, you hear a Spanish dialect borrowing many words from Quichua, the regional Native-American language. The local Quichua dialect, conversely, uses many Spanish words. South of Ecuador, in the high mountain regions of Peru, the harp is considered an indigenous instrument, although European missionaries and others in fact brought it to Peru. In rural areas of Atlantic coastal Colombia, musicians sing songs in Spanish, using Spanish literary forms, but these are accompanied by African-style drums and rhythms and by Amerindian flutes and rattles. In northern highland Ecuador, African-Ecuadorians perform the *bomba,* a type of song that features African-American rhythms, Quichua Native-American melodic and harmonic features, and Spanish language—with sometimes one or two Quichua words. Overall, in Latin America it is often hard to maintain strict cultural divisions, because the intermingling of Iberian (Spanish and Portuguese), African, and Native American strains is so profound in the Latin American experience.

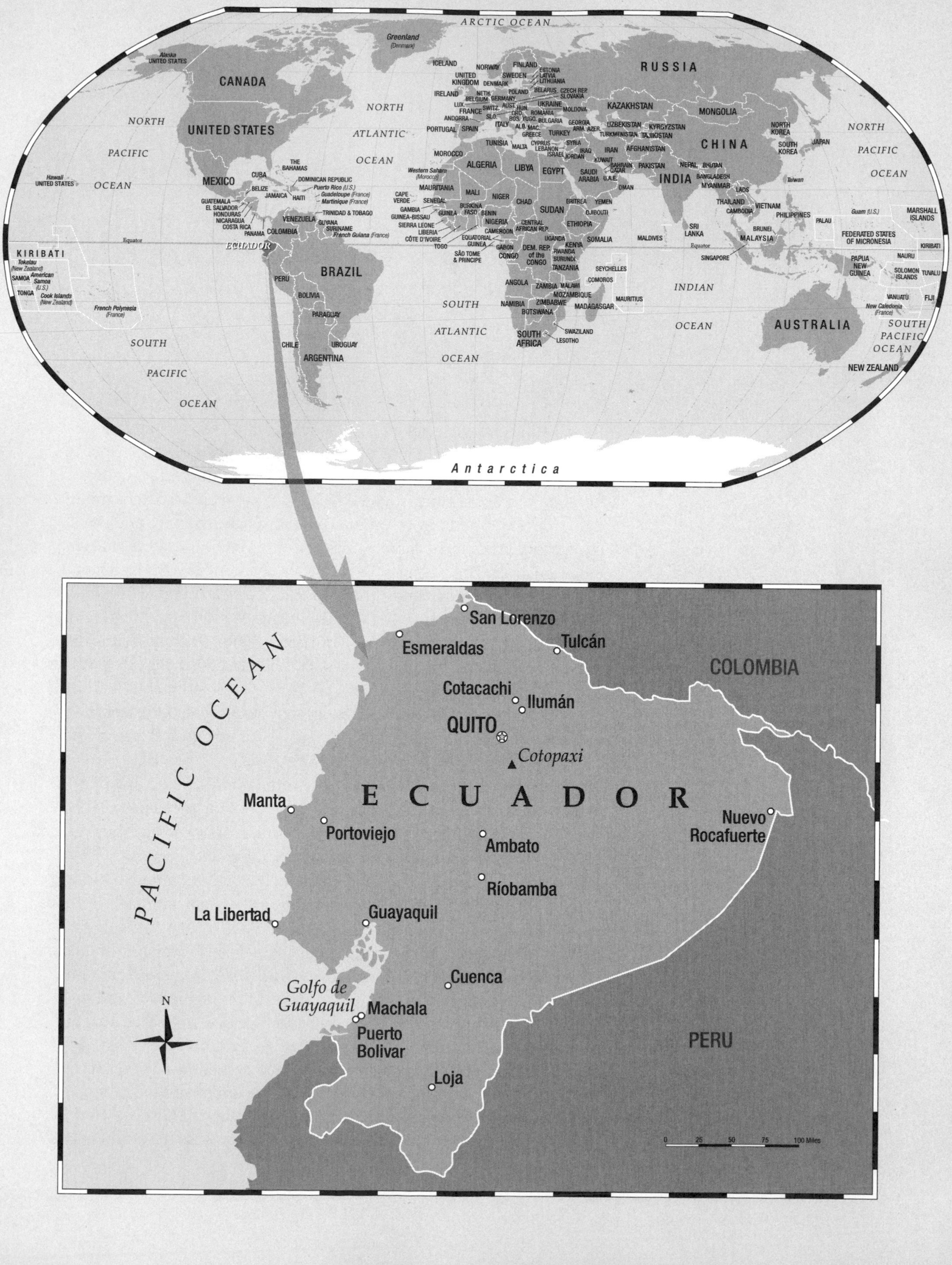
ARCTIC OCEAN
Greenland
(Denmark)
Alaska
UNITED STATES
CANADA
RUSSIA
ICELAND
NORWAY
FINLAND
SWEDEN
ESTONIA
LATVIA
LITHUANIA
UNITED KINGDOM
DENMARK
IRELAND
POLAND
BELARUS
CZECH REP.
SLOVAKIA
NETH.
BELGIUM
GERMANY
LUX.
FRANCE
SWITZ.
AUST.
HUN.
UKRAINE
MOLDOVA
ROMANIA
BULGARIA
ANDORRA
SLO.
CRO.
BOS.
YUGO.
ITALY
ALB.
MAC.
GREECE
PORTUGAL
SPAIN
TURKEY
GEORGIA
ARM.
AZER.
KAZAKHSTAN
MONGOLIA
UZBEKISTAN
KYRGYZSTAN
TURKMENISTAN
TAJIKISTAN
NORTH KOREA
SOUTH KOREA
JAPAN
CHINA
NORTH
PACIFIC
OCEAN
UNITED STATES
NORTH
ATLANTIC
OCEAN
MOROCCO
TUNISIA
MALTA
CYPRUS
LEBANON
ISRAEL
SYRIA
IRAQ
JORDAN
IRAN
KUWAIT
AFGHANISTAN
PAKISTAN
NEPAL
BHUTAN
BAHRAIN
QATAR
U.A.E.
OMAN
SAUDI ARABIA
INDIA
BANGLADESH
MYANMAR
LAOS
Taiwan
THAILAND
VIETNAM
CAMBODIA
PHILIPPINES
ALGERIA
LIBYA
EGYPT
Western Sahara
(Morocco)
MAURITANIA
MALI
NIGER
CHAD
SUDAN
ERITREA
YEMEN
DJIBOUTI
ETHIOPIA
SOMALIA
CAPE VERDE
SENEGAL
GAMBIA
GUINEA-BISSAU
GUINEA
BURKINA FASO
BENIN
SIERRA LEONE
LIBERIA
CÔTE D'IVOIRE
TOGO
NIGERIA
CAMEROON
CENTRAL AFRICAN REP.
EQUATORIAL GUINEA
SÃO TOMÉ & PRINCIPE
GABON
CONGO
DEM. REP. of the CONGO
UGANDA
KENYA
RWANDA
BURUNDI
TANZANIA
SEYCHELLES
COMOROS
MALDIVES
SRI LANKA
BRUNEI
MALAYSIA
SINGAPORE
ANGOLA
ZAMBIA
MALAWI
MOZAMBIQUE
NAMIBIA
ZIMBABWE
BOTSWANA
MADAGASCAR
MAURITIUS
SWAZILAND
SOUTH AFRICA
LESOTHO
INDIAN
OCEAN
AUSTRALIA
PALAU
Guam (U.S.)
MARSHALL ISLANDS
FEDERATED STATES OF MICRONESIA
KIRIBATI
NAURU
PAPUA NEW GUINEA
SOLOMON ISLANDS
TUVALU
VANUATU
FIJI
New Caledonia
(France)
SOUTH
PACIFIC
OCEAN
NEW ZEALAND
Hawaii
UNITED STATES
MEXICO
CUBA
THE BAHAMAS
DOMINICAN REPUBLIC
Puerto Rico (U.S.)
Guadeloupe (France)
Martinique (France)
BELIZE
JAMAICA
HAITI
GUATEMALA
EL SALVADOR
HONDURAS
NICARAGUA
COSTA RICA
PANAMA
TRINIDAD & TOBAGO
VENEZUELA
GUYANA
SURINAME
French Guiana (France)
COLOMBIA
Equator
ECUADOR
KIRIBATI
Tokelau
(New Zealand)
SAMOA
American Samoa
(U.S.)
TONGA
Cook Islands
(New Zealand)
French Polynesia
(France)
PERU
BRAZIL
BOLIVIA
PARAGUAY
CHILE
URUGUAY
ARGENTINA
SOUTH
PACIFIC
OCEAN
SOUTH
ATLANTIC
OCEAN
Antarctica
San Lorenzo
Esmeraldas
Tulcán
COLOMBIA
PACIFIC OCEAN
Cotacachi
Ilumán
QUITO
Cotopaxi
ECUADOR
Manta
Portoviejo
Ambato
Nuevo Rocafuerte
Ríobamba
La Libertad
Guayaquil
Golfo de Guayaquil
Cuenca
Machala
Puerto Bolivar
N
PERU
Loja
0 25 50 75 100 Miles

When you first think of Latin American music, you might hear in your mind's ear the vibrancy of the rhythms in salsa. There is an enormous variety of beaten and shaken rhythm instruments, such as claves, bongos, congas, and maracas, both in salsa and throughout Latin America. Or you might recall the bright, spirited sounds of today's mariachi ensemble, with its vigorous rhythms generated on guitar, *vihuela* (5-string Mexican folk guitar), and *guitarrón* (bass guitar) (Sheehy 1999). In distinctive sizes and shapes, the guitar is prominent in Latin American folk music. In Peru and Bolivia, for example, a type of guitar called the *charango* may have as its body the shell of an armadillo. There are other types of Latin American music with which you might also be familiar, including bossa nova, calypso, and tango. As already suggested, Latin America (even individual Latin American countries) reveals an enormous variety of regional musics (Schechter 1996, 1999b). But we will concentrate on the music-culture of the Ecuadorian Quichua in this chapter.

The Quichua of the Northern Andes of Ecuador

We can best appreciate the traditional nature of northern Ecuadorian Quichua music by knowing something of the traditional setting in which Quichua live. The musicians we shall be listening to have typically lived in *comunas,* or small clusters of houses, on the slopes of Mt. Cotacachi, one of several volcanoes in the Ecuadorian Andes. These *comunas* lie outside the town of Cotacachi, in Imbabura Province. The Quichua spoken in Cotacachi-area *comunas* was spoken there four hundred years ago. Today in Ecuador more than one million people speak the language.

In addition to the language, the agriculture and material culture of the Andes around Cotacachi are traditional. In this rich green countryside dotted with tall eucalyptus, at 8,300 to 9,700 feet above sea level, maize has been the principal cultivated crop for hundreds of years. The local *cabuya* cactus provides fiber for bags and sandal bottoms, and its thick trunk is used to make stools for the home. As we shall see later, the harpist who plays all night in the home of a recently deceased Quichua infant sits on a *cabuya* stool.

Quichua homes have traditionally had one room, often with a covered patio, with mud walls and a dirt floor. Regional Quichua homes have been constructed this way for four hundred years, though newer dwellings are appearing with concrete-block walls. The former home of the then twelve-year-old harpist, César, and his parents, Mama Ramona and Miguel Armando, in the *comuna* of Tikulla outside Cotacachi, is shown in Figure 9-1.

Styles of dress have also remained basically the same since the sixteenth century. Everyone covers his or her head to protect it from the intense heat and light of the near-vertical sun at midday (Cotacachi is almost precisely on the Equator). Women wear cloths, and men wear hats. Quichua women have traditionally worn embroidered blouses, over which they drape shawls (in Quichua, *fachalina*). Their two skirts, one blue and one white, are secured by two woven belts: a wider, inner belt, called the

Figure 9-1
Home of Mama Ramona and Miguel Armando in the *comuna* of Tikulla, outside Cotacachi. May 1980.

John M. Schechter

mama chumbi (mother belt) and a narrower, outer belt, called the *wawa chumbi* (child belt). You will come across this word *wawa* later, when you accompany the harpist as he plays at a *wawa velorio,* or wake for a child. These belts are designed in this region usually with names of Imbabura towns, and they are traditionally woven on home back-strap looms by Quichua families in various *comunas.* Men and boys have traditionally worn a white or blue shirt, white pants, and dark poncho, though today in Imbabura you will see Quichua teenagers wearing English-language sweatshirts and jeans. Any large gathering of Quichua, such as for weekly market or Palm Sunday procession, is still largely a sea of blue and white.

In Figure 9-2 we see three generations of father-son relationships within the same family. Of the grandfather's traditional dress, his adult son retains the white sandals, white shirt, pants, and hat, while his grandson wears Western-influenced clothes.

There is a strong sense of community among Cotacachi Quichua, arising from a common Quichua language (and regional dialect), a common dress, and common aspects of material culture. Quichua eat the same diet of beans and potatoes they grow in their own plots. They gather together regularly for weekly markets, for periodic community work projects (*mingas*), and for fiestas—such as a wedding or a child's wake.

In 1980 few Cotacachi Quichua owned vehicles; by 1990 a few community leaders possessed new pickup trucks. In any case, Quichua homes on Cotacachi's slopes are for the most part not located on roads but interspersed along a network of footpaths called *chaki ñanes.* Without telephones, in 1980 and 1990 families communicated only by foot, along *chaki ñanes.* These paths bear the weight of Quichua women carrying infants, brush, and food to and from market, and of Quichua men carrying

Figure 9-2
Three generations of Quichua men. May 1980.

John M. Schechter

potatoes, milled grain, or perhaps a harp (see Figure 9-3). For all Quichua, the way around the slopes on *chaki ñanes* is second nature; the harpist contracted to play at a *wawa velorio,* or child's wake, is able to reach the home of the deceased child, one and a half hours up Mt. Cotacachi, from his own home, at night, with no illumination other than that of the moon. Walking (in Quichua, *purina*) is so vital in daily life that, as we will see, it finds its way into speech and song.

Figure 9-3
Chaki ñan (Ecuadorian footpath). May 1980.

John M. Schechter

The Musical Tradition: Sanjuán

The common language, dress, material culture, daily labor, and importance of *purina* all find a musical echo in *sanjuán.* The term *sanjuán* may be found at least as early as 1860. At that time, it referred either to a type of song played at the festival of St. John (San Juan) the Baptist held in June or to a type of dance performed at that festival.

Today, the instrument Cotacachi Quichua often use to perform *sanjuán* is the harp without pedals, often referred to in English as the diatonic harp because it is usually tuned to one particular scale and is not capable of being quickly changed to another. Reflecting their other deep-rooted traditions, Quichua have been playing the harp in the Ecuadorian highlands for hundreds of years; in the eighteenth century, it was the most common instrument in the region (Recio [1773] 1947:426). The harp's popularity in the Andes is not limited to Ecuador; in the Peruvian highlands, as already noted, it is so widespread among Quechua that it is considered a "native" instrument.

Brought from Europe initially by several different groups of missionaries, especially the Jesuits, and even by the first conquistadors, the harp has been in Latin America for more than four hundred years. In Chile the tradition of female harpists is strong; this is a heritage of sixteenth-century Spain, when women were virtuosos on the instrument. Elsewhere in rural Latin America, including Ecuador, harp performance by folk and indigenous musicians is typically a male occupation.

The harp we discuss in this chapter is common only in Imbabura Province (Figure 9-4). It appears as an oddity among harpists in central

Figure 9-4
Harpist Raúl, playing his Imbabura harp. March 1980.

John M. Schechter

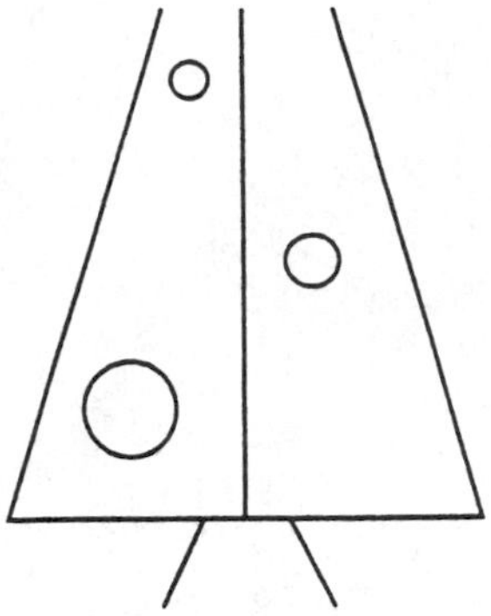

Figure 9-5
Schematic diagram showing position of soundholes in an Imbabura harp.

highland Ecuador, where musicians play a larger instrument. The type of harp Raúl plays in Figure 9-4 is made of cedar and uses wooden nails. The sound emanates through three circular holes on the top of the soundbox; they are always found in the pattern shown in Figure 9-5, on either side of the column, or pole, that connects the neck to the soundbox.

Looking at Raúl's harp, you may think that the instrument has an unusual shape compared with Western harps. The Imbabura harp's column is straight but short, giving the instrument a low "head," or top. Its soundbox is distinctively arched, wide, and deep. On older harps in this region, bull's-hoof glue was used. The tuning pegs are made of iron or wood. The single line of strings is most traditionally a combination of gut and steel. The gut strings—used for the bass and middle registers—used to be made by the Quichua themselves from the cut, washed, dried, and twisted intestinal fibers of sheep, dog, cat, or goat. Sometimes musicians use nylon strings for the middle register, or range, of notes. The steel strings, closest to the performer, play the treble register, or melody line; their bright timbre effectively makes melodic lines more audible than bass lines. Once again relying on their environment for necessary materials, Quichua musicians may use the leg bone of the sheep (in Quichua, *tullu:* bone) to tune the pegs on the harp neck.

This Imbabura harp is a descendant of sixteenth- and seventeenth-century Spanish harps, as shown by shared features of tuning, construction, configuration, and stringing. The Imbabura harp has remained essentially unchanged in appearance for one hundred to two hundred years, and possibly longer (Schechter 1992).

CD 2
Track 11

CD Selection 35 is a *sanjuán* entitled "Cascarón," played in April 1980 by the Quichua harpist Efraín (Figure 9-6). Each transcription of Cotacachi Quichua music in this chapter begins with a small stemless pitch; this corresponds either to the pitch to which that harp was tuned by that harpist on that day or to that singer's tonic pitch on that occasion. For comparison, all transcriptions of Cotacachi Quichua music are given in the key of D minor.

In general, the form of "Cascarón" is typical of Cotacachi Quichua *sanjuanes.* The *sanjuán* is fundamentally a repetitive form, in which one or

Figure 9-6
Harpist Efraín, playing his Imbabura harp outside Cotacachi. April 1980. Harpists play the treble strings with the stronger hand and the bass strings with the weaker. Left-handed, Efraín plays treble with his left, bass with his right.

John M. Schechter

two different phrases are perhaps irregularly inserted into an otherwise similar phrase pattern. In *sanjuán,* the primary motive (the A phrases in Efraín's "Cascarón") predominates. These are the melodies you identify with a particular *sanjuán.* The *sanjuán* phrase often lasts eight beats, and frequently the rhythm of the first half of the phrase is identical, or nearly identical, to the rhythm of the second half. Music Example 9-1 diagrams "Cascarón" in eight-beat phrases; A is for primary motive, B for contrasting motive, and T for the triadic arpeggiation that usually constitutes either introductory or transitional materials.

Music Example 9-1
Phrase structure, Efraín's *sanjuán* *"Cascarón."*

T 1/2T B B
AAAAAAAATBB
AAAAAT1/2TBB
AAAAAT1/2TBB
AAAAATBB
AAAATT chord

My musical transcription of Efraín's "Cascarón" performance appears in Music Example 9-2. The A motive predominates in this song. The consecutive A statements are varied by a rather fixed sequence of one, one and one-half, or two T statements followed by two B statements. Although not in quite as regular a fashion as Efraín's "Cascarón," most performances of *sanjuán* follow this general pattern, with A statements predominating, and sometimes without any B statements at all.

Music Example 9-2
Transcription by John M. Schechter of the *sanjuán "Cascarón,"* played by Efraín.

(continues)

Music Example 9-2
(continued)

Look at A1 (the first statement of the eight-beat A phrase) and sing the eight quarter-note beats. Then sing A2 and A3. You will begin to sense the feeling of *sanjuán:* eight-beat phrases, usually without rests, with the consecutive statements of the primary motive slightly varied. Note that in this case A1 differs from A2 only in the first sixteenth note of each statement. Nevertheless, the first two notes, A and D, respectively, fall within the tonic key of D minor. The A3 version partakes of the T phrase, with the

Music Example 9-2
(continued)

(continues)

first beat now identical to the first beat of T. Typically in *sanjuán* varied numbers of consecutive A phrases will alternate with two B phrases, and often these stress the note a perfect fourth higher than the tonic (here, G, related to D). In October 1990 discussions, Efraín told me that these B phrases are called *esquina* (in Spanish, "corner") phrases, reflecting the points in the *sanjuán* dance, at these B moments, when dancers turn and begin to move in the opposite direction.

Music Example 9-2
(continued)

Sanjuán also provides interesting details of interval structure and rhythm. In the A statements, the three notes D–C–A and their relationships (major second and minor third) are prominent. Compare this with the B statements, G–F–D, which represent the same intervals but are a perfect fourth higher. Listen also to the rhythm of all the statements—T, A, and B—and note that in all cases the rhythm of the eight-beat phrase is the same (Music Example 9-3).

Music Example 9-3
Rhythmic pattern of the *sanjuán* "Cascarón."

Also, the rhythm of the first four beats (the first half) of the phrase is echoed by the rhythm of the second half. Music Example 9-4 illustrates how regular these rhythmic features are. This collection, recorded in Cotacachi *comunas* in 1979–80, also gives you a dozen *sanjuanes* to learn and practice singing (Schechter 1987:35). Note the eight-beat patterning and the equal rhythm halves; "Cascarón" is number three.

Music Example 9-4
Twelve Cotacachi Quichua *sanjuanes.*

*"NI.5" refers to the fifth *sanjuán* recorded in my fieldwork with title not identified; "Ñ6"" refers to the second variant of the sixth *sanjuán* I recorded by the Quichua blind harpist, José Manuel Calapi, who was known in 1980 by his nickname, "Ñausa" (Quichua: blind).

Certain *sanjuanes,* such as "Ilumán tiyu," are often sung, while others such as "Cascarón" and "Carabuela" are typically played instrumentally. You can find words, in the original Quichua with English translation, for all the commonly sung *sanjuanes* in Schechter (1982:II:379–456). After singing or listening to all twelve of these *sanjuanes,* you will begin to sense that some combination of two (or all three) of the motives shown in Music Example 9-5 is strongly characteristic of *sanjuanes.* Just as the major second–minor third pattern is distinctive for melody in *sanjuán,* so also are these patterns distinctive for *sanjuán* rhythm.

Music Example 9-5
Characteristic *sanjuán* rhythmic figures.

As for harmonic relationships, "Cascarón's" melody and Efraín's accompanying bass line illustrate the prominence of the minor tonic key and its relative major key: the arpeggios (T) stress the minor key (D minor), the A sections emphasize the relative major (F major). The high B flat of the B statements, together with the D and F in the bass, suggest a feeling of the key of B-flat major—the subdominant key, or IV, of the relative major, F. The musics of many Andean peoples reflect this close relationship of the minor to its relative major. We will call this relationship *bimodality.*

In Cotacachi Quichua *sanjuán* the music is repetitive, with a single predominating motive, often eight-beat phrases, nearly identical first-half and second-half rhythms, characteristic pitch and rhythmic motifs, and harmonic support that demonstrates the bimodal relationship of minor to relative major. These features give many of these twelve *sanjuanes* a similar sound and provide the grammar of the musical language of Cotacachi Quichua *sanjuán.*

Sanjuán and Cotacachi Quichua Lifeways

Do Quichua speakers throughout the Ecuadorian Andes know "Cascarón"? How is *sanjuán* performed on the Imbabura harp? On which occasions is it performed? What are the characteristic verse structures of sung *sanjuanes*? How do these structures or the specific texts reflect aspects of daily Cotacachi Quichua lifeways?

For students of music-cultures, Imbabura Province and the region around Cotacachi in particular are special, even unique, sites. Many years ago an Ecuadorian musicologist commented that the Quichua of Imbabura had "a special musical aptitude" (Moreno Andrade 1930:269). An Ecuadorian anthropologist once remarked to me that the region around Cotacachi was well known as a "music box." A lyre on the flag of Cotacachi County confirms the central role music occupies in the region, and an author of a book on Imbabura traditions even suggests that to speak of Ecuadorian music is to speak of the music of Cotacachi (Obando 1988:155).

This feeling came also from the Imbabureños themselves, both Quichua- and Spanish-speaking. They insisted on the uniqueness of their own music in relation to that of every other region. In response to questions about the spread of a particular *sanjuán,* for example, Cotacachi Quichua answered, "*Cada llajta.*" *Cada* is Spanish for "every," and *llajta* is Quichua for "community." *Cada llajta* is the idea that every community has its own music, its own mortuary customs, its own dress, its own dialect of Quichua. *Cada llajta* extends even to the way Quichua is to be written in Ecuador. In 1980 meetings, representatives of various Quichua communities decided to permit the "speakers of each dialect to determine their own form of writing the language" (Harrison 1989:19). *Cada llajta* seems to operate elsewhere in Ecuador as well. In April 1980 my wife and I moved from the northern to the central highlands; I sang and played on the Imbabura harp *sanjuanes* well known in Cotacachi to Quichua speakers in this new region. Although they had never heard these songs before, they came to learn and enjoy the pieces. When *sanjuanes* are imported into other regions, the *indígenas* often name them with reference to their origin: "*Sanjuán* from Cotacachi" or "*Sanjuán* from Otavalo" (a town near Cotacachi).

Cada llajta also dictates the performance media and the performance practices. *Sanjuanes* are sung and played by Cotacachi Quichua of all ages, by women and men, girls and boys. They are performed by unaccompanied voices, by vocal duos, by voice and harp—with a *golpeador* (one who beats rhythm on the harp), by solo harp and *golpeador,* by voice and guitar, by solo *kena* (Andean vertical notched flute), by solo *bandolín* (a fretted mandolin), or by ensembles of various instruments. When you hear *sanjuán* played on the Imbabura harp, you will also see a person kneeling in front of or alongside the harp. This is the *golpeador* (in Spanish, *golpear:* to hit), who beats the lower part of the harp soundbox in rhythm to the *sanjuán.* Figure 9-7 shows Miguel Armando, the regular *golpeador* for his two harpist sons, César and Sergio, assuming a *golpeador* posture for César. Ramona, the harpists' mother, is alongside.

All Cotacachi Quichua harpists remark that the *golpeador* and his dependable, metronomic rhythm are essential to proper *sanjuán* performance. The *golpe* is the bedrock on which the harpist's concentration rests. Without it, he cannot work. Note, for example, the prominent *golpe* in Efraín's "Cascarón" performance, by his friend Martín Mateo. This rhythmic hitting of the harp soundbox is not unique to Cotacachi, Ecuador; it appears in diverse folk harp traditions in central highland Ecuador, Peru, Argentina, Chile, and Mexico.

The treble register of the Imbabura harp is tuned to a six-pitch, or hexatonic, scale in the natural minor key, omitting the second scale degree. For example, in our D-minor scale, the harpist will tune his treble register to the following pitches: D, F, G, A, B flat, C, and D (upper octave). This tuning permits him to play the full range of mostly pentatonic *sanjuanes* in his repertoire, as well as the occasional hexatonic one—for example, "Ilumán tiyu," normally played with G minor; not D minor, as tonic. The hexatonic pitches present on the D-minor-tuned harp permit the use of A, the second degree in the key of G minor, "Ilumán tiyu" requires that second scale degree. The middle register typically is also hexatonic. The bass

Figure 9-7
Miguel Armando in *golpeador* posture, with César playing harp. May 1980.

John M. Schechter

register is tuned so that the harpist may play the minor tonic triad, with upper and lower octaves, in alternation with (i.e., one or sometimes two hand positions away from) the relative major triad (Music Example 9-6). He uses four fingers of his bass hand (excluding the little finger), skipping one string between each finger, often two strings between index finger and thumb.

Music Example 9-6
Tuning of bass register of Imbabura harp.

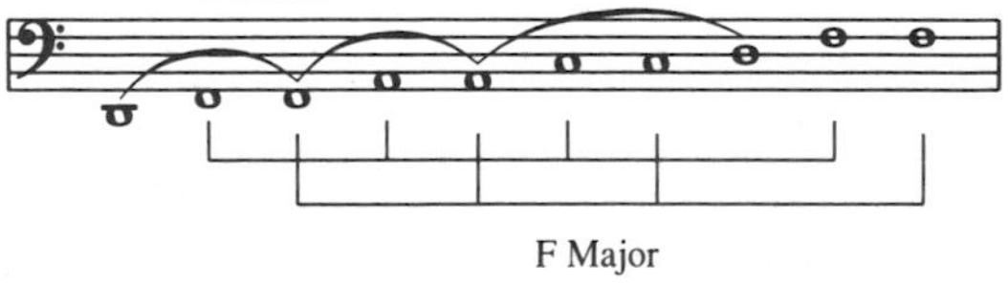

In the *comunas* outside Cotacachi, the *arpero* (harpist) and *golpeador* perform *sanjuanes* in at least three festive contexts: *matrimonio* (wedding), *misai* (private Mass), and *wawa velorio* (child's wake). Quichua in this region have traditionally celebrated a five-day wedding. Within the Saturday to Wednesday cycle, Sunday or Monday sees the *ñavi maillai,* a ritual washing of feet and face, at which harp music is present (Andrade Albuja and Schechter 2000). A *misai* is a private Mass held to a saint: After the Mass in the cantonal church, the statue of the saint—the *santo*—is returned to its altar in its owner's home; a meal is prepared for the Mass offerer, and a musical fiesta is celebrated through the night. In *wawa velorio,* held all night at the deceased child's home, *sanjuán* music predominates.

Sanjuán at *wawa velorio,* as elsewhere, is dance music. You can do the *sanjuán* dance step as you practice from your list of twelve *sanjuanes.* Men and women hold their hands behind their backs and stomp to each quarter-note beat. Step forward with your left foot, joining with the right foot on the next beat. Then move your right foot back first, followed by your left foot. When dancing *sanjuán,* keep your upper torso stiff, your knees bent, and your lower body relaxed, with a good bounce and stomp. The signal to turn around while dancing is (shouted) "*Tigrashpa!*" or "*Tigrapai!*"

We can view the *sanjuán* dance step as an emphatic back-and-forth walking, a stomp, to the music. At the child's wake, this stomping is performed all night as the *arpero* plays *sanjuanes* at length, sometimes several strung together without interruption. As a forceful walk-ing to music, *sanjuán* emphatically asserts the action of walking. It serves as a kinetic endorsement for both the walking and the Quichua way of life that depends on it. Let us delve further into Cotacachi Quichua walking, which, as we have already observed, is vital to communication, to daily tasks—in short, to survival.

Walking in Sanjuán: The Vital-Domain Metaphor

Walking as the paramount daily activity of Cotacachi Quichua emerges in expressive culture not only in dance but in song text as well. This probably should come as no surprise, for any such distinctive facet of local ecology or behavior is bound to appear in word and song. Among the Kwakiutl of Vancouver Island, for example, a person's wealth and guests were considered his or her "salmon" (Boas [1929]1940:234). For the Kaluli people of the Papua New Guinea rain forest, waterway terms are a prominent source of metaphors, including metaphors related to Kaluli music theory. In Kaluli culture, kinds of water become kinds of sound; the term for *waterfall,* in particular, is the point of departure for a series of metaphors relating to musical structure (Feld 1981:26). Other writers, too, have discussed how vital domains of experience, for particular cultures, have served as the fount for broad streams of localized metaphor. In Asturias, Spain, for example, agricultural metaphors remain strong in Asturian deepsong—among miners, who in most cases retain some ties to the land (Fernandez 1978).

Outside Cotacachi, in the *comunas,* walking is necessary for the survival of *comunas* as well as for individual sustenance. Quichua community leaders frequently say that their particular *comuna* will succeed or fail depending on whether it can obtain outside aid. Rousing *comuna* residents to support the *comuna* and searching for assistance from provincial authorities demands footwork. Their view is that *comuna*s will flourish only with persistent *purishpa* (walking) on their behalf. Moreover, on the personal level *purina* becomes to "walk" for one's educational benefit and to enable oneself to carry out family obligations. *Purina,* the inescapable daily activity of walking, becomes a positive metaphor in speech. It is behavior worthy of others' esteem because it is done on behalf of others; it is behavior leading to one's own enhanced self-respect.

In the texts of sung *sanjuán* the *purina* metaphor is "extended." In the metaphoric mechanism of extension, one takes experience from a domain where it is easily understood and uses it as the basis for domains more abstract and ambiguous. In sung *sanjuanes, purina* appears prominently in texts, notably as a verb of action. Music Example 9-7 shows *sanjuán* verse couplets, with their primary (A) motives (Schechter 1987:39).

Music Example 9-7
The Quichua verb *purina* in Cotacachi *sanjuán* couplets.

a. Kanta nishpami shamuni Kanta nishpami *purini*	I come speaking of you I walk speaking of you

b. Wawagumantallamari Wakai wakai *purini*	Indeed just because of the baby Do I walk about crying and crying
c. Solo kampa muchitawan Ayunashka *purini*	Only with your kiss Nourished, do I walk about
d. Wata wata *purini* Kanta nishpa muyuni	I walk about years and years I go this and that way speaking of you
e. Wakai wakai *purinki* Llaki llaki muyunki	You (will) walk about crying and crying You (will) go this and that way very sad
f. Na pimanta *purini* Kanmantami *purini*	Not for whomever do I walk about I walk about because of you

g. Tikumantami shamuni Kanta nishpalla *purini*	I come from (the *comuna* of) Tiku I walk about only speaking of you

h. Ima nishpalla *purinki* Mana nimanta *purinki*	Just why do you walk about? You don't walk about for nothing

i. Llaki llakilla *purijuni* Wakai wakailla *purisha*	I am walking about very sad I shall walk about crying very much

j. Karu karuta *purishpa* Llaki llakilla muyujun	Walking very far He is moving this way and that, very sad

Purina in these *sanjuán* texts "extends" to emotion. The verses express either emotional release through walking ("I walk about crying and crying") or emotional involvement through walking ("I walk about because of you"). *Purina* may be traced through its various metaphoric courses—from walking along the *chaki ñan,* to walking for the benefit of the *comuna* or for one's own betterment, to wandering for love, sadness, or as an outlet for other emotions. We notice how walking becomes extended to encompass the abstract, from physical movement for survival, to movement for broadly social purposes, to movement for personal emotional reasons.

You have looked at the musical character and the phrase structure of *sanjuán,* and you have seen how *purina* functions in *sanjuán* song text as a metaphor reflecting the vital domain of walking in Cotacachi Quichua daily life. Let us now learn two *sanjuanes* that, for different reasons, might be called classics.

Two Classic Sanjuanes

CD 2 Track 12

Two Imbabura Quichua *sanjuanes* qualify as classics in their highland region: "Rusa María wasi rupajmi" and "Ilumán tiyu." "Rusa María" (CD Selection 36) was in 1980 one of the most beloved *sanjuanes* of the Cotacachi Quichua *comuna.*

An important disc of Imbabura Quichua music, *Ñanda mañachi 1* (1977), begins side A with this *sanjuán,* and the record jacket back presents an essay, "Un país llamado Rosa María" ("A Land Called Rosa María"), in which this particular *sanjuán* becomes a metaphor for the Quichua way of life in this entire region. In our field recording, Gerónimo on vocal, Sergio on harp, and his father, Miguel Armando, on *golpe,* perform this *sanjuán* at a *wawa velorio* in January 1980. You will hear noise as the microphone is passed back and forth from singer to harpist.

Rusa María

Rusa María wasi rupajmi	Rusa María's house burning
Mas ki rupachun nishkashi,	So let it burn, she seems to have said,
Rusa María wasi rupajmi	Rusa María's house burning
Mas ki rupachun nishkashi,	So let it burn, she seems to have said,
Taita Manuilpash machashkamari	And Manuel, a father, very drunk
Manllarishkami wakajun,	Frightened, is crying,
Taita Manuilpash machashkamari	And Manuel, a father, very drunk
Manllarishkami wakajun,	Frightened, is crying,
Wambrakunapash kwitsakunawan	And young men and young women
Sirinkapajmi rishka nin,	Went to lie down together, they say,
Wambrakunapash kwitsakunawan	And young men and young women
Sirinkapajmi rishka nin.	Went to lie down together, they say.

What is it about "Rusa María" that delivers such a strong message of life in Imbabura? "Rusa María" speaks of tragedy, drunkenness, and fright, as well as courting. The first double couplet suggests resignation in the face of a disastrous house fire. Quichua homes higher up Mt. Cotacachi have thatched roofs (see Schechter 1992:141 for a photograph) instead of tile, with wooden support beams. The family meal is cooked over an open hearth, and destruction by fire is an ever-present possibility. When I asked about this verse ten years later, in September 1990, Imbabura Quichua musicians told me that "Rusa María's" home might well be small and old; she might be expressing both anger and the confidence that her neighbors, feeling sympathy, might build her a new home, larger and better. Quichua families are accustomed to disaster regarding both property and infant death.

Alcoholic beverages can be another source of social tragedy. Much of the alcohol consumed in the Cotacachi countryside in 1980 was cane alcohol (*trago*), brought as contraband from another region of Ecuador. Frequently, the owners of the small stores in the *comunas* would mix this *trago* with water, berry juice, or other substances, and the effects could be unpredictable. Consumption of *trago* or other alcohol is vital in Cotacachi rituals (such as a child's wake) and in Andean rituals in general throughout Peru and Bolivia. Yet overconsumption of *trago* can produce hallucinations, strongly emotional behavior, and in the case of adulterated *trago* blindness or death.

"Rusa María" refers also to courting. *Wambra* and *kwitsa* may mean either young man and young woman, or boy and girl. Courting begins in the schoolyard and elsewhere at age twelve or thirteen. Quichua often marry in their mid- or late teens.

"Rusa María" speaks of the inevitable in Cotacachi Quichua life: the natural environment, ritual practice in conflict with economic exploitation, and cultural expectation and human instinct. In the final analysis, "Rusa María" is a song, danced to on festive occasions; it is a source of joy and pride to all the *indígenas* of Cotacachi.

In the case of the highly popular (both in 1980 and still in 1990) *sanjuán* "Ilumán tiyu" ("Man of Ilumán"), we know the composer: Segundo "Galo" Maigua Pillajo, a Quichua composer-guitarist-singer of the Imbabura village of Ilumán. Maigua Pillajo's *sanjuán* compositions are often motivated by autobiographical forces. His fame among Imbabura Quichua is attested to by wide acknowledgment of his being the composer of highly popular *sanjuanes* and by his ensemble Conjunto Ilumán's high level of local demand and their having produced as of 1990 one commercial cassette.

My fieldwork in 1990 in Imbabura brought to light the fact that *sanjuán* may often take on the nature of a ballad, even in instances where that fact is not immediately obvious. The thoughts of a *sanjuán* text typically express the essence of a large story, making the *sanjuán* a highly distilled ballad form, the synoptic character of the text being in keeping with the elliptical character of Andean poetry dating back to Incan times. With "Ilumán tiyu," the ballad nature—the story behind the *sanjuán*—is not at all obvious. CD Selection 37 is of the composer, Maigua Pillajo, playing guitar and singing "Ilumán tiyu" together with his Conjunto Ilumán ensemble, on October 27, 1990, in the village of Ilumán, in the home of a local policeman (Figure 9-8).

CD 2
Track 13

Figure 9-8
"Ilumán tiyu" composer Segundo "Galo" Maigua Pillajo (far right), with his ensemble, Conjunto Ilumán. October 1990.

John M. Schechter

One regular member of the ensemble, a noted harpist, was unable to be present on this occasion. As with *indígena* harpists, so too was there a proliferation of *indígena* violinists in eighteenth-century highland Ecuador (Recio [1773] 1947: Chap. 21). The tradition of Quichua violinists is particularly strong today in the Otavalo-Ilumán area of Imbabura.

What had never been comprehensible, since my 1980 research when I recorded numerous versions of "Ilumán tiyu" in the environs of Cotacachi, was the nature of the lyrics. When I was informed that Segundo Galo Maigua Pillajo was in fact the composer of this *sanjuán,* I tried, during a visit to his Ilumán home on September 30, 1990, to ascertain what might lie behind words that seem merely a statement that the man singing and speaking is an *indígena* from Ilumán.

Galo described the tale behind the text. He told me that before he composed "Ilumán tiyu" he had become extremely ill with tuberculosis; the condition of his lungs had deteriorated, and he believed he was about to die. Although during 1972–73 wanderings through the *comunas* around Cotacachi he had sung the melody to a variety of words (Galo says he composes by first hearing a melody, later setting text), he now determined that he would like everyone—be they young woman or old woman, for example—to dance to this, his song, after his death. In effect, "Ilumán tiyu" was ultimately texted as Galo's final statement of his identity to posterity: "I"—the man singing, speaking—am a man from Ilumán; remember me by remembering my music: "Dance to my song." In sum, what appeared to the uninformed listener to be innocuous words came, on greater understanding, to have profound import for a composer believing himself to be on his deathbed.

Ilumán Tiyu.

Ilumán Tiyu cantanmi,	The man [not "uncle"] from Ilumán sings,
Ilumán Tiyu nijunmi.	The man from Ilumán is saying.
Ilumán Tiyu cantanmi,	The man from Ilumán sings,
Ilumán Tiyu nijunmi.	The man from Ilumán is saying.
Sultira kashpa paya kashpa,	Being a young (unmarried) woman, [or an] old woman,
Ñuka tunupi bailapai.	Dance to my song.
Sultira kashpa paya kashpa,	Being a young (unmarried) woman, [or an] old woman,
Ñuka tunupi bailapai.	Dance to my song.
Este es el indio de Ilumán	This is the *indígena* of Ilumán
Él que canta sanjuanito.	He who sings *sanjuán.*
Este es el indio de Ilumán	This is the *indígena* of Ilumán
Él que canta sanjuanito.	He who sings *sanjuán.*
Para que bailen toditos,	So that all [men] might dance,
Para que bailen toditas,	So that all [women] might dance.
Para que bailen toditos.	So that all [men] might dance,
Para que bailen toditas.	So that all [women] might dance.
Ilumán Tiyu cantanmi,	The man from Ilumán sings,
etc.	etc.
Sultira kashpa paya kashpa,	Being a young (unmarried) woman, [or an] old woman,
etc.	etc.]

Spanish speakers will note that the intermingling of Spanish and Quichua words we spoke of early in this chapter appears prominently in this *sanjuán.* The words *Tiyu, Sultira, tunupi,* and *bailapai* either represent variants of Spanish words—with either cognate or different meanings—or use Spanish roots (*bailar*) in Quichua verb forms. Moreover, the verse, "Este es el indio de Ilumán, él que canta sanjuanito," is a translation of the first, critically important, verse; Galo commented to me that a major area radio station had prompted him to produce the parallel text in Spanish. Some of his other *sanjuanes,* such as "Antonio Mocho" and "Rusita Andranga," share the distilled-ballad character of "Ilumán tiyu." Both of these *sanjuanes,* along with "Ilumán tiyu," appear on the commercial cassette *Elenita Conde,* by Conjunto Ilumán; the cassette was made in Otavalo and mass-produced in Bogotá, Colombia, somewhat prior to 1990.

The Andean Ensemble Phenomenon

Conjunto Ilumán represents a widespread phenomenon, both in the Andes and beyond: the Andean ensemble. Other Ecuadorian ensembles focusing on Quichua or *Nueva Canción (New Song)* musics over the last twenty years have included Ñanda Mañachi (Quichua: "Lend me the way"), 1977, 1979, 1983; Conjunto Indígena "Peguche" (Spanish: *indígena* ensemble from the village of Peguche [near Otavalo]), 1977; and Jatari

(Quichua: "Get up!"), 1978. The carefully and elaborately produced albums of Ñanda Mañachi, in particular, are notably evocative of the Quichua music-culture of Imbabura.

Today in the Otavalo Valley, teenagers and young men are actively engaged in music making. In Imbabura, one radio station has had an annual festival of musical ensembles, in which any and all area village ensembles may participate, each playing perhaps two songs on the radio. In July 1990 this village ensemble marathon featured enough groups for the radio festival to last twelve hours. Music making is an important means of socialization among Quichua youths who have long since ceased attending school and who find few community activities available to them except for volleyball, which is pursued with a vengeance in the village plazas and *comunas* of Imbabura. You will hear Quichua teenagers rehearsing diligently, on weekends, at a member's home, performing a few traditional *sanjuanes* and, like their counterparts in the United States, often experimenting with their own compositions.

The Bolivian ethnomusicologist Gilka Wara Céspedes has recently remarked that "the Andean Sound is becoming a part of the sonic scene from Europe to Japan" (1993:53). In Quito, the capital of Ecuador, musically polished Quichua ensembles from Ecuador and Peru are featured regularly and prominently on the main tourist thoroughfares. Where Andean *indígena* textile manufacturers and distributors have for years traveled the international byways, selling their home-woven ponchos, blankets, and scarves, today the entrepreneurial instinct remains intact but the product has frequently changed: from bulky woolens to featherweight cassettes and CDs, delicate bamboo *zampoñas* (panpipes) and *kenas*. Beyond Ilumán and Quito, one can enjoy "the Andean Sound" in mid-town New York City, in San Francisco's Union Square, in front of Il Duomo in Florence, Italy, and even on Arbat Street in central Moscow. In September 1993 a Virginia-based Bolivian ensemble, Ollantay, was featured in the annual summer concert series produced by the American Folklife Center on the plaza in front of the Library of Congress's Jefferson Building, in Washington, D.C.

The United States is unquestionably a vital part of the international Andean sonic scene. Amauta, based in Seattle, comprises Chilean and Bolivian musicians playing traditional Andean instruments; they appeared recently at the Seattle Northwest Regional Folklife Festival. *Amauta* is from the Quechua *jamaut'a,* "wise;" the *amautas* were one of three types of specialists, in the Inca Empire, responsible for preserving the memory of past Inca leaders. They created brief historical stories that were passed on through oral tradition to succeeding generations (Schechter 1979:191–92). Condor, out of Corvallis, Oregon, is an ensemble of five professional, college-educated musicians from Argentina, Peru, and Mexico; the group focuses on traditional Andean musics. Andanzas (Spanish: "wanderings") performs music from a variety of Latin American and Caribbean traditions; this widely traveled, four-member ensemble includes musicians from Argentina, Bolivia, and Mexico, as well as a classically trained harpist from the United States. Andesmanta, an ensemble of Ecuadorian musicians playing traditional highland Ecuadorian musics, including *sanjuanes,* as well as other South American folk musics, has performed at Carnegie Hall and the Metropolitan Museum of Art. Among the most well established of U.S.-based Andean groups is Sukay (Quechua: "to work furrows in straight lines," or "to whistle musically"), formed originally in 1974, with some eight albums by 1994, along with performances at Lincoln Center and major folk music festivals.

The California-based group Chaskinakuy (Quechua: "to give and receive, hand to hand, among many") is distinguished by its size—two musicians—and by the fact that both are non-Andeans: the founder Edmond Badoux of Switzerland and Francy Vidal of California. Now in their fourteenth year, Chaskinakuy is also unique in that Edmond, a careful student of Andean music-culture, performs several less common (for these U.S.-based ensembles) but important and often distinctly traditional instruments: Peruvian harp, pelican-bone flute, long straight trumpet, condor-feather *zampoña,* and *pututu* (Quechua: "conch trumpet") (Ross 1994:19–24). Chaskinakuy tours California annually and has produced two recordings. A list of selected recordings by these and other Andean ensembles can be found in Ross 1994:27.

Finally, Andean ensembles are taking root in U.S. universities. With the strong beginning of the *Nueva Canción* ensemble Toqui Amaru (Mapuche and Quechua: "chief serpent"), founded at the University of Texas at Austin in 1976 by Renato Espinoza of Chile, with Guillermo Delgado and Enrique Cuevas of Bolivia, Néstor Lugones of Argentina, and Alejandro Cardona of the United States, UT/Austin has for some years maintained an Andean ensemble among their other Latin American groups. At the University of California at Santa Cruz, students perform in intermediate (Voces [Spanish: "voices"]) and advanced-level (Taki Ñan [Quichua: "song path"]) Andean ensembles; Taki Ñan, which recorded an in-house CD in 1998 and an in-house cassette in 1992, focuses on traditional and *Nueva Canción* musics of South America, performing in Spanish and Quichua. I have recently traced the fourteen-year evolution of this ensemble (Schechter 1999a). Finally, in Berkeley, California, Chaskinakuy has now joined forces with certain Taki Ñan alumni and others to create a new Andean ensemble, Viento, dedicated to traditional South-Andean instrumental and vocal forms.

Returning from the United States to the Andes of Imbabura, the traditions of the Quichua of Cotacachi—the people, the language, the dress, the material culture, the character of *sanjuán* and the harp that plays it—have been preserved for hundreds of years. *Cada llajta* (individual character of the community) ensures the uniqueness of many aspects of their expressive culture. However, the Cotacachi Quichua share some traits with other regions and cultures of Latin America. One of these is the wake ritual for a dead child. Let us look at the *wawa velorio* to see how it accommodates *cada llajta* with broader beliefs and practices that transcend cultural and political boundaries.

Wawa Velorio

In Imbabura as elsewhere in Latin America, infants struggle to survive. In three consecutive months in 1979–80 I witnessed three *wawa velorio* rituals on Cotacachi's slopes. I observed a fourth child's wake there in August 1990. The infant mortality rate in Ecuador continues to be high; deaths are caused in large part from intestinal and respiratory diseases. Our own history has seen high infant mortality rates: in the 1620s to 1720s in Boston as many as three in ten persons died in infancy (Slater 1977:16). The death of young children in Ecuador and throughout Latin America is a daily tragedy, one that through its very frequency ironically serves to preserve dozens of unique regional traditions of genre, instrument, and dance.

We turn to one visit, with the harpist and his family, to a *wawa velorio* on Mt. Cotacachi for a two-year-old Quichua girl, January 12–13, 1980. After nightfall, Sergio, the harpist contracted to provide music for the wake (Figure 9-9), his younger brother and apprentice harpist, César, and their

Figure 9-9
Harpist Sergio. March 1980.

John M. Schechter

family leave their Tikulla home for the home of the deceased. After more than an hour's uphill winding journey on *chaki ñanes,* with their father and *golpeador* Miguel Armando bearing the family harp, they arrive. At about 9:30 Sergio sits down with his harp next to the platform bearing the deceased infant. A few candles illuminate the casket and the home. After tuning, Sergio plays a strongly percussive music called *vacación* (CD Selection 38; Music Example 9-8). The all-night *wawa velorio*—the wake for the deceased Quichua child—has begun.

CD 2
Track 14

Music Example 9-8
Partial transcription by John M. Schechter of *vacación,* played by harpist Sergio at a child's wake; this performance in February 1980.

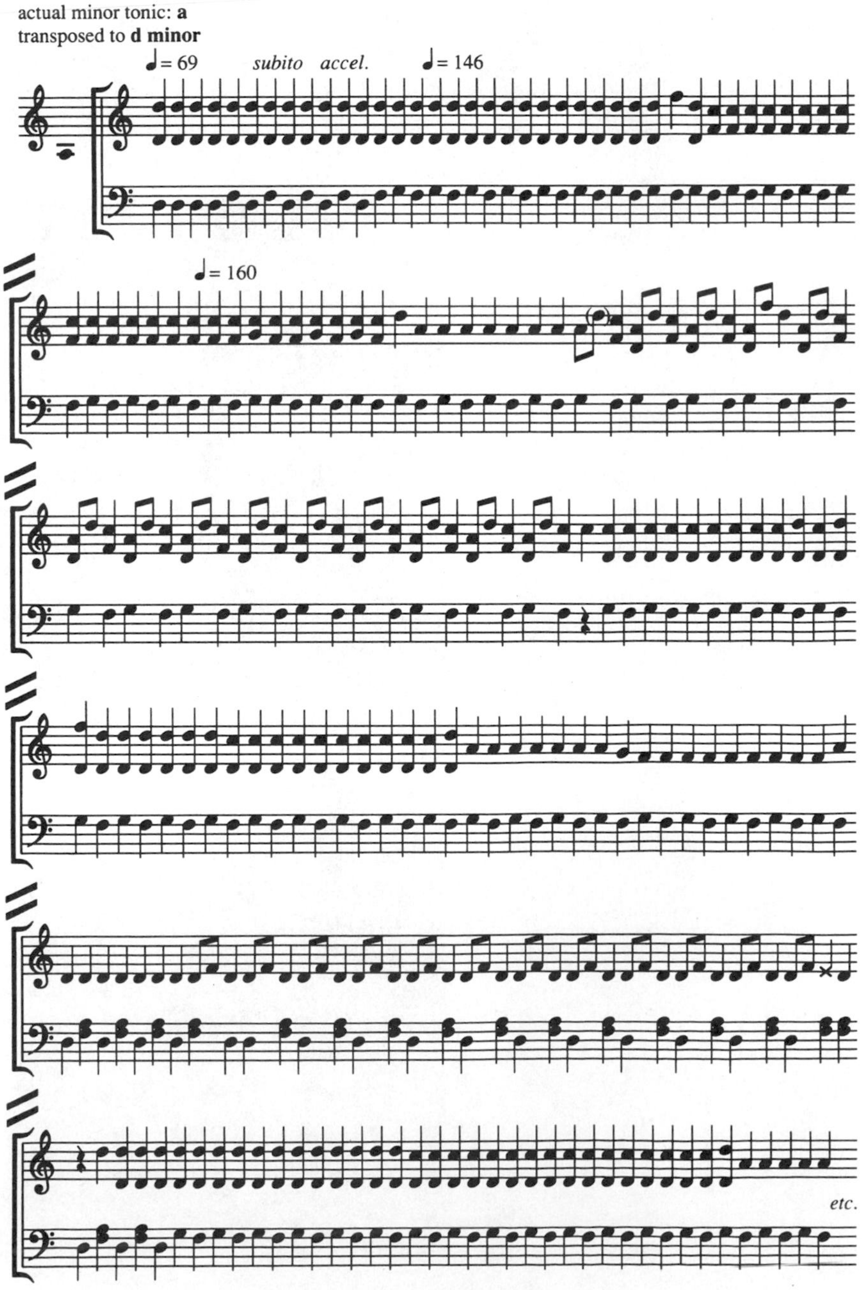

Vacación (the same term is used for both the genre and the title here) differs audibly from *sanjuán.* First, *vacación* does not require a *golpeador* but is performed by the harpist alone. Second, it is not sung but is purely instrumental. Where *sanjuán* is in simple meter, *vacación* lacks the regular stresses that characterize a particular meter. *Vacación* is not built, like *sanjuán,* in eight-beat phrases but in long, descending cycles. *Sanjuán* is dance music; *vacación* is not.

Sanjuán is performed throughout the night at *wawa velorio,* accompanying the dancing of family and guests. *Vacación* is tied to two special ritual moments: at the outset of the wake, and whenever behavior centers on the deceased child. Harpists informed me that they play *vacación* at the beginning of the ritual in order to drive out the *demonio,* or devil, from beneath the platform supporting the deceased child. The second ritual moments include the late-evening adorning of the corpse and the dawn closing of the casket.

Before playing *vacación,* after playing it, and periodically throughout the night, the harpist and his family are offered food and drink—bananas, homemade bread, barley gruel, maize gruel, stewed corn, and *trago.* I have mentioned the central importance of *trago* consumption in ritual settings both in Cotacachi and throughout the Andes. In *wawa velorio,* most of those present consume the drink. The man (never a woman) with the *trago* bottle and plastic cup goes around the room, offering a *copa* (cup) of *trago* to each man and woman: "*Ufyapai!*" ("Drink!"), he says; the one being offered the *copa* usually first asks him to drink—which he does—then accepts the offer him- or herself.

Until approximately midnight, Sergio performs mostly *sanjuanes.* By 10:30 P.M. he has played some five to ten *sanjuanes,* including perhaps "Carabuela," "Llakishamari nirkanki," "Ilumán tiyu," and "Rusa María." Occasionally, to keep the dancing going, he changes from one *sanjuán* to another without stopping. There is a distinctly regular and nearly metronomic tempo sense about this father-son duo. Miguel Armando's *golpe* is solid and reliable, invariant, and Sergio's rhythm is strong and regular. Vocalists for the duo may be Sergio's companions, Roberto and Gerónimo. One sings with Sergio. The voice-harp duo performs typically texted *sanjuanes,* including "Rusa María" and "Ruku kuskungu." To enhance the *alegre,* or happy, character of the festive ritual, the harpist likes to have near-constant chatter together with his music and *golpe.*

Around 10:30 P.M., perhaps in the middle of playing a *sanjuán,* Sergio suddenly stops and shifts into *vacación.* Now the child, in her casket, is removed from the platform where it has been prominently displayed and is placed on the floor for adorning and crowning. The infant is given to her mother, who mourns the loss of her baby with a lament. This sobbed music uses the principal notes of *vacación*: D–C–A (scale degrees 8–7–5 of D minor). A crown of flowers is put on the baby's head. Her waist and wrists are wrapped in ribbons, and bouquets of flowers are placed alongside the body in the casket. During this entire time, Sergio plays *vacación,* and he stops only when the infant and her casket are again placed on the platform.

Although dancing to *sanjuán* has been slow to start, by 1:30 A.M. everyone is dancing: With the air growing colder, at nine thousand feet, the music and the festive night are warming up. The godmother and the father might begin to dance, prompting Sergio to shout a pleased: *"Achi mamaka kallarinka ña!"* ("The godmother will begin [to dance] now!") Gerónimo shouts: *"Shinlli shinlli bailapankich' kumarigukuna!"* ("Dance really strongly, dear *comadres!*"). Sergio now hardly stops for small talk, immediately replenishing the musical warmth with one, then another *sanjuán*—maybe several strung together.

He now begins to alternate *sanjuán* with *pareja,* a slightly faster music, also for dancing but usually without text.

Very late, at about 3 A.M., Sergio leaves the harp and asks his younger brother, César, to take over (Figure 9-10). With very few people still awake, César plays a string of short *sanjuanes.* There is no banter between César and his *golpeador*-father, as there had been more naturally between musicians of the same generation, such as Sergio and Gerónimo. This is *sanjuán* without reaction—functional dance music with little function, since no one is dancing.

At about 5 A.M. everyone is awake and shares a morning meal of boiled potatoes. Before sunrise (an hour later) Sergio again takes over the harp, tuning and perhaps playing a *pareja.* Suddenly, he shifts into *vacación* and the casket is taken outside onto the patio. Sergio stops quickly, picks up the harp, and heads outside. CD Selection 39 begins with Sergio performing *vacación* as the casket is being taken outside. He then remarks, *". . . sacando para afuera"* ("[They're] taking [it] outside"). He heads at once outside and there the mother begins to sing her lament.

CD 2
Track 15

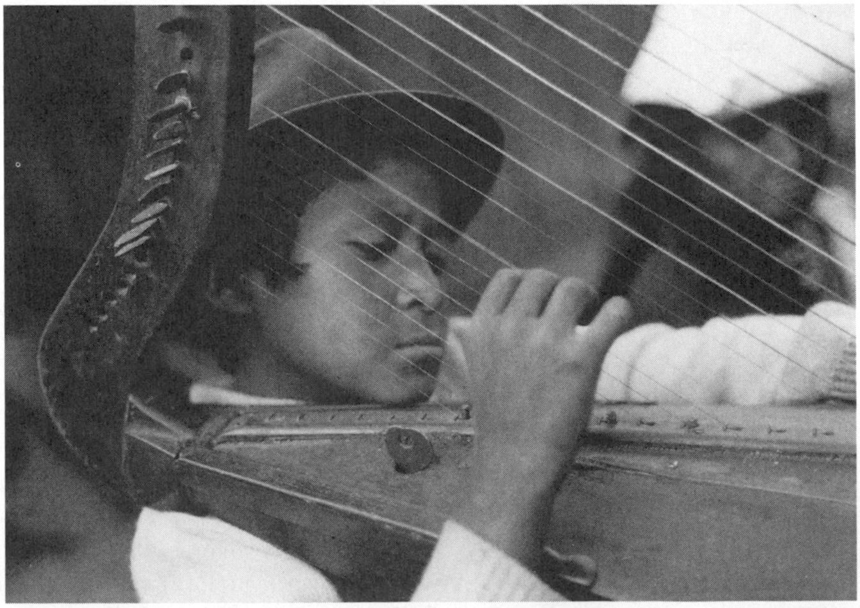

Figure 9-10
Harpist César. March 1980.

John M. Schechter

The mother bids farewell to her child for the final time. She heard cycles of *vacación* for a few minutes just before the casket's removal outside. Now, as if on cue, and almost precisely at sunrise, she expresses her heartfelt grief in a lament that, as in the night before, uses almost exclusively the same three important pitches from *vacación*: D–C–A (in Sergio's actual tuning these pitches are G♯–F♯–D♯). Soon after she begins, Sergio, also near the casket, repeats *vacación* on the harp. Both musical expressions are *of* the child: the mother's *to* the infant, the harpist's *about* the infant, marking behavior directed toward her. Because the infant is open to view for only a few more minutes, the focus of everyone's attention is on her. Although *vacación* does not "accompany" the mother's lament (they are simultaneous but independent musical expressions), nevertheless they *are* together—in time, in object focus, in musical pitch, and in structure (like *vacación,* the lament is cyclical in form, always beginning with the G♯ and descending through the F♯ to the D♯).

The mother at this point will typically sing-sob alone. On this particular morning, her sobs make it difficult to render most of the words precisely. Clearly she is addressing her baby daughter, whom she calls *warmiku* ("little woman"). She sobs-sings in short phrases that ultimately descend to the lowest pitch. (Respecting the mother in this moment of profound personal grief, I omit the transcription of this lament.)

Lamenting at dawn, the mother caresses her child's face or entire wrapped body one last time. Then the *golpeador* hammers on the lid of the casket, and when the child is no longer visible Sergio stops playing *vacación.* Just after 6 A.M. the godfather hoists the casket to his shoulder and everyone walks down the mountain to the town of Cotacachi, where the child is buried in the cemetery. After the burial the party adjourns to a *cantina* (tavern), where Sergio continues to play *sanjuanes* on the harp for dancing throughout the day.

Dancing, all night, at a child's wake. On Cotacachi's slopes and throughout Latin America, *wawa velorio*—or *velorio del angelito*—is a celebration. We find this surprising, perhaps. We might feel some of the confusion of a French baron, Jean Charles Davillier, who came upon a festive child's wake while traveling in the Spanish Mediterranean in the 1870s (1874:409; see Figure 9-11). He could not understand the merrymaking—in this case, a couple dancing a *jota,* accompanying themselves with castanets. One of the relatives informed him: "*Está con los ángeles*" ("She is with the angels"). The explanations are the same on this side of the Atlantic. For example, when nineteenth- and twentieth-century French and U.S. visitors to Argentina and Chile unexpectedly come upon children's wakes, they are consistently told that the gathering is a celebration in honor of the little angel, who is in the breast of God, or that the little angel has died in innocence and has gone to heaven. Therefore, there is to be rejoicing, not weeping (Coffin 1823:83–85; Ebelot [1890] 1943:16; Schechter 1983). The great majority of Latin Americans are Roman Catholic. In Roman Catholicism, baptism confers a vital regeneration in Christ and thus an unconditional promise of salvation to a baptized child dying in infancy. In Catholic

Figure 9-11
A festive child's wake in the Spanish Mediterranean, 1870s.

Illustration by Gustave Doré

Spain and Latin America, the deceased infant is believed to dwell among the angels—to be an angel. This is cause for rejoicing.

The joyful rite is both broad and deep in Latin America. We read accounts of children's wakes in this hemisphere going back to 1788 in Puerto Rico (Abbad y Lasierra 1788:281–82). In the nineteenth or twentieth centuries, *velorio del angelito,* or *wawa velorio,* or *baquiné* (as the rite is known among African-Antillans of Puerto Rico) was celebrated in Argentina, Brazil, Chile, Colombia, Cuba, the Dominican Republic, Ecuador, Mexico, Nicaragua, Panama, Paraguay, Peru, Puerto Rico, and Venezuela.

If we can understand something of the philosophy behind the joyful character of the Latin American child's wake, celebrating the ascension of the sinless infant into the realm of the angels, then how does *wawa velorio* fit into the category of funeral rituals? A ritual is a formal practice or custom, and rural dwellers have both calendric rituals, tied to cycles of agriculture, religion, or national celebration, and life cycle rituals, marking significant transitional moments in the life of any individual. Funeral rites are life cycle rituals.

Within the formal practice or custom, you will see actions that are prescribed—obligatory, standardized, conventional. At *wawa velorio,* I was struck by the precision with which certain prescribed actions were carried out: *vacación* always began the wake; it always accompanied movement of the corpse, usually in its open casket, from one place to another; at dawn, as the casket was brought outside for closing, the mother began her lament, almost as if on cue. Interestingly, in Hungary, laments are to be performed quite strictly at specified moments of the period after death and at burial; one of the specific points is when the casket is closed (Boilès 1978:130). During the period of immediate mourning, when all are able to view the corpse, there is always a conventionalized, dramatized outburst of grief; the corpse is usually the center of attention. There may be ritual forms of fondling the corpse—the body is sometimes stroked and embraced (Malinowski [1925] 1954:49). Thus we saw and heard, in the Cotacachi *comuna,* the child conspicuously displayed during the night, the lament seemingly almost "cued," and the Quichua mother caressing her child on the patio of their home.

Indeed, in keeping with our understanding of the prescriptive nature of ritual, we find that most accounts of Latin American (and Spanish, as well) children's wakes share certain prominent behaviors, regardless of cultural group or country. The child is always conspicuous by its presence, in the same room in which family and friends dance to the favorite music of the region (*sanjuán* in highland Ecuador, *jota* in Mediterranean Spain): thus, *cada llajta* in operation. The infant is not only present but raised: lying on the elevated platform, seated on the table, tied to a ladder placed atop the casket, suspended from the roof, or pushed back and forth between poles. Each of these types of ritual gestures symbolizes the transformation into an angel and entry into eternity. Similarly, the infant is washed and dressed in the finest clothing available and is bedecked in ribbons, flowers, and paper or cardboard wings. Upon the child's head is a crown of real or artificial flowers, and this wreath is essential: the crown is both ubiquitous (in Latin American and Spanish children's wakes) and ancient (the practice of crowning dead children dates back to the time of the ancient Greeks; Rush 1941:113). The atmosphere of the wake is always festive, with dancing, food, and alcoholic beverage.

Several Spanish and Latin American visual and literary artists have depicted the child's wake in paintings, novels, short stories, plays, and poems; many of these portrayals implicitly criticize what the native artists view as an indefensible diminution of a life, in making its extinction the pretext for merrymaking. Nevertheless, the Latin American child's wake is a deep-rooted ritual and one that embodies local cultural preferences in expressive culture—song types, dance types, instrument types. Whether or not local artists or outsiders approve of the *velorio del angelito,* the practice does serve as a reliable stamp—designed by the culture itself—of that local culture at that point in time (Schechter 1994).

Despedida (Farewell)

You have learned of the lifeways, harp, and songs of the Quichua of highland Ecuador, and you have witnessed the poignant Quichua ritual of *wawa velorio*—dancing at the wake of a child. We have singled out for recognition several individual artists, including the harpists Efraín and Sergio and the composer-singer Segundo Galo Maigua Pillajo. In their own worlds of music, these artists are highly esteemed, for they practice music-cultural traditions that their cultures prize highly and have preserved for hundreds of years.

Our sense of community is bound up with our identification with our own musics and music rituals. In one realm or another, we all obey the dictate of *cada llajta:* each of us, ultimately, is musically, linguistically, and certainly in many other respects, of *a* place.

References

Abbad y Lasierra, Fray Iñigo. 1788. *Historia geográfica, civil y política de la Isla de S. Juan Bautista de Puerto Rico.* Madrid: Imprenta de Don Antonio de Espinosa.

Andrade Albuja, Enrique, and John M. Schechter. 2000. "'*Kunan punlla rimagrinchi . . .*': Wit and Didactics in the Quichua Rhetorical Style of Señor Enrique Andrade Albuja, Husbandman-Ethnographer of Cotacachi, Imbabura [Ecuador]." In *Inscribing Andean Voices: Quechua Verbal Artistry,* edited by J. M. Schechter and G. Delgado. Manuscript submitted for publication consideration.

Boas, Franz. [1929] 1940. "Metaphorical Expression in the Language of the Kwakiutl Indians." In *Race, Language, and Culture.* New York: Free Press.

Boilès, Charles L. 1978. *Man, Magic, and Musical Occasions.* Columbus, Ohio: Collegiate.

Céspedes, Gilka Wara. 1993. "*Huayño, Saya,* and *Chuntunqui:* Bolivian Identity in the Music of 'Los Kjarkas.'" *Revista de Música Latinoamericana/Latin American Music Review* 14 (1): 52–101.

[Coffin, Isaac Foster]. 1823. *Journal of a Residence in Chili*[sic], *by a Young American, Detained in That Country, During the Revolutionary Series of 1817–18–19.* Boston: Wells and Lilly.

Conjunto Ilumán. n.d. *Elenita Conde.* Commercial cassette by this Ecuadorian Quichua ensemble. Pre-1990. Ensemble directed by Segundo Galo Maigua Pillajo of Ilumán, Ecuador.

Conjunto Indígena "Peguche" [Ecuador]. 1977. *Folklore de mi tierra.* Orion 330-0063. Industria Fonográfica Ecuatoriana (IFESA). Guayaquil, Ecuador. Dist. by Emporio Musical S.A., Guayaquil and Psje. Amador, Quito.

Davillier, Le Baron [Jean] Ch[arles]. 1874. *L'Espagne.* Illus. G. Doré. Paris: Hachette.

Ebelot, Alfredo. [1890] 1943. *La pampa: Costumbres argentinas.* Buenos Aires: Alfer & Vays. Translated by the author from *La Pampa: Moeurs Sudamericaines,* edited by Joseph Escary. Paris: 1890.

Feld, Steven. 1981. "'Flow Like a Waterfall': The Metaphors of Kaluli Musical Theory." *1981 Yearbook for Traditional Music* 13:22–47.

Fernandez, James W. 1978. "Syllogisms of Association: Some Modern Extensions of Asturian Deepsong." In *Folklore in the Modern World,* ed. Richard M. Dorson, 183–206. Paris: Mouton.

Harrison, Regina. 1989. *Signs, Songs, and Memory in the Andes: Translating Quechua Language and Culture.* Austin: Univ. of Texas Press.

Jatari!! 4. 1978. [*Fadisa.* Fábrica de Discos S.A.] Quito, Ecuador. 710129.

Malinowski, Bronislaw. [1925] 1954. "Magic, Science, and Religion." In *Magic, Science, and Religion and Other Essays.* Garden City, N.Y.: Anchor Books.

Moreno Andrade, Segundo Luis. 1930. "La música en el Ecuador." In *El Ecuador en cien años de independencia, 1830–1930,* vol. 2, edited by J. Gonzalo Orellana. Quito: Imprenta de la Escuela de Artes y Oficios.

Ñanda mañachi 1 (Préstame el camino). 1977. Prod. Jean Chopin Thermes. Llaquiclla. IFESA. Industria Fonográfica Ecuatoriana S.A. Guayaquil, Ecuador. 339-0501. Recorded in Ibarra, Ecuador.

Ñanda mañachi 2 (Préstame el camino). 1979. Prod. Jean Chopin Thermes. Llaquiclla. IFESA. Industria Fonográfica Ecuatoriana S.A. Guayaquil, Ecuador. 339-0502. Recorded in Ibarra, Ecuador.

Ñanda mañachi/Boliviamanta: Préstame el camino desde Bolivia. Música quichua del equinoccio Andino. Churay, Churay! 1983. Llaquiclla. Fediscos. Guayaquil, Ecuador. Onix L.P. 59003.

Obando, Segundo. 1988. *Tradiciones de Imbabura,* 3rd ed. Quito: Abya-Yala.

Recio, P. Bernardo. [1773] 1947. *Compendiosa relacíon de la cristiandad (en el reino) de Quito.* Madrid: Consejo Superior de Investigaciones Científicas, Instituto Santo Toribio de Mogrovejo.

Ross, Joe. 1994. "Music of the Andes." *Acoustic Musician Magazine,* June, 18–27.

Rush, Alfred C. 1941. *Death and Burial in Christian Antiquity.* Doctor of Sacred Theology diss., Catholic University of America Studies in Christian Antiquity, no. 1, edited by J. Quasten. Washington D. C.: Catholic University of America Press.

Schechter, John M. 1979. "The Inca *Cantar Histórico:* A Lexico-Historical Elaboration on Two Cultural Themes." *Ethnomusicology* 23 (2): 191–204.

———. 1982. "Music in a Northern Ecuadorian Highland Locus: Diatonic Harp, Genres, Harpists, and their Ritual Junction in the Quechua Child's Wake." 3 vols. Ph.D. diss., Univ. of Texas.

———. 1983. "*Corona y baile:* Music in the Child's Wake of Ecuador and Hispanic South America, Past and Present." *Revista de Música Latinoamericana/Latin American Music Review* 4 (1): 1–80.

———. 1987. "Quechua *Sanjuán* in Northern Highland Ecuador: Harp Music as Structural Metaphor on *Purina." Journal of Latin American Lore* 13 (1): 27–46.

———. 1992. *The Indispensable Harp: Historical Development, Modern Roles, Configurations, and Performance Practices in Ecuador and Latin America.* Kent, Ohio: Kent State Univ. Press.

———. 1994. "Divergent Perspectives on the *velorio del angelito*: Ritual Imagery, Artistic Condemnation, and Ethnographic Value." *Journal of Ritual Studies* 8 (2): 43–84.

———. 1996. "Chapter Nine: Latin America/Ecuador." In *Worlds of Music: An Introduction to the Music of the World's Peoples,* 3rd ed., edited by J. T. Titon, 428–94. New York: Schirmer Books.

———. 1999a. "*Taki Ñan:* South American Affinity Interculture in Santa Cruz, California." In *Musical Cultures of Latin America: Global Effects, Past and Present,* edited by S. Loza. Proceedings of symposium, University of California at Los Angeles, May 28–30, 1999. In press.

———. gen. ed. 1999b. *Music in Latin American Culture: Regional Traditions.* New York: Schirmer Books.

Sheehy, Daniel. 1999. "Popular Mexican Musical Traditions: The *Mariachi* of West Mexico and the *Conjunto Jarocho* of Veracruz." In *Music in Latin American Culture: Regional Traditions,* edited by J. M. Schechter, 34–79. New York: Schirmer Books.

Slater, Peter Gregg. 1977. *Children in the New England Mind in Death and Life.* Hamden, Conn.: Archon Books.

Additional Reading

Béhague, Gérard. 1973. "Latin American Folk Music." In *Folk and Traditional Music of the Western Continents,* edited by Bruno Nettl, 179–206. Englewood Cliffs, N.J.: Prentice-Hall.

———. 1979. *Music in Latin America: An Introduction.* Englewood Cliffs, N.J.: Prentice-Hall.

Olsen, Dale A., and Daniel E. Sheehy, eds. 1998. *South America, Mexico, Central America, and the Caribbean.* Vol. 2 of *The Garland Encyclopedia of World Music.* New York: Garland Reference Library of the Humanities, vol. 1193.

Additional Listening

Afro-Hispanic Music from Western Colombia and Ecuador. 1967. Rec. and ed. Norman E. Whitten, Jr. Folkways FE 4376.

The Inca Harp: Laments and Dances of the Tawantinsuyu, the Inca Empire [Peru]. 1982. Rec. Ronald Wright. Lyrichord LLST 7359.

Mountain Music of Peru. 1966. Rec. John Cohen. Folkways FE 4539.

Música andina de Bolivia. 1980. Rec. with com. by Max Peter Baumann. Lauro Records, LPLI/S-062. 36 pp. booklet.

Pre-Columbian Instruments: Aerophone [Mexico]. 1972. Prod. Lilian Mendelssohn, with Pablo Castellanos. Played by Jorge Daher, Ethnic Folkways Library FE 4177.

Additional Viewing

Benson-Gyles, Anna, prod. 1980. *The Incas.* ODYSSEY Series. Executive Producer: Michael Ambrosino; Narrator: Tony Kahn. For ODYSSEY: Producer: Marian White; Editor: David Berenson. Co-production of British Broadcasting Corporation (BBC) and Public Broadcasting Associates, Inc., Boston, MA. INCAS/ODYSSEY SERIES/Box 1000, Boston, MA 02118. PBS VIDEO, 1320 Braddock Pl., Alexandria, VA 22314.

Cohen, John, dir. 1984. *Mountain Music of Peru.* 60 min. color. 16mm film/video. Berkeley: University of California, Extension Center for Media & Independent Learning, 2000 Center St., 4th floor, Berkeley, CA 94704.

Hernández, Amalia, dir. 1989. *Folklórico: Ballet Folklórico de México.* In Spanish, without subtitles. Featured performers: Ballet Folklórico de México. Madera Cinevideo, 525 E. Yosemite Ave., Madera, CA 93638.

Schaeffer, Nancy. 1995. "Directory of Latin American Films and Videos: Music, Dance, Mask, and Ritual." *Revista de Música Latinoamericana/Latin American Music Review* 16 (2): 221–41.

CHAPTER

10

Discovering and Documenting a World of Music

David B. Reck, Mark Slobin, and Jeff Todd Titon

All of us are familiar with the tale (or movie) of Dorothy and her adventures with the Tin Man, the Lion, and the Scarecrow in the fantastic land of Oz. But most of us have forgotten Dorothy's startling discovery once she got back to Kansas: Home was where her heart was, a fascinating world of people, family, neighbors, and friends, and of things that before her adventures she had overlooked. This is a familiar theme in literature the world over. The hero or heroine (ourselves) travels to faraway places, sees and does fabulous things, meets incredible people, or searches for marvelous treasures. But invariably the rainbow leads home; the pot of gold is buried in one's own backyard; the princess is none other than the girl next door.

Music in Our Own Backyards

In our explorations of the world's musics we—both students and scholars—are fascinated by cultures and peoples greatly separated from us in geography or time, in sound and style, in ways of making and doing music. In a sense, for every one of us there is an Oz. But there is also a music-culture surrounding us, one that we see and hear only partially because it is too close to us, because we take it for granted, as fish do water. Our musical environment is held by both us (in our perceptions and memories) and other members of our community, only a fraction of whom we may know. It expands out from us (and contracts into us) in a series of concentric circles that may include family, ethnic groups, regional styles, our hemisphere, and cultural roots (Western Europe, Africa, and so on). It is available to us live or mechanically reproduced. It comes to us out of history (classical works, old-time fiddle tunes, or bebop jazz) or it is a product of the here and now (the latest hit on the pop music charts or the avant-garde "new thing"). Our surrounding musical universe seems to us multifaceted and immensely complicated.

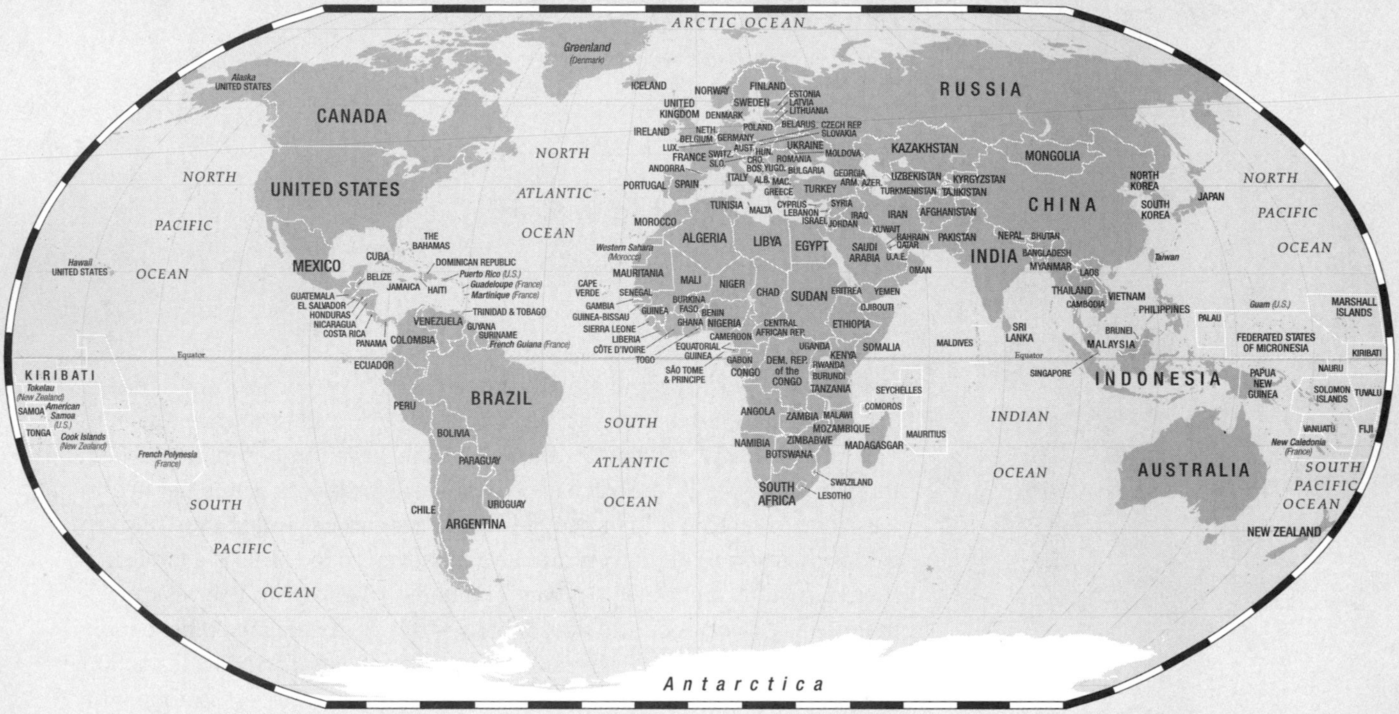

ARCTIC OCEAN
Greenland
(Denmark)
Alaska
UNITED STATES
CANADA
UNITED STATES
MEXICO
NORTH
PACIFIC
OCEAN
NORTH
ATLANTIC
OCEAN
Hawaii
UNITED STATES
CUBA
THE BAHAMAS
BELIZE
JAMAICA
HAITI
DOMINICAN REPUBLIC
Puerto Rico (U.S.)
Guadeloupe (France)
Martinique (France)
TRINIDAD & TOBAGO
GUATEMALA
EL SALVADOR
HONDURAS
NICARAGUA
COSTA RICA
PANAMA
VENEZUELA
GUYANA
SURINAME
French Guiana (France)
COLOMBIA
ECUADOR
PERU
BRAZIL
BOLIVIA
PARAGUAY
CHILE
URUGUAY
ARGENTINA
KIRIBATI
Tokelau
(New Zealand)
SAMOA
American Samoa
(U.S.)
TONGA
Cook Islands
(New Zealand)
French Polynesia
(France)
SOUTH
PACIFIC
OCEAN
Equator
ICELAND
NORWAY
FINLAND
SWEDEN
ESTONIA
LATVIA
LITHUANIA
UNITED KINGDOM
DENMARK
IRELAND
NETH.
BELGIUM
GERMANY
POLAND
BELARUS
CZECH REP.
SLOVAKIA
LUX.
FRANCE
SWITZ.
AUST.
HUN.
UKRAINE
MOLDOVA
SLO.
CRO.
ROMANIA
ANDORRA
BOS.
YUGO.
BULGARIA
PORTUGAL
SPAIN
ITALY
ALB.
MAC.
GREECE
GEORGIA
ARM.
AZER.
TURKEY
RUSSIA
KAZAKHSTAN
MONGOLIA
UZBEKISTAN
KYRGYZSTAN
TURKMENISTAN
TAJIKISTAN
CHINA
NORTH KOREA
SOUTH KOREA
JAPAN
TUNISIA
MALTA
CYPRUS
LEBANON
SYRIA
ISRAEL
JORDAN
IRAQ
IRAN
AFGHANISTAN
PAKISTAN
KUWAIT
BAHRAIN
QATAR
U.A.E.
OMAN
NEPAL
BHUTAN
BANGLADESH
INDIA
MYANMAR
LAOS
THAILAND
CAMBODIA
VIETNAM
Taiwan
PHILIPPINES
MOROCCO
ALGERIA
LIBYA
EGYPT
SAUDI ARABIA
YEMEN
Western Sahara
(Morocco)
MAURITANIA
MALI
NIGER
CHAD
SUDAN
ERITREA
DJIBOUTI
ETHIOPIA
SOMALIA
CAPE VERDE
SENEGAL
GAMBIA
GUINEA-BISSAU
GUINEA
SIERRA LEONE
LIBERIA
CÔTE D'IVOIRE
BURKINA FASO
GHANA
TOGO
BENIN
NIGERIA
CAMEROON
CENTRAL AFRICAN REP.
EQUATORIAL GUINEA
SÃO TOME & PRINCIPE
GABON
CONGO
DEM. REP. of the CONGO
UGANDA
KENYA
RWANDA
BURUNDI
TANZANIA
SEYCHELLES
COMOROS
ANGOLA
ZAMBIA
MALAWI
MOZAMBIQUE
NAMIBIA
ZIMBABWE
BOTSWANA
MADAGASCAR
MAURITIUS
SWAZILAND
SOUTH AFRICA
LESOTHO
SOUTH
ATLANTIC
OCEAN
INDIAN
OCEAN
MALDIVES
SRI LANKA
BRUNEI
MALAYSIA
SINGAPORE
INDONESIA
PALAU
Guam (U.S.)
MARSHALL ISLANDS
FEDERATED STATES OF MICRONESIA
KIRIBATI
NAURU
PAPUA NEW GUINEA
SOLOMON ISLANDS
TUVALU
VANUATU
FIJI
New Caledonia
(France)
AUSTRALIA
NEW ZEALAND
NORTH
PACIFIC
OCEAN
SOUTH
PACIFIC
OCEAN
Antarctica

Gathering reliable information on contemporary music is what this chapter is all about. We want to encourage you to seek out a nearby musical world, to observe it in person, to talk with the people involved in it, to document it with tape recordings and photographs, and to present the information in a project that will make a contribution to the body of knowledge about contemporary musical activities. If this research project is part of a course, you should check with your instructor for specifics. What follows is a general guide, based on the experience we and our students have had with similar projects at our colleges and universities.

Selecting a subject for your research is of course the first step in the project. Songs and instrumental music in North-American culture serve a great many purposes and occur in a staggeringly wide variety of contexts, from singing in the shower to the Metropolitan Opera, from the high school marching band to the rock festival, and from the lullaby to the television commercial jingle. Some of it is trivial, some of it is profound. It is all meaningful. To help you select a subject, let us impose order on our surrounding music-culture by means of a few organizing principles: family, generation, avocation, religion, ethnicity, regionalism, nationalism, and commercialization. As you read through the following brief survey you may find some subjects that interest you. Here we focus on North-American examples, but if you are using this book elsewhere you should apply these (and perhaps other) organizing principles to examples you think of from your own music-culture. Later we shall give you some specific suggestions.

Family

As is true of all cultures, North Americans first hear music in the context of family life (Figure 10-1). Much of that music comes from the records on the family stereo, radio, or television, and this "canned" music is especially important in developing children's musical taste. People often say they were very strongly influenced by the kind of music they heard before they were old enough to have their own records or choose the station on the family radio. Yet despite the parents' intentions, young people often rebel against parents' taste in music and choose to listen to what is favored by people their own age. There is usually some live music in the family as well. Many parents and grandparents sing lullabies, for example. These not only lull but promise, praise, and teach cultural values. Sometimes lullabies are the only songs in a foreign language that North-American children with strong ethnic backgrounds hear, since people (particularly grandparents) often fall back on old, familiar languages for intimate songs.

Another important family context is the automobile, where families learn songs and sing together on weekends and vacations. This is not as surprising as it appears, for the family car has become one of the basic centers of family experience, and it is one of the important places where the family gathers for an extended (some might say forced) period of time without outside distractions. The family used to have to choose between

Walker Evans. Courtesy of the Library of Congress.

Figure 10-1
A sharecropper family sings hymns in front of their home. Hale County, Alabama, 1936.

making their own music in the car or being force-fed by the radio, but now automobile cassette and CD players allow a family to have more control over what they hear when they drive.

In short, most North Americans have an early layer of songs learned in childhood in a family setting. Often they are just songs for entertaining children, with no deep cultural message to impart. What they do teach are the musical tastes and orientation of the particular social group, whether rural Quebecois, California suburban, Illinois heartland, Appalachian mountain, or New York inner-city. Children then work in harmony with (or against) this basic musical background as a part of growing up and finding their individual identity.

Generation

Much North-American music-making is organized along generational lines. Schools, church classes, scouting groups, sidewalk children's games, college singing groups, and many other musical situations include people of about the same age. Songs learned by these groups may stay with them as they grow older: imagine the twentieth or fiftieth college class reunion, where the aging ex-students keep singing the songs of their generation.

Yet the amount of generational mixing in North-American musical life has grown under the influence of television and recordings. In pop music much of the music thought to belong only to the young in the 1960s, such as the music of the Beatles, appealed to older generations as well. And today's young people like their parents' music better than their parents liked theirs. Other styles, such as country fiddling, which not long ago attracted mainly older musicians, have been picked up by young people, and now at a fiddle contest like the one held in Hartford, Connecticut, every year, the age spread of performers runs from eight to eighty. In ethnic musics too, young people have taken to learning traditional songs from their grandmothers instead of laughing at the old folks' songs as they might have one or two generations ago.

Generational blurring is part of the process of musical homogenization at work in still other areas of our music-culture. There is not so much difference between the sexes musically as there used to be. Just as women now take up sports like race-car driving and become professional jockeys, so more girls and women play instruments, such as the drums and saxophone, that used to be largely limited to boys and men. A whole genre that used to be male—barbershop quartet singing—now has a parallel female style, exhibited by groups such as the Sweet Adelines. A women's bluegrass group call themselves the All Girl Boys. We shall see the effect of regional and ethnic blurring later in this chapter.

Avocation

Music as hobby is an important part of North-American life. A barbershop quartet program lists the wives of the singers as "Thursday Night Widows"—perhaps one reason for the formation of women's quartets. Many North Americans feel the need for a strong group hobby, and of course some of this impulse is channeled into musical organizations. A local American Legion Post, or an ethnic group like the Polish Falcons, may have a band; here the music making is part of the feeling of group solidarity. Being able to field a band for the local parade or festival brings the group visibility and pride. Individual members may find performing in a fife-and-drum corps or the Governor's Footguard Band (to use Connecticut examples) a satisfying way to spend leisure time. Black youth in high school and college form extracurricular, informal singing groups whose repertoire includes rhythm and blues or gospel music hits; sometimes these groups become semiprofessional or even fully professional as they get older. Most high schools and colleges can boast a few rock bands and possibly even a jazz group, as well as cocktail pianists, folk-singing guitarists, and chamber music ensembles.

Religion

Religion is one of the better-documented areas of North-American musical life. We know about music's role in many religious movements, ranging

Figure 10-2
Music almost always accompanies formal rites of passage, such as this river baptism. Slabtown, Virginia, 1930s.

Courtesy of the Library of Congress

from the eighteenth-century Moravians through the revival movements of the nineteenth century and the founding of sects such as the Mormons. Much has been written about the appropriateness of certain types of music making in religious settings, such as organ playing in the Jewish synagogue or the introduction of folk and jazz elements to church services. The black spiritual is the object of scholarly study, while the tent revival preacher, the snake handler, and the ecstatic evangelistic churches receive attention from journalists (see Figure 10-2). But the musical activities of contemporary, mainline middle-class churches, synagogues, and mosques are little studied. Of interest also are the songs of new, unofficial religious movements, such as small meditation groups based on Christian or oriental religious thinking. These groups need to encourage solidarity and teach their message, but they have no traditional music. Often they change the words of well-known songs as a way of starting, just as Martin Luther changed the words of German drinking songs 450 years ago to create a body of sacred songs we know as Protestant chorales. The new unofficial groups may also work hard on developing an "inner music" of their members, through which the individual believer reaches the desired state of tranquility.

Ethnicity

Ethnicity is the oldest consideration in the study of the North-American music-culture in the sense that the United States and Canada are usually regarded as nations of immigrants. It is also one of the newest considerations because of the current interest in the public expression of ethnic identity, a trend that gathered force beginning in the 1960s.

Throughout North-American musical history, ethnicity has played a major role. Whether in the dialect and songs of the French Acadians in New Brunswick, the heroic *corrido* ballads sung along the Rio Grande by Mexican-Americans, the retelling of the story of hard-hearted Barbara Allen by British-American ballad singers, or the singing of a Yiddish lullaby in a Brooklyn tenement, North Americans have maintained distinctive ethnic boundaries through music. Music's function as a sign of group solidarity and common ancestry is nowhere clearer than in the variety of songs, dances, and instrumental tunes that characterize the North-American ethnic mosaic. Students in the United States whose parents or grandparents stopped public singing of Old World songs on their way to becoming "one-hundred-percent North Americans" now become enthusiastic about joining ethnic music groups or studying their group's heritage. Other parents and grandparents, of course, never stopped singing their native songs. Ethnic music in the United States has always involved transcontinental exchange. On the one hand, Greek Americans are influenced by new developments in popular music in Athens, while on the other, Polish-American records find great favor among farmers in far-off mountain villages in Poland. American jazz and country music have spread around the world, from Holland to Russia and Japan. A very complicated interplay goes on between black music in the United States and the Caribbean (Figure 10-3). A single song may show layer upon layer of musical travel. Reggae developed in Jamaica, where it represented a blend of Afro-Caribbean and black U.S. soul music. This already complicated style came

Figure 10-3
One of Boston's Caribbean steel-drum bands performs at a women's prison. 1979.

Jeff Todd Titon

to America from England, where pop groups repackaged it and exported it, and the cycle continues: Reggae is now popular in some parts of Africa.

Much of the older ethnic music of North America has changed in ways described in Chapter 5. For example, some twentieth-century fiddle contests encourage showing off in front of the crowd. Some New England contests include young fiddle players who have classical training, or who specialize in the "trick and fancy" category of virtuoso pieces instead of the standard old-time jigs, reels, and waltzes of the Northeast. Official events such as open contests push styles in directions that may be unfamiliar to older country performers, for whom fiddling meant a way to pass the time or to earn a night's pay by playing for eight solid hours of dancing.

On the other hand, folk festivals in the United States such as the Smithsonian Institution's Folklife Festival and the National Folk Festival seek out traditional singers, musicians, and craftspeople and present them insofar as possible in traditional contexts. Not that they are necessarily against change, however; at the Bicentennial Smithsonian Festival, for example, one of the staging areas was called Old Ways in the New World. Here traditional performers from various Old World countries were flown to America and presented alongside their New World ethnic counterparts: Polish-American musicians alternated with folk-singing and dancing groups from Poland; Louisiana Cajuns and French-Canadian fiddlers alternated with their counterparts from France. All learned from the musical interchange.

Regionalism

Regionalism in North America is thought to have declined with the spread of the interstate highway system, chains of fast-food restaurants, and the growth of television, all of which began in the 1950s. But just as the ethnic groups never really dissolved into the so-called melting pot, so regional homogenization never really took place in North-American life. Regionalism crops up in the names of styles, like the Chicago blues sound, the Detroit "Motown" soul sound, or even within ethnic styles, like the distinction between a Chicago and East Coast polka type. The crisp bowing, downbeat accents, and up-tempo performance of a fiddle tune in the Northeast bears little resemblance to the same tune's performance in the Southwest, with its smooth bowing and more relaxed beat. In country music today, the Nashville sound can be distinguished from the Texas sound, reflecting earlier differences between country and country-western styles. Likewise, the same hymn tune shows considerable variation even within the same denomination in different parts of the country. One Indiana Primitive Baptist was overheard to comment on the slow, highly decorated tunes of her Primitive Baptist neighbors to the Southeast: "They take ten minutes just to get through 'Amazing Grace'!" There are also local preferences for types of ensembles. The Governor's Footguard Band, formed in Connecticut before the American Revolution, is unlikely to have a counterpart in Kansas. Connecticut's fife-and-drum corps can be found in many good-sized Connecticut towns, whereas the Midwest is the heartland of the marching band.

Like ethnicity, regionalism is coming back into fashion. There are now so many local festivals that books of listings are published. In some locales, mock battles are fought again and again for tourist throngs, with appropriate live or recorded music. One very visible regional music performance is the singing of "My Old Kentucky Home" at the May running of the Kentucky Derby. In a recent year 150 thousand spectators joined in, and millions of television viewers were on hand to link the song and event to the region of its origin. The media scour the United States each year for feature stories; in the process they turn what were once regional events, like the annual celebration of an obscure southern Appalachian vegetable called the ramp, into national news, thereby making regionalism a commercial product.

In summary, if only in terms of marketing advantage and a renewed desire for local color, regional diversity has not yet been replaced by a homogenized North American music. The United States and Canada are still too large and diverse to turn all music into brand names or to have the entire population respond equally to all music, and the search for revival or for novelty continues.

Nationalism

A breakaway colony that declared its independence and fought a war to preserve it, the United States long ago began seeking ways to establish a national musical identity. We have already commented on its distinctive musical profile generated by ethnic and regional stylistic interactions. Popular national sentiment was also evoked by the frequent performance of patriotic songs, a tradition that has declined only in recent decades. Official music plays less of a part in U.S. life now than when John Philip Sousa's band and its imitators played flag-waving tunes on the bandstand for Sunday promenaders.

Perhaps the most obvious repertoire of North-American music consists of Christmas songs such as "Jingle Bells," "Deck the Halls," "Rudolph the Red-Nosed Reindeer," and the like. During the holiday season it is almost impossible to escape them. The curmudgeon who shoos away carolers from his front yard is said to lack the Christmas spirit, and he soon gains a neighborhood reputation as a Scrooge.

At the opposite end of the spectrum is public background music. There is no logical connection between event and music in a supermarket such as there is in one's own room listening to a stereo. In the case of background music of the type used in offices and factories, the employer has chosen the music, which is manufactured by the supplier to have the effect of increasing worker productivity. This of course represents a particularly powerful type of unrequested music, and there is a split among the captive audience as to whether listeners appreciate its existence or not.

Commercial Music

Much of the music in our culture is supplied by paid professionals. It is remarkable that our complex culture continues to carry on the musical situations described earlier in non- or preindustrial societies. Though a genre like the funeral lament has largely dropped out of North America, rituals like weddings and initiations (bar mitzvahs, debutante parties, senior proms) that mark a change of life still demand solemnization by music. A wedding may take place in a park with a Good Humor truck, balloons, and jeans instead of in a formal church setting, yet music remains indispensable even if it consists of pop tunes. There are other carryovers from early ritual as well. Elegant yacht clubs tend to schedule dances during full-moon evenings, continuing a practice of certain ancient cultures.

A great deal of the commercial music North Americans come into daily contact with may be described as "disembodied," by which we mean that the listener does not feel the physical presence of the performer and many times cannot even see the original musical situation (Figure 10-4). Some of this music can be partially controlled by the listener, who selects recordings from his or her collection to fit a mood. Choices are made from an entirely private domain of recordings over which the person has complete control regarding the selection of the music and the length of the listening experience. Although it is possible to imagine the original musical situation—concert or recording studio—there is no possibility of interaction with the performers, and the sound track is the same each time it is heard.

Figure 10-4
Dancing to records on a jukebox. West Virginia, 1942.

John Collier. Courtesy of the Library of Congress.

Doing Musical Ethnography

Your aim in discovering and documenting a world of music is a *musical ethnography,* a written representation and description of a music-culture, organized from the standpoint of a particular topic. (Your writing may be accompanied by photographs, tape recordings, and even videotapes that you make while documenting the music-culture.) The goal of musical ethnography is to understand a music-culture or some part of it from a native's or insider's point of view. What does that point of view encompass? Recall from Chapter 1 that a music-culture is divided into four components: ideas, activities, repertories, and material culture. Approaching a music-culture for the first time, you may feel overwhelmed; but if you organize your thinking about what you see and hear by following the outline in Table 1-1, you will be well on your way to documenting the music-culture.

The music in the repertory can be recorded for later study and analysis. Much of the social organization and material culture can be observed. By listening to musicians talk with each other, and by talking to them, you begin to understand their ideas about music, and through interviews you can learn more about those ideas, the repertory, social organization, and material culture. After all, conversations and interviews formed the basis for the musicians' life histories in this book. But discovering and documenting a world of music is not like examining an amoeba under a microscope. People will differ in how they behave, what they believe, and what they say to you. Different people will sing "the same tune" differently. Under these conditions, representing and describing a music-culture, even a single aspect of it, is a complex and subtle undertaking.

Selecting a Subject: Some Practical Suggestions

It goes almost without saying that your field project will involve you in collecting, understanding, and organizing information about music in order to present it. It differs from the usual undergraduate research paper in that its focus is on a musical situation that you seek out from people rather than from books in a library. In ethnomusicology, as in anthropology and folklore, this in-person witnessing, observing, questioning, tape recording, photographing, and in some cases performing is called *fieldwork*: work "in the field" rather than the laboratory or library. This is not to say that library research is useless or should be avoided. It may be possible to find background information on your topic in the library, and you should not overlook the opportunity to do so. But the thrust of your project takes you into the field, where you will obtain your most valuable and original information. Collecting, understanding, and organizing information about music are, of course, interrelated. You will begin with certain insights about the information you collect. As you organize it, you will gain new insights as you move toward an understanding of the musical situation from the web of information you have gathered.

You can approach the choice of a research subject in different ways. First, you might try to chart out the music you hear daily:

1. Keep a log or journal of all the music heard through three or four days, or a week. Note the context, style, and purpose of the music. Calculate how much of your day is spent with music of some sort.
2. Record, videotape, or simply describe in words several television commercials that employ music. Note the style of the music and the image it attempts to project. How is the music integrated into the message of the advertisement? Is it successful? Offensive? Both?
3. Map the uses of music in a television drama as you watch it. For comparison, select a daytime serial and a crime-fighting show, or a situation comedy and a popular dramatic series.
4. Survey the stores in your area and their uses of background music. Interview salespeople, managers, owners, customers (always obtaining their permission). See what they say about music and sales.

A second approach is to examine the music in your own background. Explore your memory of songs and music. Note how your religious and ethnic heritage influenced the music you heard and your current musical interests. How has your musical taste changed as you have grown older? Survey the contents of your CD collection for preferences in radio listening. The same questions can be asked of your brothers and sisters, your parents, or other members of your family.

A third approach is to explore music in your community—college or hometown. Here you can interview people, listen to musical performances, possibly take part in them yourself, and gather quite a lot of information. Listed below are several possible subject headings:

Ethnic groups

Piano teachers

Private instrumental instruction (music stores, private lessons in the home)

Choir directors

Church organists, pianists, and so on

School music (elementary, junior high, high school)

Music stores

Musical instrument makers

Background music in public places

The club scene (bars, coffeehouses, restaurants, clubs)

Musical organizations (community choral groups, bands, barbershop quartets, etc.)

Part-time (weekend) musicians

Professional or semiprofessional bands (rock, pop, jazz, rhythm and blues, country, gospel, and so forth)

Chamber music groups
Parades and music
Disc jockeys
Symphony orchestras

A fourth approach narrows the subject and concentrates on an individual musician's life, opinions, and music. Often we focus our attention on the musical superstars, but in the process we forget the many fine and sensitive musicians, many of them amateurs, who live in our communities. Senior citizens, teachers, owners of record or music stores, or tradespeople like the local barber, janitor, or factory worker have sometimes had rich musical experiences as professional or part-time musicians. To search out such people is not always easy. Try the musicians' union, ethnic organizations, word of mouth, school or college music teachers, radio station disc jockeys, the clergy, club owners, newspaper columnists and feature storywriters, or even local police stations and fire departments. Musicians can be approached directly at fairs, contests, festivals, concerts, and dances. Many colleges and universities have foreign student associations that include amateur musicians, and they can tell you about others in the area. Ethnic specialty restaurants and grocery stores are other resources.

The musical world that surrounds you is so diverse you may feel swamped, unable to focus your energy. But when it finally comes down to deciding on a subject for your project, two guiding principles will help you out: Choose something you are interested in, and choose something you have access to. It will be hard to succeed if you are not curious about the music you examine, and you will have to be close to it to look at it carefully.

Collecting Information

Once you have chosen a subject, your next move is to immerse yourself in the musical situation, consider what aspects of it interest you, and select a topic. Then plan how you will collect information—what questions to ask when you talk to the musicians or others involved, what performances to tape record, and so forth. Almost always you will need time and the flexibility to revise your plans as you collect the information you need. Most people will be happy to tell you about their involvement with music as long as you show them you really are interested.

Gaining Entry

Musical activities usually have a public (performance) side and a private (rehearsal) side. The performance is the tip of the iceberg; you will want to understand what lies beneath, and that is best learned by talking to the people involved. If you must approach a stranger, it may be helpful to arrange an introduction, either by a mutual friend or by a person in authority. Protocol is important in some cases. If, for example, you will be talking with musicians in an ethnic organization, it is wise to approach the president of the organization and seek his or her advice. Not only is he or she in a position to give you good suggestions, but a president needs to know what is going on; it is expected. In other situations it is best to let the people in authority know what you intend to do, and why, but to avoid having them introduce you, particularly if their authority is legal only and they do not belong to the same group as the people whose music you will be studying.

The first contact is especially important because the way you present yourself establishes your identity and role. That is one reason why it is essential to take the time to be honest with yourself and others about your interest in their music and the purpose of your project. If you are a college student, you may find yourself being assigned the role of the expert. But this is a role to avoid. The people who give you information are the experts, and you are the student who wants to learn from them. Otherwise you would not seek their help. You hope they will be willing to let you talk with them, observe, and, if it is appropriate, participate in the music.

Selecting a Topic

Usually your subject takes in several musical situations, and you will find yourself having to choose among them so as not to undertake a larger project than you can accomplish. If, for example, you are interested in Irish-American music in your community, you may find that there is so much going on that a survey of it all will be superficial, and so you will decide to concentrate on one aspect of it, perhaps the musical tradition of one family, or the musical scene in a particular club. Remember once again to choose something you are interested in and have access to.

The next step is one of the most difficult: selecting a topic. A topic is more than just a subject. It is a subject viewed from a particular angle, from a certain perspective, and with a limited goal in mind. "The Jewish cantor" is an example of a subject, something to investigate. "Musical training of Jewish cantors in New York City" is a topic. The cantor is viewed from a special perspective: training. You want to understand what the training is and what the results are. Another example of a subject is "the Outlaws, a local country music band." A topic that involves the band might be "gender and gender roles in the music of the Outlaws, a local country music band." Here the focus is on the band members' attitudes, interactions, lyrics, social scene, and so forth. By themselves, subjects cover too much ground. Topics focus your attention on specific questions that will help you organize the information you collect.

As you think about a topic, reread Chapter 1 and see how the four-part model of the music-culture can help you select aspects of your subject that you are interested in. Do you want to focus on conceptions of music, social organization, repertories, or material culture? Of course, these aspects are interrelated, and it will be difficult to ignore any of them completely; nevertheless, concentrating most of your attention on one of them will help you select a topic you can manage, and it will give you some initial ideas to think about as you gather your information.

In other words, gathering information is not simply a matter of recording it, as a sponge soaks up water. You will want to be selective in what you document, because after documentation you will need to interpret your material. Interpretation—figuring out what your documentation means—always involves answering questions about your topic. If your subject is music on the college radio station, and your topic has to do with the radio station's attitude toward women's rap groups, you will probably interview some of the people who work at the station, and in the interviews you will try to figure out a way to approach your topic. One deejay might play a lot of women's music on a particular show, and you might find out something about this deejay's attitude toward women's rap groups by asking. You would probably also try to estimate how well theory is put into practice—the station people might say they are in favor of women's rap groups, but you might find that they do not play very much of it. You might wonder why. Do the station people think the audience does not want to hear it? What does the audience want to hear, how do the station staff know, and why should they play what the audience wants to hear, anyway?

Questions like these arise during the course of your research, and they help you to select the kind of documentation that you will do—whether, for example, to survey the recordings in the radio station's library—and they also help you focus your interpretation as you go along, so when the time comes to write it up you will have some answers to your questions. Your project is not meant to be just a gathering of material but also a focusing of that material on a topic and an interpretation of the material in light of the topic you have chosen.

Library and Internet Research

Depending on the topic you have selected, it may be a good idea to visit the library and the Internet at this point to see if anyone has published research on your topic. Try the library's collection first. The online or the card catalog will be helpful; look under such headings as "music," "folk music," "popular music," and whatever categories and key words are closely related to your subject. It may be useful to spend a couple of hours in the library stacks, looking at books on the shelves and opening any that might have to do with your subject, for it is almost impossible to know where to look for everything in the card catalog alone.

After you have checked the catalog and the stacks, look for works that you might need to get on interlibrary loan. Look in the reference section for such bibliographies as the *Music Index* and online for *RILM,* as well as specialized bibliographies and reference works. There may also be discographies of recordings pertaining to your research area. For example, Richard Spottswood's *Ethnic Music on Records: A Discography of Ethnic Recordings Produced in the United States, 1893 to 1942* is a five-volume work that lists 78 rpm recordings that were made during that period (Spottswood 1990). The bibliographies will point you toward books and articles on your subject, which the reference librarian can help you find. Many of these music-related bibliographies and discographies are available electronically, some on the Internet and other on CD-ROMs.

The Internet has become a vast resource for information about music. Try searching the Internet using the key words related to your topic. You will probably have to refine your search greatly to make it efficient. Also, some of the information you find, such as website opinions about music, will not carry the authority of a scholarly book. Yet some of these specialized websites offer much useful information on topics that you may not be able to find in books. The Internet is particularly good for enabling group discussions on various subjects. If, for example, your topic has to do with bluegrass music, numerous bluegrass sites on the Internet will give you a good idea how bluegrass fans think and talk about their music. A bluegrass list (discussion group) called Bluegrass-L is open to subscribers and might even be a good place to do research. Other interest groups involving music abound on the Internet. There are several discussion lists on musics in India, for example; there is an Arab music list, and so forth. Of course, the Internet also has a great deal of music, now available in MP3 format, and who knows what the electronic future will bring?

However interesting the Internet may be, resist the temptation to focus your research efforts there. Your project chiefly involves the kind of documentation and interpretation that results from face-to-face contacts with people making music. Library and Internet research merely provides background information, and sometimes it cannot even do that—your subject may not have had attention there, or the little that has been written may not be very useful. But if research on your topic has been published, you will be able to undertake a better project if you are familiar with it; further, the people whose music you are studying will often be able to suggest good books and articles for you to read, saving you time in your search.

Participation and Observation

Returning now to the fieldwork requires a basic plan of action. Which people should you talk with? What performances should you witness? Should you go to rehearsals? What about a visit to a recording studio? If you are studying a music teacher, should you watch a private lesson? Should the teacher teach you? Will you take photographs? Videotape? What kind of tape-recording equipment can you get? Who will pay for it? You probably have been thinking about these and many similar questions, but one more than you should pay attention to at this time is your personal relationship to the people whose music you will study. Should you act as an observer, as a detached, objective reporter? Or should you, in addition to observing, also participate in the musical activity if you can?

Participating as well as observing can be useful. (It can be quite enjoyable as well.) You hope to learn the music from the inside. You will come to know some of the musical belief system intuitively. You will not have to hang around the edges of the action all the time, depending on others to explain all the rules.

But participating has its drawbacks. The problem with being a participant-observer is that you sometimes know too much. It is like the forest and the trees: The closer you are to a situation, the less of an overall view you have, and in order to address your project to an outside reader, you will need to imagine yourself an outsider, too. We tend to filter out the regularities of our lives. If we had to remember every time that we met a stranger whether our culture says we should shake hands, rub noses, or bow, we would be in constant panic, and if we had to think hard whether *red* means stop or go, driving would be impossible. This filtering process means that we take the most basic aspects of a situation for granted. So if you are participating as well as observing, you must make a special effort to be an outsider and take nothing for granted. This dual perspective, the view of the participant-observer, is not difficult to maintain while you are learning how to participate in the musical situation. In fact, when you are *learning,* the dual perspective is forced on you. The trouble is that after you have learned, you can forget what it was like to be an outside observer. Therefore it is very important to keep a record of your changing perspective as you move from outsider to participant, and this record should be written in your field notes or spoken into your tape recorder as your perspective changes.

What if you work as an observer only and forgo participation? There are some advantages to doing so. It saves time. You can put all your energy into watching and trying to understand how what people tell you is going on matches what you can actually see and hear going on. You can follow both what is said and what is done more easily with someone besides yourself. On the other hand, you do not achieve objectivity by keeping yourself out of the action. Your very presence as an observer alters the musical situation, particularly if you are photographing or tape-recording. In many situations you will actually cause *less* interference if you participate rather than intrude as a neutral and unresponsive observer.

Ethics

There is an important ethical dimension, a right-and-wrong aspect about doing fieldwork. Most colleges and universities have a policy on research with human subjects that is designed to prevent people from being harmed by the research. If your research project is part of a course, be sure to discuss the ethics of the project with your teacher before you begin and, if things change, as you proceed. Think carefully about the impact of what you propose to do. *Always* ask permission. Understand that people have legal rights to privacy and to how they look, what they say, and what they sing, even after it has gone onto your film or tape recorder. Be honest with yourself and the people you study about your interest in their music and the purposes of your project. Tell them right from the start that you are interested in researching and documenting their music. If you like their music, say so. If the project is something for you to learn from, say so. Explain what will happen to the project after you finish it. Is it all right with them if you keep the photographs and tapes you make? Would they like a copy of the project? (If so, make one at your expense.) Is it all right if the project is deposited in the college or university archive? Most archives have a form that the people (yourself included) will sign, indicating that you are donating the project to the archive and that it will be used only for research purposes. If this project is not merely a contribution to knowledge but also to your career (as a student or whatever), admit it and realize that you have a stake in its outcome. Ask the people whose music you are studying why they are cooperating with you and what they hope to achieve from the project, and bear that in mind throughout. And never observe, interview, make recordings, or take photographs without their knowledge and permission.

Today many ethnomusicologists believe that it is not enough simply to go into a musical situation and document it. The fieldworker must give back something to the people who have been generous with their thoughts, their music, and their time. In some cultures, people expect money and should be paid. It is possible for fieldworkers to act not simply as a reporter, or analyst, but also as cultural and musical advocates, doing whatever they can to help the music they are studying to flourish.

Some ethnomusicologists in the United States work for arts councils, humanities councils, and other government agencies in jobs where they are expected to identify, document, and present authentic folk and ethnic musicians to the public. Many taxpayers believe that if the government supports the fine arts, it should also support folk and ethnic arts. In fact, most European governments do more than the United States and Canada to preserve and promote their folk and ethnic music. Ethnomusicologists hear a similar kind of commercial popular music throughout the world, and many conclude that local musics—of which there are a great variety—are endangered. It is to humankind's advantage to have many different kinds of music, they believe. For that reason, they think advocacy and support are necessary in the face of all the forces that would make music sound alike the world over. This argument may at first seem remote from your project, but not when you think about your own involvement with the people and music you are studying.

Field Equipment: Notebook, Tape Recorder, Camera

The perfect fieldworker has all-seeing eyes, all-hearing ears, and total recall. But because none of us is so well equipped, we suggest you rely on written notes, tape recordings, and photographs that you make in the field. These documents serve two purposes: They enable you to reexamine at leisure your field experiences when you write up your project, and, because they are accurate records of performances, interviews, and observations, they may be included in the final form your project takes. On the other hand, field equipment presents certain difficulties: It costs money, you need to know how to work it properly, and you may have to resist the temptation to spend much of your time fiddling with your equipment when you should be watching, thinking, and listening instead.

Fifty years ago, fieldworkers relied primarily upon note taking, and today it is still indispensable. No matter how sophisticated your equipment is, you should carry a small pocket notebook. It will be useful for writing down names and addresses, directions, observations, and thoughts while you are in the field. In the days before sound recording, music was taken by dictation in notebooks. While this is still possible, it is not advisable except when performances are very brief and you have the required dictation skills. Dictating a song puts the performer in an unnatural context and changes the performance. However, notebooks are especially useful for preserving information learned in interviews, particularly if a tape recorder is unavailable or awkward in the interview situation. In addition, you should make an effort to write down your detailed impressions of the overall field situation: your plans, questions, any difficulties you meet with; as complete a description as possible of the musical situation itself, including the setting, the performers, the audience, and the musical event from start to finish; and your reactions and responses to the field experience as it takes place. Your field notebook becomes a journal or diary that you address *to yourself* for use when you write up your project.

Most university music departments and many university libraries now loan inexpensive portable cassette recorders to students for use in field collecting projects. Whether you use a tape recorder, and if so what type it is (microcassette, portable cassette, minidisc, and so forth) is largely a matter of the nature of your project and the expectations you and your instructor have. The inexpensive portable cassette recorders are best suited to recording speech (interviews, for example). Although they come with built-in microphones, the sound quality can be improved dramatically if you use an inexpensive external microphone plugged into the recorder's microphone input jack. So equipped, a portable cassette recorder may be adequate for your needs. You will need to be thoroughly familiar with its operation so that your recordings are accurate. The portable cassette or minidisc recorder is mechanically simple, and anyone can learn to operate it in just a few minutes. The most important lesson is how to put the microphone in the right spot. If the sound is soft or moderate and it comes from a small area (a solo singer, a lesson on a musical instrument, or an interview, for example), place the microphone in close and equidistant from the sources of the sounds. If the sound is loud and widely spread out (a rock band or a symphony orchestra, for example), search out "the best seat in the house" and place or hold the microphone there. Make a practice recording for a few seconds and play it back immediately to check microphone placement and make certain the equipment is working properly. Take along spare batteries and blank tapes (see Figure 10-5).

If properly used, even the simplest cameras take adequate pictures of musical performances. A picture may not be worth a thousand words, but it goes a long way toward capturing the human impact of a musical event. An instant-picture camera is especially useful because you will be able to see the photograph immediately and correct mistakes (such as standing too far from the action) at once. A close-up lens placed in front of the regular

Figure 10-5
A chief checks the quality of a recording of his musicians. Kasena-Nankani Traditional Area, Ghana.

James T. Koetting

lens will allow you to fill up the whole picture with a musical instrument. Instant pictures have another advantage: You can give them (well, not all of them) to the people you photograph.

People across the United States are in love with technology, even technology to get away from technology (backpacking equipment, for example). If you already know a lot about tape recording or photography, and you own or can borrow high-quality equipment, by all means use it. Some of the photographs in this book and the accompanying recordings were made by the authors using professional equipment; after all, fieldwork is a part of our profession. But the more sophisticated our equipment is, the more difficult it is to use it to its full potential. There is a true story about a photographer who went to a rock music festival and brought only his pocket camera. In the photographer's pit in front of the stage, he had maneuvered himself into the best position and was standing there taking pictures when a professional nudged him, saying, "Get out of here with that little toy!" The pro stood there with cameras hanging from his neck and shoulders, covering his body like baby opossums on their mama. "Well," said the amateur, yielding his position with a smile, "I guess if you need all of that equipment, you need to stand in the right spot, too!"

Interviewing

Interviews with people (consultants) whose music you are studying are a useful means of obtaining basic information and getting feedback on your own ideas. But be careful not to put words in your consultants' mouths and impose your ideas. The first step in understanding a world of music is to understand it as much as possible in your consultants' own terms. Later you can bring your own perspective to bear on the musical situation. Remember that much of their knowledge is intuitive; you will have to draw it out by asking questions.

Come into the interview with a list of questions, but be prepared to let the talk flow in the direction your consultant takes it. In his 1956 preface to *Primitive Man As Philosopher* Paul Radin distinguishes between two procedures for obtaining information: question-and-answer, and "letting the native philosopher expound his ideas with as few interruptions as possible." Your consultants may not be philosophers, but they should be given the chance to say what they mean. Some people are by nature talkative, and you will be thankful for it. Others need to be put at ease; let the person know in advance what sort of questions you will be asking, what sort of information you need, and why. Often you will get important information in casual conversations rather than formal interviews; be ready to write down the information in your field notebook. Some people are by nature silent and guarded; despite your best intentions, they will not really open up to you. If you encounter that sort of person, respect his or her wishes and make the interview brief.

Beginning fieldworkers commonly make two mistakes when doing interviews. First, they worry too much about the tape recorder, and their nervousness can carry over to the person they interview. But if you have already gotten the person's consent to be interviewed, it should not be hard to get permission to tape the interview. One fieldworker always carries her tape recorder and camera so they are visible from the moment she enters the door. Then she nonchalantly sets the tape recorder down in a prominent spot and ignores it, letting the person being interviewed understand that the tape recorder is a natural and normal part of the interview. Still ignoring the recorder, she starts off with the small talk that usually begins such a visit. Eventually the other person says something like, "Oh, I see you're going to tape-record this." "Sure," she says steadily. "I brought along this tape recorder just to make sure I get down everything you say. I can always edit out any mistakes, and you can always change your mind. This is just to help me understand you better the first time." She says that once they have agreed to be interviewed, nobody has ever refused her tape recorder. She also says that if anyone told her to shut the recorder off, she would do so.

A second problem is that beginning fieldworkers often ask leading questions. A leading question is a question that suggests a particular answer. This makes the information they get unreliable. In other words, it is not clear whether the person being interviewed is expressing his or her own thoughts or just being agreeable. In addition, leading questions usually result in short, uninteresting answers. Study this first dialogue to see how not to interview:

Fieldworker 1:	Did you get your first flute when you were a girl?
Consultant:	Yeah.
Fieldworker 1:	What was the name of your teacher?
Consultant:	Ah, I studied with Janice Sullivan.
Fieldworker 1:	When was that?
Consultant:	In college.
Fieldworker 1:	I'll bet you hated the flute when you first started. I can remember hating my first piano lessons.
Consultant:	Yeah.

The trouble here is that the consultant gives the kinds of answers she thinks are expected of her. She is not really telling the fieldworker what she thinks. She is not even giving the conversation much thought. The fieldworker has asked the wrong kind of questions. Now look what happens when another fieldworker questions the same person.

Fieldworker 2:	Can you remember when you got your first flute?
Consultant:	Yeah.
Fieldworker 2:	Could you tell me about it?
Consultant:	Sure. My first flute—well, I don't know if this counts, but I fell in love with the flute when I was in grade school, and I remember going down to a music store and trying one out while my father looked on, but I couldn't make a sound, you know!
Fieldworker 2:	Sure.
Consultant:	So I was really disappointed, but then I remember learning to play the recorder in, I think it was third grade, and I really loved that, but I didn't stick with it. Then in college I said to myself, I'm going to take music lessons and I'm going to learn the flute.
Fieldworker 2:	Tell me about that.
Consultant:	Well, I had this great teacher, Janice Sullivan, and first she taught me how to get a sound out of it. I was really frustrated at first, but after a while I got the hang of it, and she would always tell me to think of the beautiful

> sounds I knew a flute could make. I used to think a flute could make a sound like water, like the wind. Well, not exactly, but sort of. And then Mrs. Sullivan let me borrow a tape of *shakuhachi* music—you know, the Japanese flute?—and I *heard* different kinds of water, different kinds of wind! I knew then that I would play the flute for the rest of my life.

Compare the two fieldworkers' questions: "Did you get your first flute when you were a girl?" is a leading question because it leads to the answer, "Yes, I got my first flute when I was a girl." What is more, fieldworker 1 implies that most people get their first flutes when they are girls, so the consultant probably thinks she should answer yes. By contrast, the question of fieldworker 2—"Can you remember when you got your first flute?"—is open-ended and invites reflection, perhaps a story. When the consultant says "Yeah," fieldworker 2 asks for a story and gets a much better—and different—answer than fieldworker 1 did. Go over the rest of the first interview, see how fieldworker 1 injects her opinions into the dialogue ("I'll bet you hated the flute when you first started"), and fails to draw out the consultant's real feelings about her lessons, whereas fieldworker 2 establishes a better rapport, is a better listener, asks nondirective questions, and gets much fuller and truer answers.

If your project concentrates on a single consultant, you may want to obtain his or her life story (Titon 1980). For this purpose a tape recorder is a necessity. Since the way your consultants view their lives can be as important as the factual information they give, you should try to get the life story in their own words as much as possible. This means refraining from questions that direct the story as you think it should go. What is important is how your consultant wants it to go. Come back later, in another interview, to draw out specific facts and fill in gaps by direct questioning. In the initial interview, begin by explaining that you would like your consultant to tell you about his or her life as a musician (or composer, disc jockey, and so forth) from the beginning until now. Once you have begun, allow plenty of time for silences to gather thoughts. If he or she looks up at you expectantly, nod your head in agreement and try repeating what has just been said to show that you understand it. Resist any impulse to ask direct questions; write them down instead, and ask them later. For now you want the story to continue.

Not everyone will be able to tell you his or her musical autobiography, but if you are fortunate enough to find someone who can, it may turn out to be the most important part of your project. On the other hand, if your consultant's life story is a necessary part of your project, but you cannot obtain it except by direct and frequent questioning, you should certainly ask the questions. If you get good answers, the result will be your consultant's *life history,* a collaborative biography rather than an autobiography.

Interviews, then, with the people whose music you are studying (and perhaps with their audience) are important for obtaining factual information and testing your ideas. They are also important because through them you can begin to comprehend the musical situation from their point of view: their beliefs, their intentions, their training, their feelings, their evaluations of musical performance, and their understanding of what they are doing—what it is all about. Ultimately, since this is your project, you combine their ideas with your own when you write the project up using the information you have collected.

Other Means of Collecting Information

Another technique, often used in social science research, is the questionnaire. Its role in studying music is limited, but there are projects in which it can be helpful. You may wish to map out the general nature of a situation before moving into a specific subarea to focus on. For example, to work on the meaning of pop songs in students' lives, you might start by circulating a questionnaire to uncover the eventual sample you will study intensively. Questionnaires are most at home in studies of musical attitudes. To find out how shoppers react to supermarket background music, it would be hard to set up interviews but easy, if the store manager agrees, to arrange for distributing a questionnaire.

Aside from questionnaires, which seek out information, you might come upon information already gathered: autobiographical manuscripts, diaries, and tape recordings made by informants for themselves. Clubs, fraternities, schools, churches, and various organizations often store old materials that shed light on musical activities. At concerts, the programs handed out can be rich in information, ranging from description of the music to the type of advertisers that support the concerts. Membership lists and patrons' lists may be included as well.

Newspapers are enormously helpful. Hardly a day passes without journalistic commentary on the musical environment, in news stories, reviews, and advertisements. Feature stories provide up-to-date information on current concerts, trends, and musical attitudes, both locally and nationally, while advertising can furnish insights into the ideals of the North-American musical world projected by the media, ideals that influence most of us one way or another. For example, an ad for an expensive home entertainment system designed to bring music into every home offers a direct connection between musical style and the rooms of the house: "101 Strings in the greenhouse, Bach in the bedroom, Frank Sinatra in the living room, Gershwin in the den, the Boston Pops on the patio, the Rolling Stones outside by the pool." What better brief description of middle-aged, middle-class musical taste could be found?

Finishing the Project

After you have done all the hard work of organizing and collecting information, what do you do with it? Now is a good time to return to your original plan of action and list of questions you wanted to ask about the musical situation, particularly with reference to the four-part model from Chapter 1.

These questions and the information you have gathered offer a natural organization for your project. Remember that your purpose is documentation, interpretation, and understanding. Specific advice on how to write it up and what form to present it in will be available from your instructor.

Be sure to keep in mind that you are not the only one affected by your finished project. Other people's feelings and, on occasion, social position are reflected in your work. Be clear in what you say about the people you worked with. Confidentiality may be important; if people asked you not to use their names or repeat what they said to you, respect their wishes. It is possible—even customary in many anthropological works—to change the names of people or places to make certain no one is identified who does not want to be. Imagine the problems created for the member of a band who criticizes the leader if the words get back to the group, or for a school music teacher if he criticizes the school board to you in private and you quote him.

Checking back with informants is very helpful to clear up research questions. As you interview, collect information, and think about the musical situation you study, new questions always will occur to you. It is no different when you write up your project; you will probably find that it will be helpful to get back in touch with your consultants and ask a few final questions so that you will be satisfied with your project when you have finished it.

In our preface we wrote of our intention that our readers experience what it is like to be an ethnomusicologist puzzling out his or her way toward understanding an unfamiliar music. A good field project inevitably provides just that experience. Valuable and enjoyable in and of itself, discovery, documentation, and interpretation of a world of music takes on added significance because it illuminates, even in a small way, our understanding of music as human expression.

References

Spottswood, Richard K. 1990. *Ethnic Music on Records.* Urbana: Univ. of Illinois Press.

Titon, Jeff Todd. 1980. "The Life Story." *Journal of American Folklore* 93:276–92.

Additional Reading

Barz, Gregory, and Timothy J. Cooley. 1997. *Shadows in the Field: New Perspectives for Fieldwork in Ethnomusicology.* New York: Oxford Univ. Press.

Collier, John, Jr., and Malcolm Collier. 1986. *Visual Anthropology: Photography As a Research Method.* Albuquerque: Univ. of New Mexico Press.

Emerson, Robert, Rachel I. Fretz, and Lind L. Shaw. 1995. *Writing Ethnographic Fieldnotes.* Chicago: Univ. of Chicago Press.

Georges, Robert A., and Michael O. Jones. 1980. *People Studying People.* Berkeley: Univ. of California Press.

Golde, Peggy, ed. 1986. *Women in the Field: Anthropological Experiences.* 2nd ed. Berkeley: Univ. of California Press.

Hattersley, Ralph. 1978. *Beginner's Guide to Photographing People.* Garden City, N.J.: Doubleday.

Herndon, Marcia, and Norma McLeod. 1983. *Field Manual for Ethnomusicology.* Norwood, Pa.: Norwood Editions.

Hood, Mantle. 1982. *The Ethnomusicologist,* chapters 4 and 5. 2nd edition. Kent, Ohio: Kent State Univ. Press.

Ives, Edward D. 1980. *The Tape-Recorded Interview: A Manual for Fieldworkers in Folklore and Oral History.* Knoxville: Univ. of Tennessee Press.

Jackson, Bruce. 1987. *Fieldwork.* Urbana: Univ. of Illinois Press.

Marcus, George E., and Michael M. J. Fischer. 1986. *Anthropology As Cultural Critique.* Chicago: Univ. of Chicago Press.

Rabinow, Paul. 1977. *Reflections on Fieldwork in Morocco.* Berkeley: Univ. of California Press.

Sanjek, Roger, ed. 1990. *Fieldnotes: The Makings of Anthropology.* Ithaca, N.Y.: Cornell Univ. Press.

[Special issue on fieldwork in the public interest]. 1992. *Ethnomusicology* 36(2).

Spradley, James P., and David W. McCurdy. 1972. *The Cultural Experience: Ethnography in Complex Society.* Chicago: Science Research Associates.

Wax, Rosalie. 1971. *Doing Fieldwork: Warnings and Advice.* Chicago: Univ. of Chicago Press.

Wengle, John L. 1988. *Ethnographers in the Field: The Psychology of Research.* Tuscaloosa: Univ. of Alabama Press.

Index

I

J

K

P

Q

R

V

W

Y

Z